M000195977

Modern Literatures in Spain

Cultural History of Literature

Christopher Cannon, *Middle English Literature*
Sandra Clark, *Renaissance Drama*
Glenda Dicker/sun, *African American Theater*
Alison Finch, *French Literature*
Ann Hallamore Caesar and Michael Caesar, *Modern Italian Literature*
Jo Labanyi and Luisa Elena Delgado, *Modern Literatures in Spain*
Roger Luckhurst, *Science Fiction*
Michael Minden, *Modern German Literature*
Katie Normington, *Medieval English Drama*
Lynne Pearce, *Romance Writing*
Charles J. Rzepka, *Detective Fiction*
Jason Scott-Warren, *Early Modern English Literature*
Charlotte Sussman, *Eighteenth-Century English Literature*
Mary Trotter, *Modern Irish Theatre*
Andrew Baruch Wachtel and Ilya Vinitsky, *Russian Literature*
Andrew J. Webber, *The European Avant-Garde*
Tim Whitmarsh, *Ancient Greek Literature*

Modern Literatures in Spain

JO LABANYI AND LUISA ELENA DELGADO
with Helena Buffery, Kirsty Hooper, and Mari Jose Olaziregi

polity

Copyright © Jo Labanyi and Luisa Elena Delgado 2023

The right of Jo Labanyi and Luisa Elena Delgado to be identified as Authors of this Work has been asserted in accordance with the UK Copyright, Designs and Patents Act 1988.

First published in 2023 by Polity Press

Polity Press
65 Bridge Street
Cambridge CB2 1UR, UK

Polity Press
111 River Street
Hoboken, NJ 07030, USA

All rights reserved. Except for the quotation of short passages for the purpose of criticism and review, no part of this publication may be reproduced, stored in a retrieval system or transmitted, in any form or by any means, electronic, mechanical, photocopying, recording or otherwise, without the prior permission of the publisher.

ISBN-13: 978-0-7456-3495-1
ISBN-13: 978-0-7456-3496-8(pb)

A catalogue record for this book is available from the British Library.

Library of Congress Control Number: 2022932840

Typeset in 11.25 / 13pt Monotype Dante
by Cheshire Typesetting Ltd, Cuddington, Cheshire
Printed and bound in Great Britain by TJ Books Ltd, Padstow, Cornwall

The publisher has used its best endeavours to ensure that the URLs for external websites referred to in this book are correct and active at the time of going to press. However, the publisher has no responsibility for the websites and can make no guarantee that a site will remain live or that the content is or will remain appropriate.

Every effort has been made to trace all copyright holders, but if any have been overlooked the publisher will be pleased to include any necessary credits in any subsequent reprint or edition.

For further information on Polity, visit our website:
politybooks.com

Contents

Introduction 1

1 Modernity and the Singular Nation (1700–1840s) 6

2 From Sensibility to Desire: The Construction of the Modern Subject (1730s–1880s) 27

3 The Rise of the Public Sphere and the Professionalization of the Writer (1730s–1890s) 41

4 Countering Castilian: From Retrenchment to the Renaissance of Peripheral National Literatures (1710s–1890s) 62

5 The Uses of the Past: Writing the Nation (1760s–1890s) 85

6 Popular Culture: Exclusion and Appropriation (1760s–1930s) 101

7 Urban Modernity and the Provincial: Changing Concepts of Time and Space (1830s–1930s) 125

8 The Nation Called into Question (1890s–1920s) 141

9 Writers and Political Commitment (1930s–1960s) 165

10 Spain beyond Spain: Exile and Diaspora (1939–1980s) 188

11 Catalan, Galician, and Basque Literatures: Recovery and Institutionalization (1960s–1990s) 208

12 Rewriting Gender and Sexuality (1970s–2020) 223

13 Memory and Forgetting (1970s–2020) 245

14 Normalization, Crisis, and the Search for New Paradigms (1975–2021) 267

References 293
Index 317

Introduction

The title of our volume, *Modern Literatures in Spain*, recognizes Spain's particularity as a country that has developed literary markets in four languages: Castilian (whose rise to dominance as the language of state from the late fifteenth to early eighteenth centuries led to its becoming synonymous with Spanish), Catalan, Galician, and Basque (*euskara* in the Basque language). Our aim has been to offer a cultural history that is attentive to the way that "Spanish literature" has been constructed historically and came to refer solely to literature in Castilian. We have made a point of analyzing these four literatures relationally, avoiding the frequent tendency to treat them in separate chapters.

Throughout, we call into question geographic and linguistic definitions of the nation. Exile literature is explored in order to question the boundaries of the Spanish nation and its literary production; we consider exile writing in all four of Spain's literary languages. The discussion of literature in Basque covers the French as well as Spanish Basque country, since literary processes in the two territories have functioned as a continuum. The coverage of Catalan literature includes the Balearic Islands, Valencia, and the Catalan-speaking parts of Aragon. The sections on Galician literature in particular consider the fraught issue of authors from Spain's historic nationalities who write entirely or partly in Castilian. Foreign-born authors resident in Spain are mentioned at certain points, since the question of who counts as a Spanish (or Catalan or Galician or Basque) writer need not align with place of birth – or with mother tongue, for that matter.

The volume's timeline moves from the eighteenth century, in the course of which Castilian was imposed as the sole language of administration and education, to the present, with a solid publishing industry and literary output now established in Catalan, Galician, and Basque. While the minority languages still compete on an uneven playing field with Castilian, globalization has opened up opportunities for Spain's "minor" literatures. In the course of writing this book, we became increasingly aware that the timelines of the four literatures studied do not always coincide; for that reason, in certain chapters the temporal framing of the sections devoted to the various literatures differs. A major aim has been to rethink literary periodization: our chapters have a thematic focus, overlapping in their temporal coverage but gradually moving forward through time – in this way avoiding the impression that at a certain date one period ends and another starts. This has allowed us to take account of the multi-temporality of historical processes, with the coexistence at any one moment of what Raymond Williams identified as residual, dominant, and emergent tendencies (2009 [1977], 121–7). We have consequently been sensitive to the tensions and contradictions that give literary texts their dynamism and cultural relevance. The thematic focus of our chapters is organized in terms of forces of cultural change that leave their mark on, and are facilitated by, changes in literary form: we take seriously Williams's claim (2009 [1977], 128–35) that literary form does not simply mirror cultural processes but is a motor of change through its imaginative capacity to give expression to still inchoate social concerns.

There are several ways in which this cultural history of modern literatures in Spain differs from existing Spanish literary histories, in addition to its relational treatment of the country's four literatures. First, its discussion of literary movements emerges out of the exploration of literature's ability to act as a barometer of cultural change, rather than being a primary organizing principle; this avoids a view of literary history as a closed system of intertextual literary influences. Second, we have questioned the principles that underlie histories of national literature by working against the notion of a literary canon comprised by texts that are deemed worthy to represent the national – a notion that has excluded authors from certain social categories, as well as privileging certain kinds of subject matter and style. The forging of Catalan, Galician, and Basque literary canons that has been necessary to give status to minority literatures has not been exempt from such exclusions. The conception of the canon as a corpus of works deemed worthy to represent the national has meant that literary histories have often included texts that were little read or performed. We have tried in our cultural history to give a sense of what the Spanish public actually read or viewed on stage; consequently, our volume approximates to a history of literary tastes. We thus pay considerable attention to popular literary forms, many of which – especially those associated with urban culture – have been dismissed as vulgar. We have also worked against a tendency to construct "Spanish literature" (seen in the singular) in a uniformly serious register, on the supposition that the serious is better suited to represent the national. This tendency has led to the exclusion from the canon of a great deal of literary works that are huge fun – and were enjoyed by a broad public for that reason.

In this respect, we have been mindful of Pierre Bourdieu's theorization of taste as a means of constructing class distinctions, and of the process whereby, in the course of the nineteenth century, literature established itself as a (supposedly) autonomous field by defining literary merit as the inverse of commercial gain (1996a [1979], 1996b [1992]). In tracing the emergence in modern Spain of a public sphere, we have stressed the importance of journalism, not only for creating several modern literary genres but also for enabling the professionalization of the writer. We have sought to show how the literary field evolved in the course of the twentieth century with the requirement from the 1930s to the 1950s – on both sides of the Spanish Civil War – that writers commit to specific political options, and the impact since the return to democracy in 1975 of the consensus politics favored by the Spanish state and the increasing pressures of the neoliberal market, both challenged in recent years.

As should be clear from the above, we hope to have shown that, while the social and political attitudes taken by writers are hugely varied, literature is never truly autonomous; declarations of literary autonomy are themselves ideological statements. This is, therefore, a political as well as cultural history of literature, inasmuch as it situates literature in relation to political responses to, and proposals for, historical change, as well as in relation to changing social formations and experiences. In those social experiences we include the creation of new forms of subjectivity, where literature has played a vital role. A major factor here, considered throughout the volume, is the role played by literature in the construction – and critique – of gender roles. That involves much more than broadening the canon beyond the usual (heterosexual/homosocial) male suspects – though that is something we have also tried to do.

The book has been written by the two co-authors Jo Labanyi and Luisa Elena Delgado working together as a team with the three contributors: Helena Buffery for literature in Catalan, Kirsty Hooper for literature in Galician, and Mari Jose Olaziregi for literature in Basque. In some chapters, one of us has served as lead author, with one or more co-writers contributing particular sections; in others, the division of labor has been more even. Most chapters cover more than one of Spain's four literatures, in various combinations as appropriate to the topic. Chapters 1, 2, and 3 discuss literature in Castilian only. Chapters 4 and 11 deal solely with literatures in Catalan, Galician, and Basque. Buffery was responsible for all the sections on literature in Catalan, as well as for writing the frame narrative for chapter 11; she additionally wrote the sections on Spanish-language literature in chapter 10, for which she was lead author, and played a major role through her attention to the relational dimension of issues discussed in different sections of the text. Hooper wrote all the sections on literature in Galician, as well as the frame narrative for chapter 4. Olaziregi wrote all the sections on literature in Basque. The sections on literature in Castilian were shared by Delgado and Labanyi, co-writing chapters 7 and 12, and with Delgado being lead author for chapters 1 and 14, and Labanyi being lead author for chapters 2, 3, 5, 6, 8, 9, and 13. Although we have each taken responsibility for writing specific sections, the planning and rewriting of the book as a whole has been done by all of us working together, in order to produce what we hope is a coherent narrative.

We have provided English translations of quotations from Spanish, Catalan, Galician, and Basque, and of titles and organizations (where not self-evident) on first mention in each chapter. Dates of works are given on first mention in each chapter. The book's thematic organization means that many authors are discussed in more than one chapter; readers are encouraged to use the index to locate multiple mentions of particular authors. We have assumed that not all of our readers will have prior knowledge of the literatures of Spain or of Spanish history. Each chapter has a number of subheadings so as to focus discussion and allow flexibility in the positioning of the sections on the four literatures concerned.

We are keenly aware of how much has had to be excluded from our narrative for reasons of space. We have tried to make the condensed overview critical rather than descriptive. In addition, for each chapter, we have singled out a number of texts – covering the various literatures discussed in that chapter – for more detailed textual analysis, offering readings that go beyond existing criticism. We thus hope that the volume will add to scholarly understanding of the four literatures of modern Spain not just through the range of material covered, but also by offering fresh interpretations of individual texts and writers.

This book has been long in the making. We thank our editors at Polity Books – Andrea Drugan at the start and Ellen MacDonald-Kramer, Stephanie Homer, and Mary Savigar at the end – for their patience. We also thank the Production Department at Polity Books for their inspired suggestion of a mosaic for the cover picture, not only because of its evocation of Gaudí's modernist reworking of the mosaic art form, but also because the concept of a mosaic – including the gaps between the pieces – perfectly represents our attempt in this volume to produce a narrative that foregrounds cultural heterogeneity. The five authors have learned much from each other in the course of writing this book, which could not have been written by any of us on our own. The collaborative conception of the volume has been essential to the relational approach to Spain's four literatures that characterizes its structure and scope. We hope that this collaborative conception of scholarship may serve as a step towards further discussion of the diverse cultures of Spain that is based on dialogue and cooperation, allowing a rich understanding of the complexities of the country's cultural plurality.

1

Modernity and the Singular Nation (1700–1840s)

This first chapter covers the beginnings of debates around modernity in Spain in the early eighteenth century through to the Romantic period. Around 1580, German cartographer and cosmographer Sebastian Münster included in his popular work *Cosmographia universalis* a map created by Johannes Bucius in 1537 (see figure 1). Known as *Europa Regina*, it represented a queen carrying the iconology of Europe, with different parts of the body corresponding to specific territories (Dainotto 2007, 30–3). The head of *Europa Regina* was Hispania, Germany represented the heart, and France the upper chest. Italy was Europe's right arm with Sicily the orb in its hand. England, Spain's political enemy, occupied a marginal position, symbolized by a flag firmly in the grasp of the monarch's left hand. The Habsburg Emperor Carlos V (Carlos I of Spain) must have been pleased with this visual commentary on his imperial affairs.

A hundred years later, a similar anthropomorphic map would have illustrated a very different political body, as the European territories under the control of the Spanish empire began to shrink and France started to consolidate its political and cultural hegemony. The gravity of the nation's predicament had been recognized by Spanish observers even before the Peace of Westphalia (1648) in which Spain lost northern Flanders. From the first half of the seventeenth century, reformers known as *arbitristas* (from *arbitrio*, project) circulated countless proposals to improve the nation's economic situation, political cohesion, and moral character. The weaknesses threatening the stability of the vast Spanish empire's heterogeneous territories (encompassing the Americas, southern Italy and Milan, Flanders, the Philippines, and other smaller domains) were evident: a constantly bankrupt state that could not collect taxes or pay its army; conflicting internal trading policies; an unwieldy bureaucracy; unproductive lands controlled by the Church and an idle aristocracy; depopulation; massive inflation. The *arbitristas* offered a number of concrete solutions (protection of agriculture and industry; bringing water to arid areas; re-population of territories depopulated by wars; curbing of state spending; overhaul of the tax system)

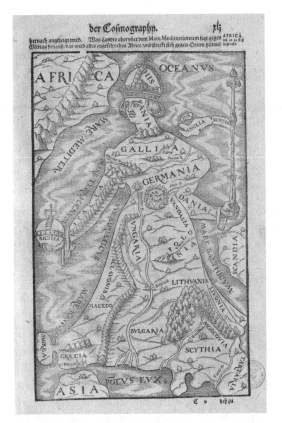

Figure 1: *Europa Regina.* Reproduced from the 1598 German edition of
Sebastian Münster's *Cosmographia universalis.*
Source: Bibliothèque Nationale de France.

that were mostly ignored. The eighteenth-century *proyectistas* (reformers)
recognized some of these *arbitrios* as valuable precedents to their own
reformist ideas (Álvarez de Miranda 1985; Dubet and García Guerra 2009).

The perception of national decadence intensified with the outcome of
the War of the Spanish Succession (1702–14), considered the first world
war of modern times. The Habsburg Carlos II's death in 1700 without
a direct heir produced a conflict between the French Bourbons' support
for the future Felipe V, grandson of Louis XIV of France, and support for
Archduke Charles of Austria by England, Holland, Prussia, and Austria,
alarmed at the threat to the continental balance of power posed by possible
union of the French and Spanish crowns. The war's conclusion marked a
major re-drawing of the political boundaries of the Spanish empire. The

Treaty of Utrecht (1713) allowed Felipe V to keep Spain's American possessions but forced him to renounce his rights to southern Flanders, Sardinia, Sicily, Naples, Milan, Menorca, and Gibraltar, most of which passed to the new emerging powers, England and Austria (Naples and Sicily would revert to Bourbon control in 1738). The war also marked a radical reconceptualization of the Spanish state, with the centralizing "Nueva Planta" (New Design) decrees of 1707–16, discussed below.

Reactive Modernity

The political and cultural implications of such losses by a previously hegemonic power were remarked upon by European thinkers in a discourse that displaced Spain's political and cultural location towards Africa, away from rationality and modernity. Montesquieu wrote a scathing attack on Spanish culture in his *Persian Letters*, asserting that the nation should be under its European peers' political supervision, thus assigning a colonial position to a nation that was (still) a colonial power (Dainotto 2007, 88). In response, eighteenth-century Spanish writers of different ideological tendencies like Father Benito Feijoo, José Cadalso, and Juan Pablo Forner wrote defensively about Spain's cultural worth, negating its symbolic "africanization" or, conversely, questioning the value of phenomena associated with modernity such as empiricism, scientific advances, secularism, and rationalism (Donato and López 2015). This kind of slanging match would become endemic to modern Spanish culture: the discussion of "Spanishness" in reactive mode, always in response to a northern European gaze (Torrecilla 1996, 11–54). The reactive mode would become increasingly emotional, whether belligerent or anguished, throughout the nineteenth century (Mariano José de Larra, Ricardo Macías Picavea, Marcelino Menéndez Pelayo, Rafael Altamira). It would peak with the thinkers writing around the time of the loss of Spain's last major colonies in 1898 (see chapter 8), captured in Miguel de Unamuno's famous statement "me duele España" (Spain hurts me), reprised and mocked by Francoist chauvinism (Franco 2005).

In practice, Spain was not the only country to be re-positioned as Europe's exotic Other. As Roberto Dainotto (2007) has shown, in the eighteenth century the European south in general became Europe's internal Other, with Spain, Portugal, Italy, and Greece (not to mention outlying nations like Russia and Turkey) seen as "deficiencies of Europeanness," located within its past. Conversely, France and other northern European countries came to incarnate the present and future, modernity and pro-gress in all their teleological certainty. Spain's ambivalent status as both an imperial and a declining power at this moment of modern European expansion presented its thinkers and public figures with an ineluctable choice: between progress achieved through a modernity viewed as foreign, and authenticity derived from intolerant, archaic traditions. The choice was an impossible one, resulting in the "split consciousness" of so many nineteenth- and twentieth-century Spanish thinkers: torn between the promise of progress and cultural prestige tied to modernity's Eurocentric master narrative and the realization that such a narrative assigned them, as members of a second-rank nation marked by its Semitic (particularly Arab) heritage, to the margins of history. This double-bind has been used to construct a tragic narrative of Spanishness, premised on the nation's sup-posed "autophagous" tendencies (Ilie 1984) – a predicament shared with all those peripheries excluded from the modern European utopia which had to eliminate the elements in their respective cultures that constituted devia-tions from the modern cultural paradigm. The irony is that, in so doing, they were often accused of imitation and lack of originality (Torrecilla 1996; L.E. Delgado, Mendelson, and Vázquez 2007).

What was specific about Spain's situation was its simultaneous position as an imperial power and a colonized country (Dussel 1995, 67; Mignolo 2012). During the eighteenth and nineteenth centuries Spain would be subject to the cultural, military, and economic imperialism of hegemonic Europe (in particular France, Holland, and England). At the same time, it was immersed in its own imperialist designs: not just in America, but also, still at this time, in South-East Asia (the Philippines) and the Pacific (Caroline Islands, Mariana Islands including Guam), all lost in 1898 (in the case of the Carolinas and the Marianas excepting Guam, sold to Germany), and in Europe (Naples and Sicily would remain under the control of a branch of the Spanish Bourbons until 1860). Spain's complex position is well illustrated by a famous quote from the *novator* (literally, innova-tor) Juan de Cabriada. The *novatores* were scientists and thinkers who, between 1675 and 1725, challenged traditional Spanish scholastic thinking and created networks of knowledge and sociability – often meeting in private *tertulias* (salons) and learned academies – in support of empiricism, secularism, and the free circulation of modern European philosophical and scientific thought (Pérez Magallón 2002). In his *Carta filosófica médico-química* (*Medical-Chemical Philosophical Letter*, 1687), Cabriada lamented: "Que es lastimoso y aun vergonzosa cosa que, como si fuéramos indios, hayamos de ser los últimos en recibir las noticias y luces públicas que ya están esparcidas por Europa" ("It is pitiful, even shameful, that we should be the last to receive news and public enlightenment already disseminated throughout Europe, as if we were Amerindians") (Sánchez Ron 2016). A mid-eighteenth-century list of Catalan grievances presented to the Spanish Crown denounced priests who only spoke Castilian with a similar argument: "¿Y van a ser los labradores catalanes y valencianos de peor condición que los indios?" ("And are Catalan and Valencian laborers to be seen as inferior to Amerindians?") (*Memorial de Greuges* 1760), the point being that Spanish missionaries often learned Amerindian languages to facilitate the conversion process, but Catalan and Valencian laborers were expected to communicate in Castilian, a language they often did not know. These two examples show the coexistence of a defense of European minority languages with an unquestioned assumption of imperialist hierarchies, thus illustrating the intersection of modernity and coloniality.

The shift in the perception of Spanishness that took place in the eighteenth century and Romantic period can be summed up by the question: Against whom is Spanishness defined? The answer foregrounds opposition to the foreign; specifically, the French. In the eighteenth century, throughout Europe, refinement and high culture were equated with French "civilization." For Spain, which had maintained its political hegemony by fighting against France for two centuries, the change of dynasty from the Habsburgs to the Bourbons had far-reaching consequences for the country's cultural self-perception. The identification of modernity, high culture, and scientific innovation with France explains why it was at this time that reactionary sectors started to monopolize the meaning of "lo español" (Spanishness). The desire to draw the boundaries of a distinct Spanish identity also led, during the second part of the eighteenth century, to the specifically Spanish cultural phenomenon of *majismo*. A *majo/a* was a well-dressed, outspoken man or woman of the working classes, particularly of Madrid (a similar term was *manolo/a*). *Majismo* refers to the appropriation by the aristocracy (particularly by women, with important ramifications for the intersection of gender and national character) of popular customs seen as manifestations of an essential national spirit (Haidt 2011; Zanardi 2016). That appropriation included dress, dance, and even linguistic usage and body language. *Majos/as* and *manolos/as* are represented in Goya's early paintings and tapestry cartoons and in the most popular plays of the century, Ramón de la Cruz's *sainetes* (one-act farces with song and dance; see chapter 6).

The literary battles fought in the eighteenth century are a consequence of Spanish reactions to French cultural hegemony. The positions in the dispute range from full acceptance of this hegemony to a defensive rejection of any tendency perceived as foreign. Around 1735, new customs imposed by the government and public officials, many of them French and Italian, came to be seen as incompatible with an essential Spanishness expressed by the term *castizo*. In Spain, *castizo* meant of good lineage; that is, unadulterated by foreign (including Jewish or Muslim) elements. The term also underpinned attempts to classify degrees of racial mixture in Spanish America and the Philippines (Carrera 2003). By extension, the term referred to what was typical of a certain region or of the nation. What was *castizo* was incompatible not only with the foreign but also with the country's non-Castilian speaking regions, unless they were assimilated into a national melting-pot, the capital Madrid being the indispensable instrument of this process. Regional specificities were viewed as local expressions of a larger whole to which they should be subordinated. From the eighteenth century on, the *castizo* came to be assigned in the Spanish national imaginary to Castile and/or Andalusia. The debate over which elements of Spanish culture were or were not *castizo* would continue through the nineteenth and twentieth centuries, with the term mobilized by Spanish conservative nationalism.

Reasons of State

Domestically, the end of the War of the Spanish Succession marked the beginning of a new political era, characterized by strongly centralized government and the aspiration to create an equally centralized national culture: a process that would continue throughout the nineteenth century. With the proclamation of the Nueva Planta decrees (Valencia, 1707; Majorca and Ibiza 1715; Catalonia 1716), the new Bourbon king Felipe V revoked the traditional institutions and charters (*fueros*) of the Catalan-speaking territories that had opposed him, ending Spain's division into the separate Crowns of Aragon and Castile. Navarre and the Basque provinces, which had supported him, kept their charters. Contrary to the fragmented character of Habsburg rule, the Nueva Planta state required the unity of all its parts, subject to a single administration. All the king's subjects would therefore be bound by Castilian law and customs; internal borders were erased, which meant, among other things, the end of the Cadiz monopoly on trade with America and beginning of Catalonia's economic expansion into colonial markets, with long-term social and economic consequences. The new political order was sustained by the creation of Spain's first permanent army and a new administrative organization that reduced or suppressed the multiple existing territorial *consejos* (councils) – of Aragón, Navarre, Italy, the Indies – while the power of the Council of Castile was increased. The territories in the Americas were subjected to parallel measures of centralization and control, which remained largely theoretical since local authorities often determined what could or could not be enforced (Guimerá Ravina 2007; Paquette 2008). Recent consideration of the Spanish and Spanish-American Enlightenment from an Atlantic perspective has challenged the premise of the movement's European uniqueness, focusing on autochthonous processes that facilitated cultural interaction and the co-production of ideas and knowledge (Cañizares-Esguerra 2001; Conrad 2012; Hill 2018; Lewis, Bolufer Peruga, and Jaffe 2020; Stolley 2020).

Felipe V's punitive centralizing measures against supporters of his Habsburg rival in the War of the Spanish Succession also extended to cultural matters, as the new king determined to make Castilian the official language of his newly designed state. Use of the Catalan language was first restricted in public areas and later eliminated from primary and secondary education, a decision that would have long-lasting consequences for Catalan culture as well as for the relationship between the Catalan territories and the state. Already in 1715, a prosecutor in the Council of Castile called for restraint in the application of the new language laws, warning that they would make Catalans of all political tendencies feel resentful (Anguera 2003, 78). The Bourbon monarchy's interest in the Castilian language was ironic, since the language of the court during the first half of the century was French and, in the second half, Italian. Ignacio de Luzán, whose *Poética* (1737; most-cited edition 1789) is considered the best Spanish expression of neoclassical aesthetics, wrote in both Italian and Spanish. The emphasis on a monolingual state, perceived as crucial for a unified citizenship, was consistent with the Enlightenment's belief in fixed universal cultural hierarchies and consequent disregard for (and fear of) difference. The new type of subject envisioned by the Bourbon dynasty was to be positioned in relation to a center from which "reasons of state" were articulated, imposed, and internalized (Medina 2009, 2013). In both politics and cultural matters, Bourbon Spain was characterized by the attempt to erase internal differences, particularly those that did not fit the imagined community of Enlightened subjects, including the poor, beggars, and vagrants. The Roma community (particularly those with a nomadic lifestyle) was subjected to increasingly repressive legislation, culminating in the 1749 order for the detention of all its members, rescinded in 1765. A 1783 royal decree granted citizenship to the Roma with the aim of achieving their full cultural assimilation, forbidding their language and traditions (Pym 2007).

Thus, it was in the eighteenth century that a particular political and cultural narrative was born: a narrative of Spanish identity whose starting point was the identification between nation and state, and the consideration of that state as politically and culturally homogeneous and centered in Castile (Albareda i Salvadó 2002). The top-down, coordinated effort to define Spanishness constituted an identity project whose far-reaching implications would surpass the economic and social projects undertaken in the century's course. The shadow that this identity project would cast on the construction of the Spanish literary canon would be very long indeed: not until the late twentieth century (1995) would a writer be awarded the Premio Nacional de las Letras (National Literature Prize) for a work in a language other than Castilian: the novel *Dins el darrer blau* (*Into the Last Blue*), written in Catalan by the Majorcan writer Carme Riera. Only in 2019 would the Premio Cervantes be awarded to a writer with a significant body of work in a language other than Castilian (the poet Joan Margarit, who switched to writing in Catalan in 1981, after early work in Castilian).

Public Spaces and the Location of Power

Part and parcel of that new narrative of unified Spanishness was the creation of physical and symbolic public national spaces. "National" meant "royal," given the absolutist equation of nation-state and crown. It was at this time that the various royal academies were founded under crown patronage (see chapter 3). Among the first collections of the Royal Library, created in 1712, were books seized from aristocrats who had supported the Habsburg side in the War of the Spanish Succession. The institution would officially become a "national library" (rather than crown property) in 1836. Academies of Letters were founded in Barcelona (1751) and Seville (1752). The Archives of the Council of the Indies (now Archivo General de Indias) were established, also in Seville, in 1785. The new dynasty additionally embarked on a process of urban modernization, particularly in Madrid, in consonance with Enlightenment ideals of the common good, social order, and sociability. This project included well-lit streets, gardens, and coffee houses (Outram 2019, 10–25). It also included new roads and infrastructure to facilitate the exchange of people and goods between the nation's symbolic center (Madrid) and the provinces, as well as between peninsular Spain and the rest of its territories. Emblematic of the new Bourbon state model is the number of royal residences, tripling those of the Habsburgs: a building boom that culminated in the construction of the vast Royal Palace in Madrid, built on the ruins of the old Alcázar after a fire destroyed it in 1734. The new Versailles-inspired building, designed mostly by Italian architects and decorated by the best artists in Europe, became a symbol of the new Bourbon dynasty and the new state (Medina 2009, 39–46). However, Felipe V would never inhabit it; the French-born monarch responsible for Spain's centralization and official monolingualism never fully adapted to life in the capital and never spoke Spanish fluently.

Despite its efforts, the Spanish state – unlike the French – was not able to shape "citizens" loyal to a common national cause in the eighteenth century or later. One reason is that in Spain, unlike France, a bourgeois public sphere independent of government and its institutions did not exist (García Díaz 2019; Kitts 2019). For the most part Spanish elites, including the aristocracy and the Church, would oppose progressive ideas as antithetical to a true national essence.

For all the state efforts to impose Madrid as cultural center of the newly designed state, the reality was that new economic, political, and cultural ideas often came from the provinces and the colonies, even if official recognition had to come from the political center. The first of the many economic societies created to promote Spain's development was the Real Sociedad Vascongada de Amigos del País (Basque Royal Society of Friends of the Nation), founded in 1765; Madrid's equivalent would be created ten years later, followed by many others in the Peninsula and other territories of the Spanish Crown. Indeed, the very notion of a Republic of Letters, a universal and timeless intellectual community from whose center (hegemonic Europe and in particular France) knowledge would circulate to the world, was challenged from the peripheries (Álvarez Barrientos 2003). Father Juan Andrés y Morell, a Valencian Jesuit who settled in Mantua (Italy) after the Jesuits were expelled from Spain in 1767, composed in Italian what is considered the first history of world and comparative literature (*On the Origins, Progress and Present State of All Literatures*, 1782–99). Andrés's work challenged the existence of universal good taste and insisted on the importance of historicizing local phenomena. His monumental work developed a comparatist approach that theorized a different Europe and a different modernity: a Europe seen from the south whose origins are found in Sicily and Al-Andalus; that is to say, in the Orient (Dainotto 2007, 105–33). The tensions between state and "regional" identities were seen as a danger to the unified nation even by "liberal" Enlightenment writers like Feijoo, whose essay "Amor de la patria y pasión nacional" (Love of the

Fatherland and National Passion, 1729) would warn against the perils of split loyalties or national allegiances considered incompatible with true patriotism, by now firmly identified with a state that was to be the sole guarantor of its citizens' interests and happiness (Valero 2002).

Cultural Identity and the Enlightenment Reform Project

In the Enlightenment, literature (meaning "letters" in the broad sense) was understood as a tool of communication and education in service of the common good; hence the predominance of didactic genres and advocacy of stylistic clarity. This was the century when the word *ensayo* started to take on its present-day sense of "essay," even if those today considered the period's best essayists (Feijoo, Gaspar Melchor de Jovellanos, Francisco Cabarrús) did not use the term (Álvarez de Miranda 1992, 285–327). Communication and exchange meant vigorous discussion, and the century is marked by innumerable public polemics. These included the bitter confrontations between the Valencian Gregorio Mayans, whose defense of a Spanish tradition which he located in the sixteenth century privileged a discursive style supported by science and erudition, and the Galician Padre Feijoo, who linked his own role as "divulgador" (disseminator) with use of the vernacular (Castilian instead of Latin) and an accessible, "natural" style. The dichotomies underscoring most of the public debates of eighteenth-century Spain – scholasticism versus innovation, tradition versus modernity, *casticismo* versus *afrancesamiento* (Frenchified customs and thought) – have carried over into critical evaluations of the period. Until recently, it was common to read that the cultural products of the Spanish Enlightenment were derivative and not on a par with their French, English, or German counterparts. Those sympathetic to the Enlightenment have justified its limited scope in Spain – what Eduardo Subirats (1981) has called its "insufficiency" – by noting that the spirit of reform could not flourish in a country with an all-powerful Church and still active Inquisition; that the creation of a true public sphere was impossible in a nation with a feudal, parasitic aristocracy; and that economic progress could not be achieved in a nation that disdained manual work and commerce and lacked an efficient communications network. Opponents of the Enlightenment have related the lack of originality of its Spanish version to what they saw as a loss of identity attributed to the secularizing reforms of the first Bourbon monarchs.

The best representative of this position is renowned philologist and historian Menéndez Pelayo, who in his *Historia de los heterodoxos españoles*

(*History of Spanish Heterodoxies*, 1880–2) consistently metaphorized the period as a deadly virus spread by foreigners. Menéndez Pelayo's strategy is clear. On the one hand, he argues that empiricism, pragmatism, and above all secularism are heterodox manifestations in the overall context of a true Spanish culture marked by a profound religiosity. On the other, he identifies what he considers the best cultural products of the time with the residues of an essential Spanish orthodoxy that has resisted foreign contagion. That logic is based on a model of cultural uniqueness, diffusion, and derivation that has been widely questioned. To engage adequately with the eighteenth century requires a major shift of focus – one that considers the Enlightenment not as a homogeneous European intellectual movement, but rather as a process of transnational and global entanglements, including the co-production, circulation, and translation of knowledge. Works like Jovellanos's *Informe sobre la Ley Agraria* (*Report on Agrarian Legislation*, 1794), Feijoo's *Teatro Crítico Universal. Discursos varios en todo género de materias para desengaño de errores comunes* (*Universal Critical Theater: Various Discourses on All Kinds of Matters to Correct Common Errors*, 1726–40), or Diego de Torres Villarroel's satirical *Sueños morales, visiones y visitas de Torres con D. Francisco de Quevedo por Madrid* (*Torres' Moral Dreams, Visions, and Excursions around Madrid with Don Francisco de Quevedo*, 1727–51) must be understood in relation to the major topics of debate at the time: censorship and free speech; women's rights, intellectual capacities, and the role of motherhood; the boundaries between emotion and reason; the social value of manual labor; the need for an equitable tax system and agrarian reform; and the definition of good citizenship and patriotism.

One of the persistent myths found in discussions of Spanish modernity, largely the result of nineteenth- and twentieth-century conservative readings, is the idea that Enlightenment reforms were abruptly introduced by the French Bourbon dynasty. The change in mentality that would lead to those reforms, continuing through to the 1812 Constitution, was in fact already visible in seventeenth-century Spanish society, especially in the peripheries. We have already referred to the *novatores*, the group of doctors and scientists who from 1675 undertook a critique of scholasticism and encouraged scientific principles and empiricism. Contemptuously called "innovators" by their opponents, figures such as Juan Caramuel, Isaac Cardoso, and Cabriada questioned the reliance on authorities and the dominant role of theology in Spanish universities. The movement developed in various parts of the country: Valencia, Seville, Cadiz, Zaragoza, as well as Madrid. The *novatores'* emphasis on pragmatism and social improvement, as well as their interest in opening Spanish debates up to French and English ideas, connects them with later Enlightenment writers such as Feijoo, Pablo de Olavide, and Jovellanos. Despite their attempts to link reform to Spanish humanism, the *novatores* were accused of being enemies of the "true spirit of the nation"; the link between Spanish tradition, militant Catholicism, and the rejection of "foreign" influences was already established in their time (Pérez Magallón 2002).

When Carlos III acceded to the throne in 1759, his enthusiastic continuation of the reforms introduced by his Bourbon predecessors was received by some sectors as drastic, revolutionary, and – again – anti-Spanish. The 1766 Motín de Esquilache (Esquilache Riot) has been used to prove the existence of an intrinsic Spanish resistance to foreign influences. The revolt was triggered by a decree issued by the Neapolitan minister Leopoldo de Gregorio, Marquis o Esquilache, banning the traditional long Spanish cape and broad-brimmed hat, but the people's anger related to several issues, not least price rises for bread and coal. The popular agitation was stirred up by the aristocracy and the Church (in particular, the Jesuits), unhappy with the Bourbon dynasty's reforms which challenged their considerable privileges. The crowd's insistence on a face-to-face confrontation with the King contested the absolutist state's control over its subjects. The traditional long Spanish cape and broad-brimmed hat had allowed citizens to conceal their identity, evading the government's increasingly controlling gaze; the new measure was perceived by the people as subjecting their bodies to intrusive surveillance (Medina 2009, 137–72). The riot's ambivalent conclusion shows that a negotiation process was necessary to resolve the tensions: Esquilache was dismissed, the short cape was eventually adopted. More broadly, the riot exemplifies the importance of collective, popular acts of protest in the (long) eighteenth century (Fuentes and Malin 2021). The Jesuits were expelled in 1767 and Carlos III continued his reform program, which included a drastic reduction in popular public celebrations and suppression of freedom of assembly. The episode, like the 1808 popular uprising against the Napoleonic occupation, would be instrumentalized for the benefit of a conservative narrative of Spanishness in the nineteenth century and beyond.

Gender and the Productive Nation

The notion of national decadence and crisis that entered the collective imaginary towards the end of the seventeenth century became embedded in it during the eighteenth, comprising an enduring structure of feeling that would reach its high point at the turn of the nineteenth and twentieth centuries. Indeed, the notion of decadence can be considered a founding myth of modern Spanish history, in the sense that it captures a very specific perception of reality linked to political agendas across the ideological spectrum. During the Enlightenment, with its belief in the potential for progress, Spain's "anomalous" position was usually interpreted as serious but solvable through practical measures. As the nineteenth century progressed, the tone became more pessimistic, metaphysical, and essentialist. Not surprisingly, given modernity's emphasis on the (re)production of normative bodies and minds as essential to society's well-being, debates around the country's decline and desired regeneration were framed through bodily metaphors (Haidt 1998; Outram 2022). From the eighteenth century on, conservatives and liberals, Spaniards and foreigners alike would figure the nation's failure to enter European modernity (that is, normalcy) as a bodily ailment or deviation (Sosa-Velasco 2010; Tsuchiya 2011). Identification of the precise locus of infection became a key concern. Whatever the source of the problem, its rhetorical presentation was always gendered: the nadir of the Spanish monarchy was often symbolized by the disabled, impotent body of the last Hapsburg king, Carlos II. If the empire's expansionist phase could be symbolized by a spectacular royal femininity (*Europa Regina*), its declining phase was consistently figured as a deficient, infertile, or queer masculinity (Penrose 2014). In the nineteenth century, nationalist discourse figured the nation in terms of motherhood, as a *mater dolorosa* or a wayward mother who ignored her obligations to her children, as was alleged of the much-maligned Queen Isabel II (Álvarez Junco 2001).

During the Enlightenment the male body signified the possibilities of reason, knowledge, and pleasure but also the limits to desire and instinct, seen as in need of control. Bodies and sexuality are key to understanding the dual nature of the period's ethos, in its normative and liberatory dimensions, discernible in the tension between a refined (elite) homosociality (which included enjoyment of erotica and pornography) and undisciplined passions or effeminacy (Harvey 2004). Spanish writers of the period construct the body as a vehicle for rational, scientific knowledge (Feijoo, Torres Villarroel) and as the site of bodily pleasure (the anacreontic poetry of Juan Meléndez Valdés and José Cadalso). Félix de Samaniego could write moralistic fables as well as racy tales to be shared with male friends; Nicolás Fernández de Moratín exalted feminine virtue in his drama *Lucrecia* (1763) and the joys of casual sex for sale in *El arte de las putas* (*The Art of Whores*, 1770); Meléndez Valdés could go from depicting idyllic scenes of pastoral life to graphic descriptions of lovemaking in *Los besos de amor* (*Kisses of Love*,

1783) (Haidt 1998, 63–102; Gies 1999, 2008; Penrose 2014, 33–110). Needless to say, erotic and pornographic materials did not circulate widely, if at all. The Inquisition was not abolished till 1834; Moratín's *El arte de las putas*, with its explicit descriptions of prostitution, was included in the Catholic Church's Index of Prohibited Books in 1790 and not published until 1898.

While Enlightenment thought emphasized universal values, the period has also been considered a watershed in European attempts to define differences between the sexes and the role of each in relation to citizenship and public life (Smith 2006; Bolufer Peruga 2016, 2018). In Spain, as in the rest of Europe, the nature of women, their role in a civilized society, and the specificities of their contribution to the public good were the subject of heated public debates and important literary works, such as Feijoo's *Defensa de las mujeres* (*Defense of Women*, 1726); Leandro Fernández de Moratín's plays *El viejo y la niña* (*The Old Man and the Young Girl*, 1790) and *El sí de las niñas* (*The Maidens' Consent*, 1805); and Josefa Amar y Borbón's remarkable *Discurso en defensa del talento de las mujeres y de su aptitud para el gobierno y otros cargos en que se emplean los hombres* (*Discourse in Defense of Women's Talent and their Suitability for Government and Other Positions Held by Men*, 1786). Mixed sociability was considered an important element of public life; hence the crucial role that many (aristocratic) women played in the period's cultural life as hosts of and participants in *tertulias* where politics, philosophy, and cultural matters were discussed. These salons were, nevertheless, private spaces. The presence of women, even aristocratic women, in cultural and educational institutions at a time when the boundary between public and private space was becoming increasingly demarcated was a different matter, exemplified in the intense 1775–87 debates over women's admission to Madrid's Sociedad Económica de Amigos del País. Despite all the restrictions on their intellectual and political contribution to the *res publica*, educated women found ways to create public platforms for their ideas. They were notable, for example, as translators, an activity that gave them intellectual legitimacy and room for creativity, since translations were often seen as textual transformations: Inés Joyes y Blake's *Apología de las mujeres* (*Apology for Women*, 1798) was written as a letter accompanying her translation of Samuel Johnson's *Rasselas*, and works by Racine and Voltaire were translated by Margarita Hickey (Bolufer Peruga 1998, 331–9; Smith 2003).

The equation of the ideal nation with a vigorous yet restrained masculinity pervades eighteenth-century Spanish literature, as it would that of the nineteenth. The link between proper gentlemanly behavior, masculinity, and national identity converged in two crucial cultural constructs of the time that exemplify the dichotomous articulation of national identity:

the *petimetre* and the *hombre de bien*. The *petimetre* (fop, from the French "petit-maître") represented a failed masculinity that exceeded the proper limits of its opposite, *hombría de bien*, by pursuing excessive pleasures and superficial appearance while lacking the civic virtues needed to build a strong nation: industriousness, self-discipline, and good judgment. As the term makes clear, the *petimetre*'s excess was intrinsically linked to the foreign and thus opposed to the *castizo*. The masculinity represented by the *hombre de bien* is a crucial theme in most of the century's best-known works: Moratín junior's *El sí de las niñas*; Jovellanos's *El delincuente honrado* (*The Honorable Delinquent*, 1773); and, most importantly, Cadalso's *Cartas marruecas* (*Moroccan Letters*, published posthumously 1789), which frame an explicit critique of the nation.

Structured in epistolary form, the 90 letters that form the *Cartas marruecas* develop an exchange between Gazel, a Moroccan diplomat who arrives in Spain, his Spanish host Nuño Núñez, and Gazel's adoptive father and advisor Ben-Beley back in Morocco. Although the *Cartas*'s configuration and subject matter bear a clear resemblance to Montesquieu's *Persian Letters* – against one of which Cadalso had written a *Defense of the Spanish Nation* (1768–71) – Cadalso's "Introduction" establishes a national literary filiation for his work, appealing to Cervantes as his predecessor. The Cervantine connection is reinforced by the fictional editor's claim to be publishing a manuscript on which he has stumbled. The editor acknowledges that his goal is to criticize the Spanish national character from a balanced position or "justo medio" (happy mean). This "happy mean" is mentioned repeatedly as the only position from which to aspire to the *hombría de bien* that undergirds the utilitarian morality of productive citizenship, equally opposed to *petimetres* and *majos*. The work's use of three narrators (two Moroccan Muslims and one Spanish Catholic) seems to sustain the cultural equanimity that the editor of the letters claims as his goal, and the work's linking of Spanish and Moroccan customs complicates the relation between Enlightenment and Europeanness.

In practice, however, the foreign interlocutors' opinions are always mediated and (in)validated by the Spaniard's voice. The text's discussion of the many ailments afflicting the weak Spanish national body is based on a notion of patriotism that regards defense of the nation's singularity as a duty. In response to the modern European emphasis on universal values and taste, the Moroccan Ben Beley states that there is nothing worse than a nation "sin carácter propio" (without its own character) (Letter XX). Nuño claims that the true Spain can still be found in the provinces (Letter XXI) but the emphasis throughout is on what Spain is not. The often-humorous account given in Letter XXVI of the cultural, linguistic, and spiritual differences between the different provinces includes recognition that, though an obstacle to "perfect union" in peacetime, the resulting rivalries can be an advantage against a common (foreign) enemy. Language – Castilian, purged of Gallicisms – is presented as a key factor in the preservation of an authentic Spanish identity.

The *Cartas marruecas* make it clear that a strong national identity rests on the concerted efforts of a community of men linked by bonds of friendship and sensibility, understood as civic virtues. The good citizen's leisure has to be carefully regulated. Letter XL criticizes an idle, ill-educated aristocracy's proclivity for hobnobbing with marginal (especially gypsy) elements of the populace for entertainment purposes: that is, for its *majismo*. By contrast, the *hombre de bien* is industrious and his productivity of public benefit.

Women (and minority ethnic groups) lack a place in the transnational society of good men that the *Cartas marruecas* celebrate. The former are discussed as reflections of their husband's merits (Letter XIX) or as examples of moral corruption and excessive consumption. The female equivalent of the *petimetre* – the *petimetra* (the century's ubiquitous symbol of unproductive femininity) – is not specifically addressed. Yet, the nation's decadence is metaphorized as effeminacy resulting from excessive luxury and idleness (blamed on wealth from the Americas) and moral laxity (blamed on new French customs). The *petimetra* would take center stage in eighteenth-century Spanish theater, in its neoclassical variants – Moratín senior's *La petimetra* (1762) – and in many of the popular *sainetes* of Ramón de la Cruz – such as *La oposición a cortejo* (*Against Male Admirers*, 1773) (Haidt 1999, 2003a; 2011).

Cadalso's fictional editor anticipates the reactions to his work in terms of the dichotomies that by then defined Spanishness: traditionalists will label him a bad Spaniard; *afrancesados* will label him a barbarian. Thus, the desired location of the good Spanish Enlightenment subject, the rational "happy mean," proves an impossibility. That Spanish patriotism could not be simultaneously self-critical and assertive would become clear with the Peninsular War of 1808–14 – one chapter of the wider Napoleonic Wars that in Spain would retrospectively, from the 1820s, come to be called Guerra de Independencia (War of Independence) and in Catalonia, Guerra del Francès (the Frenchman's War). The term "War of Independence" erases the country's internal ideological fragmentation, the conflict's international dimension, and the public debates and institutional transformations that led to the first (remarkably liberal) Spanish Constitution of 1812. Conversely, the nationalist emphasis on collective resistance to a foreign power foregrounds the alignment between patriotism and Spanishness, on the one hand, and modernity and the foreign, on the other. The consequences of such alignments became painfully obvious when Fernando VII, restored to the Spanish throne, abolished the 1812 Constitution and executed, arrested, or drove into exile those suspected of supporting liberalism. The physical and symbolic expulsion from Spanish territory of dissidents thereby became established as a legitimate action for patriots intent on saving the nation from its own citizens, a logic that would continue to be applied, with disastrous consequences, in the twentieth century.

The Myth of Two Spains

The early nineteenth century is the period that gave rise to the notion of two Spains (Juliá 2004), locked in supposedly irrevocable conflict – a notion that is as inaccurate as it is unhelpful for there are always more than two viewpoints at any historical juncture. Both progressives and conservatives have been guilty of such binary thinking. This section will stress the complexity of early nineteenth-century Spanish political and literary positions which, while differing on many counts, do not fit neatly into opposing camps.

The retrospective construction of the Peninsular War as a War of Independence against French occupation legitimized the earlier rejection of certain cultural tendencies as French imports and is largely responsible for the nineteenth century's labeling of Spain's eighteenth century as "not Spanish." In practice, the Peninsular War was a civil war of a complex kind, with both sides regarding themselves as patriots and with Spanish liberals fighting on both sides. At the time, the Peninsular War was referred to by Spaniards as "the revolution in Spain." It must be seen, not just as part of the European Napoleonic Wars, but also as intimately linked to the revolutions that broke out concurrently in Spain's American colonies, sparked by Napoleon's 1808 deposition of Fernando VII. Initially not always tied to a wish for independence, such conflicts were connected to demands for the metropolitan state to grant the overseas territories equitable political representation and greater economic independence. Fernando VII's absolutist regime and military repression on his return to power in 1813 added fuel to the fire of the by-then-entrenched independence movements in Spanish America. It is instructive to set the "revolution in Spain" in the context of the various uprisings and revolutions of the later eighteenth century on both sides of the Atlantic: the Corsican Republic (1755–70), the American Declaration of Independence (1776), the French Revolution (1789), the Haitian Revolution (1791–1804), and the Irish Rebellion (1798) were driven by republican ideals. By contrast, the aim of the fight in Spain against French occupation was to restore the absolutist Fernando VII to the Spanish throne. With the republican-inspired wars of independence in Spanish America – from Hidalgo's 1810 proclamation in Mexico to the 1826 Battle of Ayacucho – Spain lost all its continental American colonies, its empire reduced to Cuba and Puerto Rico in the Caribbean, the Philippines in South-East Asia, and Guam in the Pacific.

It is often forgotten that the beginnings of Romanticism in Spain coincide with this background of massive territorial loss. The various waves of Spanish liberal exiles, many of them writers, generally supported the Spanish American independence struggles and the new republics to which they gave birth, seeing them as counterparts to their own struggle against absolutism (Muñoz Sempere and Alonso García 2011). The fact that Spain's loss of its continental American colonies took place under absolutism helps to explain why it made surprisingly little impact on cultural production – not just because of censorship at home but also because absolutism equated the nation with the monarchy: the colonies were thus Crown property. The contrast with the much smaller territorial loss of Cuba, Puerto Rico, the Philippines, and Guam in 1898 could not be greater for, by that time, thanks to the nation-formation project consolidated in the course of the nineteenth century, the inhabitants of the national territory had internalized the idea that they were national citizens; this second phase of loss of empire was thus seen as a collective loss (see chapter 8). The impact of Spain's loss of its American continental colonies, while economically massive, was mitigated by the fact that transatlantic cultural traffic continued after the creation of the new Latin American republics.

Although Spanish liberals were tarred with the label *afrancesados*, implying collaboration with the Napoleonic occupation, their position was complex. The English-language autobiography of Joseph Blanco White (the name adopted in exile by José María Blanco y Crespo) shows the excruciating dilemma that Spanish liberals were placed in by Napoleon's appointment of his brother Joseph Bonaparte to the Spanish throne as José I. Certain that popular support for the deposed Fernando VII would not lead to reform on his restitution and equally certain that, while it was humiliating to have Joseph Bonaparte imposed as king, he would introduce liberal legislation (both predictions were accurate), Blanco White joined the struggle against Napoleon, with no illusions about the side he was fighting for. In 1810, when his native Seville fell to the French, he fled to England where he integrated into English culture, writing journalism in support of independence for Spain's American colonies. Some Spanish liberals supported José I, going into exile in France on his fall in 1813: for example, the father of the future Romantic writer Mariano José de Larra, who grew up in France till the age of 9; or the neoclassical author Alberto Lista, who on his return taught Larra and the later Romantic poet José de Espronceda. Like Blanco White, most Spanish liberals joined the anti-Napoleon struggle, only to suffer persecution on Fernando VII's return to power: the neoclassical poet Manuel José Quintana and the future Romantic dramatist Francisco Martínez de la Rosa spent the years 1814–20 in prison, the latter in a North African penal colony. To escape this fate, many liberals fled Spain in 1814, returning in 1820 when General Riego's uprising forced Fernando VII to restore the 1812 Constitution. A second wave fled overseas in 1823 when, thanks to military intervention by the restored Bourbon monarchy in France, Fernando re-imposed absolutism – turning to the French to oust liberals perceived as *afrancesados*. The Queen Consort María Cristina, who on Fernando's death in 1833 became Regent of Spain, issued amnesties in 1832 and 1834 that permitted the exiles' return.

In Spain as elsewhere in Europe, Romanticism appealed to writers with widely differing political agendas. Its literary tenets were first introduced into Spain in 1814 through a six-year press polemic between traditionalists (who welcomed it) and liberals (who defended neoclassicism) (Flitter 1992). Spanish liberal writers did not abandon neoclassicism till shortly before the second wave of exiles returned in 1833–4; there was no polemic between neoclassicism and the liberal version of Romanticism that the exiles imbibed overseas because the defenders of both – respectively supporting and opposing the Aristotelian principles of verisimilitude (unity of action, place, and time) and decorum (confinement of noble characters to tragedy and of "common" characters to comedy) – ascribed to the liberal belief in universal human rights and national sovereignty. Traditionalists who rejected liberalism could support Romanticism because of its nationalist streak. In early nineteenth-century Spain, there were two forms of nationalism: a traditionalist belief in national character, grounded in inherited local custom, for which "nation" had the pre-modern meaning of a birth group; and the new liberal belief in national sovereignty, grounded in human rights (Onaindia 2002, 29–30). These two versions of nationalism – traditional and liberal – underscored opposing conceptions of Romanticism.

The 1814–20 Spanish debate on Romanticism took place in the immediate aftermath of the War of Independence, with absolutism newly restored.

It was initiated in Cadiz, the seat of the liberal parliament responsible for the 1812 Constitution, by a German: the anti-liberal Cadiz-based merchant Juan Nicolás Böhl de Faber, who had experienced Napoleon's occupation of his native Hamburg. Böhl's promulgation of German Romantic theory was an explicit attack on neoclassicism, seen as French and thus "not Spanish." The German origin of Böhl's traditionalist ideas did not make them "not Spanish" since they were based on the defense of Spain's Golden Age drama by August Wilhelm Schlegel and of its medieval ballad tradition by his brother Friedrich (like Böhl, a Catholic convert). Böhl's initial 1814 article in the Cadiz press expounded August Wilhelm's defense of Calderón as the expression of a chivalresque Christian Middle Ages, understood as the origin of modern European civilization (Romantic) by contrast with pagan antiquity (classical). Calderón's counter-reformation Catholicism was seen as the supreme expression of this "Romantic" spirit, supposedly still alive in the Spanish *Volk* – a view echoed by the collector of medieval Spanish ballads, Agustín Durán, in his influential 1828 rebuttal of Spanish Enlightenment thinkers' dismissal of Calderón (Flitter 1992).

By contrast, the two liberal members of Böhl's literary salon who from 1814 to 1820 responded to him in the press – José Joaquín de Mora and Antonio Alcalá Galiano, both neoclassicists – saw literature as the expression of modernity, whose origins they located in the humanist sixteenth century that was snuffed out by the counter-reformation. Mora and Alcalá Galiano defended neoclassicism as an expression of liberalism; both would move easily from neoclassicism to liberal Romanticism in their post-1823 exile in London, where they became acquainted with English Romanticism in a liberal environment that saw Romanticism as the free expression of the self.

Also in London as exiles were the future Romantic writers Ángel Saavedra (from 1834 Duke of Rivas) and Espronceda, both still writing in neoclassical style; both, with Alcalá Galiano, spent the last years of their exile in Paris, where they witnessed the stage triumphs of Victor Hugo's *Hernani* (1830) and Alexandre Dumas's *Antony* (1831). The first version of Rivas's Romantic drama *Don Álvaro o la fuerza del sino* (*Don Álvaro or the Force of Destiny*) was written in Paris; his narrative poem *El moro expósito* (*The Moorish Foundling*, 1834; see chapter 5) was published in Paris with a prologue by Alcalá Galiano that stressed Romanticism as an expression of the modern age. Paris was where another exile, Francisco Martínez de la Rosa, would see the premiere of his play *Aben Humeya* (1830), formally neoclassical but Romantic in sentiment, and where he would write *La conjuración de Venecia* (*The Venice Conspiracy*) (Llorens 1979).

The critical debate on Spanish Romanticism has been as polarized as the 1814–20 polemic in its disagreement as to whether the "true" Spanish Romanticism is the traditionalist version of Böhl and his Spanish heirs (Flitter 1992), or the liberal version the exiles brought home in 1833–4 (Shaw 1963). Critics who have equated Spanish Romanticism with liberalism have ignored the pre-1833 debates in Spain and the fact that radical Romanticism was short-lived – largely confined to 1834–6 with the sensational premieres of Martínez de la Rosa's *La conspiración de Venecia* (1834), Larra's *Macías* (1834), Rivas's *Don Álvaro* (1835), and Antonio García Gutiérrez's *El trovador* (*The Troubadour*, 1836). The triumph from 1837 of the traditionalist Romantic José Zorrilla coincided with the consolidation of moderate liberalism. Conversely, the construction of a traditionalist Romantic critical legacy has omitted discussion of progressive Romantic writers and has assumed that the fashion for medieval settings supposes a rejection of modernity (see chapter 5 for rebuttal of this argument). We need to step outside this binary thinking and accept that the proponents of Spanish Romanticism occupied a variety of positions.

Even a conservative Romantic like Zorrilla has his contradictions. His redemption of Don Juan in his hugely successful *Don Juan Tenorio* (1844) has been seen as an attempt to have it both ways, depicting a rebel who dares to challenge God but offering him Christian salvation (Resina 2000). Many Romantic works are contradictory. Rivas's Don Álvaro is a rebel against the honor code, who is obsessed with restoring his family honor. Larra's journalism is a defense of liberal modernity and a critique of it (Iarocci 2006, 139–202). The exploration of religious sentiment in Enrique Gil y Carrasco's 1844 historical novel *El señor de Bembibre* (*The Lord of Bembibre*; see chapter 5) is generally viewed as traditionalist, but its vindication of the Knights Templar has satanic resonances. While Romanticism has been equated with nationalism, it also has its cosmopolitan side, incarnated by Byron whose influence on Spanish Romanticism was strong. The life of Böhl's principal antagonist in the 1814–20 polemic, Mora, was a supreme example of cosmopolitanism, moving from his 1824–6 exile in England to support political and educational initiatives in the newly independent republics of Argentina, Chile, Peru, and Bolivia (Muñoz Sempere and Alonso García 2011, 111–23). Espronceda's "Canción del pirata" (The Pirate's Song, 1835) exalts the rebel who patrols the straits between Europe and Asia, accepting no jurisdiction. Many traditionalist supporters of Romanticism regarded Christianity as the mark of the modern period (as opposed to antiquity) because it generates interiority, that is, Romantic subjectivity; the same view was held by many progressive liberals too.

2

From Sensibility to Desire: The Construction of the Modern Subject (1730s–1880s)

The period from the mid eighteenth to the late nineteenth century covered in this chapter saw the emergence and consolidation of the modern concept of the self as an autonomous individual. This process responded to developments in the political, economic, and medical spheres. Liberal political theory, deriving from Locke and Rousseau, proclaimed the doctrine of universal human rights: that is, belief in the individual's right to the pursuit of happiness in a society governed by merit rather than birthright. In the economic sphere this translated into the championing of free trade: the right to enter the market. These related developments supposed a subject who was male and middle class: only male property owners were entitled to civil rights, since only they, not being dependent on others, could exercise independent judgment. Women and workers were deemed to have voluntarily alienated their rights by entering into the marriage and wage contract respectively, accepting dependence on a husband or employer (Pateman 1988; Macpherson 1990 [1962]).

This argument was reinforced by the late eighteenth-century beginnings of modern empirical medicine, which "proved" that men and women were not (as previously thought) more and less developed versions of a single human model, but defined by radically different anatomies determined by their reproductive organs. Women were thus regarded as biologically destined for motherhood and unsuited to civic participation (Laqueur 1990). The confinement of women to domesticity was compounded in the course of the nineteenth century by capitalist development, which took production out of the household, inaugurating the modern split between public and private spheres (Davidoff and Hall 1987). According to this binary scheme, men were considered active, strong, objective, and rational; and women passive, weak, subjective, and emotional. Consequently, men were seen as driven by self-interest and women by an urge to care for others. This binary split massively disadvantaged women but gave them moral superiority.

Liberal political theory circulated in Spain, as elsewhere in the West, from the late eighteenth century. Although the Inquisition was not abolished until 1834, it failed to prevent the circulation of Enlightenment texts; Rousseau's work, particularly important for linking liberalism to sexual difference, was widely read despite being banned (Álvarez Barrientos 2005, 70). However, the political, economic, and medical factors underpinning such ideas did not translate into reality until the implementation of liberalism as the dominant political creed after the absolutist Fernando VII's death in 1833, clinched by the circulation from the 1840s of hygiene manuals written by medical experts, which mandated women's confinement to domesticity (Labanyi 2000, 71, 216–18). Capitalist development and free trade would not take off in Spain until after the 1868 liberal revolution, and particularly after the elimination of utopian socialist alternatives with the 1875 Restoration of the Bourbon monarchy, when sexual difference would become definitively consolidated. Studies of the mid-century (Burguera 2012) suggest that bourgeois women had more freedom of maneuver under the reign of Isabel II (1833–68), despite the period's neo-Catholic bent, than under the secularizing political imperatives that largely prevailed after 1868. This helps to understand why a feminist writer like Emilia Pardo Bazán could, under the Restoration, oppose political liberalism, which was responsible for consecrating the ideal of female domesticity.

These political, economic, and medical developments were accompanied by a series of shifts in the conceptualization of the emotions. The word "emoción" was first included in the Spanish Royal Academy dictionary in 1843 (L.E. Delgado, Fernández, and Labanyi 2016, 7). In the early modern period, feelings were referred to as "passions" and "affects," both of which resulted from the impact on the self of external factors, with passions being an extreme form of possession by external forces. The Enlightenment saw the emergence of the term "sensibility," which, in accordance with the new concept of the autonomous individual subject, came to be seen as the expression of an inner authentic self. "Sensibility" – grounded in sympathy for others – was regarded as a civic virtue that complemented reason; the Enlightenment subject was expected to temper self-interest with pursuit of the collective good. And sensibility had to be learned by men from women, for whom it was a "natural" disposition (Bolufer 2016).

Romanticism, with its exaltation of the (male) individual rebel, created the new concept of "emotion" as an expression of subjectivity at odds with established society and thus in conflict with reason. Emotion (e-motion) moves from the self towards the outside world; it is intrinsically linked to the Romantic concept of unfulfilled desire, which breaks with the Enlightenment ideal of sensibility as the basis of sociability. In Spain, the term *emoción* began to be used intensively in the Romantic historical novel of the 1830s, which built on the courtly love tradition of desire for an impossible object (L.E. Delgado, Fernández, and Labanyi 2016, 7). The shift to realism in the mid-nineteenth century made desire a problem rather than an ideal. The male protagonists of the realist novel tend to succeed (or fail) in achieving social integration at the price of alienation or disillusionment; its female protagonists are punished for their inability to put reason before desire. Desire thus moves from being a driving force of (largely male) subjectivity to being a female aberration. In what follows, we will trace the stages of this complex emergence and transformation of the concept of the modern self as manifested in literary texts. While many factors contributed to this process, literature – and particularly the novel, which over the period discussed came increasingly to deal with intimate behavior and is read in private – played a major role in constructing new forms of subjectivity.

Sensibility and Bourgeois Morality

Critics have tended to construct neoclassicism and Romanticism as binary opposites, encouraging a misleading association of neoclassicism with tradition and of Romanticism with liberalism. In fact, neoclassicism viewed itself as modern, since its invocation of Aristotelian verisimilitude made literature conform to notions of "the real" ratified by the new scientific empiricism. Additionally, its appeal to classical (pagan) culture, especially that of republican Rome, allowed the expression of a secularizing liberalism hostile to absolutist power. In practice, not all Enlightenment literature can be seen as neoclassical; those genres that do not fit the neoclassical label – the *comedia lacrimosa* (sentimental drama); all prose, including the sentimental and Gothic novels – is overtly emotional. But even neoclassicism is as much a vehicle of sensibility as of rational reflection: hence the predilection for pastoral in poetry. The chapter on "Tragic Passions" in Ignacio de Luzán's neoclassical *Poética* (1737) stressed the social value of tragedy's capacity to produce catharsis: a purging of the emotions effected by stimulating terror and pity. This did not mean eliminating the emotions but directing them towards social cohesion: tragedy's aim was to make audiences "más sensibles" (more sensitive) by generating the sympathy fundamental to responsible citizenship.

Sensibility and rational reflection were linked as dual manifestations of the *buen gusto* (good taste) or moral refinement that marked Enlightenment sociability. Enlightenment experimental science was connected to sensibility since it supposed that knowledge is acquired empirically via the senses, particularly sight. Consequently, it was common for Enlightenment authors to write erotic verse, while pastoral – as in the poetry of Meléndez Valdés – allowed the expression of a guilt-free sensuality. This stress on the senses as an epistemological instrument made it possible for Benito Feijoo, whose scholarly essays were published 1726–60, and the early nineteenth-century neoclassical poet and educator Alberto Lista (both priests) to reconcile the pursuit of empirical knowledge with Christian belief, since observation of nature revealed the marvels of God's creation. The resulting symbiosis of science and "wonder" allowed a space for sensationalism within experimental science. In Spain as elsewhere, scientific instruments were exploited as popular attractions, alongside magic shows (J. Vega 2010, 331–481). There is a continuum between technological developments affecting optics and the sensational effects produced by ever-more sophisticated stage machinery in eighteenth-century Spanish popular theater, including the *comedias de magia* (magic plays) that would remain crowd-pullers throughout the nineteenth century. Neoclassicism aimed to keep such sensational effects within the bounds of *buen gusto* (good taste) through adherence to verisimilitude; but verisimilitude was based on the same criterion of observation by the senses that supported sensationalism.

Between 1820 and 1840 (coinciding with Romanticism), there was a shift in the understanding of vision, with the eye no longer being regarded as a passive, objective recipient of visual information transmitted by the outside world, but as a mechanism that actively processes the sense-impressions it receives, generating subjectively inflected images. Perception thus came to be seen as a faculty of the self, rather than as an effect of the outside world (L. Fernández 2006, 136–7). Romantic poetry is characterized by an unstable relationship between subject and object, whereby the poetic "I" can no longer tell whether what it sees is real or a hallucination – as, for example, in José de Espronceda's Romantic narrative poem *El estudiante de Salamanca* (*The Student of Salamanca*, 1840), whose Satanic hero is beset by a Gothic maelstrom of phantasmatic images. The Gothic is an Enlightenment as well as Romantic form because it tests the credibility of the senses: José Cadalso's *Noches lúgubres* (*Gloomy Nights*; probably written 1771–2; published posthumously 1789–90) was massively popular in the Romantic period – 32 editions through 1848 – because of its burial-vault setting and necrophiliac plot, but in fact it represents an earlier Enlightenment understanding of vision, with the reader given rational explanations for what initially appear to be apparitions (Sebold 2000, 80–125). The stress in Cadalso's text on extreme sensations produces an intense sense of self. The self-awareness of Spanish fictional protagonists from the 1770s on was the corollary of a new narratorial omniscience able to penetrate the character's innermost feelings (Haidt 2003b).

In the Gothic texts just mentioned, the sensations are those of a male, following Edmund Burke's association of the sublime with the virile, by contrast with the "feminine" concept of beauty (pleasing rather than challenging). The female lovers in *Noches lúgubres* and *El estudiante de Salamanca* have no subjectivity except as victims (and are dead). Those literary texts that set out to express a bourgeois mindset, characterized by domestic virtue, construct a much more feminine world. In the best-known example of the late eighteenth-century *comedia lacrimosa*, Gaspar Melchor de Jovellanos's *El delincuente honrado* (*The Honorable Delinquent*, 1773, published 1787), the male hero, who weeps copiously throughout, is a perfect example of the sacrificial ethos that characterizes bourgeois domestic heroines, as well as of the Foucauldian subject whose subjectivity is constructed through the internalization of discipline. The plot is triggered by the hero Torcuato's confession that he killed his new wife's former husband in a duel. A self-made man of unknown parentage, Torcuato turns out to be the judge's illegitimate son: father and son are rewarded for their moral rectitude (the judge refuses his son preferential treatment) when the King, also reduced to tears, issues a pardon. Torcuato's reward is a double domesticity: reunion with his father and his bride. Torcuato's and Laura's marriage will be one of mutual tenderness, contrasting with her previous marriage to an abusive, profligate aristocrat. Bourgeois domesticity is thus proposed as the model of a society based on moral worth rather than rank, and on voluntary subordination through love. This play, which demonstrates the value of sentiment, was written by one of Spain's foremost Enlightenment thinkers (future prime minister of Carlos IV) and first read at the Seville literary salon of Carlos III's minister Pablo de Olavide.

The advocacy of love marriages (*matrimonios de inclinación*), based on an *amor sensato* (reasonable love) derived from both partners' appreciation of each other's moral worth, became a major topic in the late 1700s and early 1800s (Spain's "long eighteenth century" ends in 1808 with the Napoleonic occupation). Although this "reasonable love" was expected of both sexes, the key issue at stake was women's right to freely choose their marriage partner – largely because, if it could be argued that women had freely chosen their renunciation of freedom by entering into the marriage contract, then it was possible to reconcile the liberal doctrine of universal rights with women's exclusion from the public sphere. The treatment of this topic in Leandro Fernández de Moratín's successful comedy *El sí de las niñas* (*The Maidens' Consent*, written 1801, performed 1806) is anticipated in his first play *El viejo y la niña* (*The Old Man and the Young Girl*, written 1786, performed 1790). Both plays obey the neoclassical rules of verisimilitude (unity of action, place, and time) but depend on displays of sentimentality typical of the *comedia lacrimosa*, despite Moratín's criticism of the genre's excesses. In practice, a firm dividing line cannot be drawn between neoclassicism and the *comedia lacrimosa*, since both regard sensibility as the key to moral worth.

In the late eighteenth-century sentimental novel, this expression of sentiment as the basis of a modern bourgeois morality is explicitly linked to woman. A key example is *La Serafina* (1798) by José Mor de Fuentes – a military engineer, showing how scientific training and sensibility were viewed as compatible. The role of the eponymous heroine is to teach the first-person male narrator, through his love for her, the value of sentiment. The first-person epistolary form of *La Serafina* had been popularized in novels such as Goethe's *Werther* and Rousseau's *Julie ou La Nouvelle Héloïse*, which Mor de Fuentes translated in 1835 and 1836 respectively, after the Inquisition's demise allowed their publication in Spain (Bolufer 2016, 31). The cosmopolitan reading habits of eighteenth- and nineteenth-century Spanish writers should be viewed as an indication of their insertion into European intellectual circuits, and not (as so often) of their "lack of Spanishness."

The Romantic Self and the Emergence of the Woman Writer

Romanticism, with its rebellious, anti-social concept of individual desire, generated by political revolution in France and the turmoil of the War of Independence in Spain, broke this sense of reason and feeling as complementary vehicles of civility. The new stress on individual desire as the basis of the modern liberal subject was coopted by Spanish women writers – primarily poets – who emerged in the 1840s, on the grounds that, if Romanticism was the expression of feeling, women had a "natural" talent for literary expression. This required writers such as the poet Carolina Coronado and the poet, novelist, and dramatist Gertrudis Gómez de Avellaneda to walk a literary tightrope, claiming recognition in the public sphere on account of their superior capacity for emotion, while at the same time, in order to maintain female decorum, dissociating themselves from the sardonic, nihilistic subjectivity asserted by male Romantic writers such as Espronceda and Mariano José de Larra, or the authors of Spanish Romantic drama (Kirkpatrick 1989). This included distancing themselves from the male Romantic tendency to depict women as victims of Byronic male desire; José Zorrilla's *Don Juan Tenorio* (1844), in which the female victim's love saves the rebellious male subject from damnation, takes this gendered scenario to an extreme. The subjectivity constructed by these female writers is split as they navigate acceptable notions of femininity, the tension with their desires intermittently showing through.

Coronado's tactic in her *Poesías* (1843) was to draw on neoclassical pastoral, aligning woman with nature in order to position herself outside both the male world of politics and the home, and fusing neoclassicism with a Romantic exploration of the self via nature. By drawing on the Rousseaunian trope of civilization's corruption of nature's inherent goodness, Coronado was able to denounce male domestic violence. The split subjectivity produced by the attempt to claim desire while maintaining decorum shows through in the gap between the traditional feminine attributes (modesty, shyness, agreeableness) for which Coronado's male contemporaries praised her and the anger displayed in many of her texts – as in the semi-autobiographical poem "La poetisa en un pueblo" (The Small-Town Female Poet, 1843) (Kirkpatrick 1989, 195–225).

Gómez de Avellaneda's first novel *Sab* (written 1838, published 1841) explicitly opposes feminine sensibility, with its ethics of sympathy, to a calculating, competitive capitalism embodied in the heroine Carlota's fiancé, the English merchant Enrique Otway. Set in Gómez de Avellaneda's native Cuba, which she left for Spain in 1836 at the age of 22, *Sab* is also the first anti-slavery novel to be published in Spanish; indeed, written the year after slavery was abolished in the metropolis though not in Spain's remaining colonies, it anticipated Harriet Beecher Stowe's *Uncle Tom's Cabin* by ten years. Its mulatto slave hero, Sab, outdoes the two heroines Carlota and Teresa in feminine self-sacrifice, driven by his impossible love for his master's daughter, Carlota. His alliance with Teresa – another underdog, as an illegitimate child taken in by Carlota's plantation-owning family – becomes an overt critique of the capitalism represented by Enrique when they exchange Sab's winning lottery ticket for Carlota's ticket, so that she will regain the wealth whose loss had made Enrique threaten to jilt her: Sab's feminine altruism is the reverse of profit-driven (virile) Enrique. The representation of Sab's love for Carlota as noble but impossible reflects an internalization of subordination on his part: despite memories of the 1791 Haitian Revolution and his indigenous adoptive mother's appeal to Cuba's black slaves to avenge her almost extinct race, Sab represses his sense of injustice – when his master frees him, Sab's response is to kneel at his feet.

If Teresa is a hybrid of masculine intelligence and feminine altruism (she dies in a convent), Sab is a purely feminine character (he also dies): like Carlota, they are sensitive souls born to suffer. The explicit parallel drawn in the novel between the servitude of women and slaves would endure throughout the nineteenth century; when in 1891 Emilia Pardo Bazán published a translation of J.S. Mill's *The Subjection of Women* in her Biblioteca de la Mujer (Women's Library), she entitled it *La esclavitud femenina* (*Female Slavery*). The attribution to Sab of a superior feminine altruistic sensibility makes an important racial point. The emergence during the Enlightenment of the notion that Western civilization originated in courtly love supposed that only Europeans were capable of the emotional refinement involved in the courtly – and subsequently Romantic – idealization of impossible love (Passerini 1999, 188–213). Sab's capacity for impossible love gives the lie to such notions of European superiority. Gómez de Avellaneda excluded *Sab* from her 1869–71 *Obras literarias*, along with her other radical novels: *Dos mujeres* (*Two Women*, 1842–3; a critique of the indissolubility of marriage) and *Guatimozin* (1844; a tale of interracial love which attributes a refined sensibility to its defeated Aztec subjects, contrasted with the Spaniards' greed). This self-censorship tells us much about the maneuvers required of women writers when claiming a place in a public sphere defined as male; in 1853 Gómez de Avellaneda's candidacy to the Real Academia Española – the first woman to be proposed – had been rejected.

The same self-censorship is at play in a text that was not intended to see the light of day: Gómez de Avellaneda's so-called "Autobiography," a collection of letters written to her lover Ignacio de Cepeda, later published by his widow. The (male) publisher's interventions (paragraphs eliminated; correction of the author's style and spelling; refutation of her opinions; teleological ordering of the undated letters) established the criteria of intelligibility for her writing and public persona as a paradigm of tragic Romantic subjectivity, a construction that lasted until the late twentieth century. The result was a profession of identity centered on unrequited love for a man (Cepeda), her "excesses" being explained by her sex and ethnic (Caribbean) origins.

Gómez de Avellaneda's letters (those of Cepeda are not included) make obvious her constant struggle to adjust her own desires and tame her impulses and language so as to conform to a model of femininity that would please her addressee. Thus, she hides the fact that she is older than him; continuously justifies her impulsive reactions; minimizes the importance of physical desire in her past romantic relationships; and, above all, downplays the importance in her life of her literary activities. Thus, the text displays a double movement, asserting the writer's agency while preserving her desirability through her compliant confession to a masculine authority figure (Pagés-Rangel 1997). The editorial "domestication" of Gómez de Avellaneda's autobiography was rendered necessary not only by its articulation of desire on the part of a bourgeois woman, but also by its refusal to efface the corporeal. She alludes regularly to the relationship between her body and her writing, detailing specific material conditions that affected her creativity – from her frequent migraines to the very un-ladylike chilblains on her hands. She distinguishes clearly between the discourse she produces in her "healthy" state and the "anomalous" discourse resulting from her headaches; the latter expresses her unrestrained desire, remarkably for a woman writer at the time.

The multiple stages on which Gómez de Avellaneda was called to perform never quite align: "Creole" in Spain and Spanish in Cuba; defender of a woman's economic and sexual independence and yet a practicing Catholic; a writer of an anti-slavery novel who, on her death, left five emancipated slaves; Romantic and emotional in her rhetoric but rational and resilient in her actions (L.E. Delgado 2008). Her feeling of constantly being out of place is captured in one of her pseudonyms, La Peregrina (the Wanderer).

The Consolidation of Sexual Difference

Writing in the late 1850s and 1860s, Gustavo Adolfo Bécquer would become known for his sensitive exploration of love, language, and ineffability in a conversational, almost confessional style, indebted to popular poetry and music. His Rima XXI and the second of his *Cartas literarias a una mujer* (*Literary Letters to a Woman*, 1861) defined woman as the source of poetry due to her essential link to feelings. Bécquer's work may seem to offer a feminized sensibility, but the equation of poetry with femininity is tied to the poet's role as male artist sculpting his feminine material into shape. In his world, women and poetry are linked to feelings and creativity, but a male intelligence is needed to give those inchoate feelings form through language: in so doing, the poet exerts discursive control over the seductive, but menacing, power of female sexuality by denying women their own discourse. The trope of woman as enigma is recurrent in his work: she is a constant referent textualized as an absence. Bécquer's work is remarkably modern in its ability to represent subjectivity as riven with alterity, but the "you" he addresses is always an elaboration of male desire (Mandrell 1995).

Like Gómez de Avellaneda's letters, Bécquer's *Rimas* were published posthumously, in this case by a group of friends who re-ordered them to give a stereotypically Romantic (and sanitized) interpretation of his biography, presenting him as an apolitical, unappreciated, and sensitive author, unable to cope with the precariousness, vulgarity, and alienation of modern urban life. Reality was more complicated. Bécquer's work was valued in his lifetime and he published in, and was editor of, reputable journals and newspapers. Thanks to the protection of conservative politicians such as Narváez and González Bravo, he was appointed to lucrative official posts, including that of censor (Palomo and Rubio Jiménez 2015). Despite the poet's proclaimed anti-materialism, materiality is quite entangled in his work: the manuscript version of the *Rimas* was written in an accounting ledger, which included crude pornographic verses (Egea 2003, 2004). (He and his painter brother Valeriano have been identified as authors of the pornographic cartoons satirizing Isabel II, *Los Borbones en pelota* [*The Bourbons in the Nude*], published under the pseudonym SEM.) Some of his poems were published more than once, receiving multiple payments, and his work consistently thematizes the tensions and overlaps of inspiration, spirituality, and desire with materiality – as in the famous Rima XXVI which connects the symbolic value of poetry and money (Egea 2003, 2004). Despite Bécquer's popular success and posthumous association with a culture of *cursilería* (sentimental kitsch) (Valis 2003), his work has been hugely influential on modern poetry in the Spanish-speaking world, from Rubén Darío, Miguel de Unamuno, Antonio Machado, and Juan Ramón Jiménez to Luis García Montero (who edited and reorganized the *Rimas*). He is recognized for having purged Spanish poetic language of excessive rhetoric; for his musical deployment of syntax; for anticipating the metric and thematic innovations of modernism; and for his exploration of the masks and limits of desire (García Montero 2001).

Contemporaneous with Bécquer's poetry, Rosalía de Castro's novels of the late 1850s and 1860s, written in Castilian, critique the consolidation of sexual difference. *La hija del mar* (*Daughter of the Sea*, 1859) is an exploration of mother–daughter relationships that exalts female intersubjectivity. Like Gómez de Avellaneda's *Sab*, it denounces an individualistic, capitalist masculinity embodied by the transatlantic trafficker (there are suggestions that he is a slave-trader) who abuses Teresa and her adoptive daughter Esperanza, and who previously abused Esperanza's Caribbean biological mother Candora. The male characters all disappear from the novel, leaving Esperanza, Teresa and Candora to roam the Galician coast in search of each other. The novel refuses linear coherence through its discontinuous treatment of time and space; this discontinuity, reminiscent of Kristeva's notion of "women's time" (1986), functions as the projection of a feminine subjectivity that refuses individuation (separation from the mother). This precarious subjectivity is embodied by the waves of the sea, which bring the infant Esperanza at the novel's start and into which she plunges at the end. The novel's exploration of the pre-oedipal bond between mother and daughter contrasts sharply with the oedipal scenarios of male individuation, achieved through separation from the feminine, that are obsessively dramatized in the male-authored Romantic plays of the 1830s (Labanyi 2019, 25–38).

Castro's 1867 novel *El caballero de las botas azules* (*The Blue-Booted Gentleman*) mocks female subservience to man. The novel has been read as a satire of the construction of a masochistic feminine subjectivity in best-selling fiction of the time: both male-authored serialized novels and the domestic novels written as a schooling in bourgeois femininity by women authors such as María del Pilar Sinués de Marco, Faustina Sáez de Melgar, and Ángela Grassi (Kirkpatrick 1995). These women authors were professional writers, who earned a living from their writing (see chapter 3). Sinués de Marco's novelistic career spans 1854–91 (66 works); that of Sáez de Melgar 1859–89 (25 works); that of Grassi 1845–81 (10 works), with the last two publishing their first novel at the age of 19 (Sánchez Llama 2000). Their novels aim to construct a new morality for a modern society: their plots repeatedly take their bourgeois heroines through a series of adversities so as to establish their final triumph as "angel of the house." The masochistic subject-positions required by this process offered bourgeois women certain compensations by making them central to the civilizing process (Charnon-Deutsch 1994, 41–77).

The Sexualization of Desire

The women writers of the mid-nineteenth century were omitted in literary histories because they did not fit the established literary labels of Romanticism, *costumbrismo* (depiction of local customs), and realism – the exception being Fernán Caballero (penname of Cecilia Böhl de Faber), with her *costumbrista* depiction of rural life. Her most famous novel *La Gaviota* (1849; originally written in French) anticipates the realist novel's punishment of its female protagonists for putting desire before domesticity. The realist writers of the 1870s–1890s – Benito Pérez Galdós, Leopoldo Alas ("Clarín"), Emilia Pardo Bazán – provide major models of male and female subjectivity in their novels, with particular emphasis on characters who fail to conform to normative models of masculinity and femininity. What is new about the disruptive desires dramatized in their texts is their frequent explanation in terms of sexual drives, whether indulged or sublimated; not for nothing does the peak of the Spanish realist novel in the mid-1880s coincide with the beginnings of Freud's exploration of the sexual basis of neurosis. Despite the theoretical assumption that only men had an active sex drive, the concern in the realist novel, as in contemporaneous medical manuals, with female sexuality in practice sexualized the inner self of women too. Worries about women entering the market as consumers, following the implantation of capitalist consumerism in Spain with the 1868 liberal revolution's adoption of free-market policies, are figured as worries about prostitution, as exemplified in Galdós's *La desheredada* (*The Disinherited*, 1881) and *La de Bringas* (*That Bringas Woman*, 1884). Desire for power on the part of men is similarly related to sexual dysfunction, whether excessive sexual expenditure or sexual repression, as illustrated by the local Don Juan, Mesía, and the priest De Pas respectively in Leopoldo Alas's *La Regenta* (1884–5). A key theme of the realist novel is the management of sexual desire – with Pardo Bazán going against the grain by critiquing the control, or denial, of female sexuality.

In this respect, the realist novel is part of the contemporaneous nation-formation project aimed, throughout the West, at "nationalizing" the subjectivity of the nation's inhabitants (Labanyi 2000). Since women and the working classes, excluded from civic participation, were felt to threaten national cohesion, social management was seen as the task primarily of bourgeois men. Realism was conceived as a masculine project of social documentation, conducted by a controlling narrator-observer whose subjectivity must be bracketed out, in keeping with the currently dominant scientific discourses of medicine and anthropology. This "masculine" mode of narration, which constructs the subjectivity of others by asserting an authoritative "objectivity," is found even in the novels of Pardo Bazán, despite her trenchant critique of the liberal ideology of sexual difference. Determined to be accepted in the public sphere as an equal to men, Pardo Bazán was not interested in writing in the sentimental style associated with women authors and with male-authored serialized fiction, often conceptualized as "feminine" because of its appeal to emotion. Despite establishing its authors' credentials as "expert" social analysts, the realist novel also expressed concern about the new "experts" attempting to mold the subjectivity of the nation's inhabitants: doctors, social reformers (including female philanthropists who transgressed the public/private divide), and (with a social control agenda aimed at countering secular reform initiatives) priests (Labanyi 2000, 193–200, 243–4). In certain cases – most of Pardo Bazán's novels; Galdós's 1886–7 *Fortunata y Jacinta*; much more ambiguously in Galdós's other novels and Alas's *La Regenta* – this concern could develop into a defense of women's right to their own desires, even if they are still mostly punished with death or degradation. In the case of the working classes, the issue was not their right to their own desires but the need to educate them in bourgeois values so as to pre-empt social revolution.

In keeping with late nineteenth-century European degeneracy theory (Dijkstra 1986), several Spanish realist novels express worries about a "regression" to gender indeterminacy, with women developing a masculine assertiveness and men becoming effeminate. A feminist twist on this is offered in Pardo Bazán's 1886 *Los pazos de Ulloa* (*The Manor of Ulloa*), where the maternal instincts of the effeminate priest Julián are the best side of him (Charnon-Deutsch 1995). The novels of Galdós and Alas abound in disturbing gender hybrids – notably, the "masculine" philanthropist Guillermina and prostitute Mauricia in Galdós's *Fortunata y Jacinta*. And yet, in this novel, both the bourgeois "domestic angel" Jacinta and the working-class Fortunata develop a self-awareness that gives them agency without masculinizing them, since it is exercised in the domestic domain of love and motherhood. We may note that the working-class Fortunata's capacity for steadfast love counters notions of a bourgeois monopoly on sensibility. Galdós's later novels *Ángel Guerra* (1890–1) and *Nazarín* (1895) feature male protagonists who sublimate their sexual frustration or effeminacy by begetting visionary social reform projects that may be inspired or deranged. This partly marks a return to the Romantic interest in perception as a subjective projection (and in male subjectivity generally), but it also offers men a route to (spiritual) procreation that bypasses women.

As a priest, Nazarín poses the issue of emasculated masculinity in an acute way (Labanyi 1993). Alas's *La Regenta* (1884–5) is possibly unequalled in the European realist novel for its dissection of masculinity's dilemmas through its priest protagonist Fermín de Pas, as well as offering an outstanding analysis of female subjectivity through its heroine Ana Ozores (Sinclair 1998). Ana's highly developed sensibility is expressly linked to sexual frustration; it is a critical commonplace to admire the novel's anticipation of Freud's sexual reading of neurosis. The novel also anticipates Foucault's perception (1987 [1976]) that sexuality is constructed by the discourses that prohibit it and particularly through confession. The novel starts with Ana preparing for general confession with her new confessor, De Pas:

confession triggers her flashback over her past, framing the narrative construction of her subjectivity.

Ana's sensibility is matched by that of De Pas, leading to a dangerous intimacy; he will end up stifling the feminine side to his personality out of a masculine desire for power. In his review of Galdós's *Ángel Guerra*, Alas commented that the novelist should have a feminine side (Alas 1991, 213); in *La Regenta*, the narrator's point of view blurs with that of Ana in her extensive interior monologues. Significantly, the narrator distances himself from Ana during the brief period when she is sexually satisfied (by her adulterous liaison with Mesía), during which her interior monologues vanish, only to reappear once she is again condemned to sexual frustration. The implication, as Ana herself suggests at the novel's end, is that the inner self is a form of sickness (the product of sexual repression), and that the healthy, sexually satisfied body has no need for such complications. The narrator pathologizes Ana's subjectivity by subjecting her to repeated bouts of illness (described by Ana as hysteria), but, extraordinarily for a novel of the time, allows her to articulate – hesitantly – her right to sexual satisfaction.

The relation of the psyche to the body is further explored in De Pas, who, as a priest, is similarly condemned to sexual frustration. Freud is anticipated again in the depiction of De Pas's unresolved Oedipus complex, unable to free himself from his domineering mother (Sinclair 1998, 179–95). De Pas is a more clearly delineated character than Ana, in that he is split between two selves: his feminine sensibility and his masculine desire for power. Whereas she can choose only between two forms of loss of self: the psychic disintegration that results from her extreme sensibility, born of sexual frustration, and the annulment of the psyche that occurs when her brief experience of sexual satisfaction makes the inner self redundant. Although the novel clearly depicts Ana's and De Pas's sexual desires, what both are really seeking is love: an anachronistic form of Romantic love, exemplified by the incorporation as *mise-en-abyme* of Zorrilla's *Don Juan Tenorio*. *La Regenta* can be read as the swansong of a Romantic concept of desire in its expression of an elevated sensibility that has no place in an age in which the self has become irremediably sexualized.

3

The Rise of the Public Sphere and the Professionalization of the Writer (1730s–1890s)

This chapter traces the relationship, over the course of the eighteenth and nineteenth centuries, of the changing status of the writer to the development of the public sphere. The latter emerged in the course of the eighteenth century as a result of the development of the capitalist market, which separated economic production from the household, thereby creating a "sphere of private people come together as a public" (Habermas 1992 [1962], 27). In addition to those engaged in the market economy, the public sphere included professionals and holders of public office in their capacity as private citizens (Van Horne Melton 2001, 10–11). The public sphere was thus separate from both the private sphere and the state, although, in Spain's case, the overlap with the state was considerable, eroding its function as a check on the state's workings (Jiménez Torres and Villamediana González 2019, 1–24; Kitts 2019, 25–43). The expression of the public sphere was "public opinion," aired through spaces of sociability such as coffee houses, salons, debating societies and, increasingly, the press (Van Horne Melton 2001, 81–148). Being comprised of a reading public, the public sphere was closely related to the expansion of print culture.

Unlike the culture of the court, the public spaces of sociability were not dependent on social rank or economic patronage. In eighteenth-century Spain, the court continued to sponsor painting, music, and opera but not literature; the literary market would not take off in Spain till the 1830s–1840s. Hence eighteenth-century Spanish writers needed alternative sources of income, which compromised their independence (Glendinning 1972, 16–17). The growth of the press in the nineteenth century offered a lifeline to writers, but from 1875, under the Restoration, increasing state centralization and the proliferation of state functionaries produced a blurring of state and society that further eroded the public sphere's critical function (Medina 2009; Ginger 2019). At the same time, with the incipient massification and commodification of culture, public opinion started to be seen as the triumph of the mediocre. Both concerns are articulated in Benito Pérez Galdós's novels of the 1880s.

The Enlightenment Man of Letters and Spaces of Sociability

The eighteenth century was the age of the "man of letters" (*hombre de letras*). The term *letras* encompassed all print culture; only towards the century's end would the humanities and sciences start to become distinct areas of inquiry – writers such as Benito Feijoo and Gaspar Melchor de Jovellanos straddled both – and only in the nineteenth century would literature (in its modern sense of creative writing) start to be seen as a separate field within the humanities. In the course of the eighteenth century, the cosmopolitanism of the "Republic of Letters" gave way to a more national concept of culture (Álvarez Barrientos 2006, 29–37), though it was only with the European Napoleonic wars (in Spain, the 1808–14 War of Independence) that cosmopolitanism became suspect. Writers earned a living through aristocratic patronage or a career in the Church, the military, or the state administration. Feijoo was a Benedictine monk; José Cadalso, a cavalry officer; Jovellanos, a judge and major statesman; Leandro Fernández de Moratín was secretary to the statesman Cabarrús and in 1798 was appointed official state translator, becoming Director of the Royal Library under José I (Glendinning 1972, 16–17). The writer who came nearest to living off his writing was the dramatist Ramón de la Cruz, who was able to sell his popular *sainetes* (farces) and *zarzuelas* (operettas) to Madrid's theater companies at a good price (see chapter 6); nonetheless, in addition to writing over 500 stage works, he was a state accountant and relied on patronage from the Duke of Alba and Duchess of Osuna (Coulon n.d.).

The Enlightenment man of letters saw his role as contributing to the common good; this introduced a new concept of writing for the public (Álvarez Barrientos 2005, 102–3, 129–37) – that is, of culture as a good that circulates through commerce (in the term's eighteenth-century sense of social exchange, notably via the press and the new spaces of sociability). The stress on social exchange as the basis of civility explains the eighteenth-century privileging of the epistolary mode. Feijoo held *tertulias* in his monk's cell in Oviedo, as did Jovellanos in his Madrid home later in the century. The Peruvian-born reformer Pablo de Olavide's *tertulias* in Madrid and later Seville promoted theater. While many *tertulias* were spaces of homosociality, several were hosted by aristocratic women: for example, the Academia de Buen Gusto (Academy of Good Taste) hosted by the Marquise of Sarria; the literary salon of the Countess of Lemos; and the salons of the Duchesses of Alba and Osuna and the Countess of Montijo – the latter frequented by Jovellanos, Goya, and the poet Juan

Meléndez Valdés (Bolufer Peruga 1998, 310–11, 349–50). The *tertulias* held by booksellers and printers catered to a more bourgeois public, as did the new coffee houses – the first opening in Seville in 1758 (Álvarez Barrientos 2006, 113–29). Leandro Fernández de Moratín's satire *La comedia nueva o el café* (*The New Drama or the Coffee House*, 1792) is set in the coffee house of the Fonda de San Sebastián whose habitués included his father Nicolás and Cadalso.

The play stages current public debates about the need for a new national drama, linking them to the coffee house as a theater of public opinion. Coffee houses encouraged a sociability that was inclusive but more orderly than that afforded by taverns. Their social heterogeneity and provision of newspapers encouraged the free exchange of information and news; they also facilitated the circulation of rumors, scandals, and political discussion. Jovellanos's 1796 *Memoria para el arreglo de la policía de espectáculos y diversiones públicas* (*Report on the Regulation of Spectacles and Public Entertainment*) considered them an important outlet for constructive leisure time, provided they were regulated. *La comedia nueva* critiques the unrestricted circulation of opinions by depicting the conversations at a coffee house of people of diverse social backgrounds. A range of views on dramatic authorship are represented, including those of Don Eleuterio, a former scribe and accountant hoping to pay off his debts by writing neo-baroque plays, and the pedantic critic Don Hermógenes. The characters who serve as spokesmen for Enlightenment ideas persuade Don Eleuterio to take up a servant position on a country estate, in keeping with Jovellanos's view that theater was a form of entertainment best suited to the propertied classes. The play's action is framed by the *première* of Eleuterio's neo-baroque play; its flop confirms Eleuterio's lack of talent, underlining the eighteenth-century appeal to public opinion as a source of political and social legitimacy. However, not everybody's opinions are considered equally acceptable; the superficiality of coffee house chatter is mocked. In reality, it was the popular success of neo-baroque drama that prompted the state's efforts to replace it with works like that of Moratín. In this sense, *La comedia nueva* constructs a normative public sphere.

Coffee houses proliferated and became more politicized in the early nineteenth century. La Fontana de Oro, described in Galdós's 1870 first novel of that name, became a meeting place for Spanish liberals during the 1820–3 liberal interlude. Galdós's text shows that, while coffee houses represented a theoretically egalitarian space for social interaction, they were segregated by class, gender, and economic status. The tavern remained the venue for working-class sociability (Uría 2003).

The informal *tertulias* that developed during the eighteenth century were closer to the orderly, homogeneous ideal of the Enlightenment public sphere. Several would evolve into academies – conceived as debating societies with elected fellows, bringing together the best minds to undertake projects of national interest (Álvarez Barrientos 2005, 52–9). The concept of the institutionalized academy was anticipated by the Regia Sociedad Sevillana de Medicina (Royal Medical Society of Seville; founded 1700) which developed out of the learned *tertulias* organized by the *novatores* in Madrid, Seville, Valencia, and Barcelona in the late seventeenth century. The role of provincial cities was significant in this respect. The earliest academies – Real Academia de la Lengua (Royal Academy of the Language, 1713; now Real Academia Española); Real Academia de la Historia (Royal Academy of History, 1738) – also grew out of private salons. The mid-century saw the creation of Academias de Buenas Letras (Academies of Belles Lettres) in Barcelona (1751) and Seville (1752); Valladolid's Real Academia Histórico-Geográfica (Royal Historical-Geographical Academy, 1752); and Madrid's Real Academia de Bellas Artes de San Fernando (San Fernando Royal Academy of Fine Arts, 1752). In 1754 Jorge Juan's proposal for an Academy of Science was blocked by the Church. To guarantee their authority (and safeguard them against the Inquisition), academies needed royal protection; directors were frequently leading statesmen. As director of the Academy of History, in 1759 Pedro Rodríguez de Campomanes secured the Inquisition's permission for its fellows to read banned books. The Academia Valenciana, created by the Valencian historian Gregorio Mayans in 1742, foundered because of Mayans's decision to keep it independent. This institutionalization eroded the independence of the Spanish public sphere from its beginnings (Álvarez Barrientos 2006, 262; Medina 2009).

Also under royal patronage were the almost one hundred Sociedades de Amigos del País (Societies of Friends of the Nation) that sprang up all over Spain (and its colonies), pioneered, as mentioned in chapter 1, by the Real Sociedad Vascongada de Amigos del País (Basque Royal Society of Friends of the Nation, founded 1765) (Álvarez Barrientos 2005, 47–50). These societies were officially encouraged by Campomanes, then Attorney General and founder of the Madrid Royal Society of Friends in 1775. They had a practical function, promoting economic progress, particularly agricultural production, and offering scientific and technological education, bypassing the Church-controlled universities which regarded modern science as heresy. Their libraries were allowed to own the *Encyclopédie*, banned by the Inquisition. The Societies of Friends declined after the clampdown on freedom of expression following the 1789 French Revolution.

The academies and Societies of Friends were almost entirely male institutions, though a few women participated (Bolufer Peruga 1998, 351–2):
the Countess of Oropesa (mother of the Duchess of Alba painted by Goya)
was admitted to the Academy of Fine Arts as an honorary fellow in 1766,
becoming its Honorary President; María Isidra Quintina Guzmán y de la
Cerda – the first Spanish woman to be awarded a doctorate (University of
Alcalá, 1785) – was made an honorary fellow of the Royal Academy of the
Language in 1784 under pressure from Carlos III, and was a fellow of the
Basque and Madrid Societies of Friends. Josefa Amar y Borbón, known for
her translations and future author of the 1790 *Discurso sobre la educación
física y moral de las mujeres* (*Discourse on the Physical and Moral Education of
Women*), was elected a fellow of the Aragonese Society of Friends in 1782.
She was also a fellow of the Barcelona Medical Society and of the Junta
de Damas (Women's Section) of the Madrid Society of Friends, created
with Crown approval in 1787 after a 12-year polemic within the Society
(Cabarrús, Campomanes, and Jovellanos had favored women's admission
as regular fellows) (Bolufer Peruga 1998, 341–88). This minimal acceptance
of women would disappear almost entirely in the nineteenth century.

The Regulation of Theater

The Bourbon dynasty's reform program was implemented by a new cultural elite formed by high-ranking civil servants in the state administration,
who participated actively in the networks of sociability described above.
Enlightenment politicians saw culture, and particularly theater, as a key
instrument of national regeneration and unification. Jovellanos's *Report
on the Regulation of Spectacles and Public Entertainment* argued that shared
enjoyment was crucial to collective identification and cohesion; happy citizens were less inclined to revolt. The insistence with which Enlightenment
politicians and writers – Jovellanos, Moratín senior and junior, Félix María
Samaniego, José Clavijo y Fajardo – tackled the need to transform the
Spanish stage indicates that theater was understood as a metonymical
representation of the state, with the audience a microcosm of the national
public. Consequently, resistance to this transformation could take the form
of anti-government protest (Medina 2009, 83–135).

   In the eighteenth century, theater continued, as before, to serve as a
key articulation of public virtue. Now, however, civic virtue was seen as
inextricably tied to new ways of being in public that required self-control
and the cultivation of habits in the private realm; hence the importance of

theater as a school of social change. Enlightenment disdain was directed particularly at Calderón and the *auto sacramental* (morality play originally staged on street floats at Corpus Christi, moving into theaters from 1705) – a highly popular genre which Calderón had elaborated. *Autos sacramentales* were banned in 1765 for undignified treatment of religious themes and figures. For Enlightenment thinkers, religion was to be understood, not as the public manifestation of a divine order, but as a matter of private morality. As public representations of private truths, the state and theater were seen as in need of "desacralization." As the century progressed, there was considerable public hostility, on the part of the popular classes and the new bourgeoisie that prospered under Carlos III, to what was perceived as the imposition from above of foreign tastes, whether neoclassical drama (perceived as French) or Italian opera. The same French- or Italian-influenced Enlightenment reformers understood that, to be effective, the new theater had to be perceived as "national." Thus, in 1799, one of the many reform proposals took control of theater away from municipal authorities so as to strengthen the power of government ministers, judges, and censors as representatives of the central state. The new regulations included a ban on non-Spanish performers and on performances in languages other than Castilian (Gies 1994, 93). That the proposal failed (though government censorship remained) is indicative of the multiple tensions involved in efforts to control public entertainment.

The reforms proposed in the century's second half included regulating the texts chosen for performance, actors' performance styles, the appointment of theater managers, and particularly the performance space itself and who should have access to it (Andioc 1988; Medina 2009, 87–108; Albiac Blanco 2011, 473–91). The traditional *corrales* were stages constructed within rectangular courtyards enclosed by buildings, from which the plays could be seen without payment by audiences who could be hard to control. Madrid's two existing *corrales* were in poor condition; the old Corral de la Cruz was demolished and, in 1737, the first modern municipal theater, the Coliseo de la Cruz, was built in its place. In 1768 the Count of Aranda founded the Teatro de los Sitios Reales (court theater), which used the royal residences to stage neoclassical plays which the elites hoped would serve as a model for the public theaters. Theater interiors were also subject to reforms geared to maintaining social hierarchy and controlling audience behavior: seats were numbered and classified according to price; the public was required to keep quiet and still; food and drink were no longer sold; and, for security reasons, the whole theater was kept illuminated during the performance. Ticket prices were raised in 1779, with a patio (standing room) ticket being a sixth of a servant's monthly salary (Glendinning 1972, 17) – a decision consistent with the state's goal of directing the common people away from the theater toward popular street entertainment.

Despite the top-down promotion of neoclassical theater, audiences preferred neo-baroque and spectacle-based drama, and comic interludes (see chapter 6). Nicolás Fernández de Moratín's neoclassical tragedy *Hormesinda* (1770), commissioned by the Count of Aranda to renovate Spanish drama, played for only six days; his comedy *La petimetra* was never performed. It was his son, Leandro Fernández de Moratín, who would succeed in creating a neoclassical comedy that the public wanted to see: *El sí de las niñas* (*The Maiden's Consent*, 1805), written in prose rather than verse. It ran for 26 days, attracting more than 37,000 spectators (the equivalent of a quarter of Madrid's adult population) across the social spectrum, enjoying particular success with women who could afford the most expensive tickets (Andioc 1988, 497–501). The play's focus on a timely topic (free choice in marriage and female education), its humorous tone and happy ending proved to be the right combination for the moment. Moratín's liberal attitude to women's social role was shared by María Rosa Gálvez, whose successful comedies and tragedies also critiqued bourgeois norms – as in *La familia a la moda* (*The Fashionable Family*, 1805) – but went much further than Moratín in dealing with controversial issues such as spousal abuse, incest, and, in *Zinda* (1804), slavery.

Book Publishing and the Rise of an Independent Press

The eighteenth-century concern with public opinion is closely related to the increase in reading matter available to an educated public. The controls over the theater were matched by the censorship of print publications. Books had to be submitted to the Council of Castile for vetting prior to printing; the Council usually delegated book censorship to an academy or Society of Friends, further compromising those bodies' independence. Periodicals had to apply to the Council of Castile for a license. In addition, publications faced religious censorship; the Inquisition was authorized to ban publications after printing, including imported books. The Inquisition's controls were mostly ineffective – fortunately, since its Index of Prohibited Books comprised a catalog of the best works published in the eighteenth century (Álvarez Barrientos 2005, 166–74; Dufour 2003). With the clampdown after the French Revolution, a government ban on novels, aimed particularly at imported texts, was issued in 1799, and was again ineffective.

Inquisitorial trials of readers of banned books remained frequent at the century's end. Spain did not emerge from absolutism till 1833, with the Inquisition abolished in 1834. To circumvent censorship, many books in Spanish, particularly translations of foreign works, were published abroad, in France, Italy, Switzerland, and Germany, which weakened the Spanish book industry – a phenomenon that would worsen during the nineteenth century (Álvarez Barrientos 2005, 169; Botrel 1993, 590–9). Another limitation was illiteracy, which in 1768 stood at an estimated 70 percent of the population (Glendinning 1972, 14).

In 1752, the Crown ordered a report on the country's book industry which showed that only 40 Spanish cities had an outlet for selling books, the best-provided being Cadiz as a major port, able to procure Spanish books from overseas (Álvarez Barrientos 2005, 167). Book publication in Spain increased fourfold between 1730 and 1815, though creative writing accounted for a small fraction. The percentage of religious books, while still the largest category, decreased from 52 percent in 1730 to 22 percent in 1815. Printers and publishers started to become separate entities at the end of the eighteenth century. The Biblioteca Real, a copyright library, had opened to the public in 1712. After the War of Independence, bookstores started to provide reading rooms to subscribers, sometimes with borrowing facilities, mainly to read the press (Glendinning 1972, 12–13, 18).

At the century's start, the periodical press consisted of official gazettes. The first private periodicals covered literary, cultural, and economic topics, starting with the quarterly book-format *Diario de los Literatos de España* (*Spanish Literary Newspaper*, 1739–42) which reviewed recent publications. Spain's first daily was the *Diario Noticioso* (*Daily News*, 1758; from 1788–1918, *Diario de Madrid*) published by the entrepreneur Francisco Mariano Nifo who, in the mid-century, edited nine newspapers under different pseudonyms. The period 1758–71, under Carlos III, saw a flurry of new journals imitating Addison and Steel's *Spectator* in England, notably Clavijo y Fajardo's weekly *El Pensador* (*The Thinker*, 1763–7) whose cultural criticism aimed to provoke debate. Its format was continued by *El Censor* (1781–8), written unsigned by (among others) Jovellanos and Meléndez Valdés, which smuggled in excerpts from French Enlightenment thinkers and *The Spectator*, repeatedly incurring censorship. *El Correo de Madrid* (*The Madrid Mail*, 1786–91) published essays on literary, philosophical, and social topics, including Cadalso's *Cartas marruecas* (*Moroccan Letters*, 1789) (Glendinning 1972, 17–19; Álvarez Barrientos 2005, 138–52). With the panic induced by the French Revolution, all private periodicals were banned in 1791. The independent press did not recover till the War of

Independence when the Cortes de Cádiz proclaimed freedom of expression in 1810. Periodicals of all political affiliations sprang up throughout Spain in response to the conflict – not forgetting the liberal exile Joseph Blanco White's London-based *El Español* (*The Spaniard*, 1810–14). With Fernando VII's restoration of absolutism, all non-government periodicals were banned, though freedom of the press was briefly declared in the 1820–3 liberal interlude (Rodríguez Sánchez 2004).

The Original Author and the Creation of a Literary Market

The increased availability of books and periodicals, still limited to an elite, was accompanied in the mid-eighteenth century by a new concept of the writer as "author": that is, as the text's source who had "authority" over it – as opposed to the previous "authorization" of texts by a prologue, censor, or patron, and ultimately the Crown which granted the printing license (Álvarez Barrientos 2005, 166). This went together with the start of attention to intellectual property rights, confirming published texts as their author's original work, in keeping with the emergent liberal belief in property ownership as the basis of individual autonomy. In 1764, Carlos III ruled that authors' right to income from their works would pass to their heirs, this still being a privilege granted by the Crown. In 1813, the Cortes de Cádiz recognized copyright (*derechos de autor*) as residing in the author (revoked on Fernando VII's return in 1814). This concept would be elaborated by Spain's first systematic copyright legislation, the 1847 Ley de Propiedad Literaria (Literary Property Law), followed by mid-century agreements with several countries which determined that translation rights belonged to the author and not, as before, the translator. This new distinction between original author and translator downgraded the translator's role (Álvarez Barrientos 2006, 250–1). By the 1840s, print culture had become fully integrated into the market, thanks to the notion of the author as the owner of intellectual property which could and should be sold for money.

The Romantic concept of the author as original genius goes hand in hand with the capitalist concept of intellectual property rights, since both understand the author as the unique source of an original work. Pierre Bourdieu (1996b [1992]) has traced how, in the course of the nineteenth century, literature emerged as a supposedly autonomous field, distinct from other forms of print culture. As Bourdieu demonstrates, the status of the new literary field was regulated by the concept of "cultural capital," which increasingly came to be seen as existing in inverse proportion to economic capital; thus, writing that made a lot of money was regarded as "merely commercial," while "great writing" was that which was autonomous in that it did not cater to the market. The rise of a mass public in the mid-century, thanks to the serialized novel, limited the term "literature" still further to "high cultural" creative writing, consecrated by the construction of a literary canon (see chapter 6). The starving bohemian, whose literary creation went financially unrewarded, became the model for the writer of genius: in Spain, Gustavo Adolfo Bécquer and, in the *fin de siècle*, Alejandro Sawa. The five *zarzuelas* authored by Bécquer were written under a pseudonym to protect his prestige. Sawa was, in fact, sponsored by a Paris banker (P. Fernández 2003). While writers needed to earn an income to be professionals, it became unacceptable for them to admit to being good at making money.

Early nineteenth-century copyright law emerged out of pressure from playwrights, since ownership of stage works, being collaborative products, did not self-evidently lie with the writer. At the time, the word "autor" referred to the actor-manager who bought the rights to a play from the playwright, subsequently having the right to produce it (or not). Performances rarely respected the playwright's text and playwrights' names did not appear on playbills – Zorrilla was the first dramatist to have his name advertised on a theater poster in 1841. A landmark in the campaign for dramatic property rights was the audience's call for the "author" (meaning the playwright) to appear on stage after the 1836 premiere of Antonio García Gutiérrez's Romantic drama *El trovador* (*The Troubadour*), establishing the playwright, rather than the actor-manager, as the text's owner (Surwillo 2007, 41–82). The campaign for dramatic property rights was supported by Mariano José de Larra as theater critic in his 1832 press articles asking what and who is the author of a play.

The resulting 1837 royal decree giving playwrights property rights over their work had two related consequences. First, it established the notion that plays – like poetry or novels – were fixed, original texts. Second, it created the entrepreneurial figure of the theater publisher, since playwrights mostly continued to sell the rights to their work, but to a publisher who, unlike the actor-manager to whom they had sold their work previously, was legally obliged to respect the original text. This suited dramatists who could cultivate their image as original geniuses by dissociating themselves from the dirty business of promoting their work, since the theater publisher not only published their plays but arranged their performance. In old age, Zorrilla – elected to the Real Academia Española in 1882, crowned "national poet" in Granada in 1889, but financially impoverished – created the legend that he had been cheated by his publisher Manuel Delgado who had got fat on the proceeds from *Don Juan Tenorio*. In fact, Zorrilla continued to sell all his works (dramatic and poetic) to Delgado and other publishers throughout his life; Delgado paid Zorrilla the good price of 4,200 reales for *Don Juan Tenorio* and offered him advances on later works; indeed, Delgado was responsible for Zorrilla becoming one of the most widely read Romantic writers (Martínez Martín 2009, 84–92). The development from 1837 of drama publication series (*galerías dramáticas*), spearheaded by Delgado, turned theater from a performing art into literature, read as widely as it was viewed on stage (Surwillo 2007, 83–123). The downside was an increasing tendency, in the course of the nineteenth century, to write plays conceived as text rather than performance: Galdós's turn from novel to stage in the 1890s is an example.

The 1847 Literary Property Law formalized copyright for all media, granting authors intellectual ownership for life and their heirs for the next 50 years (25 for drama) – extended to 80 years by the 1879 Intellectual Property Law which remained in force till 1987. Poets and novelists had started to sell the rights to their work to a publisher from the 1830s, when the latter, who took care of sales, became a separate figure from the printer (previously, writers had contracted and paid the printer, remaining responsible themselves for publicity and distribution). In 1834, the ubiquitous entrepreneur Delgado, who had a broad overseas sales network, issued an advance contract of 6,000 reales to José de Espronceda for his six-volume historical novel *Sancho Saldaña*, in 1840 paying him the same amount for his *Poesías*. Delgado paid similarly generous sums to Larra for his 1834 four-volume historical novel *El doncel de don Enrique el Doliente* (*Enrique the Sad's Page*) and, in 1835, for another four-volume novel, never written (Martínez Martín 2009, 79–84). In 1836, a year before committing suicide, Larra signed contracts with two periodicals for annual salaries of 20,000 and 40,000 reales respectively (Gies 1994, 91). Despite these earnings, Larra was able to claim the status of literary genius by insisting that to write in Spain was like crying in the wilderness.

The writers who made good money in the second half of the century were those who retained at least partial rights to their work. One of the few to live handsomely off his writing was Pedro Antonio de Alarcón, who received around 200,000 reales for his *Diario de un testigo de la guerra de África* (*An Eye-witness's Diary of the African War*, 1859), with the publisher making a net profit of nearly two million. For his later works, Alarcón dealt with the printers himself, offering booksellers a 30 percent commission on sales (Martínez Martín 2009, 106–25). Galdós – nineteenth-century Spain's bestselling author, surpassing even the top-selling serialized fiction writer Manuel Fernández y González in the number of editions per novel – signed a contract in 1874 with his fellow Canarian Miguel de Cámara, director of the women's magazine *La Guirnalda* which had its own printing press, for exclusive publication of his works, splitting the profits equally. In 1896 Galdós unwisely sued Cámara: the verdict was that Cámara had paid Galdós more than the contract stipulated and Galdós was ordered to repay nearly 30,000 pesetas. The trial record shows that, between 1879 and 1896, Galdós had earned over a quarter of a million pesetas from his novels (the annual salary of a civil servant was 2,000 pesetas, that of a top engineer 5,000 pesetas). After 1897 Galdós tried to publish his works himself but in 1904 signed a deal with the publisher Perlado, Páez y Compañía (Sucesores de Hernando) to do it for him, in exchange for royalties (Martínez Martín 2009, 135–44). In 1911 Galdós had to appear before a notary to face his debtors; in 1914 a national subscription was set up to rescue him financially. On his death, sales of his novels stood at 1,700,000 copies – 1,250,000 corresponding to the *Episodios nacionales* (Botrel 1984, 129). How Galdós got into debt has never been clarified, but it suited his image as Spain's most respected writer. The writer considered his literary heir, Vicente Blasco Ibáñez, never acquired the same status, in part because of his origins as a writer of serialized fiction, but also because he boasted that his writing had made him rich, thanks largely to US translation and film rights.

These examples show that Spanish writers had, since the 1830s, become used to earning money from their literary works, creating the concept of the professional writer. This means that they expected to be paid for their work, not that they lived solely off their literary earnings. Several had other paid occupations, usually as state functionaries. In the mid-century, the Romantic writers Francisco Martínez de la Rosa and the Duke of Rivas both held senior political and diplomatic positions, the former being Spain's first Prime Minister in 1843–5. In the later nineteenth century, Leopoldo Alas held a university chair; the Catalan novelist Narcís Oller was an attorney; and Juan Valera was a diplomat as well as occupying senior government positions after the 1868 Revolution, including that of Minister of Public Instruction. Bécquer was employed as a censor, a position held by many writers before (Tomás de Iriarte, Nicolás and Leandro Fernández de Moratín, Jovellanos) and after (Camilo José Cela). Some writers were partly supported by private income: Gertrudis Gómez de Avellaneda from inherited land in Cuba and money-lending; Emilia Pardo Bazán from her father's landed wealth; Galdós from the fortune of his Cuban sister-in-law, with whom he lived; José María de Pereda, despite the fact that his novels extol the virtues of pre-industrial rural societies, as a factory-owning industrialist and member of the Board of Directors of the Banco de Santander.

Journalism and the Expansion of the Literary Reading Public

Whatever their sources of income, all nineteenth-century Spanish creative writers published in the press, which gave them visibility in the public sphere. The overlap between literature and journalism was considerable. Created in the 1830s, the *folletín* – literary section of a periodical, which published short literary texts or longer ones in serialized form – became the selling-point for many newspapers and magazines. The press influenced literature by accustoming writers to shorter formats and more conversational prose (Fontanella 1982, 160). Indeed, it created several short literary genres: the *artículo de costumbres* (description, often satirical, of contemporary customs), the short story, and the *crónica* (creative non-fiction, often in the form of travel writing). Throughout the nineteenth century, poetry was published in the press, only later collected in book form; this places it in a complex relationship to high and mass culture.

The early nineteenth-century prose writing that is most studied today is, in reality, journalism (Romero Tobar 1987; Seoane 1997). Ramón Mesonero Romanos's *costumbrista* sketches of urban life appeared in magazines, mostly his own *Semanario Pintoresco Español* (*Spanish Picturesque Weekly*, 1836–57), before being collected in book form. Publication in the *Semanario* allowed Mesonero to reach 5,000 subscribers: an unprecedented reading public attracted by the magazine's high-quality illustrations using the latest technology (Fontanella 1982, 31, 57–9). Larra is today known not for his plays or historical fiction but for his journalism. Many other leading literary figures of the nineteenth century were professional journalists: Joseph Blanco White, Serafín Estébanez Calderón, and Bécquer, for example. Authors such as Galdós, Leopoldo Alas "Clarín," and Emilia Pardo Bazán wrote regularly for the press and many of their works were first published in periodicals. Literature and journalism would remain intertwined through the first quarter of the twentieth century. Much of what is read today from that period (including works by "Azorín," Miguel de Unamuno, José Ortega y Gasset, Ramón del Valle Inclán, Antonio Machado, Carmen de Burgos, or Ramón Gómez de la Serna) was initially published in the press.

A broad reading public could not have developed without the huge expansion of the press during the nineteenth century. This expansion was not due to education: illiteracy figures in 1860 were worse than a hundred years before, with overall illiteracy standing at 75 percent (86 percent for women). By 1900 the figures had decreased to 56 percent overall illiteracy (66 percent for women), though lower in major cities (Viñao Fraga 1990, 578, 584). What expanded the reading public was the construction of a national railway network in the 1860s–1880s, allowing the press to reach most of the national territory – kiosks at railways stations sold periodicals and books. Also significant was the loosening of censorship from 1834, with absolutism's end and the Inquisition's abolition. In the mid-century, freedom of the press was mostly theoretical, with prior censorship reintroduced 1844–54 and 1856–68. The 1869 Constitution, after the 1868 liberal revolution, made freedom of expression its central plank, resulting in an explosion of periodical publications. It also lifted controls on the import of Spanish-language books printed abroad; France had become the hub of Spanish-language publishing aimed at the newly independent Spanish American republics. The 1875 restoration of the monarchy brought back controls on the press, though not on books. The re-establishment of freedom of expression with Sagasta's 1883 Press Law hugely increased circulation of the major dailies; the readership of *El Imparcial* (*The Independent*, founded 1867) grew in the century's last quarter from 45,000 to 140,000, its prestige enhanced from 1874 by its Monday literary supplement, *Los Lunes de El Imparcial* (Villares and Moreno Luzón 2009, 192; Davies 2018, 174–5). Sagasta's Press Law also facilitated a threefold growth in book publishing over the same period, coinciding with the heyday of the Spanish realist novel. Press freedom did not stop private denunciations, such as the Bishop of Oviedo's 1885 attack on Alas's *La Regenta*, or that which led to the 1884–5 trial of the radical naturalist novelist Eduardo López Bago for his novel *La prostituta* (he was acquitted).

Under Isabel II, when neo-Catholic influence was strong, a number of Catholic women writers were able to become professional writers through journalism. Their professional attitude to writing for money was very different from that of their admired Fernán Caballero (penname of Cecilia Böhl de Faber, whose father Nicolás had introduced Romanticism into Spain), born in the late eighteenth century, who only in 1849, faced with financial ruin, started to publish in the press her novels written in the 1820s in French and German. The creative writing of these mid-century women authors blurs literature and journalism not only because it was written for the press (mostly women's magazines) with book publication sometimes following, but also because its moralizing aim makes it a mix of literature and advice column (Blanco 2001). Women's magazines flourished from the

1830s, with features on literature, theater, science, and society as well as fashion; contributors included Larra and Bécquer.

Despite advocating female domesticity – as indicated by the title *El Ángel del Hogar* (*The Angel of the House*) of María del Pilar Sinués de Marco's 1859 novel and 1864–9 journal – these women made a living by selling articles, stories, novels, poetry, or plays to the press, as well as directing, and in several cases founding, women's magazines. In addition to creating her own journal, Sinués published over 100 books. Faustina Sáez de Melgar founded and directed *La Violeta*, while writing up to four serialized novels simultaneously for different periodicals; in 1869 she founded the Ateneo Artístico y Literario de Señoras (Ladies' Artistic and Literary Athenaeum) as an association dedicated to the education of women. Ángela Grassi wrote novels and poetry in addition to directing *El Correo de la Moda* (*The Fashion Mail*, 1867–81). Joaquina García Balmaseda was *El Correo de la Moda*'s fashion editor 1866–93 and director 1883–93, as well as running the *folletín* section of the national newspaper *La Correspondencia de España* (*The Spanish Post*, 1864–83) and translating novels by (among others) George Sand. Concepción Gimeno de Flaquer was co-editor (with Valera) of *La Mujer* (*The Lady*, 1871) and founded *La Ilustración de la Mujer* (*The Lady's Illustrated Magazine*, 1872), settling in Mexico where she directed *El Álbum de la Mujer* (*The Lady's Album*, 1883–9), continued as *Álbum Ibero-Americano* (*Ibero-American Album*) on her 1890 return to Spain. The Catholic conservatism of these women writers did not prevent them from embracing the market. All of them argued forcefully for women's education. Sinués's moral tales *La ley de Dios* (*God's Law*, 1851) and *A la luz de una lámpara* (*By Lamp Light*, 1862) became official textbooks in the state education system created in 1857, as did Faustina Sáez de Melgar's journal *La Violeta*, subtitled *Revista Hispanoamericana* (*Spanish-American Magazine*, 1862–6); Grassi's 1876 pedagogical text *Palmas y laureles* (*Accolades and Honors*) was put on the Venezuelan school curriculum. The Spanish press took on a transatlantic dimension from the 1860s, giving these women writers an unprecedentedly wide readership. With the concern after the 1868 liberal revolution to construct a more secular society, these Catholic women writers fell out of favor (Sánchez Llama 2000).

Key to the construction of literature as a specific field was the emergence of the literary (including theater) critic in the nineteenth-century press. Larra was the first outstanding example. Two hundred Spanish literary critics have been identified for the nineteenth century overall (Baasner and Acero Yus 2007). All post-1868 creative writers wrote literary reviews, usually in addition to articles on other topics. This combination of journalistic and literary writing was a good grounding for writers who would, from the late 1870s, consolidate the realist novel in Spain. Indeed, the realist novel can be seen as a fundamental element of the public sphere in its concern with social and political issues aired in the press (Labanyi 2000). Galdós's literary career emerged from a prior training in literary, theater, and political journalism, between 1865 and 1873 writing for six different periodicals, including serving on the editorial staff of the *Revista de España* (*Spanish Journal*), which he directed in 1872–3, and *El Debate*. In 1873 he was invited to write a weekly political column for the major liberal daily *El Imparcial* and started to write for the women's magazine *La Guirnalda* (*The Garland*), whose editor appointed him literary editor of his bi-weekly *El Océano* (1879–80), aimed at Latin America. From 1884–94 Galdós was contracted by the Buenos Aires newspaper *La Prensa* (*The Press*) to write a fortnightly "Carta" (letter) for 3,000 pesetas a year (more than the starting salary of a state-employed engineer); he resumed his "Cartas" in 1901–5 (Shoemaker 1973, 40). Galdós used his journalistic contacts to get advance publicity for his novels, through serialization or the publication of fragments (in *Revista de España*, *La Guirnalda*, *El Océano*, and *El Imparcial*).

Alas saw himself primarily as a journalist. He is still known in Spain by his journalistic penname "Clarín." His satirical "Paliques" (Chats) for *Madrid Cómico* paid the best, his literary reviews (despite the prestige they afforded him) the least, with his short stories (first published in the press) somewhere in the middle. Of the 11 volumes of his complete works, one is devoted to his literary reviews and six to his satirical and political journalism; to read Alas purely as a novelist and literary critic is to downgrade his importance as a political thinker, with lifelong republican convictions. From 1883 to 1901, he wrote an average of seven articles a month. In 1890 he calculated his earnings from contracts with five journals – *Madrid Cómico* (*The Madrid Humorist*), *La Ilustración Ibérica* (*The Iberian Illustrated Magazine*), *La Semana Cómica* (*The Weekly Humorist*), *El Globo*, *La España Moderna* – at 7,680 pesetas for the year, while his university chair brought him under 4,000. In total, he wrote for over 40 periodicals, including the Barcelona press and (briefly) *La Nación* (*The Nation*) in Buenos Aires and *Las Novedades* (*The News*) in New York. His sense of entitlement to payment at a competitive rate is shown in his correspondence with his journal and book editors (Botrel 1981).

If journalism enabled Galdós, on migrating to Madrid from the Canaries, to get a toehold in the capital's publishing world, it also allowed Pardo Bazán, as a young woman growing up in Galicia, to embark on a literary career via the local press. Her first novel, *Aficiones peligrosas* (*Dangerous Inclinations*), written at the age of 13, was serialized in Pontevedra's *El*

Progreso in 1866. Her early scientific articles of 1878–9 – the fruit of an auto-didact education encouraged by her father – were published in the *Revista Compostelana* (*Santiago de Compostela Journal*) and the Madrid-based Catholic paper *La Ciencia Cristiana* (*Christian Science*). In 1880, she directed the *Revista de Galicia*. Her early novels *Pascual López* (1879) and *Un viaje de novios* (*A Honeymoon*, 1881) were serialized in the national *Revista de España* and *La Época* (*The Era*) respectively. It was the serialization of her 1882 *La cuestión palpitante* (*The Burning Question*), defending Zola, in the conservative daily *La Época* that gave her national notoriety. We may note that her route to gaining a public voice as a woman was through the local and the conservative (thus respectable) press.

Pardo Bazán wrote for the press throughout her career – for *La Época* from 1881, *La Ilustración Artística* (*The Artistic Illustrated Magazine*) from 1883, the liberal daily *El Imparcial* from 1887 – to avoid depending financially on her father and to establish her name in the public sphere on an equal footing with men (Freire López 2003). The expertise gained in helping José Lázaro Galdiano launch his cultural review *La España Moderna*, to which she contributed extensively from 1889 to 1891 while also writing for the major Spanish dailies and the Argentine *La Nación*, enabled her in 1890 to use her inheritance from her father to found a monthly journal *Nuevo Teatro Crítico* (*New Critical Theater*, 1890–3), named after the *Teatro Crítico Universal* (*Universal Critical Theater*) of Enlightenment precursor Padre Feijoo, who had defended women's talents. For three years she wrote the entire contents of its 30 100-page volumes, on literary and cultural topics. From 1893 she devoted her energies to her book publishing initiative *Biblioteca de la Mujer* (*Women's Library*), making available in Spanish major European feminist works such as J.S. Mill's *The Subjection of Women* and August Bebel's *Women under Socialism*. Her involvement in international bourgeois feminism dates from 1889, when she was invited by the English *Fortnightly Review* to publish a series of articles on Spanish women (reprinted in Lázaro Galdiano's *La España Moderna* in 1890 as "La mujer española"). Pardo Bazán's professionalism is based on a sense of entitlement to recognition in the public sphere. Her nearly 600 stories, published in a range of major newspapers, allowed her to reach a much wider audience than her books.

Lázaro Galdiano's above-mentioned monthly cultural review *La España Moderna* (1889–1914), while never attaining a wide circulation, marked a shift toward the substantial essay that contributed to the emergence of the intellectual in early twentieth-century Spain (see chapter 8) – a role that would be played in Catalonia by *L'Avenç* (*Progress*). A wealthy collector, Lázaro Galdiano's aim was to raise Spain's intellectual level by commissioning original work, in all fields, with an Americanist and Europeanist vocation (Davies 2000). He paid handsomely to get top writers, offering Galdós a Goya print from his collection in return for publishing his novella *Torquemada en la hoguera* (*Torquemada at the Stake*, 1889); another scoop was Unamuno's essay series *En torno al casticismo* (*On Tradition*, 1895). More successful in terms of circulation figures were the illustrated magazines that, with new printing techniques, proliferated towards the century's end (Charnon-Deutsch 2008). Most major writers contributed to them. *La Ilustración Española y Americana* (*The Spanish and American Illustrated Magazine*, 1869–1921), which reached a readership of 25,000–35,000 including Europe and Spanish America, played a significant cultural role in making known in Spain, from 1890, the work of Latin American *Modernista* poets.

The visibility gained by creative writers through the role of the press in publishing and reviewing their work clinched the consecration of a distinct literary field. That this field was autonomous only in theory is shown by its dependence on journalism.

The Diversification of the Public Sphere

Increasingly, as the nineteenth century progressed, the public sphere would become fractured into multiple interest groups, some of which continued the Enlightenment ideal of the public sphere as a check on the workings of the state, while others resulted from the increasing disciplinary specialization that produced the new culture of professional experts identified by Foucault (1987 [1976]). This diversification of the public sphere was also driven by increased literacy, allowing a wider range of social groups to express their views publicly – particularly with the entry of an organized working class into public life after the 1868 Revolution.

The public role of theater changed substantially in the course of the nineteenth century. Romantic drama continued the Enlightenment belief in the theater as a forum for shaping public opinion. From the mid-1840s, however, theater-going became a bourgeois leisure activity; by 1871, Spain had 335 theaters, with roughly 8,000 dramatic performances nationwide (Gies 1994, 173–4, 292). Its class exclusivity was consolidated by the abolition around 1820 of the standing room that had allowed popular attendance. The improved illumination resulting from the introduction from 1845 of gas lighting and from 1888 of electric lighting (Gies 1994, 23, 32) made the theater a space of conspicuous consumption where the bourgeoisie went to view itself on display – as satirized in Alas's *La Regenta*. The confinement of women to the *cazuela* ended in the 1840s, integrating them into the display. Theater reviews start to incorporate celebrity gossip at this time (Cruz 2011, 175). Popular theater was performed at separate, cheaper venues offering lightweight fare that, with some Catalan-language exceptions, was similarly escapist (see chapter 6). From the mid-century, the novel replaced theater as the literary vehicle for airing issues of public concern – particularly, as noted earlier, with the development of the realist novel from the mid-1870s. At the century's end, theater would regain something of its earlier role as a forum for public debate with the turn to republican-inspired social drama. It is no coincidence that two of the authors responsible for the 1890s move to social drama had prior careers as realist novelists: Alas and, with a more substantial dramatic output, Galdós.

A mid-nineteenth-century beneficent society that continued the Enlightenment tradition of bringing together public figures to benefit the public good was the Sociedad Abolicionista (Abolitionist Society), founded in 1865 (with a separate Women's Section) to lobby for the aboli-tion of slavery – finally banned in Puerto Rico in 1873 and in Cuba in 1886. Its members included writers, among them the previously mentioned novelist and journalist Sáez de Melgar, who in 1879 wrote an anti-slavery drama, *La cadena rota* (*The Broken Chain*) (Tsuchiya 2015). What allowed the Abolitionist Society to admit women was its philanthropic purpose; in Spain as elsewhere, philanthropy, seen as an extension of women's mater-nal mission, allowed women (of a certain means) a limited role in the public sphere. The most notable example was Concepción Arenal, founder of the journal *La Voz de la Caridad* (*The Voice of Charity*, 1870–84), who campaigned for prison reform as Spain's first female Inspector of Women's Prisons.

By contrast, the Real Academia Española (RAE) remained resolutely male: its rejection in 1853 of Gómez de Avellaneda's candidacy was contin-ued with its refusal of Pardo Bazán in 1889, 1892, and 1912 (its first woman fellow, Carmen Conde, would be elected in 1979). The RAE's Madrid resi-dence requirement also discriminated against writers from the periphery: on his election in 1897, the Cantabrian-based Pereda had to be granted an exemption. The many specialist learned societies, likewise based in Madrid, that proliferated in the second half of the nineteenth century also excluded women, with membership limited to male professionals in the discipline concerned. Among the most visible, through their role in advising govern-ment, were the Academia de Ciencias Morales y Políticas (Academy of Moral and Political Sciences, 1857); Real Academia Nacional de Medicina (Royal National Academy of Medicine, 1861); Sociedad Española de

Antropología (Spanish Anthropology Society, 1865); Sociedad Española de Historia Natural (Spanish Natural History Society, 1871); Sociedad Geográfica de Madrid (Madrid Geographic Society, 1876); and Sociedad Española de Higiene (Spanish Hygiene Society, 1882) (Labanyi 2000, 11).

Although the Athenaeums (*Ateneos*) that proliferated in the course of the nineteenth century were not discipline-specific, they too were largely homosocial spaces. The Ateneo de Madrid – founded as the Ateneo Español at the start of the 1820–3 liberal interlude by returning liberal exiles, and reinstituted as the Ateneo Científico y Literario in 1835 on absolutism's demise – was in 1860 reorganized as the Ateneo Científico, Literario y Artístico, when, reflecting the move to disciplinary specialization, it created Chairs in its distinct fields (including one in literature) so as to foster debate in areas often not covered in the university curriculum (Ruiz Salvador 1971). Unlike the 1837–51 Liceo Artístico y Literario de Madrid, the Ateneo permitted entry to women only as guests of male members. This allowed them to be occasional invited speakers: in 1884, poet and dramatist Rosario de Acuña was the first woman to host a poetry evening; Pardo Bazán gave guest lectures in 1887 and 1897. The first woman member (Pardo Bazán) was admitted only in 1905; the following year, she was elected the first woman president of its literature section. Local Ateneos sprang up in the provinces, numbering nearly 200 by the 1880s; like the Madrid Ateneo, they functioned as debating societies. They were accompanied by the creation of local Casinos (over two thousand by 1895) which functioned more as gentleman's clubs (Cruz 2011, 198–200) – also satirized in Alas's *La Regenta*. Both Ateneos and Casinos had reading rooms; reading the national and foreign press in Oviedo's Casino allowed Alas to be Spain's top journalist without having to live in the capital.

Bourgeois public opinion was challenged, from the 1840s, by the emergence of a republican public sphere, articulated via (short-lived) utopian socialist magazines, as well as the fierce anticlericalism of much popular serialized fiction (Baena 2020). After the 1868 Revolution's institution of freedom of expression, religion, and association, a range of radical political options that can loosely be grouped under the term "republicanism" – freethinking, socialism, anarchism, freemasonry, spiritism – took off in Spain, intersecting in their rejection of class inequality and the Church. The early history of Spanish socialism has been well documented, including the founding of the Socialist Party (Partido Socialista Obrero Español) by Pablo Iglesias in 1879, and its newspapers *El Socialista* (Madrid, 1886–) and *La Lucha de Clases* (*The Class Struggle*; Bilbao, 1894–), the latter gaining a circulation of 4,000 (Unamuno was a contributor). Also well studied are the socialist and anarchist workers' cultural centers, with libraries and reading rooms and a flourishing performance culture, which proliferated in the 1890s (Tuñón de Lara 1972; Mainer 2004, 21–91). The only republican dramas of working-class life to make it into literary histories are Alas's *Teresa* and Joaquín Dicenta's *Juan José* (both 1895), the latter regularly staged on Labor Day (May 1), plus Galdós's 1901 anticlerical drama *Electra*, which triggered republican demonstrations, leading to Galdós's election as republican parliamentary deputy in 1907 and his appointment in 1910 as joint head, with Pablo Iglesias, of the Republican-Socialist Alliance.

An important lesson learned from the still limited scholarship on nineteenth-century Spanish republicanism is the major role played by republican women as political activists in the *sexenio revolucionario* (revolutionary sexennium) of 1868–75 (Espigado 2010) and, from the 1880s especially, in the republican press, where they advocated for women's rights (Arkinstall 2014). Among them was the above-mentioned Acuña: aristocrat, mason, and contributor to *Las Dominicales del Librepensamiento* (*The Sunday Freethinker*, 1885–1909) and the spiritist weekly *La Luz del Porvenir* (*Light of the Future*, 1879–99). Spanish freemasonry – which blossomed after the 1868 Revolution (López Casimiro 2011) – seems to have been unique in that certain lodges admitted women as members (rather than allowing them access under male tutelage), while some women ran their own informal lodges (Arkinstall 2014, 8). Particularly important were the Barcelona-based masons Ángeles López de Ayala and Belén Sárraga, who had close relations with the major Catalan anarchist Teresa Claramunt, founding with her in 1891 the Barcelona Sociedad Autónoma de Mujeres (Independent Women's Society; from 1898, Sociedad Progresiva Femenina / Progressive Women's Society). Sárraga would in 1897 found the Asociación General Femenina (General Women's Association) in Valencia, with centers in Catalonia and Andalusia, plus other feminist associations in Portugal and Latin America. Both López de Ayala and Sárraga founded and directed republican newspapers (with circulations of up to 20,000) and, in Sárraga's case, spoke to audiences of up to 8,000 in Spain, Algeria, and Latin America. These radical women journalists and activists wrote poetry, plays, novels, and short stories, mostly published in the freethinking press (Arkinstall 2014). The precarious archival traces of the republican public sphere should not deceive us into thinking that the bourgeois public sphere was uncontested simply because it is more amply documented.

4

Countering Castilian:
From Retrenchment to the Renaissance
of Peripheral National Literatures
(1710s–1890s)

This chapter traces the evolution of Catalan, Galician, and Basque as literary languages from the early eighteenth-century state's homogenizing measures through their respective nineteenth-century revivals. Literary histories sometimes make it appear that the mid-nineteenth-century burgeoning of Spain's three major peripheral national literatures came out of nowhere, and that medieval Basque, Catalan, and Galician had entirely given way to Castilian until some worthy intellectuals came along to revive them. While this is far from being the case, it is true that, despite the rich and diverse Galician and Catalan literary traditions that extended from the eleventh to the fifteenth centuries, enormous pressure was put on Spain's other languages by the expansion of Castilian as institutional(ized) and literary language of the emerging Castilian state. Castile's rise to hegemony from its thirteenth-century merger with León – consolidated by its 1492 conquest of the Muslim kingdom of Granada and sponsorship of Columbus's "discovery" of the Americas – was completed by the 1707–16 Nueva Planta decrees through which the new Bourbon monarchy abolished the Crown of Aragon, subordinating its territories to Castilian rule; this meant administration in Castilian. From this point, Castile became synonymous with Spain, and Castilian with Spanish.

While it has been observed that forms of Catalan continued to be used widely at all levels until the 1830s (Marfany 2004, 2008, 2017), Basque and Galician were largely eradicated in the early modern period as a presence in the public sphere. However, invisibility did not mean disappearance; most Basques and Galicians learned the vernacular language at home, adding Castilian and/or Latin as they rose through the social hierarchy. Spain's vernacular languages thus remained in widespread use, although the extent of that use varied at different levels of society. Their re-emergence, becoming symbols of the modern Basque, Catalan, and Galician national projects that took shape during the nineteenth century, responded in part to pan-European developments, such as the rise of vernacular languages and literatures inspired by German Romanticism, and the parallel rise of political nationalism that came to a head in the revolutionary year of 1848, sometimes called the "Springtime of Nations." Within Spain, the trigger was the increased political, administrative, and educational centralization that, initiated under eighteenth-century Bourbon rule, intensified in the first part of the nineteenth century, with the Spanish state continuing to look to France as a model. The territorial re-organization of Spain undertaken by Secretary of State Javier de Burgos in 1833, which fractured the historic kingdoms into provinces, was symptomatic of the central state's (counter-productive) attempt to replace local loyalties with a sense of national identity.

We start this chapter with brief historical surveys of the usage and status of the three languages concerned, so as to better contextualize their resurgence as vehicles of literary expression in the course of the nineteenth century.

Between Literary "Reconstruction" and Language Shift: Catalan in the Eighteenth and Nineteenth Centuries and Beyond

Catalan – like Castilian and Galician, a Romance language that evolved from Vulgar Latin towards the end of the first millennium AD – probably originated in the Conflent area of the eastern Pyrenees, spreading by conquest and settlement to the territories known in present-day Spain as Catalonia, Valencia, the Balearic Islands, as well as to parts of Aragon and Murcia. The rich medieval and early modern literary production to which it gave rise ranged from religious and pious literature and troubadour-esque court poetry to the eclectic writings of figures like Ramon Llull and Bernat Metge in the twelfth to fourteenth centuries, and Ausiàs March and Joannot Martorell during the fifteenth-century Valencian "Golden Age." As reflected in the great chronicles of Jaume I, Bernat Desclot, Ramon Muntaner, and Pere IV, Catalan was the language of administration of the Crown of Aragon's Mediterranean seaborne empire, which at its peak in the fourteenth and fifteenth centuries encompassed parts of southern France, Sicily, Corsica, Sardinia, Malta, Greece (in the fourteenth century), and the southern Italian Peninsula (from the mid-fifteenth century). This imperial history explains why Catalan continues to be spoken not just in the above-mentioned areas of the Iberian Peninsula, but also in parts of southern France, Andorra, and the Sardinian capital Alghero. However, its sociolinguistic status varies considerably, as a result of diverse processes of language contact, diglossia, and conflict.

Though in many ways it is as a literary language, or "language of culture" (Carner 1996), that Catalan is most uncontroversially accepted as a shared language across these different territories, its "reconstruction" as such from the early nineteenth century took place without the institutionalized support of a centralized state. Nonetheless, the shape of the Catalan cultural *Renaixença* (Renaissance) was ultimately determined by political centralization in Spain, not only because of the language shift that took place – at different speeds – in the Catalan-speaking territories, especially after the War of the Spanish Succession's end in 1714, but also because the unification of the Spanish state provided a frame for reflection on a Spanish national culture, particularly in response to the 1808 Napoleonic occupation and its aftermath.

In Catalan literary histories, the seventeenth and eighteenth centuries were long portrayed as periods of decadence – *La Decadència* – set against the literary glories of earlier centuries. This vision began to be imposed during the mid-to-late nineteenth-century period known as *La Renaixença*, generally characterized as a literary revival responsible for the seeds of recovery of Catalan language, culture, and institutions (Jorba 1986; Molas 1989). Such broad-brushstroke periodization of Catalan cultural history has recently been questioned, in particular the assumption that the *Renaixença* – elsewhere recognized as largely a conservative cultural movement – marked the beginnings of institutionalized resistance to the imposition of the Castilian language and culture from outside the Catalan-speaking territories (Fradera 2003, 2009; Marfany 2008, 2017; Domingo 2013b). Social and cultural historians have identified a more complex process of increasing diglossia amongst the dominant classes that was strengthened with the positions taken by the *Renaixença*. In practice, this periodization is a product of different struggles for hegemony: just as the scholarship of Manuel Milà i Fontanals became a source of legitimization for both the troubadour-influenced *Jocs Florals* (Floral Games) that were so central to creating an autonomous Catalan literary field and the Spanish national philology of Marcelino Menéndez Pelayo, so the poet and historian Joaquim Rubió i Ors – who published poems in Catalan under the nostalgic pseudonym "Lo Gayter del Llobregat" (The Bagpiper of Llobregat) – fathered subsequent Catalan literary histories by his descendants Antoni Rubió i Lluch and Jordi Rubió i Balaguer (Molas 1989).

Underpinned by the growing presence of the publishing industry, with daily newspapers like the *Diario de Barcelona* (from 1792) and popular novel collections like that of Mariano Cabrerizo in Valencia (from 1818) or Antoni

Bergnes de las Casas in Barcelona (from 1833), the early nineteenth century saw a proliferation of literary *tertulias*, linked to the reopening of key educational foundations from 1815 and institutions like the Real Academia de las Buenas Letras and urban Sociedades de Amigos. In the 1830s, inspired by historical Romanticism, Catalan writers and intellectuals began to excavate their linguistic and literary heritage as a way of contributing to a distinctly Spanish cultural history. So, figures like Milà i Fontanals, Ramón López Soler, and Bonaventura Carles Aribau laid the foundations for the debates over the status of the Catalan language and literature that followed over the next hundred years or so, even though they themselves often perceived a limited role for modern Catalan. Their focus on recovering high literary genres – largely turning their backs on the popular forms that continued to thrive throughout the eighteenth and nineteenth centuries – set the tone for much subsequent framing and periodization of Catalan literary history. That focus arguably contributed to language shift through the practice and legitimization of diglossia, by which the literary value of modern Catalan remained consigned to a reproduction of pseudo-medievalizing festival poetry, whilst Castilian was increasingly preferred for other written text types (Marfany 2008).

Nevertheless, the philological focus introduced in this period ultimately contributed to many of the key events and institutions that would ensure Catalan's survival as more than a local vernacular – from poetry festivals to journals and publishing ventures, culture courses, university programs, and the eventual standardization of the language overseen by Pompeu Fabra from the philological section of the Institut d'Estudis Catalans (Institute of Catalan Studies) (Vallverdú 1980; Costa Carreras 2009). The broad consensus achieved around his grammar (1912) and orthographical standards (1913), confirmed by representatives from across the Catalan-speaking territories in the Normes of Castelló (1932), indicates the extent of Catalan's acceptance as a shared standard language, as part of what Catalanists from the early twentieth century would call the "fet diferencial" (differential factor) (Prat de la Riba 1908).

After the "Dark Centuries": Re-emergence of the Galician Language

Galician emerged from the spoken Latin of north-west Iberia and was consolidated as a distinct language between the twelfth and fourteenth centuries. In its early incarnation as Galician-Portuguese, it was not only the local administrative language of modern-day Galicia and Portugal, but also the common language of lyric poetry across the Peninsula. The Galician-Portuguese troubadour school, influenced in part by its Occitan equivalent, produced almost 1,700 secular and 420 religious poems (the *Cantigas de Santa María*) during the thirteenth century (Gutiérrez García 2014). However, with the political separation of Galicia and Portugal in the twelfth century, Portuguese was established as the language of the new Portuguese Crown and Galician was left without its own administrative center, coming under increasing influence from Castilian which, as the language of the emerging Castilian state, effectively pushed Galician out of administrative use. By the middle of the sixteenth century, this process was largely complete. Galician literary historians call the period between the institutionalization of Castilian and the mid-nineteenth-century literary revival the *séculos escuros* (Dark Centuries). During this period, while other European vernacular languages were being codified into written forms, Galician remained almost exclusively oral. Consequently, the language fragmented into multiple microdialects, intensifying the loss of prestige.

The eighteenth century saw a limited revival of interest in Galicia's social and political fortunes by Enlightenment thinkers, accompanied by concern for the language (Gemie 2006; Beramendi 2007). The most prominent defender of Galician, the Madrid-based Benedictine Fray Martín Sarmiento, argued that it should be taught in schools and used in churches. His lexicographical studies of the 1740s include collections of toponyms, plant names, and examples of popular speech, and are a unique source for recovering the history of the language during this period. However, apart from some isolated early nineteenth-century political pamphlets, it was only in the 1850s that Galician began to regain ground as a literary language. The pioneering dictionary of the writer and lexicographer Xoán Manuel Pintos, comprising some 14,000 entries, remained unfinished on his death in 1856. Probably the first Galician-language dictionary to be published was Francisco Javier Rodríguez's posthumous *Diccionario gallego-castellano*, which included almost 4,000 entries. The publication in 1863 of Rodríguez's dictionary and Rosalía de Castro's Galician-language poetry collection *Cantares gallegos* (*Galician Songs*) has enshrined this date as the foundational year of the Galician literary Renaissance known as the *Rexurdimento*.

Galician public and cultural life during this period were effectively diglossic; writers and journalists in all fields other than poetry and a smattering of prose fiction continued to choose Castilian, which remained the dominant language in almost all spheres. Galician occupied a largely symbolic role until the 1880s, when the expansion of the Galician publishing industry in connection with the emerging *rexionalista* (regionalist) political movement allowed historians, linguists, grammarians, and journalists to deepen their discussion of the language's status. The first institutional focus for protection and standardization of the Galician language came in 1905, with the foundation of the Academia Gallega (now Real Academia Galega, RAG). Its inaugural President, Manuel Murguía, had advocated for production of an authoritative Galician dictionary since the 1860s. This became one of the new academy's principal projects; however, differences in the ideological and political basis for *galeguismo* during the *rexionalista* period led to disagreements over whether the dictionary should be monolingual or bilingual (González Millán 2003), and by 1928 it had reached only the beginning of the letter "c" (Santamarina 2011). No standard form of the language was agreed until 1982; the Linguistic Normalization Act, which guarantees the right to use Galician, was passed the following year, while the RAG's long-awaited *Dicionario* appeared only in 1997.

The First Modern Basque Period: Linguistic Revival

Basque – *Euskara* in standard Basque, with the dialectal variant *Euskera* also found – is the only non-Indo-European language in Western Europe and currently is spoken on both sides of the Pyrenees: in Spain, in the Basque Autonomous Community and Foral Community of Navarre; and in France, in the three Basque provinces that today belong to the Département des Pyrénées-Atlantiques. Although Basque was once spoken in an extensive zone stretching from the River Garonne and Bordeaux to the north; Rioja and parts of Soria and Burgos to the south; parts of Cantabria and Burgos to the west; and the Aran Valley to the east, its geography has been reduced dramatically over the centuries. With 900,000 speakers at present, its sociolinguistic and legal status varies considerably: it is official in parts of the peninsular Basque Country but has never been official in the French Basque provinces. Basque has no known linguistic relatives; bizarre opinions have been expressed about its origins. While little is known about the use of Basque in the Middle Ages, we know that most Basques were monolingual for much of the Basque Country's history. After the annexation of the peninsular Basque Country by Castile in the twelfth century and the definitive incorporation of the continental Basque Country into France in the sixteenth century, the Basques maintained their institutions and charters (*fueros*) but the minority and diglossic status of the Basque language increased. In the French Basque provinces, the linguistic homogenization process culminated with the 1794 Decree of II Thermidor, prohibiting languages other than French. In the Spanish Basque provinces, the process was aggravated in the eighteenth century with prohibitions on publication in Basque and penalization of the use of Basque in schools.

Recent Basque philological studies use the term First Modern Basque Period to refer to the years stretching from the 1745 publication of Manuel Larramendi's *Diccionario trilingüe: Castellano, Bascuence y Latín* (*Trilingual Dictionary: Castilian, Basque, Latin*) to Resurreccion Maria Azkue's landmark 1891 grammar *Euskal Izkindea*. These years saw the start of normalization of the Basque language with the publication of grammars and dictionaries. However, French and Spanish government centralism had started to be challenged in the early eighteenth century by the French Basque writer Joanes Etxeberri, who appealed to the Basques to cultivate their language. Larramendi's dictionary was preceded by his 1728 apology for the Basque language and his 1729 grammar, whose title – *El imposible vencido. Arte de la Lengua Bascongada* (*The Impossible Overcome: Art of the Basque Language*) – shows his awareness of the extent of diglossia, with Basque spoken by the vast majority of monolinguals but not used for administration, education, or knowledge production.

Early interest in the Basque language was stimulated by the linguist Wilhelm von Humboldt, who visited the Basque Country in 1799 and 1801. His hypothesis that Basque was the last vestige of a Basque-Iberian vernacular spoken throughout the Iberian Peninsula in antiquity gave the language a new dignity. The dialectological studies promoted by Louis Lucien Bonaparte, nephew of Napoleon III, produced the first map of the Basque language in 1863. The first proposal for the unity of the French and Spanish Basque territories had been made in the 1836 grammar of the French Basque writers Augustin Chaho and Antoine d'Abbadie, dedicated to "Zazpi uskal-herrietako uskalduner" (The Basque people of the seven Basque territories) (Urgell 2018).

In the Spanish Basque Country, diglossia was exacerbated by the 1857 Moyano Law making primary education in Castilian compulsory throughout the national territory. The Basque language was not officially used for educational and administrative purposes until the late twentieth century, becoming official in the Basque Autonomous Community in 1982 and in the Basque-speaking areas of the Foral Community of Navarre in 1986. Agreement on the creation of standard Basque – a milestone for its survival as a language of culture and science – was finally reached in 1968.

The Catalan *Renaixença*: From Provincial Revivalism to the Beginnings of Political Catalanism

When, in 1779, merchant historian Antoni de Capmany famously described Catalan as a provincial language, dead to the Republic of Letters (Branchadell 2006; Marfany 2004, 138), he was reflecting a situation in which the hegemony of Castilian as the national language, for written texts at least, was increasingly accepted by Catalan social elites. This has often been read as an indication of language shift; that is, of the increasing prevalence of Castilian in Catalonia, Valencia, and the Balearic Islands, thanks to the dominance of the language in the Habsburg court from the sixteenth century and the imposition of the Nueva Planta decrees after the War of the Spanish Succession. Yet, documents from the period show that Catalan continued to be used as the language of everyday life across the social spectrum, in spite of institutional limitations on transmission of the language introduced over the eighteenth century (Marfany 2004, 2008, 2017). Travelers refer to the monolingualism of the majority of Catalan citizens; during the Napoleonic occupation, official pronouncements in the region were issued in French and Catalan (Cassany 2009); and popular theater in Valencia and Barcelona from the early decades of the nineteenth century often portrays urban communities who find it difficult to express themselves in anything other than their local language.

The question of how and why the linguistic situation in the Catalan-speaking territories changed over the nineteenth century has given rise to continuous debate. Catalan literary histories identify four different but overlapping phases of recovery following two centuries of decadence: Romanticism (1800–40s, characterized by the excavation of the historical past to trace the region's particular cultural contribution); *Renaixença* (1840s–1880s, characterized by the revival and reactivation of this heritage in contemporary cultural practice); *Modernisme* (1880s–1900, characterized by greater critical questioning of this heritage in relation to the needs of modern society); and *Noucentisme* (1900s–1920s, characterized by the institutionalization of culture in order to provide the resources and infrastructure necessary for future cultural production). These phases share characteristics with, and mirror developments in, other regions in Spain and Europe, underlining the value of reading them comparatively and relationally (Jorba 1986). It is important to recognize the power relationships involved in this process, with lines being drawn and redrawn between the provincial and the national; the local and the universal; language and dialect; and between *patria* in its original sense of homeland or birthplace and in the sense of a political entity that the word would (like the term "nation") acquire over the nineteenth century (Marfany 2017). These oppositions help explain how Spanish writers supportive of national unity – for example, Menéndez Pelayo, Miguel de Unamuno, even José María de Pereda – could be sympathetic to "local" languages provided they remained confined to the expression of "local" matters, especially matters relating to the past (Bastons i Vivanco and Busquets i Grabulosa 2002; Balcells 2011).

These issues come to the fore in relation to the Catalan *Renaixença*. Broadly read in its beginnings as a nostalgic, medievalizing, and provincial movement that neither contributed to the development of modern Spanish letters nor presented a threat to Castilian hegemony, it later began to be seen as problematic by writers and thinkers outside Catalonia. This shift is most clearly expressed in Francisco María Turbino's *Historia del renacimiento literario contemporáneo de Cataluña, Baleares y Valencia* (*History of the Contemporary Literary Renaissance in Catalonia, the Balearic Islands and Valencia*, 1883), where recognition of the vitality of cultural practices and of the importance of incorporating their differential character into Spanish literary historiography is accompanied by criticism of attempts to cultivate modern literature in anything other than the language of the state and by concern regarding the increasing links between the cultural and the political (Rigobon 2013).

From the 1840s onwards, diverse events, initiatives, networks, and processes contributed to the emergence of modern Catalan literature. These developments were underpinned by the late eighteenth- and nineteenth-century re-discovery and re-reading of medieval and early modern history, as well as by a variety of instruments and institutions facilitated by the rapid urban development of Barcelona and Valencia. The latter included these cities' growth in importance as publishing centers, the increasing influence of the press (especially the *Diario de Barcelona*), the restoration of key educational institutions, and the creation of numerous types of civic associations (Fuster i Sobrepere 2006). The historiographical and philological focus informing these developments was framed by similar dispositions throughout Spain, in response to international events like the French Revolution and the Spanish Peninsular War. Their imbrication with a more differential Catalan nation-building project was connected to the particular socio-economic development of the Barcelona metropolitan area, and its increasing function as *de facto* capital of the Catalan-speaking regions. How and why Catalan writers, intellectuals, and, in particular, literary historians moved from celebration of regional particularism and nostalgia for a long-lost glorious past to a sense of Catalan linguistic and cultural relevance for modernity is something that can be fruitfully explored by comparison with Catalan-speaking locales where this shift was not so prevalent, such as the Balearic Islands and, to a lesser extent, Valencia (Sanchis Guarner 1981). While all three regions saw the reinterpretation of literary tradition, the national past, and the popular that is characteristic of late Romanticism, there were significant differences in the levels of importance granted to modern literature in Catalan in the construction of national identity. These differences had a far-reaching impact on efforts to create a reading public and modern culture industry, given the importance of linguistic standardization to achieve such a goal.

The case studies chosen for special attention here – the *Jocs Florals* and the canonization of Àngel Guimerà – stand at the center of more traditional accounts of the revival of Catalan culture from the 1850s onwards. However, through attention to the particular way they plot the relationship between tradition and modernity, and to their construction of a literary field determined by the operation of other social agents and fields, it will become apparent that these phenomena are conflict-ridden manifestations of a society undergoing very profound changes. The recovery of the Catalan language is often presented as taking place through the action of philologically minded intellectuals, whose aesthetic agenda and nostalgic disposition led to the privileging of poetry. In Catalonia's case, the foundational date for this revival is the 1833 publication in *El Vapor* of Aribau's ode "La pàtria," which paved the way for the appearance of other occasional poems in Catalan, notably those by Rubió i Ors in the *Diario de Barcelona* from the 1840s, or the later turn to Catalan of the proto-feminist Romantic poet Josepa Massanés. Rubió i Ors' prologue to an 1841 edition of his poems explicitly called for an end to Catalans' indifference toward their language. The same year saw the celebration of a first poetry festival in the Real Academia de las Buenas Letras in Barcelona, at which Rubió i Ors won first prize. Celebrated again in 1857, this event anticipated the *Jocs Florals* which, though framed explicitly as the revival of a historic Catalan institution, also responded to wider pseudo-medievalizing tendencies of the time, visible in the popularity of Sir Walter Scott, Wagner's *Tannhäuser*, Verdi's *Il trovatore*, and the many imitations and parodies they generated.

As will be seen in the following sections, the modern reincarnation of the *Jocs Florals* was by no means an exclusively Catalan invention. Reinstated officially by the Diputación de Barcelona in 1859, they now tend to be seen, and were already perceived by many critics at the time, as an anachronistic, nostalgic, and conservative phenomenon that may have furthered diglossic practice amongst the increasingly dominant bourgeoisie.

For contemporaries like Frederic Soler (penname "Serafí Pitarra"), they involved turning away from "el català que ara es parla" (spoken Catalan of the time), though he himself participated in them from the mid-1870s (Poblet 1967). These annual poetry festivals were far more than just another theater in which, as at the Gran Teatre del Liceu, the Barcelona elites could display their cultural capital (Ciurans 2012, 132–3). They drew together a broad spectrum of contemporary Catalan society, including philologists like Milà i Fontanals and later Menéndez Pelayo who were skeptical about the value of modern literary Catalan; conservatives like Rubió i Ors and Antoni de Bofarull; liberal federalists like Víctor Balaguer and later Valentí Almirall; and writers and intellectuals from other Catalan-speaking territories such as the Majorcan Marià Aguiló. Their broad acceptance can be seen in the emergence of similar festivals throughout Catalonia, as well as bilingual versions in Valencia and Palma de Mallorca (Domingo 2013a). If the prize "flowers" awarded – the "Viola" for poems about Faith, the "Englantina" for poems about the Patria, the "Natural" for poems about Love – enshrined a conservative worldview linking the contemporary landscape to an orthodox Christian history, the festivals did not prevent more radical and diverse voices from emerging, as with the prize awarded to Caterina Albert (better known by her penname "Víctor Català") at the 1898 *Jocs* in Olot for her powerful dramatic monologue "La infanticida" (The Infanticide). However, the predominance of patriotic odes is confirmed by the fact that, when a cross-section of judges was asked in 1924 to select the best of the "flowers" historically, the majority were in the eglantine category (Molas 2009).

Retrospectively, the resulting 1925 compilation of all-time best poems in the three categories serves to identify the key function of the *Jocs Florals* in the 65 years following their "restoration." Their commitment to presenting literature written only in Catalan, unlike similar festivals revived in Valencia and Majorca, had created a space in which the Catalan language was able to gain some cultural legitimacy, while contributing to the development of an autonomous literary field by fostering more rigorous literary critical practices, required by the judging process (Molas 2009). Furthermore, the *Jocs'* refusal to privilege any of the proposed orthographical standards developed for modern Catalan meant that it provided a space of encounter between defenders of different visions of the language. This representation of the *Jocs Florals* as a space of unity in diversity is undoubtedly somewhat idealized and nostalgic; even so, a glance at the list of prize-winners reveals the presence of many of the most significant writers in the Catalan literary field, however diverse their social origin and political allegiance. The poets selected anonymously for this 1925 volume, assembled during the ban on the *Jocs* imposed by the Primo de Rivera dictatorship, represent a range of voices – from the conservative pre-normative Aguiló to Jacint Verdaguer, Guimerà, and the more modernizing Joan Maragall and *Noucentista* normative Josep Carner – that indicates the potent legitimizing function of the annual festivals. The thematic coverage of the *Jocs* maps the changing relationship between tradition and modernity. If the early years matched the medievalizing perspective reflected in Bofarull's and Balaguer's respective troubadour collections of 1858 and 1859, their scope soon became much broader, with prizes for scholarly studies such as that of Milà i Fontanals in 1865, the emergence of Guimerà and Verdaguer as strong literary voices in the 1870s, the recognition of the authority of literary critics like Josep Yxart and Joan Sardà, and their impact on subsequent writers like Narcís Oller, himself awarded prizes for his narrative.

In the 1880s, newer generations of writers associated with the modern urban culture of the Eixample, built from the mid-1860s, distanced themselves from the *Jocs*, with more modernizing tendencies – the movement known as *Modernisme* – and debates over the standardization of the language emerging around the magazine *L'Avenç*. With the development of more permanent institutions for the promotion of Catalan culture, such as the Institut d'Estudis Catalans (1907), the *Jocs Florals* largely lost their legitimizing function, especially after their rejection of the orthographical standards proposed by Pompeu Fabra and disseminated by *Noucentista* writers, intellectuals, and organs. However, the festivals continued to have influence in the early twentieth century, with the participation of new generations of writers such as Carner, Guerau de Liost (penname of Jaume Bofill), and Josep Maria de Sagarra, and they took on a resistant quality under the Primo de Rivera dictatorship that was reprised in the years following the Spanish Civil War. Other institutions paved the way for the relative hegemony achieved by the Catalan language and literature in 1930s Catalonia: Pompeu Fabra's work on standardization of the language; the libraries, university studies, publishing houses, and journals that flourished under *Noucentisme*; and the political commitment to provide legitimizing structures for cultural production in Catalan (Murgades 1987). Even so, the *Jocs Florals* created a space for the development of a Catalan literary field and brought together many figures that might otherwise appear somewhat incompatible in social, political, and cultural outlook.

The case of Àngel Guimerà, declared a Mestre en Gay Saber (Master in the Art of Poesy) during the same *Jocs Florals* (1877) at which Verdaguer received a prize for *L'Atlàntida* and Josep Yxart presented his critical essay on contemporary Catalan theater, is indicative of the festival's central role in fostering the development of a diverse literary field in Catalan. Born in Tenerife, Guimerà moved with his family to Catalonia as a child and studied in Barcelona. He started to write in Catalan only in the 1870s when he began to gain a name as a poet, winning numerous prizes. Influenced by the modernizing literary critics Yxart and Sardà, Guimerà turned his hand to dramatic writing after 1877 (Miracle 1990). His early plays followed the Romantic historical models that had been so central to the Catalan literary revival, drawing on medieval and early modern Catalan history, as in his immensely popular *Mar i cel* (*Sea and Sky*, 1888). Yet his engagement with wider social and political debates via Almirall's Centre Català (the first political Catalanist platform, created in 1882) and his later political affiliation to the more conservative Lliga de Catalunya, together with the impact of northern European realist theater on the Catalan cultural scene of the 1890s, led him to draw on contemporary social conflicts for subsequent plays, culminating in the celebrated trilogy *Maria Rosa* (1894), *Terra baixa* (*Lowlands*, 1897), and *La filla del mar* (*Daughter of the Sea*, 1900). Focusing on three different aspects of the modern Catalan landscape – the urban proletariat, rural society, the coastal world – and characterized by a combination of romantic melodrama and more realist popular dialogue, these plays were translated and adapted into numerous languages, often via the mediating versions of the Spanish playwright José Echegaray, and generated film adaptations in Catalan, Spanish, English, and German (Gallén 2012). Guimerà's cultural prestige gave him great political weight. He was one of the signatories who took the Memorial de Greuges (Report of Grievances, in defense of Catalonia's moral and spiritual interests) to Madrid in 1885 and was elected president of the Lliga de Catalunya in 1889; his 1895 speech in Catalan as president of the Ateneu Barcelonès was a landmark moment in the shift toward institutional use of Catalan (Cassassas 2016). Like his contemporary Verdaguer (see chapter 5), Guimerà embodies many of the conflicts and contradictions of the Catalan cultural field of his time (Fradera 2007, 76–7), veering between nostalgia for a lost past and recognition of the complexity of the modern sociocultural landscape, between traditional literary forms and aesthetic and linguistic innovation. The rootedness of both writers in romantic nostalgia led to their rejection as models by the *Noucentista* movement, with its espousal of Mediterranean classicism. However, their contribution to the dignification of the Catalan language was never questioned, nor their capacity to speak beyond the circles of the *Renaixença* intelligentsia, reflected in the power of Manelic's struggle in *Terra baixa* against the corruption of the dominant classes; in the major homage organized in Guimerà's hometown of Manresa in 1909; and in his election to the Institut d'Estudis Catalans in 1911. The enormous popular turnout for Guimerà's burial in Montjuïc cemetery in 1924 confirms his canonicity and underlines literature's powerful representational function for Catalan culture and society; at a time of heightened repression of Catalan social, cultural, and political institutions under the Primo de Rivera dictatorship, such events provided an opportunity for broad societal resistance. Together these case studies illustrate a process of literary reconstruction played out across the boundaries between the provincial and the national, the local and the international. They show how the same sites authorized to perform a primarily nostalgic relationship to a distant past can become stages on which to explore the limits of contemporary cultural relations, transmission, and community.

A Nation Finds Its Voice: The Galician *Rexurdimento*

Although the beginning of the Galician cultural, linguistic, and literary revival known as the *Rexurdimento* is often formally dated to 1863, the first recognized calls for a coherent Galician identity within Spain came three decades earlier in 1833, in response to the Spanish government's administrative dismemberment of the historic Kingdom of Galicia. The movement to resist the kingdom's division into provinces called for the establishment of a unified province of Galicia and so came to be known as *provincialismo* (provincialism; the term carries none of the dismissive overtones of the English). Galician historians consider *provincialismo* (*c.*1840–80) the first formal stage in the journey of modern Galician political identity from its beginnings to *rexionalismo* (*c.*1880–1920) to *nacionalismo*.

The *provincialista* movement, whose most prominent figure was the young journalist Antolín Faraldo, had its base in the university city of Santiago de Compostela and was focused around two organizations: La Sociedad Patriótica (Patriotic Society) and Acción Literaria (Literary Action). Faraldo and his collaborators, conscious of Galicia's low literacy rates, lack of industrialization, and geographical isolation, were strong advocates for social reform and economic modernization, although this never fully solidified into a political agenda. The movement's cultural and literary dimension was much more visible, creating dozens of journals with evocative titles such as *La Aurora de Galicia* (*Galician Dawn*) or *El Emancipador Gallego* (*The Galician Emancipator*). *Provincialismo* came to a head and premature end in 1846, when Faraldo and his colleagues joined Colonel Miguel

Solís's military uprising against the increasingly centralist reforms of the Spanish minister General Narváez. On April 15, the rebels announced the creation of a Junta Superior del Reino de Galicia (Supreme Assembly of the Kingdom of Galicia), with Faraldo as its secretary. While the uprising was quashed within weeks by superior Spanish forces, the Spanish government's disproportionately vicious response gave the event a symbolic charge which it retains today. Twelve of its leaders, including Solís, were executed in the village of Carral, and are still celebrated throughout Galicia as the "Carral Martyrs." Faraldo was exiled to Portugal, later settling in Granada where he died at the age of 30. His symbolic role in the emergence of a modern Galician cultural and political identity would be consolidated in Manuel Murguía's iconic 1886 *Los precursores* (*The Precursors*), which considers Faraldo "el primero y el mejor" (the first and the best).

The legacy of the Carral disaster was to shift the *provincialista* movement away from political activism and toward literary and cultural activity, with increasing attention to the Galician language. Despite the lack of a strong autochthonous written culture, some Galician-language texts, chiefly those drawing strongly on oral culture, had been in circulation since the century's start. Until very recently (see chapter 6), the first printed book in Galician was believed to be José Fernández de Neira's political dialogue *Proezas de Galicia* (*Galician Feats*, 1812), written like so many other early Galician works as a propagandistic response to the 1808 Napoleonic occupation. Early works did not always circulate in print, and the efforts of the 1840s consisted partly in recovering this early heritage. For example, Antonio Benito Fandiño's pioneering drama *A Casamenteira* (*The Matchmaker*, 1812) would be printed for the first time in 1849, as part of a homage to Fandiño in Ourense. Throughout the 1840s and 1850s, Galician-language texts and fragments increasingly appeared in journals and newspapers, as did several key texts, including the compendium of Galician language and customs in epistolary form, *A gaita gallega* (*The Galician Bagpipe*, 1853) by Xoán Manuel Pintos, mentioned above for his lexicographical work.

While the 1840s and 1850s had seen a gradual increase in Galician-language cultural production, the foundational events of 1861 and 1863 sparked the *Rexurdimento* proper into life. In 1861, inspired by Barcelona's example two years earlier, A Coruña hosted Galicia's inaugural *Xogos Florais* (Floral Games). Of the 12 prizes awarded, only one was for a Galician-language composition: the exiled poet Francisco Añón's poem "A Galicia" (To Galicia), which begins by exhorting Galicia to awaken from its slumber and embrace the future. The following month, Pontevedra held its inaugural *Xogos Florais*, again with only a few Galician-language prize-winners, notably Francisco Fernández Anciles, whose poem "A noite de San Xoán" (St John's Night) celebrates the traditional revelries. Each event generated a publication, but it is the Coruña publication that has survived as a foundational text. This mammoth 500-page anthology, *Album de la Caridad* (*Charity Album*, 1862), places the prize-winning works alongside a lengthy selection of other pieces described as a "mosaic" of contemporary Galician poetry. Like the games themselves, the anthology is dominated by Castilian-language writing but is noteworthy for including a handful of Galicia's female writers, including Concepción Arenal, Emilia Calé, Elisa Lestache, Joaquina López de la Vega, Elvira Luna, Narcisa Pérez Reoyo, and, writing in Galician, the woman who would change everything: Rosalía de Castro.

Rosalía de Castro has many faces. Born in Santiago de Compostela in 1837, her early death in 1885, just as the *rexionalista* movement was emerging, made her an ideal symbol for the modern Galician consciousness taking shape in the hands of her widower, Manuel Murguía. Murguía's influence over Castro's personal and professional legacy created a contradictory figure whose personhood, beyond the stereotypical figure of devoted mother and wife, was firmly subordinated to her political role as a precursor of Galicia's emerging nationhood and her place as the "mother" of Galician literature. This reading would dominate Galician literary historiography for more than a century after Castro's death (Rodríguez 1990). Paradoxically, and uniquely for a figure so closely identified with a peripheral literature, Castro is also one of a handful of women writers who would be admitted into the twentieth-century Spanish literary canon. This is largely thanks to the attraction of the so-called "1898 Generation" to the existentialist themes of her last, Castilian-language poetry collection *En la orillas del Sar* (*On the Banks of the Sar*, 1884). It was only toward the end of the twentieth century that scholars were able to recognize and reclaim Castro's personal, political, and literary complexities (Miguélez-Carballeira 2013; 2014, 175–94).

Castro's decision to write and publish in a language with such a fractured public history was no accident (Rábade Villar 2011). Her fluency in Galician, which distinguished her from most Galician intellectuals (even Murguía), arose from her unusual personal background, whose details Murguía sought to keep hidden after her death. The illegitimate daughter of a woman from Galicia's rural aristocracy and a priest, she spent her earliest years living with her godmother in the countryside, where Galician was the language of daily life. By the age of 10, she had moved to Santiago de Compostela to join her mother, who ensured she was educated as a proper young Spanish lady. The teenage Castro was an active member of Santiago's literary and theatrical scene until in 1856, at the age of 18, she moved to Madrid. After marrying Murguía in 1858, Castro followed him to government posts in Castile and Galicia, swiftly establishing herself as a Castilian-language essayist (*Lieders*, 1858), poet (*La flor/ The Flower*, 1857; *A mi madre/ To My Mother*, 1862), and novelist (*La hija del mar/ The Daughter of the Sea*, 1859; *Flavio*, 1861). By the time she entered the Galician literary scene, she was an established writer with a clear voice of her own.

While both Galician and Spanish literary historians tend to celebrate its "naïve" or "ruralist" character (Miguélez-Carballeira 2013; Murado 2008), Castro's first Galician-language poetry collection *Cantares gallegos* is far from the work of a novice. The collection opens with a prologue that is not only the first piece of prose published by a woman in Galician, but a strongly worded denunciation of Castilian colonialism in Galicia. As Castro acknowledges in this prologue, no standard written form of the Galician language existed as she was writing, and so she had to forge her own. Twentieth-century literary historians often saw the peculiar nature of Castro's written Galician as an embarrassment, something to be standardized away, but more recent critics have recognized the powerful creative charge of a language emerging from centuries without material form (Rábade Villar 2011). The collection draws heavily on the Galician oral tradition, specifically on popular songs; she acknowledges the influence of Antonio Trueba's *El libro de los cantares* (*The Book of Songs*, 1852). The poems follow a standard pattern: a short refrain based on a Galician popular song, followed by Castro's own verses. The subjects range from rural life with its labor and festivities, to contemplation of nature, to the impact in Galicia of key social problems such as poverty and emigration. It is very clear where Castro lays the blame for Galicia's troubles: the famous poem "Castellanos de Castilla" (Castilians of Castile) overtly blames Spain for the conditions faced by Galician seasonal migrants to Castile, drawing a parallel between the suffering of Galicians and of the slaves whose condition was then being vociferously debated throughout Spain and its colonies. *Cantares gallegos* established the primary markers of Galician identity that remain in force today: language, culture, and territory, the latter often inseparable from its "dark other," emigration.

After *Cantares gallegos*, Castro continued writing, critiquing her homeland's social problems in both Galician and Castilian. Her 1866 article "Las literatas" (Literary Women) is an acute and often angry denunciation of the experience of female writers in Spain. The following year, she published the novel that remains her best known, *El caballero de las botas azules* (*The*

Blue-Booted Gentleman), a heavily ironic and stylistically innovative social critique, which deconstructs rigid models of female behavior. In 1880, Castro's second Galician-language poetry book *Follas novas* (*New Leaves*) brought together poems written over the previous decade while Castro was living, as she states in the prologue, in "o deserto de Castilla" (the Castilian desert). Castro thus not only takes up the subject position of an emigrant herself but also, underlining the intrinsic contribution of emigration to Galician literary history, dedicates the collection to the Galician community in Cuba, who had funded the publication and raised money to support Castro and her family when they were living in poverty. *Follas novas* addresses many of the same social questions as *Cantares gallegos*, including social injustice, emigration, and the status of women, but from a more reflective perspective. The opening section, "Vaguedás" (Vagaries), reflects on Castro's creative process as a woman who does not write of the typically feminine "pombas y . . . frores" (doves and . . . flowers); its self-reflective, even metaphysical concerns take the Galician language into previously uncharted areas.

Despite the relative success of *Cantares gallegos* and *Follas novas*, Castro's career as a Galician-language writer came to an abrupt end in 1881. In her article "Costumbres gallegos" (Galician Customs) published in the Madrid newspaper *El Imparcial*, Castro described an ancient custom in some parts of coastal Galicia, whereby a family might show hospitality to a foreign sailor by permitting him to spend a night with a female member of the household. The article caused a scandal in Galicia, much of it directed at Castro herself. Offended, she vowed never to write in Galician again. Her final poetry collection, which gained her admission into the Spanish literary canon, was *En las orillas del Sar* (1884), which continues the metaphysical, even existentialist line of *Follas novas* but now, of course, in Castilian. Scholars today recognize Castro as a complex, often contradictory writer, a powerful and original creative force, and an intense, extremely well-informed critic of the social injustices of nineteenth-century colonial Spain. She remains an essential interlocutor for women writing not only in Galician, but in Spanish and in other languages.

Castro may have become the face of the *Rexurdimento* but she was far from its only literary figure. Two other poets are commonly identified as shaping Galicia's lyrical resurgence, albeit in very different ways: Manuel Curros Enríquez and Eduardo González-Pondal Abente, commonly known as Pondal. Curros, like Castro, left for Madrid in his teens and took his first literary steps there while working as a clerk and, later, journalist. His career as a Galician-language poet began, and he returned to Galicia, after his extensive narrative poem "A Virxe do Cristal" (The Virgin of the Crystal) was awarded a prize at a local competition in 1877. Like Castro, Curros often took inspiration from Galician popular culture: "A Virxe do Cristal" is based on a seventeenth-century origin tale for the Sanctuary of the same name in his mother's hometown, Vilanova dos Infantes. Also like Castro, Curros was a vociferous critic of social injustice and a convinced anticlericalist. His first and best-known poetry collection *Aires d'a mina terra* (*Airs of My Homeland*, 1880), which criticizes the Church's elitism and lack of support for the poor, was banned and Curros excommunicated by the Bishop of Ourense. He followed it up with the equally extensive and equally anticlerical *O divino sainete* (*The Divine Farce*, 1888), a satire on Dante's *Divine Comedy* that is also a spirited defense of the *Rexurdimento* and its literature. Although largely ignored by contemporary Galician critics, it has been almost continuously in print since Curros's death in 1908 in Cuba, where he had emigrated in 1894.

In contrast to Castro and Curros, Pondal was less concerned with the injustices of Galicia's present than with the reclamation of its past. From a relatively wealthy family, he trained as a doctor, moving in the same literary circles as Castro and Murguía. While Pondal's Galician-language poem "A Campana de Anllóns" (The Bell of Anllóns) is included in the *Album de la Caridad* arising from the 1861 *Xogos Florais*, it was with his discovery in the 1870s of James Macpherson's *Ossian* cycle of epic poems that he found his own distinctive path. Inspired by Macpherson and by the growing interest of ethnographers and historians, such as his friend Murguía, in Galicia's hitherto largely forgotten Celtic origins (Miguélez-Carballeira 2013), Pondal aimed to create his own poetic mythology out of the surviving fragments. Writing in both Spanish and Galician, he increasingly moved toward the latter, reworking the bilingual *Rumores de los pinos* (*Murmurs of the Pines*, 1877) into the monumental, monolingual *Queixumes dos pinos* (*Laments of the Pines*, 1886). His unfinished masterwork, begun in 1857 and unpublished in his lifetime, is the epic poem on the discovery of the Americas, *Os Eoas* (*Children of the Dawn*), strongly inspired by Camões's *Lusiad*, whose dozens of fragments he legendarily handed to the Real Academia Galega in a suitcase shortly before his death. Although *Queixumes dos pinos* and, since its reconstruction, *Os Eoas*, are both widely read, Pondal's most visible legacy is "Os pinos" (The Pines), his 1890 collaboration with the composer Pascual Veiga, which was chosen as the Galician national anthem and premiered at Havana's Centro Gallego in December 1907. Frequently performed by emigrant communities as an act of resistance while banned in Spain during the Franco dictatorship, the anthem was formally adopted in a newly standardized edition by the Xunta de Galicia in 1984.

Similarly to the Catalan case, traditional readings of Galicia's nineteenth century as ruralist, sentimental, and inward-looking miss the point. The works of Curros, Pondal, and especially Castro demonstrate the extent to which the Galician literary *Rexurdimento* was not only an intensely political movement, but also one forged in relation: between Galicia and Castile, Galicia and Cuba, Galicia and the wider Celtic world. As we will see, these connections continue to shape Galician literature – and life – today.

Euskal Pizkundea: The Basque Renaissance

The Basque Renaissance follows a different timeline from the Catalan *Renaixença* or Galician *Rexurdimento*. The term *Pizkundea* (Renaissance) covers the period from the sociocultural resurgence triggered by the 1876 abolition of the *fueros* in the peninsular Basque Country, after the central state's victory in the third and last Carlist War, through the first three decades of the twentieth century. The early twentieth century is discussed in chapter 8. This chapter discusses the first half of this period, which saw the emergence of a Basque-language literature thanks to various earlier developments, notably the Floral Games (*Lore Jokoak*) initiated in the French Basque Country 26 years earlier than in the Spanish Basque Country (and six years before their institutionalization in Catalonia), and of a mostly Spanish-language, clearly political, pro-foral literature, which fed into the Basque nationalism that would take shape from the 1890s (Igartua and Zabaltza 2012, 67).

Estimates for 1879 show that roughly half of the Basque territories' inhabitants were Basque speakers but that their distribution varied widely, ranging from 96 percent of the population in Gipuzkoa to 10 percent and 20 percent respectively in Álava and Navarre, where Basque had declined considerably in the eighteenth and nineteenth centuries (Urgell 2018, 610). The elites boasted of knowing Spanish or French and of not knowing Basque. The majority of the population was monolingual and uneducated; for that reason, many early texts in Basque are devotional works, written in the only language known to the populace at large.

Although the first known literary publication in Basque dates back to 1545 (Bernard Etxepare's volume of poetry *Linguae Vasconum Primitiae*), the early nineteenth century marks the start of the creation of a new Basque-language literary corpus with works like Bizenta Mogel's 1804 *Ipui onak*

(*Moral Tales*), the first female-authored published work in Basque, which also signals the birth of children's literature in Euskara. A translation and adaptation of Aesop's fables, it inspired a school of fabulists, mostly writing in verse. Bizenta's case is exceptional since it is estimated that only 15 percent of Basque women were literate at the time. Humboldt's Romantic concept of the people as guardians of the language and national spirit inspired her uncle Juan Antonio Mogel's *Peru Abarka*, written in 1808 but published posthumously only in 1880. Its dialogues contrast the "wisdom and authenticity" of the eponymous farmer protagonist with the ignorance of the urban barber Maisu Juan, initiating a long line of literary works that would extol the traditional life and mindset of authentic rural Basques. Basque-language publications increased from the mid-nineteenth century. Many chronicled popular customs; for example, Juan Ignazio Iztueta's 1847 *Guipuzcoaco provinciaren condaira edo historia* (*History of the Province of Gipuzkoa*), which equated the survival of the Basque language with that of the *fueros* (Madariaga Orbea 2006, 159). The *fueros'* abolition in 1876 encouraged the beginnings of a *costumbrista* literature, as in Jean Baptiste Elizanburu's 1888 *Piarres Adame, saratarraren zenbait historio Laphurdiko eskuaran* (*Stories of Piarres Adame, from Sara, in the Lapurdan Dialect*), serialized in the republican periodicals *La Nivelle* and *Le Reveil Basque* – a humorous account in dialogue form of a visit to the fiestas of Olheta. The first novel in Basque, Domingo Agirre's historical fiction *Auñemendiko lorea* (*The Flower of the Pyrenees*, 1898), grew out of the development, from the mid-nineteenth century, of a Spanish-language literary tradition rooted in Basque legend (see chapter 5).

The *Lore Jokoak*, established in 1853 in the French Basque town of Urruña by the previously mentioned d'Abbadie, were instituted in the peninsular Basque Country in 1879, under d'Abbadie's patronage until 1897. They included folkloric competitions in traditional sports, dance, and *irrintzi* (deep-throated yodeling), together with literary contests termed *Koplarien guduak* (literally, versifiers' wars). The Basque festivals held in Donostia-San Sebastián and other Basque towns between 1893 and 1936 were an extension of the Floral Games and helped to stimulate narrative and drama in Basque. Unlike the focus on learned literary forms in the Catalan *Jocs Florals*, folklorism prevailed with priority given to the *bertsolaritza* tradition (oral improvisation of rhyming compositions; see chapter 6). The topics prescribed by the Floral Games prior to 1879 emphasized a conservative vision of Basque society, close to the foralist movement with a strict Catholic morality and focused on the peasant or farmer – and on women, seen as virtuous, hardworking, and the lynchpin of the domestic sphere, a gender politics that Basque nationalism would perpetuate in subsequent decades. This vision lay behind the award of first prize, at the 1853 first Floral Games, to Jean Martin Hiribarren for his composition *Montebideoco berriac* (*Montevideo News*) on Basque emigration to South America and its dangers for Basque religious believers, generating a string of texts that transformed the Americas into Basque nationalism's despised Other. The various topics proposed by the jury for later competitions continued the defense of tradition; for example, "Village Patron Saints' Festivals" (1852), "In Praise of Farmers and the Farming Life" (1854), "Women Who Drink" (1855) (Haritschelhar 2012, 126).

After 1879, in response to the abolition of the *fueros*, the topics proposed for the Floral Games changed dramatically, emphasizing the decline of Euskara and perceived threats to the Tree of Gernika as a symbol of the Basque spirit. Major poetic compositions were Gratien Adema ("Zaldubi")'s proto-nationalist call for union "Zazpi euskal herriek" (The Seven Basque Provinces), indebted to Herderian Romanticism; and the nuanced bucolic poetry of Jean Baptiste Elizanburu, whose idealized Basque landscape with its green valleys and scattered white farmsteads established the prototypical setting of the later Basque *costumbrista* novel (see chapter 8). Other significant French Basque poets included Jean Baptiste Larralde, a descendant of *bertsolaris* (oral poetic improvisers), who won the prize in 1856, 1859, and 1864. Also notable is Felipe Arrese-Beitia's "Ama euskeriaren azken agurrak" (Farewell to Mother Basque), awarded first prize at the 1879 Floral Games held in Elizondo, Navarre; in this elegiac poem, which draws formally on the *bertsolaritza* tradition, the *fueros'* suppression is seen as heralding the certain death of the Basque language. The trope of "ama euskeria" (Mother Basque) would become central to the construction of Basque national identity in the late nineteenth century (Bijuesca 2010, 177).

Also key to the consolidation of Basque-language writing was the development of a Basque-language press. Like the Floral Games, this dates back to the mid-century with the French Basque Augustin Chaho's bilingual journal *Ariel* (1844–52) and short-lived *Uscal-Herrico Gaseta* (1848), the first journal exclusively in Basque. Chaho also anticipated the compilations of oral texts that would blossom in the late nineteenth century. Around 140 Basque-language or bilingual (Basque/Spanish or Basque/French) periodicals were founded between 1876 and 1936. Among them, *Eskualduna* (1887–1944), published in the French Basque Country, was the first Basque weekly and for 30 years enjoyed considerable success, with a print run of 7,000 copies in 1908. José Manterola, known for his Basque songbook, founded and directed the journal *Euskal-Erria* (1880–1918), which became a platform for many writers. Other key journals were Juan Iturralde y Suit and Arturo Campión's *Revista Euskara* (Pamplona, 1878–83); Fermín Herran's *Revista de las Provincias Euskaras* (Vitoria, 1878–89); and Vicente de Arana's *Revista de Vizcaya* (Bilbao, 1885–9). Also influential was the periodical *Euskalzale* (Bilbao, 1897–9), founded by the ever-active Azkue, holder of the first Chair of Basque Language established by Bizkaia Provincial Council in 1888, who in 1896 would help found a Basque-language school, *Ikastetxea*, in Bilbao. This flourishing Basque-language press was accompanied by the institutionalization of Basque language and literature through the creation of awards, associations, and university chairs.

This cultural effervescence must be set in the context of the massive influx, in the last third of the nineteenth century, of Spanish-speaking immigrants to industrialized Bilbao. In the same period, Biarritz and later Donostia-San Sebastián became important European centers of the new leisure industry. The resulting conflict between rural and urban worlds would form the core of literary expressions of Basque nationalism, as we will see in chapter 8.

5

The Uses of the Past:
Writing the Nation (1760s–1890s)

This chapter examines the ways in which literature contributed to nation formation in the decisive period of Spain's insertion into modernity, through its depiction of a national past with which readers or audiences were invited to identify. Benedict Anderson (1983) has famously traced the ways in which, from the mid-to-late nineteenth century, state education and the extension of print produced a cultural homogenization that gave inhabitants of the national territory a sense of belonging to a shared "imagined community," despite the fact that most of them would never meet. In the process, the term "nation" shifted its meaning from its pre-modern sense of a birth group, whose identity was based on inherited local ties and customs, to its modern sense of the nation-state as a shared political project to which all citizens were invited to subscribe. The friction between these two concepts of the nation – traditionalist and liberal – accounts not only for the three Carlist Wars of the 1830s to the 1870s but also, given the overlap between the traditionalist defense of inherited local customary law and certain strands of the regionalist movements that emerged in the mid-century, for much of Spain's political instability in the modern period.

In Spain, cultural homogenization did not get underway until the mid-nineteenth century, with a national press developing from the 1830s and compulsory state education instituted in 1857. Previously, national identity – reinforced by the 1808–14 war against Napoleonic occupation – was a largely traditionalist concept. But Spanish liberals, in exile under the absolutist Fernando VII and in power after his death in 1833, began to develop a notion of national identity as a project in which citizens had to be persuaded to invest; that is, as something to be created (Álvarez Junco 2001, 119–49). The nature of that project was contested, with utopianism ceding to more conservative models from the 1840s, and from 1875, under the Restoration, with conservative liberals arguing for tight central controls and progressive liberals defending local and individual autonomy. It was not until 1884, with traditionalism defeated in the last Carlist War and both conservative and progressive liberals firmly embracing the notion of nation formation, that the term "nation"' entered the Spanish Royal Academy dictionary with its modern meaning of "nation-state" (Boyd 1997, 65).

Traditionalist visions of the nation could take it for granted that the present was authorized by the past. Precisely because it broke with inherited authority, liberalism needed to legitimize the modern "imagined community" by grounding it in a prior "invented tradition" – to use Eric Hobsbawm's term (Hobsbawm and Ranger 1984, 1–14). Hence the importance of historiography which, in the mid-nineteenth century, established itself as a privileged discipline through its ability to construct a narrative of the nation. Not for nothing was the architect of the Restoration, Antonio Cánovas del Castillo, a historian and author of a historical novel, *La campana de Huesca* (*The Bell of Huesca*, 1852), set in the twelfth century. Of the national histories written at this time, mostly from a liberal standpoint, the most influential was Modesto Lafuente's 30-volume *Historia general de España* (*General History of Spain*, 1850–67); like most other histories of Spain of the period, it placed Castile at the center of a providential narrative leading inexorably to national unity (Pérez Garzón et al. 2000, 95–105). The Catalan writer Joan Cortada's earlier histories of Spain and Portugal in the 1840s strove instead to highlight the contribution to the nation of the Peninsula's diverse kingdoms, counties, and regions, a vision to which he remained committed in later volumes intended for use in the education system. From 1856, the production of national histories was accompanied by the state-run National Art Exhibitions' promotion of history painting, addressing primarily national but sometimes regional topics, from a range of conservative and progressive perspectives. The choice of historical subject matter should not be seen as a rejection of the present for the past, for the aim is to produce reader identification with a "we in the past" whose values offer a blueprint for the present (Manzano 2000, 50–1; Labanyi 2019, 13).

Neoclassical Tragedy: The Past as National Allegory

In fact, the literary depiction of national history to construct a particular model of the nation goes back to the 1760s, with allegorical drama aimed at critiquing the abuse of absolutist power (Andioc 2012). The use of past (and sometimes non-Spanish) settings had the advantage of deflecting censorship. Recourse to the conventions of neoclassical tragedy, reserved for "noble" subject matter, dignified the fight against tyranny, while affecting audiences through Aristotelian catharsis. As in revolutionary France,

Spanish neoclassical tragedy turned to ancient Rome to reinforce secular, democratic values. A favorite topic was the rape of Lucretia, revenge for which instituted the Roman Republic – as, for example, in Nicolás Fernández de Moratín's 1763 *Lucrecia* or the 1769 Catalan-language *Lucrècia* by Menorcan Joan Ramis i Ramis, which is punctuated with calls for freedom.

In the 1770s, national historical topics became increasingly common, making the struggle against tyranny a patriotic duty by conflating it with the defense of the national territory against racial Others, as in Nicolás Fernández de Moratín's treatment of the Christian "Reconquest" from Islam in *Hormesinda* (1770) and *Guzmán el bueno* (1777), anachronistically taking Spain's origins as a nation back to the eighth century. The Lucretia motif and the equation of tyranny with occupation by racial others come together in the repeated treatment of the rape of Florinda by the last Visigoth king Rodrigo which, according to medieval chronicles, prompted her father (governor of Tangiers) to facilitate the 711 Muslim invasion of Spain. Pedro Montengón's novel *El Rodrigo* (1793) – written in exile in Italy where he read Locke, Rousseau, Voltaire, and Diderot – criticizes absolutism through its depiction of Rodrigo's abuses. In the epic poem *Florinda*, also written in exile in 1824–5 by Ángel Saavedra (future Duke of Rivas, still writing in a neoclassical vein), Rodrigo stands for the absolutist Fernando VII. María Rosa Gálvez's play *Florinda* (1804) has its heroine emulate Lucretia by committing suicide as an act of civic duty, asserting her female agency. Another female victim – of gender and racial scapegoating – is the Jewish protagonist of Vicente García de la Huerta's tragedy *Raquel* (written 1765, performed 1778), in which the mutinous populace blames the ruinous state of the nation on the twelfth-century Alfonso VIII's infatuation with a Toledan Jewess.

The Romantic Interest in the Multicultural Past

A very different take on Spain's multicultural medieval past would develop in the 1830s, as liberal exiles returned to Spain on the absolutist Fernando VII's death in 1833, bringing with them the Romantic exoticization of the oriental. A related factor was the renewal, in the late eighteenth and early nineteenth centuries, of Arabic studies in Spain, with scholarship on Spain's Islamic past seen as a tool of secularization (Rivière Gómez 2000, 13). This positive attitude to the Islamic past changed with the 1859–60 African War, which initiated Spanish colonial expansion in Morocco. From that date, Spanish Arabists increasingly reverted to constructing Spanish Arabs as negative Others. The Middle Ages were the favorite topic of mid-nineteenth-century national histories, since they represented the crucible out of which the nation (united by the Catholic Kings) was forged, and since the emergence of a medieval vernacular literature was seen as the expression of a Spanish *Volksgeist*. The Middle Ages equally served the purposes of those who, across the political spectrum, were concerned to preserve local freedoms, since they preceded national unification.

If the late eighteenth century defined patriotism as the defense against racial Others, by the 1830s Spanish Arabists realized that they had a golden opportunity to refute the "Black Legend" of Spain's backwardness and intolerance by revealing the advanced cultural achievements of Muslim Spain. This appropriation of the "Moors" as "Spanish," integrating them into the national narrative, would in the late nineteenth and early twentieth centuries (and under the Franco Dictatorship) be hijacked by the political right to argue that Spain's Muslims were quickly "hispanicized" and thus Arabic culture's contribution to Spain was negligible. Spanish liberal exiles in London played a key role in Spanish Arabism, with the pro-Bonapartist José Antonio Conde's *Historia de la dominación de los árabes en España* (*History of Arab Domination in Spain*, London, 1820–1), which stressed the tolerance enjoyed under Arab rule, and Pascual Gayangos's recovery of Spanish Arabic texts in London and from the 1830s in Spain, taking up the new Chair of Arabic at Madrid's Universidad Central in 1843 (Monroe 1970, 50–3, 67–80). The study of Arabic literature in Spain was also boosted by the earlier proposition, advanced in the 1782–99 history of world literature of the exiled Spanish Jesuit in Italy, Juan Andrés (see chapter 1), that Provençal courtly love poetry (seen as the origin of European vernacular literature) was derived from Spanish Arabic poetry, thus positioning Spain as central to the rise of European civilization – a reversal of the topos of Spanish culture's belatedness and derivative nature.

The 1830s revitalization of Spanish Arabic studies coincided with a number of Spanish Romantic texts that depict Muslim Spain or the Moriscos (the "Moors" who stayed on after the 1492 Conquest of Granada until their 1609 expulsion). A largely negative view of Muslim Spain remains in Juan Eugenio Hartzenbusch's play *Los amantes de Teruel* (*The Lovers of Teruel*, published 1836, performed 1837), but Francisco Martínez de la Rosa's drama *Aben Humeya o la rebelión de los moriscos* (*Aben Humeya or the Morisco Rebellion*) makes Spanish Muslims its main characters. Premièred (in French) in Paris the week the 1830 July Revolution broke out, its sixteenth-century Morisco rebels against the despotism of Felipe II were hailed as heroes of the struggle against absolutism. The play presents the murder of the cultured, tolerant Morisco leader, Aben Humeya, as the snuffing out of lost historical potential. Imprisoned from 1814 to 1820 and exiled from 1823 to 1833 under Fernando VII, Martínez de la Rosa would in 1834–5 serve as Spain's first Prime Minister on Fernando's death. His 1837–46 historical novel *Doña Isabel de Solís*, on the Castilian wife of the penultimate King of Granada, similarly expresses an attachment to the utopian potential of lost historical objects.

Ángel Saavedra, Duke of Rivas, exiled in England, Malta, and France from 1823 to 1834, had in 1816 written an anti-Muslim and anti-Jewish neoclassical tragedy, *Aliatar*. However, his 700-page narrative poem *El moro expósito* (*The Moorish Foundling*, 1834) empathizes with its mixed-race protagonists: Mudarra, illegitimate love child of the Castilian Señor de Lara and the sister of the tolerant Caliph of Córdoba, where he is held captive; and Kerima, born of the rape of a Christian captive by the tyrannical Arab governor. Like Martínez de la Rosa, Rivas stood on liberalism's political right, but his text serves as a melancholic memory of tenth-century Córdoba (Rivas's birthplace) as the capital of a still unified Muslim Spain at the height of its cultural splendor. Córdoba is depicted as a center of philosophy and science while Castilian Burgos is backward and ignorant. Although the protagonists leave Córdoba for Castile, the poem refuses a celebratory ending as Kerima, converted to Christianity by her zealot Christian slave, jilts the brave and generous Mudarra at the altar in Burgos cathedral to become a nun. The narrator describes cultivated tenth-century Córdoba as an empire on the wane, and intolerant, warlike Castile as an "estado naciente" (state-in-the-making), recognizing the modern nation-state's foundation on cultural exclusion (Labanyi 2019, 11–24).

Ethnic diversity is rehabilitated also in the Duke of Rivas's Romantic drama *Don Álvaro o la fuerza del sino* (*Don Álvaro or the Force of Destiny*, staged 1835). Set in the eighteenth century, its mixed-race protagonist's parents (a Spanish viceroy accused of treason against the absolutist Crown and an Inca princess) are pardoned – too late. In Antonio García Gutiérrez's *El trovador* (*The Troubadour*, 1836), set in the Middle Ages, the protagonist's gypsy mother is also treated sympathetically, despite her horrendous crime of infanticide.

From the Romantic Historical Novel to the *Folletín*

The medieval period is massively favored by the Romantic historical novel, beginning with early examples written in English by the Spanish liberal exiles in London, Valentín Llanos Gutiérrez and Joaquín Telesforo de Trueba y Cosío, where they read Walter Scott (Llorens 1979, 260–84). Scott is the inspiration also for the considerable number of historical novels written in Spain, the best-known being Ramón López Soler's *Los bandos de Castilla o el caballero del Cisne* (*The Castilian Feuds or the Knight of the Swan*, 1830), Mariano José de Larra's *El doncel de don Enrique el Doliente* (*King Henry the Sick's Page*, 1834), José de Espronceda's *Sancho Saldaña o el castellano de Cuéllar* (*Sancho Saldaña or the Lord of Cuéllar*, 1834), and Enrique Gil y Carrasco's *El señor de Bembibre* (*The Lord of Bembibre*, 1844). Although all four novels choose Castile as their setting, as do most historical novels of the period other than those published in Catalonia, they depict it as racked with civil strife. *Los bandos de Castilla*, by a Catalan author, contrasts Castile negatively with the Crown of Aragon. In Larra's and Espronceda's novels, the depiction of civil war mirrors the first Carlist War of 1833–40. However, the stress on a lawless Castile allows treachery and brutality to mingle with a sublime individualism, explicitly contrasted by Larra with a prosaic nineteenth-century modernity. The selfless idealism of the heroes of these novels – commoners or less wealthy nobles who aspire to a lady beyond their reach – vindicates the liberal defense of individual rights against tyranny and inherited privilege at a time when, with absolutism defeated, it was starting to mean the triumph of the bourgeois self-made man. Espronceda's novel depicts sympathetically the Jew Abraham (whose scientific knowledge is contrasted with the Christian nobles' illiteracy) and the Moorish captive Zoraida (who turns out to be Abraham's daughter), rescuing both from the inquisitor's pyre; the novel was published the year the Inquisition was abolished.

From the late 1830s, particularly with the shift to moderate liberal government in the 1840s, a more sanitized, nostalgic vision of Spain's past becomes dominant, as, for example, in the Arabist Serafín Estébanez Calderón's *Cristianos y moriscos: Novela lastimosa* (*Christians and Moriscos: A Sentimental Novel*, 1838) or Rivas's *Romances históricos* (*Historical Ballads*, 1841). These texts give an antiquarian view of the past, valued because it is gone. This dissociation from the past shifts easily into its equation with the fantastic, as in the verse *leyendas* (folktales) of José Zorrilla (written 1837–84) – a genre that Gustavo Adolfo Bécquer would perfect in his prose *leyendas* of 1858–64.

The much-maligned *folletines* (serialized novels, see chapter 6) of the mid-nineteenth century, many of them historical, continue the identification with the past's utopian potential found in the earlier Romantic historical novel. The bandit novels of the prolific *folletín* writer Manuel Fernández y González lament the eradication of Robin Hood figures under modernity. His *Los monfíes de las Alpujarras* (*The Monfíes of the Alpujarras*, 1859) – a melodramatic account of the mid-sixteenth-century Morisco rebellion, with erudite footnotes probably facilitated by his Arabist scholar brother, Francisco – attacks the religious intolerance of Felipe II and celebrates the main characters' dual Arab–Spanish cultural allegiance. An extraordinary alliance is formed between the Monfíes (Muslims who, after the fall of Granada, literally go underground) and Calpuc (king of an unconquered Mexican tribe), who join forces against the Spanish. The heroine is triply mixed-race: native-American/Spanish/Arab. Although the novel assumes the necessity of conversion to Christianity, its pro-Morisco and anti-colonial stance – remarkable since its publication coincided with the African War in Morocco – is made possible by the novel's anticlericalism. The strength of anticlericalism in mid-nineteenth-century popular fiction should not be forgotten. This is history not as progress but as loss.

Catalan Historical Literature and Scholarship: Conflicting Nationalist Projects

Historical writing played a key role in nineteenth-century Catalonia, whether through the embrace of ideas associated with Romanticism in historical novels like the previously mentioned López Soler's *Los bandos de Castilla* (1830) or Cortada's *Tancredo en el Asia* (*Tancred in Asia*, 1833), *La heredera de Sangumí* (*The Heiress of Sangumí*, 1835), and *Lorenzo* (1937), or, later, theater and even epic poetry. The institution of the *Jocs Florals* (Floral Games; see chapter 4), so often placed at the heart of the Catalan literary revival, was a response to the literary-historical scholarship of the period and the nostalgia for Catalan literature's glorious medieval past that animated it. The Romantic equation, in Cortada's novels, of medieval history, mystery, and love contributed to his impassioned speech in Catalan at the Real Academia de Buenas Letras on behalf of the troubadour "courts of love" in December 1840, and to the first such celebration within that institution in 1841. If the poetry of Bonaventura Carles Aribau, Joaquim Rubió i Ors, and the early decades of the *Jocs Florals* was primarily nostalgic (see chapter 4), the emergence of Jacint Verdaguer toward the century's end reveals a more complex affective negotiation of Catalan historical material, projected onto a contemporary landscape riven by conflicting nation-building projects.

Significant work on Catalan cultural and linguistic historiography had been undertaken in the eighteenth century thanks to figures like Antoni de Capmany – such as the four-volume *Memorias históricas sobre la marina, comercio, y artes de la antigua ciudad de Barcelona* (*Historical Reports on the Seafaring, Commerce, and Arts of the Ancient City of Barcelona*, 1779–92) – and later Antoni Puigblanch and Josep Pau Ballot. This was boosted in the early 1800s in response to the patriotic national realignment that followed the Peninsular War and the influx of Romantic philological ideas and debates from other parts of Europe. The shape and development of Catalan historical writing was greatly influenced by sociopolitical events throughout the century, with the Carlist Wars, Joan Prim y Prats's celebrated achievements in the African War (1859–60), and Catalan political involvement in the 1868 Revolution and its aftermath feeding both regional conservative and more federal and liberal progressive responses.

In the early nineteenth century the work of Herder and the Schlegel brothers was particularly influential, transmitted through writers and intellectuals such as Antoni Bergnes de las Casas, Aribau, López Soler, and later Manuel Milà i Fontanals and Rubió i Ors (Jorba 1986). Through European-oriented periodicals – *El Europeo* (1823–4), *El Vapor* (1833–6), and the later *Museo de las Familias* (1843–67) in Barcelona; *La Palma* (1840s) in Majorca – writers, intellectuals, and publishers sought to influence the literary taste of the growing reading public. Celebration of the historical novels of Walter Scott, together with Shakespeare-influenced historical dramas and tragedies, joined with a renewed historiographical urge to recover the Catalan literary and cultural heritage through engagement with past texts and histories, and excavation of the popular poetic tradition by Catalan and Majorcan philologists such as Pau Piferrer, Marià Aguiló, and Josep Maria Quadrado from the 1840s onwards. Yet, just as the historical novels written during the first half of the nineteenth century (whether based on Catalan themes or exotic evocations of ethnic others, as in Cortada's *Tancredo*) were published in Castilian, many of the medieval Catalan literary-historical archives and literary institutions were administered from Madrid.

Gradually, however, writers who had begun to excavate Catalan history turned to the Catalan language to construct their versions, often from radically opposed ideological perspectives. Thus, with the publication in Catalan of *L'orfaneta de Menargues* (*The Orphan Girl of Menargues*, 1862), set in the fifteenth century, Antoni de Bofarull espoused the kind of conservative vision of Catalan heritage that would culminate in the more moralistic writings of the influential ecclesiastical figure Josep Torras i Bages. In contrast, Bofarull's contemporary Víctor Balaguer, who alongside pioneering histories of Catalonia and the Crown of Aragon produced essays and plays in Catalan on historical themes, identified with more progressive federalist ideals that would be expressed most coherently in the work of the federal republican politician, journalist, and essayist Valentí Almirall. After the 1873–4 First Republic's failure, the latter went on to become a key figure in the development of political Catalanism, founding the Centre Català in 1882 and publishing his landmark essay *Lo catalanisme* (*Catalanism*) in 1886. The interface between historiography, narrative, and political writing in authors such as Balaguer, Bofarull, Torras i Bages, and Almirall determines the emergence in the late nineteenth century of a double tradition – conservative versus republican – of Catalanist thought. From the late 1860s onward, the majority of Catalan historical novels focused on more recent periods of sociopolitical conflict: the War of the Spanish Succession in Francesc Pelai Briz's *Lo coronel d'Anjou* (*The Colonel of Anjou*, 1872) and Maria Bell-Lloch's *Vigatans i botiflers* (*Partisans of Charles III versus Partisans of Philip V*, 1878); the French revolutionary wars in Joaquim Riera i Bertran's *Història d'un pagès* (*History of a Peasant Farmer*, 1869); the Peninsular War in Josep d'Argullol's *Les òrfenes de la mare* (*Maternal Orphans*, 1872), Josep Martí i Folguera's *Cor i sang* (*Heart and Blood*, 1860), and Josep Feliu i Codina's *Lo Bruch* (*The Bruch*, 1880); and the Carlist Wars in Frederic Soler's *L'any 1835* (*The Year 1835*, 1874), Argullol's *La guerra* (*The War*, 1877), and later Marian Vayreda's *Records de la darrera carlinada* (*Memoirs of the Last Carlist War*, 1898).

The paradoxes of the uses of the past in nineteenth-century Catalan literature are encapsulated in the work of Jacint Verdaguer, born in the provincial town of Vic and trained as a priest, not normally associated with the academic philological tradition and its uses of history. His most famous work, the epic poem *Canigó: Llegenda pirenaïca del temps de la Reconquesta* (*Canigó: Pyrenean Legend from the Time of the Reconquest*; written 1879–86, published 1886 and translated into Spanish that same year), brings to the fore many of the characteristics and contradictions of the uses of history in nineteenth-century Catalan literature. His first epic poem had been *Atlàntida*, completed in 1876, whose acclaim at the 1877 *Jocs Florals* presaged the impact Verdaguer would have on the developing legitimacy of Catalan as a literary language. Structured around the parallels between the legend of the fall of Atlantis and its redemption through Columbus's discovery of the Americas, *Atlàntida* enshrined the Spanish providentialist vision that characterized the political outlook of many of the fathers of the *Renaixença*.

Employed as a family chaplain by the Marquis of Comillas from 1877, Verdaguer combined his personal interests in recovering local popular traditions with the rediscovery of Catalan history and geography characteristic of the period. In writing *Canigó* he returned to the mythical beginnings of the Catalan tradition, setting the poem in the French-Catalan Pyrenees at the end of the first millennium AD, with Mount Canigó personified as "a giant of Spain, / Of Spain – and Catalan" (Canto IV). Inspired by his own *excursionisme* (hiking expeditions to explore the Catalan landscape), the poem draws links between history, landscape, and spirituality that affirm the central thematic pillars of Patria–Fe–Amor (Homeland–Faith–Love) at the heart of the *Jocs Florals*, while anticipating the more programmatic frame of Torras i Bages's *La tradició catalana* (*The Catalan Tradition*, 1892).

The disorder represented in the poem by the pull of pagan myths and the threat of saracen conquest, resulting in the death of Gentil (the poet's alter ego) and the rage of Guifré (the founding hero of Catalonia), is redeemed by the wisdom of the Catholic Church, re-Christianization, and the foundation of the Romanesque monasteries that would be rediscovered and restored from the late nineteenth century. Although the poem's narrative espouses a world view underpinned by reaffirmation of the medieval past and renewed Christianization of Catalonia, in contrast with Almirall's more progressive *Lo catalanisme*, the aesthetic and affective landscape it negotiates is far more complex, combining a wide range of different verse forms, fusing classical and Romantic elements, and revealing a relationship with landscape that exceeds the moral and the redemptive. After Verdaguer's ecclesiastical fall from grace in the 1890s, he rewrote the poem, removing the dedication to his former mentor Bishop Josep Morgades from Canto XI, and adding an epilogue entitled "Els dos campanars" (The Two Bell-towers) which brings home the conflict between modernity and the conservative Catholic vision of Catalan nation-building, raising questions about the relationship between past and present. The pull between the different desires and visions of Catalan culture now reaches elegiac rather than celebratory resolution (Torrents 2004, 130), introducing a tone of reflective nostalgia that might help to understand Verdaguer's popularity with radically different social sectors, from conservative regionalists to the republican and anarchist working class (Torrents 2002; Subirana 2018, 43–59).

Galician Historiography and Fiction:
Constructing a Pre-Modern Past

Galicia first emerged as a discrete subject for historical scholarship in the mid-nineteenth century, in works such as José Verea y Aguiar's *Historia de Galicia* (1838), whose theory of Galicia's Celtic origins was taken up by the provincialist politician Antolín Faraldo in the 1840s; and Leopoldo Martínez Padín's *Historia política, religiosa y descriptiva de Galicia (Political, Religious, and Descriptive History of Galicia*, 1849), restricted by the author's early death to a single volume. These early works modeled the close connection between ethnic origin and proto-national legitimization that would be foundational in the new, committed model of Galician history that emerged alongside the *Rexurdimento* in the 1860s (Beramendi 2007). Its most prominent early exponents were Benito Vicetto and Manuel Murguía. Their common aim was to establish Galicia's historical difference from Spain, largely through celebration of the country's non-Latin roots, drawing on scholarship in the new linguistic, archaeological, and ethnographic sciences to seek evidence of Galicia's Swabian and Celtic origins (Miguélez-Carballeira 2013).

Vicetto, son of a Genoese soldier, was a prolific reproducer of the past and already firmly established as a writer of heady Romantic novels and poetry when the first of his *Historia de Galicia*'s seven volumes appeared in 1865. His prologue to this volume makes clear his history's debt to his literary career. A country's history, he claims, is its biography. His work places Galicians at the heart of a pan-European family, celebrating their connections with the Celts of Celtiberia, the Gauls of France, and the Brigantes of England and Ireland. Galicia's history, he argues, is that of the first people of Europe. This view of a fully European Galicia of international significance would be central to the Xeración Nós group of nationalist intellectuals in the 1920s.

1865 was a transformative year for Galician historiography, with the launch of a second multi-volume account of the country's past in Manuel Murguía's *Historia de Galicia*, whose publication would eventually span the *rexionalista* period, the last of its five volumes not appearing until 1911. Like Vicetto, Murguía strategically endorses Galicia's connection to the pan-European Celtic history so much in vogue since the eighteenth century; his version, which engages closely with the latest archaeological and linguistic research, would underpin the development of *galeguista* intellectual and cultural production for more than four decades (Miguélez-Carballeira 2013). If Vicetto's writing was inspired by Romantic mystique, Murguía's was heavily influenced by his day job as an archivist, making him attentive to the practical realities of preservation and access to the past. In the prologue to the first volume, he laments Galicia's lack of autochthonous institutional spaces such as a general archive or archaeological museum, while private archives are inaccessible to the public or lost forever. Murguía's attention to the material and ideological dimension of the past is fundamental to his promotion of Galician history as a legitimizing institution for the emerging Galician *rexionalista* movement, in which he and his wife Rosalía de Castro were key players (see chapter 4).

The Romantic fascination with Spain's medieval past surfaces in Galicia only in the 1890s, due to the tardy emergence of the Galician-language novel. Its most prominent exponent was the Santiago-born priest and novelist Antonio López Ferreiro whose three novels – published under the pseudonym "K" – grew out of his work in the Santiago cathedral archives. The novels, first serialized in Galician regional newspapers, move backwards chronologically, providing a panoramic vision of pre-modern Galicia, from *A tecedeira de Bonaval* (*The Weaver-girl of Bonaval*, 1894), set in Santiago in 1543, to *O castelo de Pambre* (*Pambre Castle*, 1895), set in fourteenth-century Melide, and *O niño de pombas* (*The Dove's Nest*, 1905), which opens in Lalín in 1134. López Ferreiro's project had several key elements: to promote the Galician language, hitherto used only sporadically as a medium for prose; to bring to life the region's history as researched and reclaimed by Murguía, Vicetto, and others; and to infuse this history into the Galician geographical imagination. To this end, his novels combine romantic plotlines with learned historical, geographical, and philological footnotes and digressions, paying particular attention not only to the landscape (so familiar from Rosalía de Castro's poetry), but also to the built environment of Santiago de Compostela and the small towns where much of the action takes place.

Basque Literature: Myths of Origin

Defeat in the three Carlist Wars fueled the nostalgic historical gaze of much nineteenth-century Basque literature, with historiography drawing on the past to elaborate a sense of Basque identity. Historical scholarship in the continental Basque Country, dating back to the early nineteenth century, had tended to treat the Basque Country as a whole, as for example in J.A. Zamacola's *Historia de las naciones bascas de una y otra parte del Pirineo septentrional . . .* (*History of the Basque Nations on Both Sides of the Western Pyrenees . . .*, 1818; issued in French and Spanish), and Augustin Chaho's *Histoire primitive des euskariens-basques; langue, poésie, mœurs et caractère de ce peuple* (*Primitive History of the Basques; Language, Poetry, Customs, and Character of That People*, 1847), which devotes a chapter to Basque unity. Peninsular Basque historiography – concerned to refute central government attacks on the legitimacy of the *fueros*, as in the Royal Academy of History's 1851 *Diccionario geográfico-histórico de España* (*Geographical-Historical Dictionary of Spain*) – tended to focus on the Spanish Basque provinces, as in Pedro Novia Salcedo's response of that year, *Defensa histórica, legislativa y económica del Señorío de Vizcaya, y provincias de Álava y Guipúzcoa* (*Historical, Juridical, and Economic Defense of the Lordship of Biscay and Provinces of Álava and Guipúzcoa*) (Agirreazkuenaga 1992).

Historiographical work designed to justify the *fueros* was largely based on legends and traditional myths, in line with Romantic trends. A key figure of the Romantic period, Chaho had studied oriental languages in Paris and wrote literary, philosophical, and historical works as well as studies on Basque grammar. His 1843 *Aitor. Légende Cantabre* (*Aitor: A Cantabrian Legend*) invented the myth of Aitor as the progenitor of the Basque people who had supposedly led them westward, as distinct from the Iberians, descended from the Semitic Tubal. Chaho's writings would spawn an abundant legendary literature in Castilian, including José María de Goizueta's *Leyendas vascongadas* (*Basque Legends*, 1851) and Juan Venancio Araquistáin's *Tradiciones vasco-cántabras* (*Basque-Cantabrian Legends*, 1866). With the literary renaissance following 1876, this fascination with primitive Basque legend would generate a series of Spanish-language historical novels influenced by Walter Scott, including, most influentially, Francisco Navarro Villoslada's *Amaya o los vascos en el siglo VIII* (*Amaya or the Basques in the Eighth Century*, 1879), set during the Muslim invasion, and Vicente de Arana's *Jaun Zuria o el Caudillo Blanco* (*Jaun Zuria or the White Chieftain*, 1887), on the mythical first Lord of Bizkaia.

Similar legendary literature in Basque developed from 1879, anticipated by translations into Basque of Basque-themed historical works in French such as Francisque-Eugène Garay de Monglave's Ossian-inspired poem *Le chant de Altabiscar* (*The Song of Altabiscar*, 1835), recounting the victory of the Basques against Charlemagne at Roncevaux; or Jean-Baptiste Daskonagerre's 1870 self-translation into Basque of his 1867 French-language novel *Les échos du pas de Roland* (*Echoes of Roland's Steps*), whose French text claims to be translated from a Basque original. The first novel in the Basque language, Domingo Agirre's romantic historical narrative *Auñemendiko lorea* (*The Flower of the Pyrenees*, 1898), set in the seventh century and clearly influenced by Navarro Villoslada's *Amaya*, narrates the origins of Christianity in the Basque Country. This legendary literature, constructing a fiercely independent Basque people, would influence Sabino Arana's 1892 *Bizcaya por su independencia* (*Bizkaia for Independence*), the first expression of Basque nationalism by its founder.

Narrating the Nineteenth Century: From Patriotism to Entertainment

Moving back to Spanish-language historical writing, Galdós's *Episodios nacionales* (*National Episodes*) turn to the immediate past. Written 1873–9 (first and second series, covering the Battle of Trafalgar, War of Independence, and the reign of Fernando VII) and 1898–1912 (third, fourth, and fifth series, covering the first Carlist War, the reign of Isabel II, and the so-called "revolutionary" years from the 1868 Revolution to the restoration of the Bourbon monarchy), they comprise a major, albeit critical, contribution to Restoration nation formation. They were begun during the cantonalist secessions of the First Spanish Republic, suggesting that Galdós felt a need to provide Spaniards with a unified vision of nineteenth-century national history. They were resumed a few months before another historical crisis: Spain's 1898 loss of her last major colonies, with military defeat by the United States in Cuba and the Philippines. The first series gives a heroic vision of the War of Independence against the French but starts with Spain's defeat by the British at the Battle of Trafalgar, in tune with Galdós's stress in the first series on how popular aspirations, manifested by the common people's participation in the nation's history, have repeatedly been dashed. By the end of the second series, and increasingly in the last three series, the common people – meaning the middle classes – have been reduced to the role of historical onlookers. Galdós's negative view of mid-nineteenth-century Spain – together with his similar depiction of the Restoration in his contemporary novels, many of which weave recent historical events into their plots – would shape the diagnosis of Spain's ills by late nineteenth- and early twentieth-century Spanish intellectuals (see chapter 8).

The *Episodios'* insistence on the everyday life of their fictional characters – what Galdós calls "la historia chica" (microhistory) – illustrates his project of creating an "imagined community" through readers' identification with the many (largely middle-class) characters who act as focalizers or narrators. This is not only "history from below" but a concept of the nation constituted by its subjects. Despite their evolution from patriotism to ironic detachment laced with fantasy, the *Episodios nacionales* throughout refer to their subject matter as "la nación." For this reason, the *Episodios*, unlike Galdós's other work, would be exempted from censorship under the Franco dictatorship.

Galdós's depiction of the Carlist Wars in the *Episodios'* third and fifth series decries the violence that is undoing national unity. Unamuno's early historical novel *Paz en la guerra* (*Peace in War*, 1897) depicts the third Carlist War (1872–6) as a complex conflict between bourgeois liberal modernity and popular attachment to the land. Researched and written from 1887 to 1896, *Paz en la guerra* overlaps with Unamuno's writing of *En torno al casticismo* (*On Tradition*, 1895; see chapter 8) in which he elaborates the concept of *intrahistoria* (intrahistory): the everyday life of the peasantry which subtends "superficial" historical events. *Paz en la guerra* ends with the liberal Juan José, on the 1876 abolition of the Basque *fueros* by the liberal state he had supported, adopting the Basque nationalism that was an heir to Carlism's rejection of state centralization. Nevertheless, the novel's final message is the need for exclusivist nationalisms to dissolve in a supranational concept of popular community, in keeping with Unamuno's mid-1890s socialist internationalism. In 1892 Unamuno had argued that socialism and Carlism had a common ground since both channeled deeply rooted popular aspirations. In *Paz en la guerra*, it is the Carlist shopkeeper Pedro Antonio who achieves transcendence of all exclusivist forms of nationalism by finding peace in the Basque countryside, implying a rejection of Bilbao's massive industrialization in the years between the period depicted and 1897 when the novel was published.

Historical fiction on the nineteenth century would continue into the first three decades of the twentieth century but serious investigation of national history gives way to an aestheticization of the past. While Valle-Inclán's novel trilogy *La guerra carlista* (1908–9), set in his native Galicia and Navarre, can be read as a critique of bourgeois modernity, it largely uses the third Carlist War to produce striking linguistic effects. History becomes a succession of visual tableaux. In his *Ruedo Ibérico* (*Iberian Bullring*) trilogy of 1927–32, which satirizes the generals plotting the 1868 Revolution (the remaining six novels going up to the 1895–8 Cuban War were never written), narrative almost completely disappears beneath the avant-garde prose. With the 22 novels of Baroja's historical series *Memorias de un hombre de acción* (*Memoirs of a Man of Action*, 1913–35), loosely focusing on his liberal conspirator ancestor Aviraneta (1792–1872), the national frame of reference is eroded by the representation of the Spanish and French Basque Country as a continuum, with much of the action set in a multilingual, cosmopolitan Bayonne. History becomes a pretext to tell a proliferation of adventure stories. The abandonment of any attempt to use the past for the purposes of nation formation is complete by the time of José Ortega y Gasset's 1929 creation of Espasa Calpe's series of novelized biographies, *Vidas Españolas e Hispanoamericanas del Siglo XIX (Nineteenth-century Spanish and Spanish American Lives)*, designed to compensate for the flop of his earlier avant-garde fiction series *Nova Novarum*. The series' success was probably due to its selection of non-exemplary historical subjects: the Madrid bandit Luis Candelas (Antonio Espina, 1929); Sor Patrocinio, the stigmata-bearing nun who advised Isabel II (Benjamín Jarnés, 1929); Teresa Mancha, the lover abandoned by Espronceda (Rosa Chacel, not published till 1941), to list a few (Soguero García 2000). We can read this move from the literary use of the past to instill values in Spanish citizens to its use as a vehicle of entertainment as a sign of the growing disillusionment with the nation-building project of the Restoration – a disillusionment that will be discussed in chapter 8.

6

Popular Culture: Exclusion and Appropriation (1760s–1930s)

This chapter traces the construction – and transgression – of the divide between popular and learned culture from its late eighteenth-century beginnings to the twentieth-century avant-garde. The term "popular culture" is used by those who identify with learned culture to designate those cultural forms they regard as "not learned." It is often pejorative, as the alternative binary "high" and "low" culture makes clear. The boundary between learned culture and popular culture is a product of modernity; as Peter Burke has shown, the previous participation of the learned in popular culture diminished across Europe over the period 1500–1800 (1978, 270–81). The end of that participation made possible, in late eighteenth-century Europe generally, the "discovery" of popular culture as something exotic.

Under modernity, rural popular culture (folk culture, produced by the people) has tended to be seen as positive (a survival from a supposedly "authentic" pre-modern era), and urban popular culture (mass culture, produced for the people by the culture industries) as negative (a loss of "the natural"). In Spain, this dichotomy was exacerbated by the Franco regime's exaltation of folk dance and song and denigration of urban popular culture (except in folksy *costumbrista* versions). The negative view of mass culture was aggravated by Theodor Adorno and Max Horkheimer's influential 1940s Marxist analysis of mass culture as indoctrination by the culture industries (2002 [1947]). However, in the mid-1950s Raymond Williams (1980 [1975]) and Richard Hoggart (2017 [1957]), drawing on the insights of Antonio Gramsci, endowed mass culture with the agency implicit in the term "popular culture," arguing that the working classes strategically select and rework aspects of the cultural repertoire available to them. This rethinking of mass culture encouraged the study of workers' culture by Spanish Marxist historians (notably, Tuñón de Lara 1972). If in English the term "popular culture" has since the 1950s subsumed mass culture, with both being seen as conferring agency, in Spanish the distinction between "cultura popular" and "cultura de masas" persisted until relatively recently, given the continuation of rural cultural traditions into the late twentieth century, when the dwindling rural populace was assimilated into mainstream culture by television.

In practice, the term "popular culture" has often been used to refer to cultural forms consumed by the middle-class majority rather than by the lower classes; in such usage, the term "popular" merges with that of "popularity." With the development of the culture industries, "popularity" became synonymous with "commercially successful." As Pierre Bourdieu notes (1996b [1992]), in the late nineteenth century high culture came to be seen as opposed to commercial culture: to obtain cultural capital, writers had to present themselves as commercial failures.

The Construction of a Spanish Literary Canon

Bourdieu further proposes that class is not determined merely by economic status but by the cultural capital derived from the consumption of particular cultural products (1996a [1979]). The creation in the course of the nineteenth century of a literary canon meant singling out certain works or types of literature as conferring cultural capital on their readers. The canon originally consisted of writing in verse (much drama continued to be written in verse till well into the nineteenth century). Prose fiction, regarded as mass culture, was mostly – with exceptions such as *Don Quixote* – excluded from the canon till the later nineteenth century when Spanish realist writers were promoted as creators of a national novel.

Popular culture cannot be equated simplistically with what gets excluded from the canon; women's writing has been excluded but is not necessarily popular culture. The canon is the pantheon of works considered worthy to represent the nation; that is, in Spain's case, works seen as reflecting an essential "Spanishness" continuous over time and across the national territory. Nineteenth-century Catalan, Galician, and Basque writers initially explored their cultural history in texts written in Castilian (in the continental Basque Country, French) to give it national status. From the mid-nineteenth century, with increased journalistic and literary use of Catalan especially, the construction of a Spanish literary canon became a way of excluding literary production in languages other than Castilian. Conversely, the construction of a Catalan (and later, Galician and Basque) literary canon became an instrument for creating a distinct cultural heritage.

As part of the "invention of tradition" that accompanied the consolidation of the nation-state and the emergence of sub-state nationalisms across Europe, canon formation posited origins in the distant past. Just as the mid-nineteenth-century Catalan *Renaixença* looked to the medieval poetic tradition of the Floral Games, so the Spanish canon claimed as its founding moment the medieval oral ballad tradition (*romancero*), a popular corpus which thereby acquired high-cultural status. Oral literary origins were chosen since the corpus of medieval written texts in Castilian was thin compared to those in Catalan (with substantial production in poetry and prose) and Galician (which had been the language of lyric poetry across the peninsula) (see chapter 4).

John Guillory (1993) has shown how the construction of a national literary canon was tied to developments in education; the canon is what is taught in schools and universities. The construction of a Spanish literary canon coincided with the mid-nineteenth-century organization of a state education system. The canon taught at school or university had a double function: to inculcate supposedly essential Spanish values and to create a standard vernacular. Those who learnt to speak and write "proper" Spanish would enjoy superior social status. The creation of a literary canon was accompanied by the rise of philology as a discipline; Spanish university departments of literature are still called "Departamentos de Filología." Spanish literature was included in the centralized state educational curriculum, regulated at secondary and higher level by the 1845 Plan Pidal and subsequently the 1857 Moyano Law which also introduced free, obligatory primary education (6–9 years). Needless to say, education was exclusively in Castilian (as decreed by Carlos III in 1768).

A key figure behind the Plan Pidal was Antonio Gil y Zárate, whose 1844 *Manual de Literatura* (*Literature Handbook*) comprised the syllabus of his course as holder of one of the Chairs of Spanish Literature created at Secondary Education Institutes in 1836. Gil y Zárate's textbook explicitly articulates the circular logic whereby the literary historian starts with a notion of Spanishness which he will then find in the works selected for inclusion. His handbook was a rejoinder to existing histories of Spanish literature written by foreigners: Friedrich Bouterwek's 1804 volume on Spanish literature in his German-language *History of New Poetry and Rhetoric* and the Swiss Jean-Charles-Léonard Simonde de Sismondi's 1813 French-language *History of Southern European Literature*. Neither had been to Spain and Bouterwek did not know Spanish. They would be followed by Harvard professor George Ticknor's 1849 three-volume *History of Spanish Literature*. Ticknor had briefly lived in Spain. The earlier 1769–91 *Historia literaria de España, desde su primera población hasta nuestros días* (*Literary History of Spain, from Its Earliest Inhabitants to Our Times*) by the priests Rafael and Pedro Rodríguez Mohedano had reached only the end of the

Roman period by its final tenth volume (Ríos-Font 2004, 16–19). The exiled Jesuit Juan Andrés's 1785–1822 Italian-language *On the Origins, Progress, and Present State of All Literatures* (see chapter 1), although giving a prominent place to Spain, was a comparative study begun before the invention of national literary history. This is generally attributed to Friedrich Schlegel's 1812 University of Vienna lectures, "History of the Old and the New Literature," which elaborated the Herderian theorization of the *Volksgeist* as a framework for the writing of national literary histories. The notion that each nation's literature expresses its people's "soul" allowed literary works to be classified as "national" (suitable for inclusion in the canon) or not, contributing to the concept of the "two Spains" that has played such a negative role in Spanish history. As seen in chapter 1, Friedrich Schlegel posited the medieval Spanish ballad tradition as the expression of an essential Spanish chivalresque spirit, supposedly still alive in Golden Age theater (championed by his brother August Wilhelm).

While Gil y Zárate's textbook is generally regarded as the first history of Spanish literature written by a Spaniard in Spanish (Ríos-Font 2004, 27), that distinction was claimed by José Amador de los Ríos, holder of Spain's first university chair in Spanish literature, in his 1861–5 *Historia crítica de la literatura española* (*Critical History of Spanish Literature*). Although Spanish writers of national literary histories through to the early twentieth century insist on the need to correct earlier foreign histories, they largely agree with them in constructing Spanish literary history as an exaltation of the nation's past glories. In internalizing the Schlegel brothers' love of Spain's medieval ballad tradition and Golden Age drama because they were not contaminated by modernity, they perpetuated the Black Legend of a "primitive" Spain that they were keen to dismiss. Amador de los Ríos put such emphasis on Spain's medieval literature that the final volume of his unfinished literary history stopped at the reign of the Reyes Católicos. His work's nationalist intention was made clear by its dedication to Isabel II.

The canon was consolidated also by the edition of anthologies and collections of "classic" authors. From the early nineteenth century, admirers of the oral ballad tradition collected it in volumes aimed at high-cultural readers – for example, Agustín Durán's 1828–32 *Colección de romances castellanos anteriores al siglo XVIII* (*Collection of Castilian Ballads before the Eighteenth Century*). The year following the Plan Pidal saw the creation of the Biblioteca de Autores Españoles (BAE; Library of Spanish Authors), compiled 1846–80 by Manuel de Rivadeneyra and Bonaventura Carles Aribau, limited to Spanish-language authors although both were Catalan. The literary corpus constructed by the BAE makes evident the contradictory nature of what was regarded as worthy of canonization: while its volumes included the *Romancero general* (*Ballad Compendium*), the eighteenth-century writers selected were overwhelmingly high-cultural Enlightenment figures, in many cases little read. What counted to the BAE's compilers was ultimately conformity with "universal" criteria of approval, which meant that popular literature could enter the canon only if it had been praised by foreign scholars.

Popular Theater in the Eighteenth Century

Although canon formation did not get seriously underway before the organization of a centralized state education system, the term "national literature" started to be used in Spain in the 1730s. The term emerged in the context of worries about the "vulgarity" of the adaptations or imitations of Golden Age drama that remained crowd-pullers. Enlightenment critics – starting with Ignacio de Luzán's *Poética* (1737) – dismissed them as "popular theater" for not conforming to the neoclassical rules of good taste (Álvarez Barrientos 2005, 209–13). Plays that catered to the demand for visual spectacle were audience favorites: theatergoers started to be called spectators ("espectadores") at this time (Doménech Rico 2012, 127). "Popular theater" meant both commercially successful theater and theater that did not serve the Enlightenment aim of inculcating civic values. Although the theater is generally seen as having become an industry in nineteenth-century Spain, commercial theaters were created from the late sixteenth century to finance hospitals and orphanages (Ruano de la Haza 2012, 57–61). This remained a requirement of Madrid's two municipally owned eighteenth-century theaters, the Teatro de la Cruz and Teatro del Príncipe, and of Barcelona's Teatre de la Santa Creu. Complaints about the commercial fare of Madrid's municipal theaters were made by the neoclassical dramatists Nicolás and Leandro Fernández de Moratín, who had difficulty getting their own (unprofitable) works staged.

The major crowd-pullers were the *comedias de magia* (magic plays), which exploited visual illusion (Gies 1994, 70–87). They were banned to no avail in 1765, 1788, and 1800 for promoting superstition. Magic comedies remained popular till the late nineteenth century, their special effects paving the way for Romantic drama: the author of the hugely successful 1829 magic play *La pata de cabra* (*The Goat's Hoof*), Juan de Grimaldi, managed Madrid's municipal theaters from 1823 to 1836, producing Mariano José de Larra's *Macías* (1834), The Duke de Rivas's *Don Álvaro* (1835), and Antonio García Gutiérrez's *El trovador* (*The Troubadour*, 1836) (Gies 1988, 22–134). Bandit plays were a bugbear of Enlightenment thinkers since they suggested that Spain was a lawless country. *Comedias de santos* (plays on saints' lives), like the *autos sacramentales* mentioned in chapter 3, were banned for irreverence in 1765.

In 1759, Carlos III expelled the famous *castrato* Farinelli who had in 1737 been invited by Fernando VI to manage musical spectacles at the court theaters of the Buen Retiro and Caños del Peral (future Teatro Real), dominated by Italian opera and *zarzuela* – a homegrown form of mythological or pastoral musical theater that included spoken dialogue, dating back to the 1640s performance at La Zarzuela royal palace of musical dramas by Calderón. The result was the move of *zarzuela* to Madrid's commercial theaters, where it enjoyed a boom from 1769 when the dramatist Ramón de la Cruz introduced everyday Spanish settings and popular Spanish song (Lamas 2008, 78–9). This brought *zarzuela* close to the *sainete* (comic one-acter with singing and dancing) – the most popular dramatic genre of the 1760s–1780s, of which Cruz wrote over 500, as well as almost 70 *zarzuelas*.

Like the Golden Age *entremés*, the *sainete* was performed between the acts of the main play. In the 1760s the introduction of theater wings facilitated scenery changes, with entr'actes no longer restricted to the space in front of the curtain. This allowed Cruz's *sainetes* to develop complex choreography, with multiple actions offering a performance of heterogeneous community. His plays often disrupt neoclassical hierarchies and lack any didactic intention (Medina 2009, 130–2). Many have a metatheatrical dimension, their characters being actors and spectators who argue about their tastes; in *El pueblo quejoso* (*The People Protest*, 1765), the actors and *autora* (female actor-manager; actor-managers were often women) engage with a cross-class selection of spectators who invade the stage. *Manolo* (1769) uses popular Madrid characters to parody French-influenced neoclassical tragedy. The reaction against foreign influence in eighteenth-century Spain was enhanced by the vogue, from the 1740s, for *majismo* (see chapter 1). Cruz's *majo* characters declare themselves an "españolísimo gremio" (hyper-Spanish fraternity), identifying with their neighborhood (often Lavapiés). The districts where Cruz's *majos* live were inhabited by rural immigrants; his *majos* flaunt their regional accents and Andalusian, Galician, or Murcian origins (Haidt 2011). This constructs a fantasy of national community in which the national capital Madrid contains the diversity of the peripheries. That fantasy was encouraged by the state, as seen in the "typical" (*castizo*) regional types depicted in the *Colección de trajes de España* (*Collection of Spanish Costumes*, 1777–89) of Cruz's brother, the state-employed engraver Juan de la Cruz. In 1789, Cruz was commissioned to script a performance to celebrate Carlos IV's coronation, titled *Las provincias españolas unidas por el placer* (*Spain's Provinces United in Pleasure*). The spectacle presented "types" from Spain's provinces and colonies who paid homage to the new king by displaying their regional costumes, songs, and dances. Cruz's *sainetes* form part of the same cultural project as Goya's tapestry cartoons depicting *majos* (1775–88), commissioned to decorate the royal palace (Medina 2009, 186–97). Goya's pastoral figures have little in common with the streetwise popular types in Cruz's *sainetes* but both represent a fantasy of popular community "united in pleasure."

Cruz's *sainetes* initiate the Spanish cultural mode of *costumbrismo* (depiction of local customs) that would find its best-known manifestation in Ramón Mesonero Romanos's *Escenas matritenses* (*Madrid Scenes*, 1832–42; see chapter 7), which again depict the capital as a microcosm of the nation. This nationalist focus has allowed *costumbrismo* to be assimilated by the canon, despite its popular subject matter. Mesonero would be the first of many nineteenth-century Spanish-language writers to lament the loss of regional diversity with the homogenization brought by modernity. Such laments were the other side of the contemporaneous nation-formation project, whose view of the capital as melting pot was predicated on disavowal of a flourishing urban popular culture in peripheral cities such as Barcelona and Valencia.

Folk Culture

The nostalgia for a regional diversity perceived as under threat boosted the Romantic exaltation of rural folk culture, following Juan Nicolás Böhl de Faber's dissemination of Friedrich Schlegel's "recovery" of the country's ballad tradition. The valorization of the Spanish ballad tradition from the Romantic period on was schizophrenic. *Romances viejos* (old ballads) were admired as unspoiled survivals of the past preserved through oral transmission, while the *romances de ciego* (blindman's ballads) sold as broadsheets (*pliegos de cordel*) by blind peddlers were considered degraded because they were transmitted in print and sold commercially. In fact, *romances de ciego*, dating back to print's beginnings, assimilate material from the medieval oral tradition. *Romances de ciego* were also transmitted orally, sung to guitar accompaniment by their blind peddlers. What made *romances de ciego* suspect was their sensationalism and implicit challenge to the law, their stock repertoire being tales of crimes, generous bandits, and victims of injustice (Caro Baroja 1980). Their blind peddlers, denigrated as a sign of

Spain's backwardness, were pioneers in the modern commercialization of print culture. Another kind of broadsheet, developed in the nineteenth century, was the *aleluya*, which told a story through a sequence of 48 printed images with verse captions, arranged on a single sheet (ballads had a single image above the text). Both *pliegos de cordel* and *aleluyas* included adaptations of literary texts, popular and canonical, Spanish and foreign (Marco 1977; Botrel 2011).

Ballads set in the past became a major Spanish Romantic genre, dovetailing with the *leyenda* (folktale, often fantastic, in verse or prose). The Grimm brothers' folktale collections (1812–57) inspired Fernán Caballero (penname of Böhl de Faber's daughter Cecilia) to publish her *Cuentos y poesías populares andaluces* (*Andalusian Folktales and Folksongs*, 1859). The Duke of Rivas's narrative poem *El moro expósito* (*The Moorish Foundling*, 1834; see chapter 5) and Juan Eugenio Hartzenbusch's play *Los amantes de Teruel* (*The Lovers of Teruel*, 1837) were based on medieval legends; Rivas's *Romances históricos* (*Historical Ballads*, 1841) were *leyendas* in ballad form. 1840 saw a glut of verse *leyendas*: José de Espronceda's Gothic *El estudiante de Salamanca*; José Joaquín de Mora's *Leyendas españolas* (*Spanish Legends*), written in Bolivia, which exceptionally question heroic versions of the national past; and José Zorrilla's *Cantos del trovador* (*Troubadour Songs*). Zorrilla published *leyendas* through the 1880s; their nationalist agenda takes refuge from modernity in a fantastic bygone world.

The same impulse motivates Gustavo Adolfo Bécquer's prose *Leyendas*, published in the press 1858–64; like his unfinished archaeological project *Historia de los templos de España* (*History of the Temples of Spain*), they are a song to ruins. The fantastic elements in these folktales, drawn from Spanish, European, and Oriental sources, partake of the Gothic – a genre exploited by Agustín Pérez y Zaragoza's massively popular 12-volume *Galería fúnebre de historias trágicas, espectros y sombras ensangrentadas . . .* (*Funereal Gallery of Tragic Stories, Specters, and Bloody Shadows . . .*, 1831) (P. Fernández 2016). The *Galería fúnebre*'s sensationalism anticipates the popular serialized novel that would engage a broad readership from the 1840s to the century's end, peaking 1850–70.

The Serialized Novel

There were two forms of serialization: the *folletín*, published in successive issues of a newspaper; and the *novela por entregas*, sold in weekly fascicules through home delivery to subscribers. The term *folletín* is often used of both. The major realist novelist Benito Pérez Galdós, despite lambasting serialization in 1870 (Pérez Galdós 1972, 119), used both methods. The press also regularly published short stories by major authors, a practice that challenges classifications: should the realist novelist Emilia Pardo Bazán's nearly 600 short stories be considered "popular literature" because she wrote them for the press?

The *novela por entregas* was a major innovation with its large print runs of around 12,500 copies (occasionally 25,000). It flourished in the publishing industry's major centers: Madrid, Barcelona, and Valencia. Jean-François Botrel (1974) has described the coordination between publishers, writers, and salesmen that made this industrialization of literary production possible. Publishers commissioned works from writers: the contract stipulated the amount to be written per week and payment per installment (eight pages), with rights assigned to the publisher. A sophisticated publicity machine went into operation on issue of the first installment, including a nationwide network of door-to-door salesmen. The price remained steady at one *real* per weekly delivery of two installments: slightly less than the cost of a loaf of bread. The number of installments (written from week to week) was often unspecified, allowing successful novels to be extended; the average duration was 20–40 weeks. For publishers it was a win–win situation, generating a regular income and allowing print runs to be tailored to demand. For working-class subscribers, the low weekly outlay was attractive; however, the amount paid for the whole novel was roughly equivalent to buying five bound books. The supposition that most readers of *novelas por entregas* were women is unlikely given the 1860 female illiteracy rate of 86 percent (Viñao Fraga 1990, 578).

The much-maligned writer of serialized novels, Manuel Fernández y González, hired amanuenses to whom he dictated his texts, allowing him to write an average of 3.5 novels per year from 1845 to 1888. The 16-year-old future Valencian novelist Vicente Blasco Ibáñez worked for him in 1883. Writers would frequently subcontract to others, undermining the notion of individual authorship. The annual income of a writer in demand could reach five to six times the salary of an Assistant Professor at Madrid University. Assuming 3.5 readers per copy, Botrel estimates that individual serialized novels may have reached 42,000–55,000 readers (1974, 132). Many more heard them read out loud, their hyperbolic prosody lending itself to oral performance; public or private readings to a group remained common throughout the nineteenth century.

A pioneer of the *novela por entregas* as writer and publisher was the republican Wenceslao Ayguals de Izco, from Catalan-speaking Vinaroz in

Castellón, who in 1843 set up his Sociedad Literaria (Literary Society) to disseminate radical literature. His inspiration was the Europe-wide popularity of Eugène Sue's *Le juif errant* (*The Wandering Jew*, 1844), which Ayguals translated. His own anticlerical serialized novels – beginning with *María, la hija de un jornalero* (*María, a Day-Laborer's Daughter*, 1845–6; see chapter 7) – formed part of the cycle of Spanish imitations of Sue's *Les mystères de Paris* (*The Mysteries of Paris*, 1842–3), as did those of his fellow radical republican Ceferino Tresserra, whose *La judía errante* (*The Wandering Jewess*, 1862) is a riff on Sue's novel. After the 1868 liberal revolution, when there was a concerted effort to construct a high-cultural "national novel," serialized fiction was increasingly denounced as a foreign imitation.

The Commercialization of Theatrical Culture

Late nineteenth-century complaints about commercialization focused largely on theater: specifically, the *género chico* (short genre), also known as *teatro por horas* (one-hour theater), which dominated the Madrid stage from the 1860s to 1920s, providing a cheap, entertaining alternative to the moralizing melodramas that played to respectable audiences. Impresarios realized they could maximize profits by offering four one-hour shows instead of a full-length performance. This led to a revival of the *sainete*, now performed as an independent work. The *zarzuela* had enjoyed a revival since the 1850s (Madrid's Teatro de la Zarzuela opened in 1856); from the 1880s, one-act *zarzuelas* largely took over. Both of these forms of *género chico* mixed song with dialogue; the *sainete*'s attraction was its fast-paced popular repartee, while that of the *zarzuela* was its modern musical hybridity, borrowing from Italian opera and French *opéra bouffe*, and assimilating central European and, after 1903, US and Latin American rhythms (Salaün 2011, 42, 87–115). Spanish-language *sainetes* and *zarzuelas* were overwhelmingly set in Madrid's popular districts, with *sainetes* more likely to feature the *lumpenproletariat* while *zarzuelas* straddled shopkeepers, servants, the service sector, and the odd industrial worker. Both were hailed as expressing the *castizo* spirit of Madrid's popular classes, but audiences were middle-class, as were the writers and composers.

The Madrid-based *zarzuela* gave a cozy picture of the city's "typical" neighborhoods, depicting courting rituals at a time marked by growing worker protest. The depiction of Madrid "types" in the *sainetes* of their most prolific Spanish-language writer, Carlos Arniches, is less saccharine, with its racy use of lower-class slang and *lumpen* characters, echoing turn-of-the-century Spanish criminologists' interest in the figure of the *golfo* (petty delinquent). Despite their conservative agenda, Arniches's plays convey the popular classes' energy and wit. In this respect they have aged better than the Andalusian-based *sainetes* of the Álvarez Quintero brothers, Serafín and Joaquín, in which playboy *señoritos* (landowners' sons) are entertained by gypsies and other low-life characters, who speak in comically exaggerated Andalusian accents.

Género chico came to be seen as "popular," despite largely catering to establishment views of "the people" (at least in its Spanish-language versions), because it was commercially successful. Between 1890 and 1900, the 11 Madrid theaters devoted to *género chico* premiered 1,500 new works; in 1901 the Teatro Apolo, known as the "cathedral of *género chico*," sold four and a half million tickets (Madrid's population was half a million) (Salaün 2011, 48). In practice, *género chico* was populist, convincing middle-class audiences that the lower classes existed to entertain them.

From 1900 the *género chico* gave way to the *género ínfimo* (minimal genre): musical spots with a solo female singer, performed in cheaper, more disreputable venues (Salaün 2011, 53). The *café cantante* (cabaret) and *teatro de variedades* (music hall) offered (male) audiences singing and dancing with naughty female stars. The solo songs became known as *cuplés* (from the French *couplet*), and their singers as *cupletistas*. Verbal *double-entendre* and insinuating gesture were crucial to the *género ínfimo*'s success, massively boosted by the 1894 opening of Barcelona's Paral·lel district: a two-kilometer stretch devoted to entertainment, making Barcelona the nation's popular entertainment capital. *Cuplé* culture – whose stars often had spectacular international careers – contributed to the renovation of Spanish stagecraft by incorporating foreign theatrical innovations, with dramatic lighting effects and sophisticated sets (Salaün 2011, 233–48).

Performing and Containing Catalan Popular Culture: Theater and the Satirical Press

The privileging of poetry by the *Renaixença* movement – and by the histories that have made it central to Catalan culture's revival – tends to ignore the period's more varied social and cultural characteristics as well as continuities with previous centuries. This marginalized popular literature, except for that deemed to express values associated with the troubadour tradition or some essential folk spirit collected and preserved by nostalgic literary historians. Even so, satirical theater, pamphlets and songs, which remained popular throughout the eighteenth century, maintained their presence in Catalan-speaking areas; some 250 works of popular literature in Catalan were published between 1801 and 1833. These were largely moral and devotional texts, short *entremesos* and *sainets*, and popular poetry.

Catalan-language production mirrored many of the nineteenth- and early twentieth-century popular literary developments witnessed in Madrid. The *folletín*, equally popular in Barcelona and Valencia, did not, however, further Catalan-language fiction since the economic interests of a growing publishing industry prioritized publication in the language of the state to maximize dissemination. It did, however, insert Catalan writers into the commercial mainstream, with the earliest translations of Eugène Sue, George Sand, and Víctor Hugo published by Catalans in Castilian (Martí-López 2002). The first of Sue's novels, *Los misterios de París* (*The Mysteries of Paris*), was translated and published in Barcelona in 1844, one year after its French original, by the same Joan Cortada who was a pioneer of the Romantic historical novel and proto-champion of the *Jocs Florals*. Sue's novel spawned numerous Castilian-language imitations in subsequent decades by Catalan writers like Pere Mata, Ferran Patxot, Antonio Altadill, Víctor Balaguer, and above all Manuel Angelon, including Nicasio Milà de la Roca's copycat *Los misterios de Barcelona* (*The Mysteries of Barcelona*, 1844) and Angelon's *Los misterios del pueblo español* (*The Mysteries of the Spanish People*, 1858–60). Much of Angelon's work circulated in serial and book form, the most popular being the 800-page *El pendón de Santa Eulalia o los fueros de Cataluña* (*Saint Eulalia's Banner or The Charters of Catalonia*, 1858), named after the emblem used historically to call Barcelona's citizens to arms. Although Antoni de Bofarull's Catalan-language *L'orfaneta de Menargues* (*The Orphan Girl of Menargues*, 1862) can be placed within this serialized tradition, the Catalan-language *fulletó* began to make headway later in the century, with a growing vernacular press from the late 1860s that published popular fiction and theater (especially *sainets*) as supplements.

Barcelona enjoyed a flourishing popular performance culture throughout the eighteenth century, focused on the Teatre de la Santa Creu. Staples were Italian and French traveling companies and, later in the century, *sainets* in the style of Ramón de la Cruz. A new theater space was inaugurated at the Santa Creu in 1787 after a fire during the performance of a bilingual version of Cruz's *El café de Barcelona* (*The Barcelona Café*). Vernacular theater in Valencian in this period is thought to have been limited to the *col·loqui* (dialogue) form enjoyed by the urban populace of Valencia and Alicante (Sansano 2005, 2009).

Throughout the nineteenth century, theater remained the most dynamic Catalan popular cultural form, with the one-act comic and satirical plays of actor-playwrights Francesc Renart, Josep Robrenyo, and Joaquim Dimas i Graells in the early decades, and later the *sainets* and *sarsueles* of Frederic Soler ("Serafí Pitarra") and his followers (Curet 1967). These works' enduring popularity led to attempts to ban them due to their rabble-rousing potential and the obstacle that theater in the "dialects" supposedly presented to the efficient spread of Castilian as the national language (Branchadell 2006). They were also viewed with suspicion by Barcelona's elites for their alleged lack of literary quality and, later, for their linguistic chaos (Ciurans 2012). Nevertheless, such popular genres provided an important representational platform for a growing industrialized society and influenced other forms, such as the *quadres de costums* (*costumbrista* prose sketches) that began to emerge in the Catalan press from the 1860s (Triadú 1950).

In the nineteenth century, Barcelona had more theaters than Madrid. Comic theater especially flourished in both Barcelona and Valencia. From the century's start, drawing on a rich secular and festive theatrical tradition and influenced by late eighteenth-century models, especially Ramón de la Cruz, there was a proliferation of bilingual works – in Catalan with intercalated dialogue in Castilian – by dramatists such as Renart, Robrenyo, Dimas, and, in Valencia, Josep Bernat i Baldoví and, later, Eduard Escalante. Unlike the nostalgic vision promoted by *Renaixença* intellectuals, these works do not shy away from political contestation, transmitting a republican worldview and often pointing to the linguistic and social diversity of the time, with encounters between Catalan speakers and visitors from other parts of Spain and examples of diglossic practice. A key example is Robrenyo's *El Sarau de la Patacada* (*The Patacada Carnival Festival*, 1805), while sociolinguists have used Escalante's works to analyze nineteenth-century language usage in urban Valencia. Generally, these plays poke fun at misunderstandings between Catalan and Castilian speakers, and at attempts by middle- and upper-class characters to switch to Castilian as a perceived prestige language. Bernat i Baldoví's 1845 *El virgo de Visanteta* (*Visanteta's Virginity*) stands out for its irreverent subject matter and liberal use of sexually explicit taboo language typical of informal Valencian speech.

Escalante's Barcelona-based contemporary Soler ("Pitarra") became particularly popular in Catalonia from the late 1850s for his short comic *sainets* and *sarsueles* in Catalan, which mocked *Renaixença* mores with satires of medieval histories, as in the legend of the birth and minority of Jaume I in *L'engendrament de Don Jaume* (*The Conception of King Jaume*, 1856); parodied patriotic plays about the African War, as in *La botifarra de la llibertat* (*The*

Sausage of Liberty, 1864); sent up the rivalry between patrons of the Liceu and the Teatre de la Santa Creu in *Liceistes i cruzados* (1864); or lampooned the exaltation of the rural in *L'esquella de la torratxa* (*The Cowbell in the Turret*, 1864). Like Robrenyo's plays at the century's start, some plays were overtly political, usually progressive and republican – examples include Abdó Terradas's *Lo rei micomicó* (*King Comicoco*, 1838), Rossend Arús's *Mai més monarquia* (*Monarchy Never Again*, 1873), and later the Catalanist republican plays of Josep Burgas, such as *Jordi Erin* (1906) whose eponymous fictional hero's name links Catalonia and Ireland – or reflected ongoing political or social conflict, including plays based on notorious crimes such as Jaume Piquet's *La monja enterrada en vida* (*The Nun Buried Alive*, 1885). Many of these popular dramatists additionally critiqued contemporary social practice through pamphlets, press articles, poems, and songs. Their plays were the staples of the theaters that lined the Rambla, the open-air spaces along the Passeig de Gràcia, and later the Paral·lel, as well as district associations and labor athenaeums. This tradition may be traced through to the social theater of Felip Cortiella, Ignasi Iglésias, and Juli Vallmitjana toward the century's end, as well as to the creation of workers' theaters and choral societies such as that of Josep Anselm Clavé and, later, the *Orfeó Català*.

The gulf between this popular performance tradition and the writers discussed in chapters 4 and 5 is by no means absolute, with Soler later participating in the *Jocs Florals* and joining the crusade to create serious theater in Catalan that led to the 1865–6 foundation of the Teatre Romea. His skill in creating realistic dialogue based on modern dialectal Catalan influenced many "serious" writers, while his prose sketches in periodicals like the *Diario de Barcelona*, *La Renaixensa*, and *L'Avenç* provided models for the later development of narrative fiction in Catalan, alongside regular contributors of *quadres de costums* like Robert Robert and Emili Vilanova (Triadú 1950; Poblet 1967). The wide acclaim received by Guimerà's plays (see chapter 4) would be unimaginable without this urban theater tradition; nor were the aesthetic and ideological positions of the *Renaixença's* proponents adopted in a vacuum. Jocfloralista idealization of the rural world would begin to be supplanted by the growing strength of liberal and federal republican positions, resulting in greater cross-fertilization between high and popular forms and movements.

The *Modernista* approach to the popular from the late 1880s is more cognizant of contemporary social realities, reflecting both the real harshness and hypocrisy of contemporary rural society and engaging with a broad spectrum of urban society. A similar shift can be detected in popular poetry and folktale collections. Whereas in the early nineteenth century the purpose of this anthologizing practice was to recover some eternal *genus loci*, by the century's end it was to gather authentic examples of modern Catalan, culminating in the work of Antoni Alcover to recover the diverse forms of Catalan spoken across the Catalan-speaking regions. The *Noucentista* vision that gained prominence from 1906 also benefits from being seen in terms of its attitude to social and aesthetic diversity. Its rejection of *Modernisme* constitutes a shift away from spontaneous manifestations of the popular, associated in conservative political Catalanism with turn-of-the-century anarchist bombs, to the more systematic aim of controlling and civilizing contemporary Catalan society (Murgades 1987, 2020). *Noucentisme* was long held responsible for producing "a generation without a novel" (Yates 1975) because of its rejection of the realist depiction of contemporary Catalan society for translations of European fiction that might provide more appropriate civilizing models.

The Catalan satirical press deserves special attention, not only because it predates the major dailies of the late 1870s and 1880s, but also because it spans the key period of consolidation of Catalan literary culture (1860s–1930s). It was undoubtedly one of the most popular literary forms, with a range of journals published across the Catalan-speaking territories, from the *fallera* genre in Valencia and its links to the dominant modes of popular theater and festivity since the start of the nineteenth century, to the long-lasting journals *La Campana de Gràcia* (*The Bell of Gràcia*, 1870–1934) and *L'Esquella de la Torratxa* (1872–1939, named after the previously mentioned 1864 play), which remained popular throughout their timespan (McGlade 2016). Both were inspired by the short-lived 1865–6 weekly *Un Tros de Paper* (*A Piece of Paper*), which sold 4,000 copies before being closed down for political reasons. Both combined journalism, theater, and a commitment to contemporary dialectal Catalan, positioning themselves against the *Jocs Florals'* medievalizing tendencies and aligning themselves with the republican, anticlerical, and federalist politics of the early 1870s. They would sell 8,000–10,000 copies in Barcelona in the first four hours of publication, with the remainder transported to the rest of Catalonia. As precursors of a viable daily press in Catalan, with Almirall's pioneering *Diari Català* first appearing in 1879, they had a central role in the emergence of broader social commitment to a distinctly Catalan cultural field. Their range of influence made them prone to government backlash, suffering countless fines and suspensions. Although both magazines remained influential into the 1930s, during the Second Republic *El Be Negre* (*The Black Sheep*) took on the mantle of wide-ranging counter-cultural satire. *La Campana* was closed down after Generalitat President Lluís Companys' aborted declaration of an independent federal state in October 1934, which led to the suspension of Catalan autonomy, while *L'Esquella* was taken over by the UGT (Unión General de Trabajadores / Socialist Trade Union) at the start of the Civil War and later handed to the Sindicato de Dibujantes Profesionales (Draughtsmen's Trade Union), where its contributors included key antifascist writers and cartoonists like Avel·lí Artís Gener ("Tísner") and Pere Calders, both of whom went into exile in Mexico at the war's end. The ensuing repression completely obliterated this tradition until the emergence of counter-cultural magazines in the 1970s.

Basque Popular Culture: Oral Literature and Theater

The importance of oral literature in the Basque context has rightly been stressed. Pastorals (*pastorala* or *trageria*) – dating back to the medieval mystery play, characteristic of the French Basque province of Zuberoa (Soule) – continue to be staged annually in open-air productions involving an entire village. The masquerades (*maskarada*) popular across much of Europe in the sixteenth century are still performed in the same region. *Bertsolaritza* – the oral improvisation of *bertsos* (rhyming compositions) – dates back to at least the fifteenth century (Mitxelena 1988 [1960], 25) and has a wide following today (see www.bertsozale.com). *Bertso-paperak* (broadsheets of *bertsos*), sold at fairs and markets, were popular from at least the early nineteenth century, with the first documented performance of improvised *bertsos* being in 1802 and the first sound recording in 1935 (Garzia 2012, 47). They blossomed during the nineteenth century, particularly following the Third Carlist War (1872–6). *Bertsolaris* (improvisers of *bertsos*) enjoyed huge cultural prestige. At the time of the poetic revolution led by the Basque modernist poets "Lizardi" and "Lauaxeta" during the Second Spanish Republic, intellectuals such as "Aitzol" (penname of José Ariztimuño) considered *bertsolaritza* the standard-bearer of the Basque cultural renaissance and encouraged the creation in 1935 of the Bertsolari Eguna (Bertsolari Day).

Bertsolaritza metrics and techniques strongly influenced mid-nineteenth-century Basque poets, such as Jean Martin Hiribarren whose eulogy "Euskaldunak" (The Basques, 1853) comprises 5,428 *bertsos*; José María Iparragirre whose "Gernikako arbola" (Tree of Gernika, 1853) would become the Basque anthem par excellence; and "Bilintx" (penname of Indalecio Bizkarrondo). In the French Basque region, Pierre Topet ("Etxahun") was, like Bilintx, inspired by traditional Basque love poetry.

These *bertsolaris* were seen as bards whose songs revealed the Basque soul (Aldekoa 2004, 81). Many award-winners at the Floral Games were influenced by *bertsolaritza* forms.

Compilations of Basque popular literature, in the German Romantic tradition, flourished. Wilhelm von Humboldt's studies of the Basque language led him to collect traditional songs. Building on the work of late eighteenth- and early nineteenth-century pioneers Juan Antonio Mogel and Juan Ignazio Iztueta, later anthologies of popular songs were compiled by Francisque Michel (1857) and Jean Dominique Julien Sallaberry (1870). Collectors of folktales and legends in the 1870s and 1880s were mainly foreign, including Jean François Cerquand, Wentworth Webster, and Julien Vinson. The monumental *Cancionero Vasco* (*Basque Songbook*, 1877–80) of José Manterola included popular and more elaborate poetic compositions.

The purist view of the Basque language taken by the founder of Basque nationalism, Sabino Arana, expounded in the appendix to his *Lecciones de Ortografía del Euskera Bizkaino* (*Lessons in Bizkaian Basque Orthography*, 1896), drove a wedge between high and popular culture. Over time, the opposition of philologists such as Julio de Urquijo and Arturo Campión, defenders of literary tradition and popular speech, prevailed. Important in legitimizing popular linguistic forms was the prodigious compilation work of Resureccion Maria Azkue in his *Cancionero popular vasco* (*Popular Basque Songbook*, 1918–21) and four-volume *Euskalerriaren Yakintza* (*Popular Basque Knowledge*, 1935–47). However, the reading matter of most Basque speakers continued to be religious texts, *bertso-paperak*, and almanacs, generally read aloud to an audience, usually in the home. The reading of almanacs, shared by the pro-Basque cultural elite and sectors of the general public, provided non-conventional forms of education; they were read widely by women and rural smallholders, including those who had migrated to the industrialized urban areas. From 1924 the *Euzkel-Egutegiya* (*Basque Almanac*, 1909–34) had a print run of 10,000 copies in Gipuzkoan Basque and 2,000 copies in Lapurdian Basque (Eizagirre 2008, 253).

Theater, which accounted for 51 percent of all Basque literary publications, was readily embraced by a public with limited reading habits in Basque. The Basque theatrical renaissance was centered on Donostia-San Sebastián which by the nineteenth century's end had become a cosmopolitan tourist destination. Under Toribio Altzaga's directorship, the Academy for Basque Declamation (Euskal Iztundea), created by the Donostia-San Sebastián City Council in 1915, promoted Basque-language theater in the city and surrounding Gipuzkoa province. As well as serious social dramas,

Altzaga's own theatrical output included popular comic skits, such as
Burruntziya (*The Saucepan*, 1926).

Basque-language performance culture operated across a broad continuum, with the same authors writing not only serious plays and lightweight
sketches but also operas and *zarzuelas*. Marcelino Soroa, in addition to
writing humorous *costumbrista* sketches, authored the popular *zarzuela*,
Iriyarena (*Of the City*, 1876). In Bizkaia, Azkue wrote two operas in the early
twentieth century, having in the late 1890s written the libretto and music
for several *zarzuelas*, published in his journal *Euskalzale* and performed by
his students as holder of the Chair of Basque in Bilbao and by members of
Bilbao's Choral Society. Altzaga wrote the libretti for three operas: *Txanton
Piperri* (1899), *Amboto* (1906), and *Gli kornamenti* (*The Horns*, 1906). Basque
zarzuela and opera attracted popular audiences because of their use of the
Basque language and creation of a repertoire of Basque "types," in the case
of opera also because of the frequent deployment of amateur performers
(often members of local choral societies) and popular Basque melodies
and dance forms (Morel Borotra 2003, 72–83). Forty operas in Basque
were produced from 1884 – the first, *Pudente*, having being written in 1878
by Serafín Baroja, father of novelist Pío Baroja – to 1930. Their historical-
romantic dramas helped to shape a vision of the Basque people grounded
in tradition, as in *Mendi Mendiyan* (*On the Mountain*, 1909), *Maitena* (1909),
and *Amaya* (1910); industrialization is entirely absent, even in those operas
premiered in Bilbao. Although the same authors and composers wrote *zarzuelas* and operas, the two genres had different functions: while *zarzuelas*
denounced the increasing use of Spanish in Basque society, operas promoted Basque history, culture, and language to a wide public.

Popular Culture in Galicia: The Dilemmas of Diglossia

In 2018, the historian Julio González Montañés discovered a printed play
in a Galician archive which not only pushed the date of the earliest known
Galician-language publication back by a century, but also provided new
information about the existence of a popular theatrical culture during
Galicia's so-called "Dark Ages." *Entremés gallego* (*Galician Interlude*, 1701),
by Salvador Francisco Roel, written (and presumably performed) entirely
in Galician, is unusual in a history of early Galician-language theater hitherto constructed largely from Galician-language interpolations in plays
such as *Comedia de la invención de la sortija* (*Play about the Invention of the
Wedding Ring*, 1594), the Jesuit-authored *Entremés de los gallegos* (*Interlude of

the Galician People, *c.*1640), or the work conventionally considered the first Galician drama, *Entremés famoso sobre la pesca del rio Miño* (*Famous Interlude on Fishing in the River Miño*, 1671). As González Montañés demonstrated (2018), Roel's play was performed in A Coruña as part of the festivities celebrating the birth of the royal heir Prince Luis Felipe, and was part of a lively history of popular spectacles and performances in Galicia. The *entremés* and the dialogue were especially popular formats, inspiring the propagandistic texts that responded to the Napoleonic invasion. The identification of popular spectacle with a distinctively Galician language and identity came into its own with the *Rexurdimento* and especially with the *Xogos Florais* of 1861. However, after the *Rexurdimento*, Galician cultural histories go surprisingly quiet.

The *Rexionalista* period (*c.*1880–1920) is generally considered an anomaly within the teleological narrative of Galician literary history, a low point between the great peaks of the *Rexurdimento* and the fully-fledged nationalist culture of the Xeración Nós in the 1920s (Rodríguez 1990). As in the Catalan case, conventional literary histories have paid little attention to publications in genres other than poetry during this period, allegedly on grounds of aesthetic quality but in practice because of the onus to promote a legitimizing narrative of elite monolingual cultural production. This elides the complex bilingual cultural output of this fertile period when Galician-identified writers, journalists, and publishers were actively participating in and creating new popular forms. In practice, as during the *Rexurdimento*, most writers moved between Galician and Castilian in their fiction and non-fiction work; access to the Galician language was not universal for writers or the reading public. Much popular "Galician" cultural production during this period is in Castilian, such as the commercial illustrated *Biblioteca de Escritores Gallegos*, founded in 1910 by the Madrid-based Galician writers Luis Antón del Olmet and Prudencio Canitrot, whose contributors included Manuel Murguía, Valle-Inclán, Alberto Insúa, and Sofía Casanova. One of the most striking consequences of the elision of *fin de século* Castilian-language production from Galician national literary history is the erasure of Galicia's women writers, all of whom wrote bilingually, and who were thus doubly marginalized as not Galician enough for Galician literature and not Castilian enough for Castilian literature (Hooper 2003).

A consequence of the retrospective preference for elite cultural production, assessed according to the modernist criteria of the 1920s and the culturalist criteria of the 1950s, has been the dismissal of work considered insufficiently modern, intellectual, and universalist. The author who has suffered most from this is Francisca Herrera Garrido, whose *Néveda* (1920), Galicia's first female-authored novel, was dismissed by the Xeración Nós as *costumbrista*, sentimental, and as offering little advance on the writings of Rosalía de Castro four decades earlier. The very existence of *Néveda's* female-voiced, female-centered narrative, with its abundant depictions of popular culture, demonstrates the germ of an alternative path for Galician-language narrative. The institutionalized practice of using folkloric and localist elements to elaborate a distinct Galician identity expressed in Spanish rather than Galician, so distasteful to later politicized Galician intellectuals, can be traced back to Emilia Pardo Bazán. Her foundation of an explicitly apolitical *Sociedad del Folk-Lore Gallego* at the height of the *Rexionalista* movement in 1884 owed much to her correspondence with Antonio Machado y Álvarez ("Demófilo"), who had promoted the foundation of similar societies across Spain. The simultaneous rise of politicized programs of lexicographic and ethnographic research as part of a proto-nationalist political project meant that the question of ownership of Galicia's folklore and popular culture, and of the uses to which it could be put, was never straightforward (Miguélez-Carballeira 2013). As will be shown in chapter 8, the intellectualization of Galicianist culture, and above all the 1920s foundation of the magazine *Nós*, were a reaction to this.

Kiosk Literature, Politics, and "Sicalipsis"

Returning to popular cultural production in Spanish, the early twentieth century saw a publishing and cultural revolution with the introduction of cheaply printed, generally small-format novella series known as "literary magazines," issued weekly and sold at newsstands (hence the alternative term "kiosk literature") or by mail-order subscription (Zamostny and Larson 2017). The pioneers were *El Cuento Semanal* (*The Weekly Story*, 1907–12) and *Los Contemporáneos* (*Contemporary Writers*, 1909–26), both directed by erotic fiction writer Eduardo Zamacois. Among their many successors were *La Novela Breve* (*The Short Novel*, 1910–20); *El Libro Popular* (*The Popular Book*, 1912–14); *La Novela de Bolsillo* (*The Pocket Novel*, 1914–16); *La Novela Corta* (*The Short Novel*, 1916–25); the anarchist *La Novela Ideal* (*The Ideal Novel*, 1925–38) and *La Novela Roja* (*The Red Novel*, 1922–3); *La Novela Semanal* (*The Weekly Novel*, 1922–30); the Catholic *Nuestra Novela* (*Our Novel*, 1925–6); *La Novela Mundial* (*World Novel*, 1926–8); and *La Novela de Hoy* (*Today's Novel*, 1922–32) whose director Artemio Precioso decimated competition by signing writers up on exclusive contracts. These series sometimes included plays; certain series, such as *La Novela Teatral* (*The Dramatic Novel*, 1916–25) and *La Farsa* (*Farce*, 1927–36), specialized in drama; *La Novela Semanal Cinematográfica* (*The Weekly Cinema Novel*, 1922–30) published novelized versions of films. Essays, poetry, and biographies also featured in certain series. Several of these "literary magazines," notably the anarchist *La Novela Ideal*, were published in Barcelona, although, as with the nineteenth-century serialized novel, in Castilian to allow nationwide distribution; copycat Catalan-language equivalents also appeared. Print runs regularly reached 50,000; the first issue of *La Novela Corta*, Galdós's play *Sor Simona*, sold a record 200,000 copies. Similar series continued on a smaller scale through the 1930s and, in tamer form, after the Civil War. The pioneer *El Cuento Semanal* sold at 30 céntimos per issue, the price of a liter of table wine; the average cost of a novel was 3.5 pesetas. *La Novela Corta* slashed prices to 5 céntimos per issue. Covers and inside line drawings were mostly modernist, often risqué; the contents were highly varied in function and quality. Established names (Galdós, Pardo Bazán, Blasco Ibáñez, Felipe Trigo, Concha Espina, Pío Baroja, Ramón del Valle-Inclán, Ramón Gómez de la Serna) appeared alongside new talent. They were accessible to working-class or new readers in price, language, and format (short length, illustrations) and because they could be bought at newsstands (Zamostny and Larson 2017, 3–27).

This accessibility was not lost on revolutionary militants. Anarchist, Communist, and socialist activists published novellas and essays under the label "revolutionary kiosk literature" on overtly political topics (anticlericalism, police and military repression, republicanism) (Santonja 1993). Some novellas by anarchist writers, who promoted an advanced sexual politics, adapted the "novela rosa" (romance fiction) format to challenge traditional views on marriage, female sexuality, and the family. The sister series *La Novela Ideal* and, from 1933 to 1937, *La Novela Libre* (both published under the imprint of the anarchist journal *La Revista Blanca*) are crucial to the development of Spanish anarcho-feminism, thanks to writers like Soledad Gustavo, Federica Montseny (later Republican Minister of Health), Antonia Maymón, Margarita Amador, María Solá, Ángela Graupera, and Regina Opisso (Prado 2011). The Catalan anarcho-syndicalist leader Salvador Seguí wrote for *La Novela Roja* and *La Novela de Hoy*. A prolific contributor to several series was Carmen de Burgos, who used their mass readership to campaign for divorce and to discuss adultery, male and female homosexuality, and transvestism.

Kiosk literature was tied to the vogue for eroticism, known as "sicalipsis," dating back to *cuplé* culture. Eroticism was seen as incompatible with

"Spanishness" by many early twentieth-century intellectuals (Unamuno, Gregorio Marañón, Santiago Ramón y Cajal, José Ortega y Gasset), despite which, from 1900 to 1936, erotic materials comprised up to 20 percent of Spanish publications (Zubiaurre 2012; Rodríguez de Rivera 2017). Several erotic authors – of novels as well as novellas – attained unprecedented popularity and earnings. "Sicaliptic" material, sometimes openly pornographic, also pervaded magazines and postcards, advertising, films, and sex-advice manuals. Some writers justified their erotic subject matter by aligning it with scientific and social concerns (Davis 2017), as in Trigo's highly successful novels and novellas which combine explicit eroticism with denunciation of Spanish sexual mores and regenerationist social critique. Gregorio Marañón's prologue to a short story collection by the decadentist (and openly queer) writer Antonio de Hoyos justified his erotically charged pessimism as the diagnosis of a social pathology (L.E. Delgado 2003).

"Sicalipsis" is key to the vibrant artistic atmosphere of Madrid and Barcelona in the 1920s and under the Second Republic. Its most prominent celebrity was Álvaro Retana: contributor to several novella series, novelist, illustrator, *cuplé* writer, scenographer, and costume designer, who cultivated a (contradictory) bisexual public persona. Bisexuality, homosexuality, cross-dressing, and references to what he called "the third sex" are present in most of his work. Other names in the sicaliptic genre are Joaquín Belda, El Caballero Audaz, and Alberto Insúa; the few female names are mostly pseudonyms for male writers. While "sicalipsis" did not treat political topics, it had political consequences: Retana was tried for public obscenity twice before the Civil War, sentenced to death in 1939, and imprisoned till 1948; Hoyos died in a Francoist jail. After 1939, Spanish newsstands would not see a similar public display of explicitly erotic and political material – for the two are linked – until the late 1970s.

The Modernist Cooption of Popular and Mass Culture

Early twentieth-century anxieties at the invasion of "sicalipsis" triggered attempts to "rescue" popular culture from commercialization. Already in the 1880s, the previously mentioned "Demófilo" (folklorist father of poets Antonio and Manuel Machado) had lamented the hybridization of *cante jondo* (flamenco, literally "deep song") with other popular song forms in the new *cafés cantantes*. In 1881, he created El Folklore Andaluz (Andalusian Folklore Society) and published his *Colección de cantes flamencos (Flamenco Song Collection)*. Manuel Machado's penchant for Madrid's *cafés cantantes* is evident in his bestselling 1912 *Cante hondo*. By contrast, Antonio Machado's interest in *Campos de Castilla* (*Castilian Earth*, 1912) and *Nuevas canciones* (*New Songs*, 1917) in popular proverbs shows an appreciation of folk culture as a form of popular knowledge. Between 1926 and 1932 Antonio and Manuel jointly wrote a series of Andalusian folk dramas, including the highly successful *La Lola se va a los puertos* (*Lola Goes to Sea*, 1929).

Folk culture is a minor presence in the work of the Catalan avant-garde, which focused mainly on urban modernity – an exception being Joan Salvat-Papasseït's *El poema de la rosa als llavis* (*Poem of the Rose on the Lips*, 1923) which draws on popular motifs and forms. It plays a major role in the work of the Madrid avant-garde poets, Federico García Lorca and (in his early work) Rafael Alberti, both originating from rural Andalusia. For both, popular poetry functions as modernity's Other (racialized in Lorca's case), its appropriation generating cultural critique. The dialogue and choral refrains of folksong in Alberti's 1924 *Marinero en tierra* (*Sailor on Land*) counter an alienated modernity. Lorca was irked by his reputation as a "gypsy poet" after the success of his *Romancero gitano* (*Gypsy Ballads*, 1928); the book's publication by Ortega y Gasset's *Revista de Occidente* indicates that it coopts the ballad form to produce high-cultural effects. Lorca's *Poema del cante jondo* (*Poem to Cante Jondo*, published 1931) was written during his and composer Manuel de Falla's preparations for their 1922 *Cante jondo* contest in Granada, designed to "save" flamenco from commercialization in the *cafés cantantes*. The competition's subtitle – "canto primitivo andaluz" (Primitive Andalusian Song) – signals its high-cultural primitivist conception. Lorca's preceding talk bewailed flamenco's assignment since the 1870s to taverns and brothels. The contest's exclusion of professional (i.e., commercial) singers ruled out the best performers (Mitchell 1994, 160–96).

Dramatists created modernist estrangement through the appropriation of puppet theater. Lorca authored several puppet plays and, in his 1933 drama *La zapatera prodigiosa* (*The Prodigious Shoemaker's Wife*), the shoemaker returns disguised as a puppeteer who performs *aleluyas*. A puppeteer opens Valle-Inclán's *Los cuernos de don Friolera* (*Lieutenant Friolera's Horns*, 1921), while his play collections *Tablado de marionetas para educación de principles* (*Puppet Play for the Education of Princes*, 1926) and *Retablo de la avaricia, la lujuria y la muerte* (*Puppet Theater of Avarice, Lust, and Death*, 1927) echo the 1920s European avant-garde's fascination with the automaton. Valle-Inclán's novel trilogy *El ruedo ibérico* (*The Iberian Bullring*, 1927–32) dehumanizes its characters by drawing on mass culture – the satirical press – as well as broadsheets and *aleluyas* (Sinclair 1977).

The 1920s saw the consolidation of cinema as a form of mass cultural entertainment in both Barcelona and Madrid. Fascination with the new medium permeates the Catalan magazines *L'Amic de les Arts* (1926–9), *Hèlix* (1929), and *Mirador* (1929–38). The Madrid avant-garde's interest in cinema was channeled via Luis Buñuel's 1927–8 programming of experimental foreign films at Madrid's elite university hall of residence, the Residencia de Estudiantes, continued 1928–31 by Ernesto Giménez Caballero's Cine-Club Español (Gubern 1999). Alberti's *Yo era un tonto y lo que he visto me ha hecho dos tontos* (*I Was a Fool and What I've Seen Has Made Me Two Fools*, 1929) pays homage to the absurdism of Hollywood silent comedies, as does Lorca's sketch *El paseo de Buster Keaton* (*Buster Keaton's Promenade*, 1928). César M. Arconada, film critic for Giménez Caballero's *La Gaceta Literaria* (*Literary Gazette*), published avant-garde biographies of Hollywood stars in 1929 and 1931. Hollywood cinema is pastiched in Gómez de la Serna's 1923 novel *Cinelandia* (1923) and Concha Méndez's 1931 play *El personaje presentido* (*A Character Foretold*); Méndez wrote the screenplay for Carlos Emilio Nazarí's film *Historia de un taxi* (*Tale of a Taxi*, 1927). The impact of cinema on avant-garde stagecraft was substantial, particularly in the use of projections and lighting. Nonetheless, the theater director who made the most striking use of film projection, cinematic special effects, choreographed silent scenes, and popular film genres was the prolific Enrique Rambal, whose spectacles span the 1920s to 1950s (M. Delgado 2003, 67–89). His stage productions remind us that, as in the case of the *cuplé*, popular theater has frequently played a leading role in formal innovation. The following chapter will discuss the avant-garde appropriation of cinematic techniques in relation to the city.

Urban Modernity and the Provincial: Changing Concepts of Time and Space (1830s–1930s)

This chapter considers literature in Spanish and Catalan, focusing initially on Madrid and Barcelona as pockets of urban modernity in the decisive period for Spain's economic, social, and cultural modernization. Its second part reminds us that such pockets were an exception in a country that remained overwhelmingly rural and provincial.

Constructing the Capital

Already in the 1830s life in the capital Madrid starts to be depicted as a process of incessant change, thanks to urban rebuilding and immigration from the provinces. The realist novel, which documents contemporary life, builds on the *artículo de costumbres* (sketch of local customs) that was developed as a journalistic genre by Mariano José de Larra from 1828 and consecrated by Ramón de Mesonero Romanos's *Escenas matritenses* (*Madrid Scenes*, published weekly in the press 1832–42; in book form 1835, 1842, 1845, and 1851). The realist project, being part of the nation-formation process, focuses on life in the capital. It is logical that it should have developed out of journalism, since both the press and the novel played a major role in creating a national "imagined community." The mid-nineteenth-century expansion of the press, conditional on urban growth, created a broad reading public: Mesonero's *Semanario Pintoresco Español* (*Spanish Picturesque Weekly*, 1836–57), whose title constructs its readers as "Spaniards," was distributed nationwide.

This journal's quality illustrations are consonant with the centrality of vision to the experience of the modern city; the *artículo de costumbres* is also called an *escena* (scene) or *cuadro* (tableau). The genre's visuality echoes the popular magic lantern shows (mentioned by Mesonero) that simulated motion, and the panoramas (Mesonero's first collection was titled *Panorama matritense*) that simulated the simultaneity of different spaces: both are experiences intrinsic to the modern city. The panoptical urge encouraged by the panorama – the desire for total control through surveillance – is illustrated in Mesonero's "Paseo por las calles" (Stroll through the Streets), as he moves from the fragmented vision of the city seen from street level to the view from above, anticipating Leopoldo Alas's *La Regenta* (1884–5) which starts with De Pas surveying Vetusta from the cathedral tower. The panoptical impulse governs Mesonero's complementary role as Spain's major town-planner of the time, with his *Rápida ojeada sobre el estado de la capital y los medios de mejorarla* (*Quick Glance at the State of the Capital and How to Improve It*, 1835) and *Proyecto de mejoras generales de Madrid* (*Project for the General Improvement of Madrid*, 1846, partly implemented in the 1840s–1850s as described in Benito Pérez de Galdós's *Fortunata y Jacinta*). Mesonero's 1861 *El antiguo Madrid* (*Old Madrid*) is a guide to the city he helped to demolish.

In his *costumbrista* articles, Mesonero is a *flâneur* surveying urban mores. He critiques the introduction of foreign customs, despite modeling his urban reforms on Paris and London, which he visited for that purpose in 1833–4. He admires these capital cities' efficient organization of time and space but enjoys Madrid's chaotic sociability. This ambivalence towards modernization allows *costumbrismo* to encompass the description of rural life – as in Serafino Estébanez Calderón's *Escenas andaluzas* (*Andalusian Scenes*, 1847), which serve nation formation by incorporating rural dwellers into the national "imagined community." Mesonero's stress on Madrid's role as compendium of the nation thanks to migration from the provinces serves the same end.

The urge to "write the city" is the salient feature of Wenceslao Ayguals de Izco's *María o la hija de un jornalero* (1845–6), whose documentary detail – tracing the history of Madrid's landmarks – interrupts the narrative for pages at a time, including lengthy footnotes. Ayguals's concept of the *historia-novela* (history-novel) outlined in the epilogue to *María* is encyclope-dic but not panoptical because it refuses a unified narrative structure. The narrator takes us, with the characters, on a guided tour of Madrid (stress-ing institutions requiring reform like the hospital, orphanage, and prison) and of recent historical events in the city, in an unruly account that mirrors the novel's anticlerical, anti-monarchist defense of popular sovereignty (Labanyi 2019, 41–51).

Although Galdós's first two novels – *La Fontana de Oro* (1870), *El audaz* (*The Conspirator*, 1871) – were set in the capital, it was not until *La familia de León Roch* (1878) that he turned to contemporary Madrid, and only from *La desheredada* (*The Disinherited*, 1881) that he set about documenting the whole social spectrum. The period 1877–1900 saw another wave of urban growth thanks to migration from the countryside, with many cities more than doubling their population (Shubert 1990, 48). The Madrid described by Galdós is the modern consumerist city that enthralled Walter Benjamin via Baudelaire's reflections on Paris, in which people and things have gone into circulation as commodities (Fernández Cifuentes 1988).

In *La desheredada*, the mobility of the modern city permits the protagonist Isidora to traverse Madrid from the outlying lunatic asylum and rope-factory to the center with its stores and avenues, art museum, and prison. All these spaces foster circulation, whether of people (the institutions of social control aiming, theoretically, to recycle the unfit back into the system) or things (via production but especially consumption). What dazzles Isidora as a rural immigrant is a city governed by visual display. Vision is paramount since display, and not birthright or inherent value, determines status. The market economy turns things and people into signs by assigning them an abstract monetary value determined by demand. As elsewhere in Europe, anxieties about the market system are figured by the prostitute: the woman who makes herself into a commodity. Gender anxieties are at stake here: the prostitute acquires agency by entering the masculine public sphere of the market but also becomes a social outcast. Isidora's brother Mariano, as child vagrant, also inhabits the public space of the street. The coincidence of Isidora's first act of (high-class) prostitution with the 1873 declaration of the First Republic, plus Mariano's attempted assassination of Alfonso XII, link their moral decline to new lower-class political demands. The novel praises the socialist printer Juan Bou (from industrialized Catalonia) for ascribing to a bourgeois work ethic but ridicules his desire to ban property and money. Bou's socialist utopia, founded on the exchange of labor and produce, would restore persons and things to their use value, overcoming their conversion into arbitrary signs by the market – a key concern in Galdós's Madrid-based novels from *La desheredada* through *Fortunata y Jacinta* (1886–7), and again in the *Torquemada* novels (1889, 1893–5) which depict the vertiginous social ascent of a Madrid moneylender.

In criticizing an urban economy in which consumerism outweighs production, Galdós's novels feed into contemporaneous degeneracy theory, which supposed that modernity was exhausting natural energies. In the 1890s, Galdós would experiment with "saviors" (Ángel Guerra, Nazarín, Halma) who leave the city to undertake (failed) rural communitarian projects. Alas's *La Regenta*, set in a provincial capital (a fictionalized Oviedo), moves regularly between city and country. The blurring of the boundary between the two suggests that there is no "outside" to capitalist modernity: nature has been commodified whether in the city (parks and conservatories) or the country (leisure homes); the unruly working classes are within (the workers' demonstration) and without (the mines which by the 1880s had become Asturias's hallmark).

Galdós and Alas depict urban modernity from the standpoint of the bourgeois reformer, keen to avoid social revolution. Socialism was growing in the urban centers, with anarchism attracting a strong following in Catalonia and among landless peasants in the south. The start of the twentieth century saw a shift from bourgeois to socialist or anarchist perspectives. Pío Baroja's 1904–5 urban trilogy, *La lucha por la vida* (*The Struggle for Life*), depicts Madrid exclusively via the lower classes. The last novel in the trilogy, *Aurora roja* (*Red Dawn*), portrays how, in the early 1900s, workers' movements start to bypass parliamentary politics through direct action, with considerable fluidity still between anarchism and socialism. The city has become a political laboratory. However, the exploited offer few redemptive qualities, echoing contemporary studies of Madrid's *lumpenproletariat* influenced by degeneracy theory. Disillusionment with the bourgeois dream of progress impacts profoundly on perceptions of time and space. For Baroja, the city is a chaotic space of degrading poverty, in which people live from day to day, with no sense of spatial or temporal direction. Its lack of cohesion is mirrored by Baroja's impressionistic cityscapes, perceived from Madrid's bleak outskirts and echoing the paintings of his brother Ricardo.

The fascination with Madrid's shanty towns in the trilogy's first novel *La busca* (*Low Life*) is echoed in *La horda* (*The Hordes*), published the following year (1905) by the Valencian republican activist Vicente Blasco Ibáñez – better known for his rural novels, discussed below. Written when Blasco Ibáñez was living in Madrid as a republican parliamentary deputy, it ends with a utopian fantasy in which the "hordes" inhabiting the shanty towns encircling Madrid descend on the city. But, as in Blasco Ibáñez's other novels, political idealism gives way to a pessimistic view of human egoism.

The nihilism of Baroja and Blasco Ibáñez is countered by Carmen de Burgos ("Colombine") whose novel *La rampa* (*The Ramp*, 1917), focusing on the attempts of working-class women to negotiate modern urban life, stresses their agency against all the odds.

The Madrid Avant-Garde:
The Metropolis as the Shock of the New

Most of the members of the 1920s Madrid avant-garde migrated to the capital from the periphery, experiencing the modern city as the "shock of the new" (Hughes 1991). Their break with realism was anticipated by

Madrid-native Ramón Gómez de la Serna's 1914 *El Rastro*, which, following its narrator-*flâneur* round Madrid's flea market, focuses rather on the material detritus discarded by the modern city in its obsession with the new. The random juxtapositions of unwanted objects mirror the avant-garde cult of the *objet trouvé*, offering a cubist vision in which things, no longer contained by a single viewpoint, assert their autonomy by staring back at the narrator. Their lack of monetary value refuses the abstraction – conversion of material things into signs – of the market economy. They do, however, have sentimental value; the narrator stresses the human relations behind these objects (the people who have made and used them), resisting commodity fetishism (Highfill 2014).

In this text Gómez de la Serna first developed the *greguería* he would make his trademark: somewhere between the Japanese *haiku* and Lautréamont's chance encounter of an umbrella and sewing machine on a dissection table, and described by Surrealist filmmaker Luis Buñuel as the verbal equivalent of film montage. The experience of the modern city dovetails with early cinema's modes of spectatorship since both require the viewer to process a rapid succession of fragmentary visual images. The avant-garde fascination with film (Albert 2005, 407–520), introduced in the previous chapter, is most evident in texts that deal with the city. The visual distortions of Ramón del Valle-Inclán's *esperpentos*, coinciding with German expressionist cinema of the time, are linked to urban viewing habits in his avant-garde drama *Luces de bohemia* (*Bohemian Lights*, 1920, revised 1924), which uses streetlamps to bisect the mise-en-scène into geometric blocks of light and shadow, and depicts its characters via refracted café-mirror reflections.

Antonio Espina's 1927 *Pájaro pinto* (literally *Speckled Bird*, a reference to the children's nonsense rhyme "La pájara pinta") puts into practice Vertov's notion of the cine-eye as well as José Ortega y Gasset's 1925 essay *La deshumanización del arte* (*The Dehumanization of Art*), in a paradoxical coexistence of materiality and abstraction that he called "cinegrafía" (cine-writing). The text's dislocated episodes mimic experimental film montage. Its protagonist is an automaton numbed by city life, who watches his actions as if on a screen. César M. Arconada's 1928 poems *Urbe* convey everyday urban life through a montage of visual images, drawing incongruous parallels between city and country through the use of metaphor. Each poem sets up a syncopated dialogue between two rhythms – one fast (the left-hand column printed in black), the other slow (the right-hand column printed in red), simulating jazz. The poems depict typists, factory workers, office workers, with a strong eroticization of the working woman, in a landscape of motorcars, trams, trucks, factory windows, electric pylons, and power plants.

In his 1929 *Indagación al cinema* (*Inquiry into Cinema*), Francisco Ayala marveled at cinema's ability to engage popular audiences while using sophisticated montage techniques. Nonetheless, his 1930 novella *Cazador en el alba* (*Hunter in the Dawn*), while focusing on a popular protagonist (a rural migrant who makes good in the city), uses a densely metaphorical language aimed at expert readers. First published in Ortega's *Revista de Occidente*, *Cazador en el alba* illustrates Ortega's *La deshumanización del arte* in proposing a "new art" accessible only to a cultural elite. However, Ayala's text does not so much dehumanize its protagonists – the peasant Antonio Arenas and his urban girlfriend Aurora – as animate things in the city, releasing new energies. Conversely, the women Antonio sees in the city are described as technological marvels. Antonio becomes a boxer: the body as efficient machine.

A similar awe at the energies unleashed by the modern metropolis underscores Federico García Lorca's *Poeta en Nueva York* (*Poet in New York*, written 1929–30, published posthumously). Lorca's stay in New York coincided with the October 1929 Wall Street Crash, which made evident the arbitrary nature of monetary value. The poems indict the dehumanization of advanced capitalism, casting African American culture as a source of vitality stifled by the abstractions of the monetary economy, as well as by racial oppression. The equation of African Americans with the primitive – monkeys and crocodiles – associates them with a physical sensuality that, while contrasting positively with a deathly white culture, reproduces stereotypes about the animality of people of color. This is especially unfortunate given that Lorca's stay coincided with the Harlem Renaissance. In practice, Lorca's view of capitalism is ambivalent. In the poem "Danza de la muerte" (Dance of Death), an African mask invades Wall Street, representing not only the revenge of primitive natural forces on the monetary economy but also a harnessing of untamed natural energies to the equally wild energies unleashed by technology: "El ímpetu primitivo baila con el ímpetu mecánico" (The primitive beat dances with the mechanical beat). The most vital aspect of Lorca's New York poems is their rhythm, for the city sets everything in motion. The disjointed visuality of the modern city finds its maximum expression in the Surrealist montage of Lorca's 1929 filmscript, *Viaje a la luna* (*Trip to the Moon*), written in New York.

Avant-garde aesthetic effects combine with social criticism in José Díaz Fernández's 1929 novel *La Venus mecánica* (*The Mechanical Venus*), which juxtaposes the frivolity of the roaring twenties with a redemptive view of class struggle. Social commitment and avant-garde aesthetics also mark the fiction of Luisa Carnés. Self-taught and starting to work at the age of

11, Carnés would become a journalist, writer, and activist. Her novel *Tea Rooms. Mujeres obreras* (*Tea Rooms: Working Women*, 1934) offers a choral narration of the daily routines of the female employees of a Madrid tea room, capturing the fast-paced rhythms of the modern city whose leisure rituals are built on precarious female labor.

The references in Spanish avant-garde writing to modern urban leisure rituals are ubiquitous. Jazz bands are celebrated in Guillermo de la Torre's poetry collection *Hélices* (*Propellers*, 1923), and in Gómez de la Serna's "Jazzbandismo," performed by him in blackface at the 1929 screening of *The Jazz Singer* at the Cineclub Español. Spectator sports are referenced in Rafael Alberti's 1928 ode to the Hungarian Barcelona Football Club player Platko; the rugby player in Lorca's 1931 drama *Así que pasen cino años* (*When Five Years Pass*); boxing in Ayala's *Cazador en el alba*, as we have seen; and the tennis players, skaters, athletes, rowers, and swimmers in the 1920s poetry of Concha Méndez (herself a swimming champion). Her 1928 *Surtidor* (*Fountain/Gas Pump*) and 1930 *Canciones de mar y tierra* (*Songs of Sea and Land*) speak of motor cars (she drove her own), dance halls, and the fairground with its mechanical thrills. The fairground also appears in Alberti's *Cal y canto* (roughly translatable as *Bricks and Song*, 1926–7) and in Ernesto Giménez Caballero's *Julepe de menta* (*Mint Julep*, 1929) and his avant-garde film *Esencia de verbena* (*Essence of the Fairground*, 1930). Founder of the Cineclub Español and editor of the avant-garde magazine *La Gaceta Literaria*, Giménez Caballero had, in 1928, converted to fascism in Mussolini's Italy. In the 1930s, avant-garde writers on the political right would repudiate the modern city, now seen as degenerate. The early 1930s urban novels of Samuel Ros and Antonio Botín Polanco, founding members of Falange Española (Spain's fascist party, created in 1933), denounced modern technology for destroying man's soul. In *Arte y Estado* (*Art and the State*, 1935), Giménez Caballero decried as racial regression the jazz he had celebrated in *Julepe de menta*.

Barcelona: Modernity and Cosmopolitanism

The nineteenth century's last decades witnessed major political and economic shifts in modern Catalan culture, with the labor movement's emergence from clandestinity after the 1868 Revolution and the evolution in and around Barcelona of collectivist anarchism and eventually anarcho-syndicalism, together with economic prosperity. This prosperity was underpinned by the vertiginous growth of Barcelona, as it expanded beyond its constricting medieval walls. The city's rapid urban development and increasing interconnectedness with other parts of Catalonia and Spain began to reconfigure its role as an alternative capital – industrial, coastal, European-looking, and cosmopolitan – and led to diverse attempts to represent its relationship to the Catalan landscape.

If the politician and historian Víctor Balaguer had ensured that the streets of the newly built Eixample district were inscribed with the names of heroes and places associated with the Crown of Aragon's glorious past (Michonneau 2002), the promoters of the 1888 Barcelona Universal Exposition aimed to style the city as the Paris of the south (Resina 2008, 41–6). The writers and artists associated with *Modernisme* sought to move beyond the more nostalgic dispositions of the *Renaixença* to bring Catalan culture into dialogue with contemporary European ideas and trends (Marfany 1975). This generally meant a shift away from rural idealization to recognition of contemporary social progress, diversity, and inequality, mediated by readings of modern European realist and naturalist fiction, socially progressive political and educational tracts, and the theater of Ibsen, Strindberg, and even Maeterlinck. Above all, it meant that Catalan debate over the relationship between tradition and modernity was increasingly focused on Barcelona, which, together with the city's growing capacity to sustain the development of the various institutions and instruments necessary to underpin an increasingly autonomous cultural field, contributed both to exacerbate external resentment of Catalan particularism and to foment internal resistance, whether through the conservative Bases de Manresa (1892) or their more progressive precursors, the Centre Català (1882–94) and the Memorial de Greuges (Report of Grievances, 1885).

The velocity of social change and the co-existence of different temporalities began to be reflected in literary chronotopes from the 1870s onwards, in *costumbrista* chronicles like those of Emili Vilanova, influenced by the writings of Robert Robert published in satirical papers like *Un Tros de Paper* (1865–6). Yet it is above all the novels of Narcís Oller that portray the impact of the increasing abstraction of the capitalist economy on time and space. Oller, considered the most important Catalan-language novelist of the nineteenth century, was born in 1846 but did not begin to write novels in Catalan until the 1880s, influenced by the literary critics Sardà and Yxart who were concerned with Catalan culture's relationship to modernity (Yates 1998). Oller's first novel *La papallona* (*The Butterfly*, 1882) was translated into Spanish and hailed as a pioneer of Spanish literary naturalism – an evaluation questioned by Émile Zola in his introduction to the novel's French translation, who pointed to its moralizing character. Set in Barcelona, the novel only grants glimpses of the urban backdrop, characterized by the anonymous multitudes likely to have marked his own encounter with the city as a student from provincial Valls. The novels that followed center on the fictional town of Vilaniu, presenting the effects of rapid urban, economic, and technological change on provincial life, and exploring the effects of the city's increasing pull. Novels like *L'Escanyapobres* (*The Usurer*, 1884) and *Vilaniu* (1885) show how the introduction of the railway led to the bypassing of provincial towns, which descended into sleepy obsolescence or obsession with the past, and how new forms of capital accumulation led to a shift away from the more traditional family industries that had fueled Catalonia's industrial revolution. In a later protofeminist vision of the same seismic change, Dolors Monserdà's Barcelona-based *La fabricanta* (*The Female Factory Worker*, 1904) would portray a nineteenth-century working-class woman who ends up running her own factory, thus imagining an alternative genealogy for the industrial bourgeoisie.

The telescoping of temporal-spatial relations, thanks to the impact of new technologies, economic growth, and rapid urbanization on Barcelona's urban fabric, is more fully explored in Oller's *La febre d'or* (*The Gold Fever*, 1890–2), often considered his masterpiece, although it was criticized at the time for focusing on individual morality rather than the social and economic impact of the new urban environment. With its complex network of hypotextual interconnections between different characters and social strata, it presents a vision of the boom (and 1886 bust) of Catalan culture up to the 1888 Universal Exposition, exploring the effect of stock market speculation on social relationships. Its central character, a former provincial artisan who builds enormous wealth through successful ventures on the Barcelona stock exchange, represents the burgeoning class of nouveaux riches who challenged the old bourgeoisie. His fall in the novel, as a spendthrift increasingly dedicated to buying social prestige through superficial embellishments and the pursuit of false titles, is set against what for Oller was the bedrock of Catalan society: hard work and a rejection of pomposity (Resina 2008, 611). Later novels like *La bogeria* (*Madness*, 1899) and *Pilar Prim* (1906) give a greater sense of the effects of these social changes on the protagonists' psychological make-up.

If Oller's novels show the impact of nineteenth-century capitalist modernization, the literature of *Modernisme* marks the emergence of a discourse about Barcelona as a cosmopolitan city, with many of its foremost writers choosing to live in the modern Eixample rather than in the labyrinthine streets of its medieval center. In poems like Joan Maragall's "Oda nova a Barcelona" (New Ode to Barcelona, 1909), the city is constructed as "la gran encisera" (the great enchantress), a potent symbol of modern times. However, the poem also recognizes it as a space of social and cultural conflict, as do the articles Maragall wrote in response to the violence of the 1909 Tragic Week (Benet 1992). This conflictual relationship with the modern city is reflected in other writers of the period, although it is in the more politically committed writings of figures like Jaume Brossa and those associated with the anarchist movement, as well as the social drama of Juli Vallmitjana, Ignasi Iglésias, and Felip Cortiella, that we begin to see representation of the subaltern classes (Casacuberta and Gustá 2010). Vallmitjana's work in excavating the peripheral world of Barcelona's gypsies in novels like *La Xava* (*The Gypsy Girl*, 1909) and his journalistic writings in *L'Esquella de la Torratxa* (see especially number 1789 in 1913), was immensely influential on turn-of-the century visual culture and on the growing myth of the city's Districte Cinquè (Fifth District) or Barrio Chino (Chinese Quarter), as it was christened in 1925 by crime writer Francisco/Francesc Madrid (McDonagh 1987). This urban underworld would become the main focus of early twentieth-century popular fiction, with titles like Madrid's *Sangre en atarazanas* (*Blood in the Docks*, 1926), and of the emerging sensationalist press, such as *El Escándalo* – a world that is depicted in the writings of foreign visitors to the city from Henri de Montherlant to Jean Genet and Georges Bataille. Its exotic pull is central to the proliferation of urban texts in the jazz-age Barcelona of the late 1920s and 1930s (Davidson 2009), such as Josep Maria Planes' *Nits de Barcelona* (*Barcelona Nights*, 1931), Carme Montoriol's *Teresa o la vida amorosa d'una dona* (*Teresa or a Woman's Love Life*, 1932), and, most famously, Josep Maria de Sagarra's *Vida privada* (*Private Life*, 1932).

This is the world on which the writers of the *Renaixença* had turned their back in their excavation of an idealized medieval past; yet it is also a world that in the early twentieth century was distasteful to a new generation of writers focused on the professionalization of Catalan literary culture. With the increasing local hegemony of *Noucentisme* from 1906 onwards, there was an attempt to placate social conflict and resolve the tension between unruly cities and a traditional rural hinterland through a synthesis – la Catalunya Ciutat (Catalonia City) – based on notions of civility and an appeal to the values of Mediterranean classicism, as exemplified in Lliga Regionalista leader Enric Prat de la Riba's *La nacionalitat catalana* (1906); the writings of Eugeni d'Ors in the Catalan daily *La Veu de Catalunya*; the poetry of Josep Carner and Guerau de Liost, especially the latter's *La ciutat d'ivori* (*The Ivory City*, 1918); and in urbane satirical writing (Murgades 1987, 2020). In two key texts, *La ben plantada* (*The Elegant Woman*, 1911) and

Gualba la de mil veus (*Gualba of the Thousand Voices*, 1915), d'Ors explored a civilizing alternative to social fragmentation and aesthetic escapism. The former creates an ideal muse of classical proportions in Teresa, whose impeccable taste and decorum span city living with leisurely sojourns in the provinces, combining local Mediterranean and cosmopolitan roots. The latter shows the moral and social disorder visited upon the irresponsible pursuit of art for art's sake. The reaction against *Noucentisme*'s idealist call to order would emerge in the avant-garde's attack on the classical, most notoriously in the *Manifest groc* (*Yellow Manifesto*, 1928) of Salvador Dalí, Sebastià Gasch, and Lluís Montanyà, which embraced an anti-artistic urban modernity (Buffery and Caulfield 2012). It can be found also in the work of writers who combine aesthetic innovation with socially progressive ideas, such as Majorcan journalist Gabriel Alomar, a habitual collaborator in the republican press, whose 1904 lecture "El futurisme" (Futurism) pre-dated Marinetti's use of the term, and especially working-class avant-garde poet Joan Salvat-Papasseït, whose *Poemes en ondes hertzianes* (*Poems in Hertzian Waves*, 1919; illustrated by Joaquim Torres-Garcia) draw on the symbols, sounds, and spaces of the modern industrial city to call for social change (Molas et al. 2005; Keown 2008). The prose poems of J. V. Foix published in *Gertrudis* (1927) and *KRTU* (1932) sometimes evoke a phantasmagorical city, criss-crossed by chance encounters, absurd juxtapositions, and violent images (Venuti 2019). Drawn from a 1918 dream diary and thus anticipating Surrealist ideas, their syncopated glimpses of the city contrast with the long cinematic tracking shot that is the 1918 novel *Un film (3000 metres)* (*A Film [3000 meters]*) by Caterina Albert ("Víctor Català"), better known for her 1905 rural novel *Solitud* (*Solitude*), discussed below. Both provide evidence of the engagement of Catalan writers with the asynchronous rhythms of modern life.

A Provincial Nation

The repudiation of urban life is, of course, a well-established literary topos. In 1900 only a tiny fraction of Spain's population lived in cities. Historian Juan Pablo Fusi has claimed, echoing Ortega y Gasset, that Spain was entirely provincial, since even its capital was marked by a decidedly non-cosmopolitan *casticismo* (1994, 89–90).

In practice, the majority of Spain's realist novels take place in provincial towns or rural settings: Alas's *La Regenta* in a fictionalized Oviedo, as we have seen; Emilia Pardo Bazán's *Los pazos de Ulloa* (*The House of Ulloa*, 1886) and *La madre naturaleza* (*Mother Nature*, 1887) in rural Galicia and *La tribuna* (*The Tribune*, 1883) in a fictionalized La Coruña; José María de Pereda's *Peñas arriba* (*Among the Peaks*, 1895) in the Cantabrian mountains; Juan Valera's *Pepita Jiménez* (1884) in an Andalusian village. While Pedro Antonio de Alarcón's *El sombrero de tres picos* (*The Three-cornered Hat*, 1874) also takes place in an Andalusian village, his greatest success, *Diario de un testigo de la Guerra de África* (*Diary of an Eye-Witness of the African War*, 1860), depicts Spanish-occupied Tetuán in Morocco. One of the most popular writers of the time with Spanish and foreign readers, Armando Palacio Valdés, set his novels in his native Asturias, with his bestselling *La hermana San Sulpicio* (*Sister San Sulpicio*, 1889) located in Andalusia. The attitudes to the city/country binary vary hugely: for Pardo Bazán, the countryside is barbaric though she deplores the unhealthy upbringing of city women; for Valera, the ideal is the "marriage" of civilization and agriculture; for Pereda, the goal is local autonomy to maintain patriarchal community. If Madrid could serve as a metaphor for the nation, it was because it represented the contradictions of Spain's recalcitrant modernity. The capital's best chronicler, Galdós, was a native of the Canary Islands whose narrative gaze depicts it as a space both familiar and foreign. In his 1897 speech on Pereda's reception into the Spanish Royal Academy, Galdós insisted that Pereda's work, set mostly in Santander province, was no more regional than his own depiction of Madrid, for Spain was characterized by its geographic localism (Pérez Galdós 1972, 195–6). Both Galdós and Pereda considered this diversity a positive feature for writers. Pereda's traditionalist defense of regionalism was anchored in a rejection of modernity as a homogenizing process. On these grounds he lamented the lack of attention paid in Madrid to the renaissance of Catalan literature. Recent critical studies have asserted the need, when studying Spain's nineteenth century (and its literatures), to abandon the emphasis on the nation-state and on the capital as metaphor for the nation (Martí-López 2000), and to focus instead on how transcontinental mobility and colonial entanglements are always present in its multilingual cultural production (Enjuto-Rangel et al. 2019; Martí-López 2020).

   A map of regional locations depicted in literary texts of the early to mid-nineteenth century would include, for example, the "provincial" poetry of Extremadura-based Carolina Coronado and Rosalía de Castro's remarkable *Cantares gallegos* (*Galician Songs*, 1863). Gustavo Adolfo Bécquer's *Cartas desde mi celda* (*Letters from my Cell*, 1864) is considered the first cartography of what today has become known as "empty Spain": the nation's desolate, underpopulated interior (see chapter 14). In conveying to readers of Madrid's conservative newspaper *El Contemporáneo* the isolated mountainous area of Aragon where his text was written, the Andalusian Bécquer erased economic reality and social and historical change in favor of fantasy, myth, and timelessness – a frequent tendency in his *Leyendas* and the drawings of his brother Valeriano. An essentialist, ahistorical reinterpretation of Spain's rural interior can also be found in the turn to the Spanish landscape to understand the nation's cultural specificity by Miguel de Unamuno, an enthusiastic hiker whose *Por tierras de Portugal y España* (*Traversing Portugal and Spain*, 1911) and *Andanzas y visiones españolas* (*Spanish Walks and Visions*, 1922) explore the rural interior's ignored landscapes, inhabitants, and oral literature.

The concepts "provincial," "regional," and "local" often overlap and are somewhat slippery. During the Spanish *fin de siècle*, they relate directly to debates about national identity, colonialism, modernity, and cultural deficiency. Postcolonial and transatlantic critical approaches have displaced the logic of center and periphery, origin and diffusion, bringing to light circuits of cultural exchange not only between Spain and Europe but also between Spain and Latin America, Africa, and the Philippines (Tsuchiya and Acree 2016; Murray and Tsuchiya 2019). The binaries urban–rural, capital–province, metropolis–colonies, cosmopolitanism–rootedness are just some of the limiting dichotomies that have structured the study of Spanish literature of the period covered in this chapter. It is more productive, as Fredric Jameson proposes in relation to nineteenth-century realism (2013), to study such antinomies in relation to the inextricable tensions they represent.

The Critique of Rural Spain

The dire economic circumstances, as well as the social and political struggles of rural life in Extremadura, at the time an extremely poor region of Spain, are reflected in the best-known novels of the prolific and successful Felipe Trigo, *El médico rural* (*The Country Doctor*, 1912) and *Jarapellejos* (1914), the latter ironically subtitled *Vida arcádica, feliz e independiente de un español representativo* (*Arcadian, Happy, Independent Life of a Representative Spaniard*). Both texts focus on the dire circumstances of the region's peasants, in which they were ensnared by *caciquismo* (the control of local political bosses), *latifundismo* (the monopoly of land ownership by large landowners), and hostility to change caused by both of these as well as the Church. The region's backwardness would be notoriously portrayed in Luis Buñuel's pseudo-documentary *Las Hurdes. Tierra sin pan* (*Land without*

Bread, 1933). In his Valencian rural novels, Vicente Blasco Ibáñez deploys regionalism without the romanticized filters of Pereda, Valera, or Palacio Valdés. *Cañas y barro* (*Reeds and Mud*, 1902) recreates the beauty of the Valencian landscape and the region's ancestral popular traditions, while also revealing extreme poverty, patriarchy, violence, and ignorance. In keeping with his radical republican activism, these are depicted as the result of social and economic factors, including abusive working conditions, lack of education, and control by a few of the resources on which the livelihood of entire communities depend. The most negative character (Cañamel, owner of the town's tavern) spent years as a civil guard in Cuba and is described as coming from Castilian-speaking lands. Valencian agriculture was a model of efficiency compared to Andalusia, as depicted in Blasco Ibáñez's *La bodega* (*The Winery*, 1909) set in Jerez, which tackles the region's agrarian problem: the existence of large estates (often under-cultivated) with absentee or abusive landowners and a population of landless seasonal workers.

A key author for the depiction of "empty Spain" is Concha Espina, who in 1914, already a recognized author and journalist, published *La esfinge maragata* (*Mariflor*). Espina's alignment from 1934 with the Falange (Spanish fascist party) and her unabashed Catholicism have led to a one-dimensional interpretation of her multifaceted career. Her writings always adhered to a conservative view of culture, social order, and the Spanish nation, but they also overtly denounced social injustice, with particular emphasis on the situation of women.

La esfinge maragata recounts the journey of Florinda / Mariflor, raised in a Galician coastal town, to her father's birthplace in the Maragatería (León) on his emigration to Argentina to save the family from bankruptcy. He hopes Florinda will help solve the family's economic problems by marrying an older, wealthy cousin. On the train to León, she encounters a young poet, Terán, and they fall in love. Their literary projections onto the fleeting landscape from the train (the quintessential symbol of modernization) are demolished by Florinda's discovery that her family homeland is an impoverished, arid terrain inhabited only by women, children, and older men since adult males have had to emigrate to the city or overseas. Espina establishes a link between the natural and human environments, both abandoned, both oppressed. The novel adopts the perspective, typical of the regional novel, of an external gaze trying to make sense of unfamiliar territory. But there will be no idyllic reconciliation or break with the new environment. Despite her impulse to rebel, Florinda, faced with her family's imminent ruin, agrees to marry her cousin. What determines her decision is acknowledgment of her role in a community of women who, despite their destiny as female serfs, forge bonds of solidarity and resilience.

Espina's later novel *El metal de los muertos* (*The Metal of the Dead*, 1920) recreates the 1917 miners' strike in Río Tinto (Huelva), where the British owners of the Río Tinto Company Limited exercised colonial rule over the local population, from which they were separated physically (by a wall), legally (by armed guards and surveillance mechanisms), and culturally (the area followed British customs and calendar). The only presence of the absentee Spanish state is the Civil Guard's patrol of the main roads. As in *La esfinge maragata*, *El metal de los muertos* relates the exploitation of the local population to the destruction of the natural environment, which Espina again figures in gendered terms: the mining is compared to a recurrent act of rape that leaves the land sterile. Exploration of the rural interior did not lead Espina to abstract meditations on the nation's essence, as in many male-authored narratives, but to broken bodies, ruined communities, and a destroyed landscape.

Symbolist Poetics and the Catalan Landscape

The Catalan rural novel of the period too was shaped by the changing relationship between tradition and modernity, presenting a corrective to previous idealized visions of Catalonia's landscape (Castellanos 1983). Novels like Raimon Casellas's *Els sots feréstecs* (*Dark Vales*, 1901), Joaquim Ruyra's *Marines i boscatges* (*Sea Paintings and Forestscapes*, 1903), Marian Vayreda's *La punyalada* (*The Stabbing*, 1904), Prudenci Bertrana's *Josafat* (1906) set in Girona but confronting rural savagery with the superficial containment of urban civilization, and Josep Pous i Pagès's *La vida i la mort de Jordi Fraginals* (*The Life and Death of Jordi Fraginals*, 1912) focus on the often harsh relationship between the Catalan landscape and its inhabitants, frequently trapped in past customs and primitive superstition. However, rather than embracing the determinism associated with European naturalism, these novels prefer a Symbolist aesthetic that privileges the overcoming of tensions and contradictions through the individual artist's poetic vision (Castellanos 2013). They also tend to objectify female characters, who are troublingly excessive in their sensual abandonment. The depiction of the Catalan landscape becomes central to exploring the nature of Catalan identity and its relationship to modern forms; no longer representing a nostalgic looking back to a more harmonious past, it offers a more melancholic and often tragic reflection of spatio-temporal disjunction. If in Àngel Guimerà's play *Terra baixa* (*Lowlands*, 1896) we already witness the encounter between urban poverty and provincial hypocrisy, conflict is heightened in Caterina Albert's extraordinary 1905 *Solitud* (*Solitude*).

Better known by her penname, Víctor Català, Albert is considered one of the most influential Catalan writers of the twentieth century; *Solitud* has been described as the Catalan *Pedro Páramo* (Bosch 2009). From a family of rural landowners in the fishing village of L'Escala, Albert was largely self-educated and for a long time rejected Pompeu Fabra's codification of the Catalan language, placing her in conflict with the *Noucentista* ideals of the twentieth century's first decades. Her early fiction, like that of other novelists associated with *Modernisme*, depicts the individual's struggle against a brutal rural world, focusing, however, on the often violent marginalization of women and the effects of contemporary social, economic, and political conditions on the development of female subjectivities. The central character of *Solitud* is forced into extreme physical isolation and psychological introspection when her husband takes a post in the mountains. Mila's sensual response to her environment, transmitted through the novel's exploration of bodily changes and the eroticization of a landscape that is marked as female (Bartrina 2001), contrasts with the *Modernista* concern with the male artist's capacity to impose aesthetic order on a chaotic reality. With its narrative condensation and often disconcerting combination of Symbolism and psychological realism, Albert's novel is an unprecedented exploration of the imbrications between gender, nation, and landscape that will provide a model for many of the Catalan women writers discussed in chapter 12. As with Concha Espina, it is a woman writer who is most able to critically probe the dark side of rural Spain through heightened attention to the relation between the female body and the land.

8

The Nation Called into Question (1890s–1920s)

Turn-of-the-century Spain saw an unprecedented questioning of the state of the nation, exacerbated by the loss in 1898 of its remaining colonies in the Caribbean, South-East Asia, and the Pacific (Cuba, Puerto Rico, the Philippines, Guam) in devastating naval defeats by the United States off Manila and Santiago de Cuba – a political and cultural crisis that anticipated the wider European crisis of humanism in the wake of World War I. This chapter will be concerned with the soul-searching resulting (largely) from this humiliation, which made Spain a second-class citizen of Europe at a time when other European powers were carving up the globe. To compensate, Spain would embark on a wave of Spanish colonial expansion in Morocco, Western Sahara, and the Gulf of Guinea. The nationalist pro-war sentiment that flooded the Spanish press was fueled by the dependence on Cuban, Puerto Rican, or Philippine markets of economic elites, who could buy their sons out of military conscription, and by fear that the emergent sub-state nationalisms would use the Cuban and Philippine independence struggles to further their own aspirations. Indeed, Spain's diminished geopolitical status reinforced the loss of trust in the Spanish state by many thinkers in the historic nationalities, politicizing the cultural revivals in those territories. The strong feelings aroused by opposing nationalisms have made the literary history of this period susceptible to simplifications.

The first such simplification is the division of writers into members of the "1898 Generation" (defined by concern with the situation of Spain) and *Modernistas* (rough Spanish equivalent of Symbolists, seen as influenced by transnational aesthetic trends). This categorization has long been criticized for dissociating the aesthetic from the political – a dissociation that further separated Spanish-language *Modernismo* (Latin American and Spanish), seen as a renovation of literary form, from Catalan *Modernisme*, recognized as an expression of post-1888 Barcelona's turn toward European (particularly French) modern projects. But the "father" of Latin American *Modernismo*, Rubén Darío, praised Catalan *Modernisme*, whose cultural nationalism he appreciated (Martí-Monterde 2016); Darío's own work, like that of many

Latin American *Modernistas*, reflects critically on capitalist modernization and cultural imperialism. The term "1898 Generation" was coined by one of its members, Azorín (penname of José Martínez Ruiz), in 1912. José Ortega y Gasset is generally seen as a member of the "1914 Generation" but he shares many concerns with earlier writers. This chapter treats the period from the 1890s to the 1920s as a continuum since all the writers discussed are concerned with Spain's place in the world.

A key feature of the turn of the century was the emergence of the intellectual as an arbiter of public opinion, whose views on the state of the nation were disseminated via the press (Serrano 2000; Juliá 2004, 9–20; Martínez del Campo 2018). Intellectuals created nationalist sentiment by making the nation – whether Spain or the historic nationalities – the object of public interest. From around 1890, the *ensayo* (essay) blossomed as a major journalistic genre. Political thinkers had contributed to public opinion since the late eighteenth-century beginnings of the periodical press (see chapter 3); what was distinct about the turn-of-the-century intellectuals was their rejection of the central state and national party politics, presenting themselves as independent thinkers. The birth of the European intellectual is generally attributed to the 1898 Dreyfus Affair in France. This was predated by the Spanish equivalent, the 1896–7 Montjuïc Affair: the national and international press outcry – including protests by Miguel de Unamuno, Pío Baroja, Ramiro de Maeztu, and Azorín – over the torture in Montjuïc fortress of anarchists unjustly accused of bombing the Barcelona Corpus Christi procession, plus the ensuing persecution of many Catalan republicans. By the 1930s, the position of the independent intellectual had become untenable, forcing writers of all political persuasions to commit to a particular political grouping (see chapter 9). Few of those who had proclaimed themselves independent intellectuals at the turn of the century negotiated that transition successfully.

Turn-of-the-century Crisis

The term "1898 Generation" refers to those turn-of-the-century writers whose work is seen as determined by Spain's 1898 defeat by the United States, known within Spain as "el Desastre" (the Disaster). Until recently, its members have generally been listed as Unamuno, Ángel Ganivet, Baroja, Azorín, and Maeztu; sometimes Antonio Machado; less often Ramón del Valle-Inclán. The term "generation" is unhelpful since Baroja, Azorín, and Maeztu's collaboration in radical protests and journals was mostly limited to 1901, with their trajectories diverging after 1905; their relationship with Unamuno, Machado, and Valle-Inclán was never close. This all-male cast omits the numerous women writers who addressed similar concerns about the state of Spain: Blanca de los Ríos, Rosario de Acuña, Emilia Pardo Bazán, Concha Espina, Carmen de Burgos, Carmen Baroja, María Goyri, María de Maeztu, among others.

For the so-called "1898 Generation," that date was only one (especially traumatic) moment in a longer trajectory. Unamuno's study of Spain's historical decline, *En torno al casticismo* (*On Tradition*, 1895), and almost all Ganivet's work were written before 1898, while discussion of decadence and regeneration goes back to at least the 1880s. Such concerns – like worries about degeneration elsewhere in Europe – were bound up with racial, gender, and class anxieties. With the boundaries of the nation redrawn by military defeat, the symbolic withdrawal to rural central Spain – whose backwardness was explicitly attributed by Ganivet to empire's draining of the nation's energies – was a retreat from cultural, racial, and linguistic contact zones. The resulting *abulia* (loss of will) diagnosed by Ganivet is represented as a crisis of masculinity in the novels of Unamuno, Baroja, and Azorín, whose male protagonists lack direction.

The wider debate on the state of the nation took many forms and positions, spanning popular and high culture, and celebrating, condoning, or questioning empire. The popular stage of the 1880s and 1890s saw a vogue for blackface *zarzuelas* and *sainetes*, in Castilian and Catalan, which used Afro-Cuban characters as butts of humor to bolster a sense of white superiority (Soria 2019). In Acuña's play *La voz de la patria* (*The Voice of the Fatherland*, 1892), an Aragonese mother opposes her son's enlisting to fight in the 1893–4 Melilla War, challenging the meaning of patriotism, honor, and national glory. Pardo Bazán's press articles *De siglo a siglo* (*From One Century to Another*, 1902) deplore Spain's declaration of war on the United States but support empire from a position of white superiority. The fantasy of a bounded nation is undermined in several late nineteenth-century realist novels by the use of *indiano* characters (returnee emigrants to the Americas) whose new riches produce a kind of reverse colonialism. Galdós's novels critique Spain's colonial project by using Cuba and the Philippines as a dumping ground for his unsavory characters. Even after 1898, popular erotic fiction is shaped by an enduring coloniality in the fondness for exotic locations, as in Felipe Trigo's bestselling début novel *Las ingenuas* (*The Ingenues*, 1901), set in the Philippines.

In fact, with the exception of Maeztu's *Hacia otra España* (*Towards Another Spain*, 1899), the writers labeled as the "1898 Generation" wrote little about "the Disaster." What concerned them was the broader issue of the moral bankruptcy of the Restoration regime instituted in 1875. The critique of the Restoration was, in turn, part of a Europe-wide questioning of liberal democracy that would become acute after World War I, when various non-democratic political options, of right and left, emerged. This, in turn, went back to Bénédict Morel's 1857 *Treatise on Degeneracy*, compounded by Max Nordau's 1892 *Degeneration*, which feared that excessive modernization was producing a retrogression to an earlier stage of evolutionary development. Constancio Bernaldo de Quirós and José María Llanas Aguilaniedo's ethnographic study of degenerate "types," *La mala vida de Madrid (Madrid Low Life*, 1901), was a source for Baroja's novel *La busca (Low Life*, 1904).

Another label for the so-called "1898 Generation" is *regeneracionistas*. This links their work to the Krausist reform movement of the 1870s–1890s, concerned to moralize the population through education. Denunciation of the Restoration political system for its endemic *caciquismo* (rigging of elections by local political bosses) was common to late nineteenth-century realist novelists of all political persuasions. In the case of turn-of-the-century literary authors, the term "regenerationist" is largely inappropriate since, apart from Maeztu, they do not propose practical solutions. Those who did so were professionals: the mining engineer Lucas Mallada, the geographer Ricardo Macías Picavea, and the lawyer Joaquín Costa who advocated collectivist solutions and educational reform, as well as irrigation and reforestation schemes. The label "regenerationist" could be extended to Catalan political thinkers such as Enric Prat de la Riba and Francesc Cambó, whose proposals for a regionalist restructuring aimed to make Catalonia an economic driver for a revitalized Spain (Cacho Viu 1998).

The overwhelming focus by literary authors on spiritual rather than material solutions has a geopolitical explanation. The 1898 disaster is the lynchpin that connects the concern with Spain's decadence to the broader crisis of European liberal democracy. The Spanish–American War marked an epochal shift in the world system, with the United States' entry onto the world stage as an imperial power ending the period of Western European hegemony instituted in 1492. Spain's defeat in 1898 was a crucial factor in the "decline of the West" that Spengler would proclaim in his 1918–22 work of that name. This epochal shift was a challenge not just to Western Europe's political and economic hegemony but also to the "universality" of European culture. When certain turn-of-the-century Spanish writers talk of the "universality" of Spanish culture and of the possibility of Spain offering a cultural model for Europe, they are positing Spain as a repository of universal European values that are under threat from a new technological and capitalist model of modernity epitomized by the United States. Other writers would look to France or Germany as a repository of European values felt to be lacking in Spain.

What united all Spanish writers was hostility to the utilitarian conception of modernity attributed to the United States. This led to exaltations of "brotherhood" between Spanish and Spanish American writers in the face of a common enemy – an imagined spiritual community that would by the late 1920s come to be called *hispanidad* (Hispanicity). From the 1930s, the term *hispanidad* would be commandeered for a reactionary Spanish nationalist agenda, of which the major expression is Maeztu's 1934 *Defensa de la hispanidad* (*Defense of Hispanicity*). Maeztu's aim is to vindicate Spain's historical role in bringing Christian salvation to all peoples; Spain must join forces with the European Catholic right to stop Latin Americans from looking to the Soviet Union or the United States. In its origins, however, *hispanidad* referred to an imagined spiritual community in which the writers associated with Latin American *Modernismo* played a central role. As the first Latin American literary movement to exert an influence on Spain, *Modernismo* was conceived as a New World aesthetic hegemony formulated in opposition to the rival threat of New World technological and commercial hegemony represented by the United States. This – forcefully expressed in the Uruguayan essayist Enrique Rodó's *Ariel* (1900), praised by Unamuno – supposed that a now independent Latin America was taking up the torch of European civilization that was faltering in the Old World. Thus, Latin American *Modernistas*, like their Catalan counterparts, looked to Paris as a source of cultural modernity able to counter the new "Yankee" imperial threat. The rise of peripheral nationalisms was part of the larger remapping of centers and margins signaled by the emergence of the United States and Latin America as new sources of political and cultural influence respectively.

The Problem of Castile

The most practical turn-of-the-century writer was Maeztu from industrial Bilbao, who had in 1891–4 worked in Cuba in the family sugar mill and a tobacco factory. His trajectory from youthful admiration for Nietzsche to authoritarianism was held together by a lifelong belief in the need to develop an industrial bourgeoisie. *Hacia otra España* was published during his early Madrid years when he wrote for the republican and socialist press. The lesson he draws from Spain's defeat by the United States is that

Spaniards must overcome their aversion to capitalist enterprise. He attributes separatist urges at home to the lack of development of Castile, whose political control is resented by an industrialized Catalonia and Basque Country. The capitalist enterprise of those regions is proposed as a national model; the answer will not come from politicians or spiritual solutions. His years in London in 1905–19 led him to advocate a kind of guild socialism, melding capitalist enterprise with Catholic values, anticipating the Opus Dei technocrats of 1960s Spain (Villacañas Berlanga 2000). Swinging to the far right, he served in General Primo de Rivera's civilian directory in 1927 and in 1931 founded Acción Católica, modeled on Charles Maurras's Action Française. He was executed in Republican Madrid at the start of the Civil War for supporting insurrection.

The spiritual response to Spain's decadence that Maeztu criticized in 1899 is exemplified by Ganivet and Unamuno. The former's *Idearium español* (1897) triggered his 1898 public correspondence with Unamuno (book version *El porvenir de España* / *The Future of Spain*, 1912), coinciding with Spain's military debacle. Ganivet's views are riven with contradictions. While arguing that Spain's imperial ventures in the Americas and Europe have drained its energies, leading to national lethargy (*abulia*), and that it should now turn inwards to recuperate its strength, he praises Spain's evangelization of the Americas as a selfless enterprise, unlike the mercantile British empire. He blames Spain's historical decline on the foreign Habsburg dynasty for ending the municipal freedoms of Castile, allowing him to posit Castile as the embodiment of a Spanish national character (independence, defined on geographical rather than historical grounds) that lies intact waiting to be reactivated. Having argued that Spain's imperial ventures were a mistake, he concludes that the nation's future lies in its spiritual influence over a fraternity of Spanish-speaking peoples and in the colonization of Africa. This "civilizing mission" is implemented in Ganivet's 1897 novel *La conquista del reino de Maya por el último conquistador español Pío Cid* (*Conquest of the Kingdom of Maya by the Last Spanish Conquistador Pío Cid*), whose narrator-protagonist imposes himself as advisor to a Rwandan tribal ruler, introducing liberal reforms but sanctioning violence. Its 1898 sequel, *Los trabajos del infatigable creador Pío Cid* (*The Labors of the Indefatigable Creator Pío Cid*), narrates Pío Cid's regeneration attempts back in Spain, ending with his vision of himself leading an Arab army to free the African peoples from the corrupting yoke of Europe. The endorsement of the man of action in these novels anticipates the rise of charismatic political figures after World War I.

In his correspondence with Unamuno in *El porvenir de España*, Ganivet rejects economic solutions for idealism, while Unamuno denounces imperialism as material greed. Unamuno's solution is the communitarian ethos of the common people, continuing the message of *En torno al casticismo*, serialized in the regenerationist journal *La España Moderna* in 1895 (book version 1902). *En torno* already gestures towards his break with Marxism in favor of a renewed spirituality after his 1897 mental breakdown. Rejecting positivist historiography, it dismisses "superficial" historical events (the choppy ocean waves) for the nation's "eternal tradition" or "intrahistory" (the still ocean bed): that is, the emotional sediment accrued over time that shapes a nation's belief system. This is a theorization of historical memory. Underlying the concept of an "eternal tradition" is the search for common values that can provide a basis for collective life, by contrast with the attention given in political histories to particularities, which Unamuno sees as exclusionary; hence his plea for Spain to open itself to Europe. *En torno* excoriates the exclusionary features of the Spanish national character (egocentric individualism, religious uniformity and intolerance, adherence to a rigid honor code) enshrined in Golden Age drama, advocating instead the inner self-questioning of the Spanish mystics.

Unamuno's search in *En torno* for common values supposes a concept of national unity, with Castilian culture at its core. On the one hand, he argues that true unity requires the recognition of diversity, endorsing a dialectical concept of history driven by the tension between opposing forces. In this respect, he finds positive the rise of regionalist sentiments and the cosmopolitan urges they entail. On the other hand, he insists that regionalist sentiments must not be exclusionary. This means that the nation-state must prevail. A native of Bilbao, he supported study of the Basque language and customs but criticized Sabino Arana's Basque nationalism for its Catholic traditionalism and exclusionary rejection of Castilian-speaking immigrants to industrial Bilbao. He opposed Arana's standardization of Basque since it ignored popular usage, implying that Basque is suitable for the expression of local but not universal concerns; hence his controversial 1901 speech proclaiming Basque a language unable to adapt to modernity. In the 1932 parliamentary debates on the Catalan Autonomy Statute, under the Republic, Unamuno opposed Catalan nationalism for being exclusionary.

Unamuno's 1897 mental breakdown led to a rejection of Europeanization, equated with rationalism and technological modernization, in favor of faith as the basis of self and community. Remaining hostile to Catholicism, he proposed an ethics based on faith, elaborated in *Del sentimiento tragico de la vida* (*The Tragic Sense of Life*, serialized in *La España Moderna*, 1911–12, book version 1913). A better translation would be *The Tragic Feeling of Life* for the book is a passionate defense of the primacy of emotion. Unamuno defines life as agonistic: a struggle to maintain faith against all reason. This is a performative concept of identity, in which one creates a self through the will to be. It is inherently tragic because one's will to be conflicts with that of others. This is the dilemma faced by the protagonists ("agonists") of Unamuno's literary works – notably the novel *Abel Sánchez* (1917) and play *El otro* (*The Other*, written 1926, published and performed 1932) – written mostly in 1914–21 after being dismissed as Rector of Salamanca University and in 1927–9 while exiled in France. (See chapter 5 for his 1897 *Paz en la guerra*.) Their absurdism and self-reflexivity – most apparent in *Niebla* (*Fog*, 1914) and *Cómo se hace una novela* (*The Making of a Novel*, 1927) – align them with European modernism. They can also be read as reflections on a self-doubting masculinity or, in *La tía Tula* (*Aunt Tula*, 1921), on a Catholic-induced female fear of sexuality. *San Manuel Bueno, mártir* (*Saint Manuel Bueno, Martyr*), published a month before the April 1931 declaration of the Republic, whose priest protagonist conceals his loss of faith to his parishioners, suggests that the individual realizes himself through community.

After his 1897 mental breakdown, Unamuno continued to be involved with workers' associations (Rabaté and Rabaté 2009). One of the few intellectuals to oppose General Primo de Rivera's 1923 coup, his return from exile in 1930 met with a multitudinous reception. Elected for the Republican-Socialist Coalition at the 1931 municipal elections that brought down the monarchy, it was Unamuno who declared the Republic from the balcony of Salamanca's City Hall. An active parliamentary deputy 1931–3, he began from 1932 to criticize what he saw as the Republic's drift towards intolerance and, to the consternation of many, welcomed Franco's July 1936 military coup. Faced with the execution of colleagues and friends in Salamanca, he denounced the Nationalists at the October 1936 Día de la Raza celebration at Salamanca University, where Franco had reappointed him as Rector, provoking the Africanist general Millán Astray's famous outcry "¡Abajo los intelectuales! ¡Viva la muerte!" (Down with Intellectuals! Long Live Death!). He died two months later under effective house arrest.

A Basque like Unamuno, Baroja similarly declared the Basque language unsuited to modernity and criticized Basque nationalism for its Catholicism, links with Carlism, and racist rejection of immigrants, while praising a supposed Basque racial disposition to action as an antidote to the degenerate Latin or Semitic character of other Spaniards, in particular Catalans whose culture he dismissed as superficial. His ideas on degeneration are expressed in his Castile-focused novels *Camino de perfección* (*Way of Perfection*, 1902), *César o nada* (*Caesar or Nothing*, 1910), and *El árbol de la ciencia* (*The Tree of Knowledge*, 1911); the first of these starts by denouncing the sexual inversion resulting from urban modernity, with predatory females emasculating enervated men. But the rural interior provides no antidote. Castile is written off as irremediably hostile to change; his protagonists fail to become men of action – a pessimism offset by lyrical descriptions of the Castilian landscape. Baroja's colonial fable *Paradox, rey* (*Paradox Rules*, 1906) charts the implantation in the Gulf of Guinea of an anarchist utopia rejecting parliamentary democracy, ended by the invading French colonial army. His mix of anarchism and admiration for the political strongman did not fit either side in the Spanish Civil War.

Perhaps the most "angry young man" of the period was the young Azorín; from 1905, however, he moved to the right. In his anarchist phase (1895–7), he defended revolution and translated Kropotkin. After 1897, his work expresses a disillusioned anger, with despondency prevailing from his 1901 *Diario de un enfermo* (*Diary of an Invalid*). His best-known novels – *La voluntad* (*Will*, 1902), *Antonio Azorín* (1903), and *Las confesiones de un pequeño filósofo* (*Confessions of a Minor Philosopher*, 1904) – center on the semi-autobiographical character Antonio Azorín, whose last name he took as his penname. They portray a desolate, backward Castile stifled by a repressive Catholicism, to which the lethargic protagonist succumbs. His travel literature written for the press – *La ruta de don Quijote* (*The Route of Don Quixote*, 1905), *Los pueblos: Ensayos sobre la vida provinciana* (*Provincial Life*, 1905), and *Castilla* (*Castile*, 1912) – expresses a melancholic attachment to a land without hope. Only in "La Andalucía trágica" (Tragic Andalusia; included in *Los pueblos*) does he capture the revolutionary anger of the landless; elsewhere, aestheticization preempts protest. From a Catalan-speaking village in Alicante, Azorín was, of the writers discussed so far, the most sympathetic to linguistic and cultural diversity.

Although a contemporary of Maeztu, Baroja, and Azorín (Ganivet and Unamuno were some ten years older), Antonio Machado, born in 1875, came to the topic of Spain's decadence late in his 1912 *Campos de Castilla* (*Castilian Earth*; expanded in later editions). His early Symbolist-influenced poetry, *Soledades, Galerías, Otros Poemas* (*Solitudes, Galleries, Other Poems*, 1907) – written 1899–1902 during stays in Paris – anticipates his later poetry in its interest in folksong, inherited from his folklorist father Demófilo. *Campos de Castilla* evokes Castile's past imperial hegemony via its harsh landscape, contrasting its warrior past with present-day provincial apathy. The folk wisdom expressed in the ballad "La tierra de Alvargonzález" (Alvargonzález's Land) is developed in the "Proverbios y cantares" (Proverbs and Folksongs) sections of this book and his 1917 *Nuevas canciones* (*New Songs*; expanded in later editions). For Machado, a lifelong high-school teacher, education is not about imparting expert knowledge to an ignorant populace but about developing the knowledge they already have. In 1919, as a teacher in Segovia (till 1931), he co-founded its Universidad Popular (People's University).

From 1924 Machado switched largely to prose, with the aphoristic pronouncements of his heteronyms, Abel Martín and Juan de Mairena, presented in *De un cancionero apócrifo* (*From an Apocryphal Songbook*, 1924–6). They propose an ethics based on dialogue and collective authorship. Machado would be a member of the governing body of the Misiones Pedagógicas (Pedagogical Missions) set up by the Republic in 1931 to take culture to the rural hinterland (see chapter 9). His respect for folk culture as a form of knowledge allowed him, unlike the intellectuals discussed so far, to make the transition to political commitment to the Republic, participating fully in its wartime cultural project and dying shortly after crossing the French border into exile in February 1939. Nonetheless, he refused to join a political party, insisting on the need to create self-questioning individuals. In contrast to the elitism of most early twentieth-century Spanish intellectuals, Machado can be considered an example of the organic intellectual theorized by Gramsci in his contemporaneous *Prison Notebooks* (1929–35): the intellectual identified with an emergent class or group who gives voice to their not yet fully articulated thoughts and feelings.

All the writers discussed so far focus on Castile's failings. While rejecting it as a model, they continue to see it as the key to the nation's future, sidelining the sub-state nationalisms that were becoming increasingly vocal.

An Idiosyncratic Critique of the Nation: The Case of Valle-Inclán

While critiquing national politics, Valle-Inclán never wrote about Castile. Much of his work is set in his native Galicia but he had no involvement with the Galician regionalist movement; when it morphed into Galician nationalism in the 1920s, he abandoned Galician settings. The only constant in his work is his critique of bourgeois modernity, embodied by the moral bankruptcy of the Restoration; its stylistic corollary was a rejection of realism for the cultivation of aesthetic effects. That critique would take him in many directions, including Carlism, an interest in popular culture (rural and urban), anarchism, and in his last days admiration for Mussolini. His only active political involvement was with Carlism, especially in the period 1908–15. What held together his sympathies for authoritarian solutions and anarchism was his rejection of liberal democracy. Most of his plays were not performed in his lifetime but, despite his bohemian protestations of poverty, he was well paid for the work he published in the press or in the contemporary cheap novella series; his late 1920s experimental novels sold well, and his early *Sonatas* were enduring bestsellers (Alberca 2015, 479–88).

Valle-Inclán's links with pro-absolutist Carlism – expressed in his 1905 *Sonata de invierno* (*Winter Sonata*), 1908–9 novel trilogy *La guerra carlista* (*The Carlist War*), and his 1911 drama *Voces de gesta* (*Epic Voices*) – continued till at least 1931 when he received a Carlist decoration. Yet, throughout his life he mixed in progressive circles, including the *tertulia* of republican leader Manuel Azaña. Like Unamuno, he was one of the few Spanish intellectuals to reject Primo de Rivera's dictatorship from the start; his 1927 play *La hija del capitán* (*The Captain's Daughter*) was confiscated for satirizing Primo's coup. In 1931, under the Republic, he stood as unsuccessful election candidate for Lerroux's Radical Republican Party. When, in early 1933, Republican president Azaña named him Director of the Spanish Academy in Rome, he dismayed his paymasters by praising Mussolini in interviews (Alberca 2015, 603–5).

The rejection of bourgeois values is expressed in the nostalgic aristocratic atmosphere of his early *Sonatas* (1902–5), presented as the memoirs of the aging Casanova figure, the Marquis of Bradomín. Their decadent eroticism and cosmopolitanism (set in Italy, Mexico, Galicia, and Carlist Navarre) echo *Modernismo*, which Valle-Inclán had imbibed in Mexico in 1892–3. His fiction and drama set in an archaic rural Galicia, written 1904–9, combine nostalgia for local community with exaltation of a feudal aristocracy that places itself above the law. Decadence is the result of incipient modernization, fostering economic greed. This archaic Galicia is aestheticized through its millenarian popular religiosity (very different from the fundamentalist Catholicism of Carlism). On his death bed in January 1936, Valle-Inclán refused religious rites; he was given a civil burial.

The 1919 play *Divinas palabras* (*Divine Words*, performed 1934) returns to this archaic rural Galicia, but the aesthetic effects are now grotesque as the villagers squabble over profitable exhibition rights to a hydrocephalic child. The *esperpento* formula (aesthetics of systematic distortion) that Valle-Inclán developed in the 1920s uses dehumanization as an instrument of trenchant social critique. The theorization of the *esperpento* in *Luces de bohemia* (1920, revised 1924) as taking the classical hero for a walk down Madrid's Callejón del Gato, known for its distorting mirrors, creates an aesthetics of dissonance by subjecting high art to the crude buffoonery of popular street entertainment. (For his use of cinematic effects, see chapter 6.) The three plays re-issued in 1930 as *Martes de carnaval* (a play on words translatable as "Carnival Gods of War") – *Los cuernos de don Friolera* (*Lieutenant Friolera's Horns*, 1921, revised 1925), *Las galas del difunto* (*The Dead Man's Finery*, 1926), *La hija del capitán* – mock the military, linking them to the former colonial wars in Cuba and the Philippines, in overt provocation of Primo de Rivera's military dictatorship.

The 1924 edition of *Luces* added two scenes with a Catalan anarchist prisoner, referencing Primo's brutal repression of anarcho-syndicalism in Barcelona in 1922–3. The anarchist's dream of revolutionary destruction of the bourgeoisie is echoed by Bakunin who appears in the *Ruedo Ibérico* series' unfinished third novel, *Baza de espadas* (*Trick of Spades*, 1932). The grotesque linguistic pyrotechnics of the *Ruedo Ibérico* trilogy (1927–32) mock the Bourbon monarch Isabel II and the bourgeois generals who depose her in equal doses.

Ortega y Gasset and the *Revista de Occidente*

The philosopher Ortega y Gasset is distinguished from the previous generation of intellectuals – largely of petty bourgeois origin – by his social class, coming from a family of press magnates: his maternal grandfather was founding editor of the liberal daily *El Imparcial* (1867–1933) and top illustrated weekly *La Ilustración Española y Americana* (1869–1921); his father became *El Imparcial*'s editor from 1900, having directed its literary supplement since 1879. This pedigree gave Ortega a confidence in his public role that contrasts with his predecessors' pessimism. And yet Ortega's political ventures were short-lived failures. His key contribution was as a cultural entrepreneur facilitating the dissemination of ideas through his many journalistic and publishing endeavors.

Having studied philosophy in Germany in 1905–7, Ortega promoted Europeanization. His first book *Meditaciones del Quijote* (*Meditations on the Quixote*, 1914) argues that Spain should not forget its Germanic (Visigoth) inheritance (profound and intellectual), seen as superior to its Mediterranean (Latin) roots (superficial and sensual). His advocacy in this book of the nation's return to primal racial origins enabled the future founder of the Spanish fascist party, José Antonio Primo de Rivera, to declare himself his disciple. Ortega was, however, a lifelong defender of secular liberal democracy. By this he meant acceptance by the uneducated majority of rule by a select minority. His vision of himself as mentor of the masses went down badly with the Socialist Party to which he made overtures in 1909–10. His first political initiative was his 1913 foundation of the short-lived Liga de Educación Política (League of Political Education) as a national forum of the best minds outside the political party system. Moving on to create the political magazine *España* (1915), he abandoned that for the one-man journal *El Espectador* (1916–34). Much more significant was his contribution to the liberal daily *El Sol*, founded with his help in 1917, which would serialize his major works *España invertebrada* (*Invertebrate Spain*, 1920, book version 1921) and *La rebelión de las masas* (*The Revolt of the Masses*, 1929–30, book version 1930). Both argue that Spain's problem is the masses' lack of respect for the ruling minority: *España invertebrada* attributes this to Spain's weak feudalism, meaning that the people never learnt to obey; *La rebelión*, written when communism and fascism were in the ascendant, sees it as a Europe-wide phenomenon. It is hard not to read this as Ortega's explanation of his personal failure to achieve intellectual leadership in the political sphere.

This elitism helps understand why Ortega initially supported General Primo de Rivera's 1923–30 military dictatorship. From 1929, however, he became a vocal opponent of the dictatorship and the monarchy that supported it and, in 1931, co-founded the Agrupación al Servicio de la República (Association in Support of the Republic) to push for the monarchy's end. Elected to Congress for the Agrupación in June 1931, in September Ortega dissociated himself from the Republic, having realized it was not his dream of a supra-party elite but, precisely, the entry of the masses into political life. Dissolving the Agrupación in 1932, he abandoned politics for the Chair of Metaphysics he had held at Madrid's Central University since 1910. Opting for exile at the start of the Civil War, spent successively in Paris, Buenos Aires, and Portugal, he was marginalized on his return to Spain in 1945 (Elorza 1984; Gray 1989). His intellectual legacy would be reclaimed in the late 1970s by the architects of the transition from dictatorship to democracy.

Ortega's political failure was offset by his immense contribution as a cultural entrepreneur. From 1922 he directed the book series *Biblioteca de Ideas del Siglo XX* (*Library of Twentieth-Century Ideas*) of the publishing house Calpe (from 1926, Espasa-Calpe), introducing Spaniards to major European philosophical and scientific works. In the same year, he was responsible for Biblioteca Nueva translating Freud's complete works, making Spain the first country to do so. His crowning achievement was his creation and direction of the *Revista de Occidente* (*Review of the West*, 1923–36), one of the great European cultural magazines of the early twentieth century (Sinclair 2009, 40–7). Its prospectus explicitly excluded coverage of politics. Like his Calpe book series, its aim was to form a cosmopolitan intellectual elite.

The "West" in the journal's title meant Europe, with occasional inclusion of the Americas thanks to Ortega's visits to Argentina in 1916–17 and 1928–9, where he established links with Victoria Ocampo's prestigious journal *Sur*. In Europe, the *Revista* had agreements to share material with T. S. Eliot's *The Criterion*, *Nouvelle Revue Française*, *Nuova Antologia*, and *Europäische Revue* (Rogers 2012, 29–64). Its contributors comprise a Western intellectual and literary star system: among others, Georg Simmel, Einstein, Carl Schmitt, Bertrand Russell, Virginia Woolf, Faulkner, Kafka, Thomas Mann, Pirandello, Cocteau, and from South America Ocampo, Borges, and Neruda. Almost all Spanish writers of the day published in its pages, Rosa Chacel and María Zambrano being among the few women contributors.

Equally important was the *Revista de Occidente*'s publishing house, with its various book series in philosophy, history, and sociology, plus its poetry collection and experimental prose series Nova Novarum which promoted the Spanish avant-garde. Ortega's own theorization of the avant-garde, *La deshumanización del arte* (*The Dehumanization of Art*, 1925), insists that modern art is unpopular – that is, incomprehensible to the masses – and argues for a playful self-reflexivity whereby art points only to itself. The apoliticism of Ortega's theorization of modern art might appear to contradict the concern with national regeneration in his other essays, but it is itself a political statement.

Ortega's elitist project for national regeneration supposed the incorporation of the provinces into a "vertebrated" national life. In the historic nationalities, very different regeneration projects were being proposed.

Galicia: Between Languages and Continents, a Nation Takes Shape

The rise of *rexionalismo* in Galicia from the 1880s brought the country's political future, its relationship with Madrid and the wider Peninsula, and – crucially – the Americas into the spotlight. Having developed out of the *provincialista* movement (see chapter 4), *rexionalismo* took its name from its belief that Galicia's linguistic, cultural, and political autonomy should be protected, while remaining a region of Spain (Beramendi 2007). Galician *rexionalistas* were deeply influenced by their Catalan colleagues, as leading *rexionalista* Alfredo Brañas recognized in his foundational *El regionalismo* (1889). The most successful strand of *rexionalista* thought, which would form the basis for the early twentieth-century institutionalization of Galician language and culture, was the liberal strand based in A Coruña. Led by Manuel Murguía, husband of Rosalía de Castro, it generated diverse cultural and political initiatives such as the *Biblioteca Gallega* (1885), the *Asociación Regionalista Gallega* (1891), *Revista Gallega* (1895), and the *Liga Gallega* (1897). In 1905, Murguía became founding president of the new Academia Gallega (now Real Academia Galega). As the names of these organizations demonstrate, although *rexionalista* thought embraces the Galician language's Herderian role as the expression of a Galician spirit, Galician cultural and public life remained dominated by Castilian throughout this period. Galician self-identified writers and intellectuals like Brañas and Murguía saw no contradiction in writing in Spanish. Consequently, the *fin de século* has generally been dismissed by Galician-language critics as a period of stagnation between the foundational high points of the 1860s *Rexurdimento* and the Xeración Nós in the 1920s.

In fact, *fin de século* culture and literature was vibrant; bilingual but multi-centered and outward facing. In the rapidly industrializing southern city of Vigo, a group of *rexionalista* businessmen and journalists led by Enrique Peinador, Federico Barreras, and Jaime Solá used maritime links with Britain to develop Anglo-Galician historical ties into a modern relationship of mutual economic, social, and cultural benefit that circumvented Madrid (Hooper 2020). Meanwhile, intensive Galician emigration to the Caribbean and Southern Cone since the mid-nineteenth century created large, permanently settled communities, above all in Havana, Buenos Aires, and Montevideo. These communities attracted entrepreneurial Galician journalists and publishers, who set up Galician-focused periodicals such as *Follas novas* and *Eco de Galicia* (Havana), *Suevia* (Buenos Aires) or *Terra* (Córdoba, Argentina). Strong connections between these and "home" periodicals such as *Revista Gallega* (A Coruña), *Patria Gallega* (Santiago de Compostela), or *Vida Gallega* (Vigo) meant that literary and artistic works by Galician writers in both Castilian and Galician crossed and re-crossed the Atlantic, printed and reprinted in multiple periodicals. The resulting multilingual, multi-centered complexity of early twentieth-century Galician cultural production is encapsulated in the first comprehensive history of Galician literature, written by Eugenio Carré Aldao, a close collaborator of Murguía from A Coruña *rexionalista* circles. His study and anthology *Literatura gallega* (1911) includes writers in Galician and Castilian from Galicia, the wider peninsula, and the Americas.

The status of the Galician language was transformed with the rise of the proto-nationalist Irmandades da Fala (Brotherhoods of the Language) from 1916. Their socially liberal platform included autonomy for Galicia, equal rights for men and women, and, crucially, co-official status for the Galician language in Galicia. This program opened the door to the theorization of a monolingual Galician national culture during the 1920s. Two works were key to shaping this process: Vicente Risco's 1920 *Teoría do nacionalismo* (*Theory of Nationalism*), and Manuel Antonio and Álvaro Cebreiro's 1922 manifesto ¡*Máis alá!* (*Further Still!*).

Risco was a prolific journalist, intellectual, and schoolteacher who had studied with Ortega y Gasset in Madrid. Having joined the Irmandades da Fala in 1917, he swiftly became a valued contributor to the nationalist newspaper *A Nosa Terra* (*Our Land*), his Europeanist ambitions for Galician culture evident in his articles on Apollinaire, Rimbaud, and Verlaine. *Teoría do nacionalismo* extends Murguía's regionalist project to produce a resounding defense of Galicia as a fully articulated nation determined by its geography, ethnography, language, and character. If Risco's book provides the first explicit theorization of Galician nationalism, Antonio and Cebreiro's manifesto is its defining cultural expression: a vibrant, angry text that violently ejects Castilian-speaking intellectuals such as Valle-Inclán from Galician literature, formally rejecting the earlier tolerance of bilingualism.

In 1920, Risco founded the journal *Nós*, a strongly nationalist publication with a distinctive visual identity, committed to the normalization of the Galician language; all its advertising, from books to bars, was in Galician only. Risco, who remained the journal's driving force throughout its life, adopted a bipartite editorial strategy. On the one hand, he sought to modernize *galeguista* thought, bringing the latest literary, linguistic, ethnographic, and anthropological scholarship to bear on contemporary debates about Galicia's identity, history, and future. On the other, he sought to connect Galicia to its European neighbors. The journal had a keen sympathy for other minority nations, frequently discussing the Irish, Catalan, Breton, Portuguese, and Valencian cases, but also kept a close eye on European (especially German and French) high culture. Thanks to Risco's enlightened support for translation, *Nós* provided Galician readers with direct access to English-, French- and German-language literature and thought. Despite an enforced break (1923–5) during the Primo de Rivera dictatorship, the journal – which circulated widely among Galician communities throughout Spain and the Americas – survived until 1936.

Risco and *Nós* were at the center of the Ourense-based intellectual circle known as the Xeración Nós (Nós Generation), whose most prominent members included the geographer and novelist Ramón Otero Pedrayo and the artist and humorist Alfonso Daniel Rodríguez Castelao. Like Risco, Otero Pedrayo was a social conservative from a privileged background who had little contact with Galician culture during his formative years; Castelao had grown up with less material wealth but much exposure to Galician language and culture. These social differences inflected the group members' works and would have real political consequence for the *galeguista* movement during the 1930s (Carballal 2017). The combination of social conservatism and the push toward creation of a high literary culture contributed to the group's rejection of outsiders such as Galicia's first female novelist Francisca Herrera Garrido (see chapter 6).

Despite the Xeración Nós's influence, it must be remembered that they were an elite minority and that the majority of educated Galicians at this time were happily reading popular fiction, much of it in Spanish. Of all the Xeración Nós, it is Castelao whose work has stood the test of time. His theorization of art and humor as a form of resistance, his biting political cartoons, and especially the illustrated vignettes known as the *Cousas* (*Things*) offer a powerful reinterpretation of the rural as a site of social and political critique.

Euskal Herria: The Homeland of the Basques

The late nineteenth century saw tumultuous changes in the sociopolitical life of the Basque Country. The nationalism of Sabino Arana, replacing the nostalgia of *fuerismo* (the movement to reinstate the Basque *fueros* [charters] that historically guaranteed a measure of local decision-making), burst onto the scene with his 1893 proclamation "Euzko tarren aberria Euzkadi da" (Euskadi [the Basque Country, spelt Euzkadi by Arana] is the homeland of the Basques). From then until well into the twentieth century, Basque-language writing would focus on creating the Basque nation. The major industrialization, especially in the province of Bizkaia and to a lesser extent Gipuzkoa, that had attracted waves of immigrants from other areas of Spain made this period one of labor conflict, with the Bilbao working class having founded the Basque section of the Spanish Socialist Workers' Party (PSOE) in 1886. Sociocultural life in the French Basque Country was conditioned by debates between secular republicans and conservative Catholics who, after World War I, embraced French nationalism, publishing in the Catholic newspaper *Eskualduna* (1887–1944). Unlike the industrialized peninsular Basque Country, the economy of the continental Basque provinces was – with the exception of the transformation of the *Côte Basque* into a leisure playground for international elites – grounded in the primary sector, resulting in major emigration to the Americas in these decades.

The unionist slogan "Zazpiak Bat" (The Seven Provinces Form One Nation), present at certain Floral Games in the early 1890s, found its political embodiment in the nationalism of Arana, who in 1895 founded the Partido Nacionalista Vasco (Eusko Alderdi Jeltzalea [Basque Nationalist Party], PNV). Traditional Catholicism, anti-liberalism, anti-socialism, and an essentialist racial vision marked Arana's ideology, disseminated through his creation of periodical publications (*Bizkaitarra*, 1893; *Baserritarra*, 1897; *Euzkadi*, 1901–15) and Basque centers such as the Batzokija (1894) in Bilbao. His slogan "Jaungoikoa ta Lagi Zarrak" (God and the Old Laws) dominated his personal and political life which, like the PNV itself, combined a pro-independence stance with more moderate positions. Arana's symbolic world of invented tradition drew on the nineteenth-century Romantic legendary literature that fed the foralist imaginary (see chapter 5). Having learnt Basque, in 1888 he had competed with Resurreccion Maria Azkue and Unamuno for the first Chair of Basque Language created by Bizkaia Provincial Council (won by Azkue). The urgent need to foster Basque-language literacy led to the creation of kindergartens in Bilbao and, in the 1920s, of *ikastolas* (Basque-language schools) in Donostia-San Sebastián, together with the publication of grammars for children such as Arana's *Umiaren lenengo aizkidia* (*First Grammar for Children*, 1897) and Ixaka Lopez Mendizabal's *Umearen laguna* (*The Child's Friend*, 1920) and *Xabiertxo* (1925), widely read until the 1960s.

Arana's poetics, outlined in the previously mentioned appendix to his 1896 *Lecciones de Ortografía del Euskera Bizkaino* (*Lessons in Bizkaian Basque Orthography*), was implemented in his posthumously published *Olerkijak* (*Poems*, 1919). This prescriptive literary program, which would exert a powerful influence on the 1930s generation of poets known as Olerkariak (The Poets; see chapter 9), sought to elevate Basque-language poetry, felt to be overly influenced by the metrics of oral improvisers (*bertsolariak*). Arana expressed his traditionalist Basque supremacism in the misogynist histori-cal melodrama *Libe* (1903), set at the time of the 1471 Battle of Mungia against Castile, in which the female protagonist redeems her betrayal of the Basque race (by falling in love with a Castilian count) through her self-sacrificial contribution to Basque victory. What prevails at the play's end is Basque virility (Aresti 2014).

Greater literary impact was enjoyed by Katalina Eleizegi's historical drama *Garbiñe* (1917), whose eponymous protagonist sacrifices herself for love at a time when women's views and solidarity were starting to be expressed. Associations like the Emakume Abertzale Batza (Nationalist Women's Association, 1922–3 and 1931–6) allowed the incorporation of women into the Basque nationalist project, albeit with subaltern status and exaltation of their sacred function as mothers (Ugalde 1993). Female members like Tene Mujika, Julene Azpeitia, Errose Bustintza, and Sorne Unzueta contributed extensively to the journals *Euskal Esnalea* (1908–31) and *Euskalerriaren alde* (1911–31), both created in Donostia by protagonists of a flourishing Basque philological movement. Arturo Campión's extensive *Gramática de los cuatro dialectos literarios de la lengua euskera* (*Grammar of the Four Basque Literary Dialects*, 1884) was followed by significant publications by Azkue and Julio de Urquijo. In addition to his 1891 landmark grammar and other cultural activities (see chapters 4 and 6), Azkue published a dictionary (1905–6) and a study of Basque morphology (1923), also helping to found various educational and cultural journals and initiatives. Urquijo's *Revista Internacional de Estudios Vascos* (*International Journal of Basque Studies*, 1907–) attracted contributions by eminent European linguists and philologists; under his chairmanship, the Euskaltzaleen Biltzarra (Assembly of Basque Experts, 1908) debated the standardization of the Basque language, following conferences on the need for a standardized orthography in Hendaia in 1901 and Hondarribia in 1902 (Haritschelhar 2012, 133). The standardization of Basque finally agreed in 1968 was made possible by the creation in 1918 of Euskaltzaindia (Royal Academy of the Basque Language), together with the scientific-cultural institution Eusko Ikaskuntza (Society of Basque Studies).

While Basque was denigrated as a language confined to the rural world, Spanish was bolstered by the state education system and its use expanded by the late nineteenth-century influx of Spanish-speaking immigrants to Basque urban and industrial centers. These conflicting worlds form the core of the stereotypes and fantasies feeding Basque literary nationalism. The *costumbrista* novels of Domingo Agirre – *Kresala* (*Salt Water*, 1906), *Garoa* (*The Fern*, 1912) – portrayed "authentic" Basque lifestyles rooted in the farmstead (*baserri*) or the sea. *Kresala* describes fishermen's traditions, defending folk culture against modern civilization's onslaught. *Garoa* depicts two distinct geographic, moral, linguistic, and ideological worlds: the idealized Basque hills and hamlets and the urban world overrun with immigrants who lack moral and patriotic virtues.

This *costumbrista* focus was continued by José Manuel Etxeita's *Josecho* (1909) and *Jayoterri maittia* (*Beloved Homeland*, 1910), incorporating elements of the serialized novel and adventure story. The *costumbrista* folk novel *Piarres* (1926–9), by French Basque writer Jean Barbier, pays tribute to the 6,000 Basque soldiers who fought in World War I, criticizing the foreign bourgeoisie settling on the Basque coast. The *costumbrista* short fiction of Jean Etxepare (*Buruxkak / Ears of Wheat*, 1910; *Berebilez / By Car*, 1934) and Pedro Miguel Urruzuno (*Ipuiak / Stories*, 1930), together with Gregorio Mujika's popular *Pernando Amezketarra: Bere ateraldi eta gertaerak* (*Pernando Amezketarra: His Witticisms and Life Stories*, 1927), developed a fluid prose style that broke with the purist tendencies of Arana and his followers, resonating with their target audience of readers from rural backgrounds. The French Basque Pierre Lhande authored one of the few historical novels of the 1920s, *Yolanda* (1921), as well as *Le Pays basque à vol d'oiseau* (*The Basque Country: A Bird's Eye View*, 1925) which offers a historiographical reading of Basque literature, understood as literature written in the various languages of the Basques. By contrast, Nikolas Ormaetxea ("Orixe")'s *Euskal literaturaren atze edo edesti laburra* (*A Brief Look Back or A History of Basque Literature*, 1927) considered only works published in Basque, a practice that from the 1960s would be institutionalized by the philologist Koldo Mitxelena (Mitxelena 1988 [1960]).

In Search of a Cosmopolitan Nation: Catalan Nationalism and European Modernity

The development of the Catalan literary field was deeply imbricated with the wider sociopolitical turmoil of the nineteenth century, leading to different and often competing readings of the region's past and present physical and political landscape; the role and status of the Catalan language; the relationship between high and popular culture; and attitudes to Barcelona's emergence as an industrial capital and burgeoning urban metropolis rivalling Madrid in cultural significance. The divide between conservative, Catholic, traditional and more liberal, federal positions was exacerbated by the failure of Catalan politicians, during the 1868 liberal revolution and 1873–4 First Republic, to achieve lasting political influence in the Spanish capital. It also reflects emerging cultural debates around Spanish culture's relationship to modernity, at their most polarized in Catalonia in the tension between followers of Josep Torras i Bages's defense of *La tradició catalana* and the more modernizing, Europeanizing dispositions of the writers associated with Jaume Massó i Torrent's journal *L'Avenç* (*Progress*), who often joined republican satirical organs such as *L'Esquella de la Torratxa* and *La Campana de Gràcia* in attacking the conservatism of *Renaixença* institutions like the *Jocs Florals*.

Catalonia's openness to modern aesthetic trends is evidenced by the *Festes Modernistes* of the 1890s – which saw the first performance in Spain of a play by Maeterlinck, in Catalan translation – and the Barcelona International Expositions of 1888 and 1929. The cultural receptivity of Barcelona audiences would be applauded by twentieth-century aesthetic modernizers like Federico García Lorca, whose theater was better received in Barcelona than in Madrid (George 2002; M. Delgado 2003). Yet other figures who cautiously approved Catalan artists' negotiation of the relationship between tradition and modernity tended to be ambivalent about the Catalan language's place in such developments (Bastons i Vivanco and Busquets i Grabulosa 2002; Balcells 2011). Attitudes ranged from incomprehension at the decision to write in Catalan, expressed in personal correspondence between writers of Catalan and non-Catalan origin, to the increasingly hostile positions taken by intellectuals associated with the 1898 Generation, especially Baroja, who wrote in *El Mundo* on "El problema catalán. La influencia judía" (The Catalan Problem: The Jewish Influence, 1907), and Unamuno, whose doubts about the modern relevance of "regional" languages such as Basque and Catalan developed into opposition to the threat they posed to Spanish national unity.

From the 1880s, attitudes towards the Catalan language shifted from the nostalgic and provincial outlook prevalent throughout much of the nineteenth century to appreciation of the need for standardization to fulfill the needs of contemporary cultural production, thanks to the writers, thinkers, and educators who collaborated on *L'Avenç*. Their articles on the function and status of Catalan, alongside reflection on modern aesthetic developments in the arts in general, initiated a campaign for the modernization of Catalan grammar and orthography that drew on philological theory and practice current elsewhere in Europe, as well as engagement with experts from across the Catalan-speaking territories. Fruits of this campaign were the First International Congress on the Catalan Language, held in Barcelona in 1906 with 3,000 delegates; Prat de la Riba's expression of the language's centrality to the Catalan nation's future in *La nacionalitat catalana* (*The Catalan Nationality*, 1906), echoed in other contemporaneous *Noucentista* writings; and the dedication of former engineer Pompeu Fabra to the standardization of Catalan under the auspices of the Institut d'Estudis Catalans (Institute of Catalan Studies). The Institute was the first of the educational and cultural institutions created after the 1906 formation of Solidaritat Catalana, a broad Catalanist coalition which brought together the more economically and socially conservative Lliga Regionalista with a range of Catalan republican parties (such as the Centre Nacionalista

Republicà, Unió Catalanista, and part of Unió Republicana) and rural Carlist representatives in the region (Rubí and Espinet 2008). Responding to the repression of the Catalan-language satirical publication *Cu-Cut* in November 1905 and the enforcement of military impunity in the region, the movement aligned the modernizing culturalist policies of conservatives and republicans and achieved broad success in both general and local elections in 1907. Although short-lived, the alliance laid the foundations for the creation from 1914 of a range of educational and cultural institutions by the Mancomunitat de Catalunya (Commonwealth of Catalonia, comprising the four Catalan provincial governments), including public schools and libraries to support wide community access to education and literacy in Catalan. Despite political disagreement about the kind of citizenship such institutions were designed to facilitate, these developments – together with the wider range of initiatives sponsored by republicans, anarchists, and private associations – ensured a rapid increase in literacy and the consequent social diversification of Catalan writing. The Primo de Rivera dictatorship's suppression of the Mancomunitat and other Catalan institutions from 1923 would generate even wider social support for the alignment of cultural and political Catalanism, from the late 1920s creating allegiances between a range of left-wing, republican, and separatist formations that would shape the positioning of writers and intellectuals in the 1930s.

The chronological coincidence at the turn of the century of these cultural developments with social and political turbulence meant that Catalonia's *Modernista* flirtation with modernity was seen with suspicion in other parts of Spain. This was compounded by the perceived anarcho-syndicalist sympathies of some of the writers associated with *L'Avenç* – notably Jaume Brossa and Pere Coromines, forced into exile in the repressive aftermath of the 1896 Barcelona Corpus Christi bombings – and above all by the consolidation of conservative political Catalanism in response to Spain's 1898 loss of its last American and Asian colonies (Ucelay da Cal 2003). Baroja and Unamuno were not alone in equating *Modernisme*'s perceived superficiality with the Spanish nation's modern decline; in the Catalan-speaking territories, too, the national mythologies formulated through *Modernisme*'s dialectical synthesis of tradition and modernity were perceived as inimical to the political vision of a civilized, harmonious Mediterranean society that emerged with the new century. Particularly problematic was the relationship between society and the artist, conceived within *Modernisme* as an oppositional figure who aims to transform society whilst resisting assimilation by bourgeois ideology, as exemplified in novels like art historian and painter Raimon Casellas's *Els sots feréstecs* (*Dark Vales*, 1901), although its sensitive, enlightened protagonist, exiled to a rural backwater by Church authorities, is defeated by the community whose lives he seeks to improve. By contrast, *Noucentista* intellectuals, led by their principal ideologue Eugeni d'Ors ("Xènius"), defended the need to forge an alliance with political power in order to construct a cultural community based on neoclassical ideas of measure and classicism of form, as anticipated in the poetry of the *Escola Mallorquina* (Majorcan School). In the daily *Gloses* that "Xènius" published in the Lliga Regionalista organ, *La Veu de Catalunya*, he developed a vision of the quotidian dispositions that needed to be developed in order to build Prat de la Riba's projected Catalan nationality, rooted in Mediterranean civilization and cultural imperialism. Such an outlook was hostile both to the socially committed writing of anti-bourgeois radicals like Brossa, Ignasi Iglésias, Felip Cortiella, and Juli Vallmitjana and to the decadent Symbolist work of Santiago Rusiñol, Casellas, and Adrià Gual. Yet it is perhaps the position of the relatively liberal writer Joan Maragall that best indicates the effects of shifting geopolitical alignments.

Maragall is generally associated with *Modernisme* in Catalan literary histories because of his relationship with the *Avenç* group and his pioneering translations into Catalan of Goethe, Nietzsche, Novalis, and Ibsen from the late 1880s, even though his poetry is imbued with a neo-romantic flavor, expressed in his celebration of the poetic spirit in language in lectures at the Ateneu Barcelonès from 1903 (Terry 2003). He also had close friendships with intellectuals elsewhere in Spain, notably Unamuno (Bastons 2006). His case highlights the conflicting interests involved in reconciling developments in national discourse with the social, political, economic, and cultural imperatives of modernity. Originally destined to work in his father's textile company, Maragall chose to study law in Barcelona while participating increasingly in the literary institutions of his day. In the 1890s – as well as publishing poems that combined a realist and romantic tone, such as "La vaca cega" (The Blind Cow) in *L'Avenç* – he won a prize at the 1894 *Jocs Florals* for a poem on the *sardana*; published regular articles in Spanish in the conservative *Diario de Barcelona*, including sensitive critiques of contemporary European Symbolist art; and penned the first translations and commentaries in Spain of excerpts from Nietzsche's work. His personal spirituality attracted him to the conservative Catholic accounts of the Catalan tradition promulgated by Torras i Bages, but his writings also displayed a strong social conscience, from his lament at colonialism's destructive force in his 1898 "Oda a Espanya" (Ode to Spain) to more complex consideration of the causes and effects of urban violence in "Nueva oda a Espanya" (New Ode to Spain, 1909) and the newspaper articles "Ah, Barcelona" (October 1, 1909), "L'església cremada" (The Burnt-out Church, December 18, 1901), and "La ciutat del perdó" (The City of Forgiveness, December 18, 1909) – the last censored by Prat de la Riba in *La Veu de Catalunya* (Benet 1992; Subirana 2018, 69). His complex aesthetic and sociocultural positioning between the pulls of the local and the universal, Catalan and Spanish, tradition and modernity situate him in a radically different camp from the more medievalizing, nostalgic viewpoint associated with the *Renaixença*, as well as from the more programmatic, institutional outlook of *Noucentisme* which, through the critical writings of d'Ors, marked him as a thing of the past. By recovering him as a more resistant figure, through his work as translator and mediator of foreign culture as well as his cultural commentaries and participation in debate with intellectuals in other parts of Spain (Škrabec 2017, 33–80), it becomes possible to appreciate his fluid stance with regard to both the modern European repositioning of the individual in relation to society and the local context of Catalonia's shifting relationship to Spain; that is, to see him as a key mediator of the competing nationalisms at the turn of the century.

9

Writers and Political Commitment (1930s–1960s)

The 1931 declaration of the Second Republic and the 1936–9 Civil War required writers to commit to a specific political option. The Franco dictatorship's brutal repression and censorship, too, required writers to take a stand. Juan Goytisolo noted in *El furgón de cola* (*The Rear Carriage*, 1967) that when there is no freedom, everything becomes political. This chapter treats the 1930s to the 1960s as a single unit, despite the vast political differences between the prewar and postwar periods, since both were characterized by the overt politicization of culture. The rise in the 1920s and 1930s of fascism in Italy and Germany and of communism worldwide introduced new collectivist political options that broke with the liberal defense of individual rights – the Spanish Communist Party was founded in 1921, splitting from the Socialist Party (PSOE) which favored social democracy; the Spanish fascist party Falange Española was founded in 1933 by José Antonio Primo de Rivera, son of the 1923–30 dictator General Miguel Primo de Rivera. Anarchism too – known as *comunismo libertario* (libertarian communism) – supported collectivization, while rejecting the state. These collectivist political developments challenged belief in the autonomous individual and, by extension, the autonomy of art. The excitement of being caught up in collectivist movements was felt by writers at both ends of the political spectrum.

Feminist Intellectuals

Feminist commitment anticipated other forms of political commitment that would become the norm in the 1930s. Many feminist activists of the twentieth century's first decades, concerned with a relational rather than individualist concept of the self, were socialists or anarchists; they would become increasingly politicized in the 1930s. Carmen de Burgos ("Colombine") collaborated with socialist and republican parties, having since 1904 campaigned for divorce in the liberal press and in her books

El divorcio en España (*Divorce in Spain*, 1904) and *La mujer en España* (*Women in Spain*, 1906). The height of her activism was in the 1920s, as founder of the Cruzada de Mujeres Españolas (Spanish Women's Crusade, 1921) and president of the Liga Internacional de Mujeres Ibéricas e Hispanoamericanas (International League of Iberian and Spanish-American Women, 1923). With her novels and many contributions to the various cheap novella series of the day (see chapter 6), she took the topic of women's rights to a mass audience (Louis 2005).

If Carmen de Burgos advocated an equality feminism that previously had few champions in Spain, María Martínez Sierra built on nineteenth-century difference feminism to argue for women's participation in the public sphere. She started to publish under the name María Martínez Sierra (keeping the surnames of her cultural entrepreneur husband Gregorio Martínez Sierra) with her 1931 *La mujer ante la República* (*Woman and the Republic*), initiating a political commitment that would lead her to serve as Socialist Party parliamentary deputy 1933–4. She had been appointed Spanish secretary to the International Women's Suffrage Alliance in 1914, and in 1931 founded the Asociación Femenina de Educación Cívica (Women's Civic Education Association). Her five volumes of feminist essays published in the press 1915–30 (book versions 1916–41) appeared under the name of her husband Gregorio, whose status as a public figure gave authority to her controversial ideas (Blanco 2003). In 1947, on Gregorio's death and needing the income from the intellectual property rights, she revealed that she had authored the prolific dramatic output performed and published under his name until 1929. Her feminist essays anticipate today's "ethics of care" by proposing that women's capacity for emotional relationship is superior to male competitive individualism, blamed for World War I.

Martínez Sierra was a founding member of the Lyceum Club – created in 1926 by María de Maeztu (sister of Ramiro de Maeztu, discussed in chapter 8) as an all-female space for debate. While it nurtured many women writers and intellectuals, it was a bourgeois feminist club. The only woman elected to parliament in all three elections under the Republic, Margarita Nelken, was refused membership because she was a single mother living with a married man. In the 1920s Nelken authored three feminist studies and a 1930 history of Spanish women writers, plus a novel and several popular novellas with a feminist slant. As with Martínez Sierra, the Republic would channel her energies into political militancy, championing peasants' rights in her Badajoz constituency. A similar trajectory from literature to politics was taken by anarchists Lucía Sánchez Saornil and Federica Montseny, whose radical feminism broke with bourgeois norms. Sánchez Saornil had since 1919 contributed to Ultraist poetry magazines under the male penname "Luciano de San-Saor." In the 1920s she abandoned poetry for anarchist journalism and during the Civil War co-founded the anarchist organization Mujeres Libres (Free Women), initiating a lifelong lesbian relationship. The Barcelona-based Montseny would in the 1920s, tailing off in the 1930s, pen three novels and over 50 popular novellas, mostly in the series *La Novela Ideal* and *La Novela Libre* published by her parents' anarchist journal *La Revista Blanca*. Her fiction promotes the new revolutionary woman, advocating free liaisons between equals and the right to motherhood outside marriage. Under the Republic she became a charismatic orator for the anarchist union CNT, continuing to prioritize women's rights with her 1932 study *La mujer, problema del hombre* (*Woman, A Male Problem*) and, as Republican Minister of Health between November 1936 and May 1937 (the first Spanish woman to hold a ministerial position), by drafting Spain's first abortion bill (not passed).

Taking Sides

Many male writers whose careers had begun in the 1920s reoriented or abandoned their literary production in response to increased politicization in the 1930s. Rafael Alberti moved from the expression of subjective crisis to committed poetry and drama in 1931, when he and his partner María Teresa León joined the Communist Party. *El poeta en la calle* (*Poet in the Street*, 1931–5) exhorts peasants and workers to unite in revolution, coopting Lope de Vega, as a writer of popular verse, to their cause. Alberti's prewar plays repurpose popular forms for political ends: the *auto sacramental* in *El hombre deshabitado* (*The Derelict Man*, 1931); ballads in *Fermín Galán* (also 1931); puppet theater in *Bazar de la providencia* (*Bazaar of Providence*) and *Farsa de los Reyes Magos* (*Farce of the Three Kings*, both 1934). After 1930, Federico García Lorca moved almost entirely from poetry to theater so as to engage audiences directly; with his rural trilogy – *Bodas de sangre* (*Blood Wedding*, 1933), *Yerma* (1934), and *La casa de Bernarda Alba* (*The House of Bernarda Alba*, 1936) – he abandoned the hermetic Surrealist work written from 1929 to 1931 for more accessible, though no less poetic, social dramas.

Under the Republic, Francisco Ayala dropped avant-garde fiction for political journalism, resuming creative writing only in exile. The avant-garde writer César M. Arconada also joined the Communist Party in 1931, resigning from Ernesto Giménez Caballero's avant-garde magazine *La Gaceta Literaria* and turning to Soviet-style socialist realism from his 1930 novel *La turbina* (*The Turbine*, 1930), as well as writing for the Communist magazines *Octubre* (1933–4) and *Nueva Cultura* (1935–6, 1937). The move from avant-garde experimentalism to socialist realism was theorized in José Díaz Fernández's 1930 *El nuevo romanticismo* (*The New Romanticism*), which dismissed as bourgeois play José Ortega y Gasset's advocacy of self-reflexive abstraction. Díaz Fernández had embraced revolutionary commitment himself with his 1929 novel *La Venus mecánica* (*The Mechanical Venus*). After his 1931 election to parliament for the Radical Socialist Party, he too abandoned creative writing for political journalism.

The shift to political commitment was made in the opposite direction by Giménez Caballero, who in 1928 converted to fascism in Rome. Italian futurism had shown the avant-garde's compatibility with fascism; if political commitment led left-wing writers to shun literary experimentalism, Giménez Caballero's view of fascism as irrationalist "exaltation" allowed him to transition seamlessly from his experimental early work – Surrealist exploration of the abject in *Yo, inspector de alcantarillas* (*My Self, Sewage Inspector*, 1928); futurist celebration of modern mass culture in *Hércules jugando a los dados* (*Hercules Playing Dice*, 1928) and *Julepe de menta* (*Mint Julep*, 1929) – to the fascist panegyric *Genio de España* (*Genius of Spain*, 1932). *Genio de España* posits Spain, with its cultural mix of East and West, as the cradle of a fascist rejuvenation achieved by violently melding the Genius of the East (oriental despotism, including Soviet Communism) and the Genius of the West (individualism). In *Arte y estado* (*Art and the State*, 1935), Giménez Caballero theorized modern mechanically reproduced mass culture – cinema, radio, the graphic arts – as an instrument of state propaganda; he served in the Nationalist propaganda apparatus during the Civil War.

Those authors whose literary career began around 1930 took the political function of literature for granted. Ramón J. Sender joined the anarchist trade union CNT in 1929, from 1932 moving close to the Communist Party. His mix of journalism and fiction deals with controversial political topics: in *Imán* (1930), the Moroccan colonial war, drawing on his experience of military service; in *Viaje a la aldea del crimen* (*Journey to the Village of the Crime*, 1934), the Republican government's repression of the 1933 anarchist peasant uprising in Casas Viejas (Cadiz), on which he had reported as a journalist. His historical novel *Mr. Witt en el cantón* (*Mr. Witt in the Canton*, 1936), on the 1873 cantonalist uprising in Cartagena under the First Spanish Republic, is a parable of the need to take sides. Sender's 1932 *Teatro de masas* (*Theater for the Masses*) theorized the proletarian theater that he and others would put into practice during the Civil War. The self-educated Luisa

Carnés drew on her personal experience as a working-class woman for her novels *Natacha* (1930) and *Tea Rooms* (1934). She would establish herself as a journalist in the 1930s Communist press, contributing to the Republic's wartime agitprop theater.

Like Antonio Machado (see chapter 8), the philosopher and essayist María Zambrano – a student of Ortega y Gasset – maintained her defense of liberal values while remaining committed to the Republic. Her first book *Horizonte del liberalismo* (*Horizon of Liberalism*, 1930) refutes Ortega's elitism. Critiquing avant-garde "dehumanization," she proposes the concept of "poetic reason," based on compassion. Writing in the 1930s for the *Revista de Occidente*, José Bergamin's liberal Catholic *Cruz y Raya* (1933–6), and the Communist *Nueva Cultura* (1935–7), she returned to Spain from Chile at the start of the Civil War to serve on the Republic's Propaganda Council and Council for Child Evacuees, and on the editorial staff of *Hora de España* (see below).

The Cultural Program of the Second Republic

Zambrano had also, from 1933, participated in the Misiones Pedagógicas (Pedagogical Missions) created by the Republican government in May 1931. Aimed at granting the people access to culture, the Missions formed a national-popular project in the Gramscian sense of incorporating the masses into the nation as historical agents. They implemented the late nineteenth-century Krausist intellectuals' dream of reform via educa- tion; many of the Republic's ministers had been educated at the Krausist Institución Libre de Enseñanza. From April 1931 to the right-wing CEDA's election victory in November 1933, the Republican government created an average of 2,000 schools per year, plus over 13,500 new schoolteacher positions. The Misiones Pedagógicas were the centerpiece of this cultural program (Mendelson 2005, 93–123; Otero Urtaza 2006). Serviced largely by student volunteers, the Missions took culture to rural areas, playing record- ings of classical and folk music, screening films, and exhibiting copies of masterpieces in the Prado. The use of mechanically reproduced art forms, which allowed materials to be left in the villages visited, broke with the bourgeois notion of the original artwork. Their Teatro del Pueblo (People's Theater), directed by playwright Alejandro Casona, included a student choir that performed folk songs. As director of La Barraca, the additional student-volunteer theater founded in 1932, Lorca aimed to return theater to its pre-modern roots in popular spectacle, bypassing bourgeois realism by presenting mostly Golden Age classics with avant-garde costumes and backdrops (Rodríguez Solás 2014). From 1935, Max Aub's student theater group El Búho toured the Valencian region. Villages without road access were serviced by a Retablo de Fantoches (Puppet Theater), directed by Rafael Dieste and transported by mule. Over their five years (1931–6), the Missions created over 5,500 village libraries, as well as bussing books to remote areas; a major participant was the lexicographer María Moliner. Writers active in the Missions included Miguel Hernández, Luis Cernuda, and Pedro Salinas.

Extraordinarily, the Republic's cultural program was stepped up in wartime. Literacy was brought to the civilian population by the Flying Literacy Brigades (Brigadas Volantes de Lucha contra el Analfabetismo) and to the troops by the Cultural Militias (Milicias de la Cultura), teaching an estimated 300,000 civilians and 70,000 soldiers to read and write. Battalions were equipped with libraries (Escolar 1987, 137–44). Soldiers were encouraged to write poems about the war, with their texts pinned on battalion noticeboards or published in the over 1,300 magazines produced by Republican political parties, trade unions, and military units (Salaün 1985). The Spanish Civil War has been called the "Poets' War" because of the volume of poetry written on the Republican side by common soldiers and recognized poets (Spanish and foreign). Poetry was privileged because it lent itself to live performance (often sung to guitar accompaniment) and connected with the still strong folk ballad tradition. As narrative verse, ballads told the story of the war, though in a highly formulaic manner. Principally, they served an agitprop function, raising the troops' morale.

The magazine of the Communist Alliance of Antifascist Intellectuals, *El Mono Azul* (1936–9), named after the blue boilersuits donned by committed intellectuals as "cultural workers," encouraged soldiers to submit their poems to its column "Romancero de la Guerra Civil" (Civil War Ballad Book). After May 1937, *El Mono Azul* published poems only by professional poets, as did the more intellectual, government-subsidized *Hora de España* (1937–9). Directed by Rafael Alberti, *El Mono Azul* published work by virtually every pro-Republican writer, including Latin American poets Pablo Neruda, Vicente Huidobro, César Vallejo, and Octavio Paz. *Hora de España*, directed by Antonio Machado, reflected the tensions between liberal and Marxist positions, including debates on artistic autonomy versus commitment.

Among the poets who gave battlefront recitals were Rafael Alberti and Miguel Hernández, the latter a Commissar in the Republican army. Hernández's 1937 poetry collection *Vientos del pueblo* (*Winds of the People*) equates his voice with that of the people. His nickname of *pastor-poeta* (goatherd poet) was cultivated for propaganda purposes (he had had a good Jesuit education till age 14, tending his father's goats subsequently) (Becerra Mayor and Antón Fernández 2010, 16–28). Having joined the Communist Party in 1936, he abandoned his previous baroque poetry, largely adopting the ballad form. The "singability" of his wartime poems ensured their popularity with late 1960s anti-Franco *cantautores* (singer-songwriters). In *El hombre acecha* (*Man at the Ready*, written 1937–9), the emphasis, as the Republic suffered increasing military losses, is on violence and death. He died in a Francoist jail in 1942.

Hernández also wrote plays for performance at the front. In August 1936, Alberti and León created the theater company Nueva Escena (New Stage) as an organ of the Alliance of Antifascist Intellectuals. In her prewar *Huelga en el Puerto* (*Dock Strike*, 1933), written after the first of her and Alberti's three visits to the Soviet Union, León had appropriated the innovative stagecraft of Soviet agitprop. It was as theater director and entrepreneur that she would make a major mark during the war. In Fall 1937 she founded Nueva Escena's successor, the Teatro de Arte y Propaganda (Art and Propaganda Theater), based in Madrid but also taking performances to the front, as did the Guerrillas del Teatro (Theater Guerrillas) that León created in February 1938. The Theater Guerrillas collaborated with the Fifth Regiment's agitprop unit Altavoz del Frente (Frontline Loudspeaker), which had its own Teatro de Guerra (War Theater); its first performance included one-acters by Carnés and Alberti. Republican war theater – what Alberti termed *teatro de urgencia* (emergency theater) – consisted mostly of one-acters, exhorting men to join the Republican war effort, ridiculing the Nationalist enemy, or paying tribute to the Republican dead. In addition to Hernández, playscripts were contributed by Sender, Aub, Arconada, Dieste, and the poets Manuel Altolaguirre, Pedro Garfias, and José Herrera Petere (Mundi 1987). The plays that have aged best are those that draw on the popular traditions of vaudeville, circus, and puppet theater, blending with the comic Golden Age curtain-raiser (*entremés*), as in Arconada's 1937 farce *La conquista de Madrid* (*The Conquest of Madrid*); Dieste's *Nuevo retablo de las maravillas* (*New Theater of Wonders*, 1937); or Alberti's 1938 *Radio Sevilla* which stages a spoof flamenco show sending up Nationalist General Queipo de Llano, notorious for his brutally misogynistic, drunken broadcasts on Seville Radio.

Falangist Intellectuals: From Victory to Disillusionment

If the Republic's cultural program – before and during the war – can be seen as national-popular, Nationalist wartime culture was national-populist in seeking to integrate the people into a unified, hierarchical state. The Nationalist Press and Propaganda Service, based in Burgos, was controlled by the Falange. In an exception to the Nationalists' overall anti-intellectualism, its Director of Propaganda, the poet Dionisio Ridruejo, assembled a team consisting largely of writers: poets Luis Rosales, Luis Felipe Vivanco, Leopoldo Panero, and José María Alfaro; novelists Juan Antonio Zunzunegui and Ignacio Agustí; dramatist Gonzalo Torrente Ballester; fascist ideologue Giménez Caballero; plus the medical scholar Pedro Laín Entralgo. In 1937, Torrente Ballester called for a "national theater" that would return drama to its liturgical roots. The Teatro Nacional created by Ridruejo in 1938 performed morality plays (*autos sacramentales*) synchronized with the religious calendar and choreographed as open-air rallies. Torrente Ballester's own morality play *El viaje del joven Tobías* (*The Young Tobías's Journey*, 1938) was banned for sacrilege. The monarchist José María Pemán, who would after the war be responsible for purging pro-Republican teachers, penned the best-known example of militant Nationalist verse, the apocalyptic *Poema de la Bestia y el Ángel* (*Poem of the Beast and the Angel*, 1938). The major Falangist journals were the Mussolini-influenced *Jerarquía* (1936–8), the luxury illustrated *Vértice* (1937–46), and the postwar literary and cultural magazine *Escorial* (1940–50), founded by Ridruejo with Laín Entralgo as deputy editor.

After their victory in 1939, fascist intellectuals realized that Franco's aim was not the revolutionary destruction of a discredited liberalism, but defense of the wealthy and the imposition of a virulently anti-modern Catholicism. Their tone would shift from imperial exaltation to disillusion-ment, especially when Allied victory in World War II ended their dream of a new fascist world order. The successive issues of *Escorial* chart the evolution of Falangist intellectuals from fascist enthusiasm to existential depression. *Escorial* has been seen as a liberal haven within the Franco regime (Gracia 2004, 217–26), but the evolution of certain Falangists (including Ridruejo and Laín Entralgo) to a liberal humanist position would not take place till the 1950s; in the 1940s their veiled (in Ridruejo's case, open) critique of Francoism stemmed from their fascist commitment.

Escorial's first editorial explained that it was named after the Monastery of the Escorial outside Madrid (the burial place of Spanish kings) as the emblem of a religious-military state. The first issue famously published

Ridruejo's article "El poeta rescatado" ("The Poet Salvaged") "reha-bilitating" Antonio Machado, who had briefly taught him. Far from recognizing Machado's liberal values, the article insists that, without knowing it, Machado – who had died in exile – had supported Falangist ideals. *Escorial* would, in a policy of "integration" that should not be confused with tolerance, coopt as contributors liberal intellectuals who passively accepted the Franco regime, hiring as managing editors Antonio Marichalar, who had managed Ortega's *Revista de Occidente*, and Rosales, formerly associated with Bergamín's liberal Catholic *Cruz y Raya*. *Escorial* was hospitable to young Catholic writers who would, in the 1950s, move to the left, such as José Luis Aranguren, José María Valverde, and Blas de Otero. But, as its opening issue stated, its hospitality extended only to those who had not reneged on their Spanishness. Ortega was consistently attacked for his secularism.

What most strikes today's reader of *Escorial* is its intense Catholicism, even in its early days under Ridruejo who, in 1942, on returning from fight-ing with the Blue Division of Spanish Falangists alongside Hitler's troops in Russia, passed the magazine's editorship to the deeply religious Laín Entralgo and resigned from his regime positions. The poems published in its pages move from an initial crusading spirit to spiritual anguish. The abandonment of politics for a poetics of intimacy (*intimismo*), while a con-sequence of fascist disillusionment, was promoted as a "re-humanization," rejecting the prewar avant-garde "dehumanization" advocated by Ortega. This initially took the form of a return to the sixteenth-century neoclas-sicism of the soldier-poet Garcilaso de la Vega, promoted especially by the magazine *Garcilaso* (1943–46). After Alfaro replaced Laín Entralgo as *Escorial*'s editor in November 1942, *Escorial* almost entirely dropped politics for literature. This depoliticization intensified with Allied victory in 1945, when Franco removed the Falange from major office. The resulting Church hegemony was reflected, in poetry published in *Escorial* and elsewhere, in an increasingly solipsistic search for divine consolation. *Escorial* fell silent in 1947–9 and ceased publication in 1950.

The importance of religion for pro-regime poets in the 1940s suggests that it was a substitute for a politics too difficult to handle. Vivanco's 1940 *Tiempo de dolor* is not about the suffering caused by the recent war but mystical love poetry. Panero's 1949 *Escrito a cada instante* (*Written Every Day*) addresses poems to Vallejo and Lorca with a total disconnect from the political. The postwar period lent itself to existentialist anguish given the impossibility of realizing authentic selfhood through a freely chosen project – an obvious impossibility for the war's losers but felt keenly by

Falangist intellectuals who had expected victory to empower them. A supreme example of religious existentialism is Dámaso Alonso's *Hijos de la ira* (*Children of Wrath*, 1944), whose reputation as precursor of the social poetry of the 1950s needs qualifying: its title is a quote from Paul's Epistle to the Ephesians, referring to those not converted to Christianity. Despite its famous first line "Madrid es una ciudad de más de un millón de cadáveres (según las últimas estadísticas)" (Madrid is a city of over a million corpses [according to the latest statistics]), it does not address political or social injustice but is an anguished appeal to an unresponsive God. Where *Los hijos de la ira* does anticipate 1950s social poetry is in its rejection of inflated Falangist rhetoric and the stilted poetic language of *garcilasismo* for everyday diction.

The Emergence of a Literary Opposition

The existential frustration of all postwar intellectuals allowed slippage between political positions. The first oppositional stirrings came from disenchanted Falangists and Catholics whose values clashed with the reality of Francoism. Otero would move from his 1942 *Cántico espiritual*, inspired by St. John of the Cross, to become one of the most outspoken regime opponents from his 1950 *Ángel fieramente humano* (*Proudly Human Angel*). Joining the illegal Communist Party in 1952, he lived for long periods in Paris and revolutionary Cuba and visited the Soviet Union and China. Otero's poetry through the 1950s addresses the "inmensa mayoría" (vast majority) of those struggling against a God who makes them suffer. He fears they may not be listening – indeed, from 1955 his work, banned in Spain, was published abroad.

Gabriel Celaya's acceptance of worldly and bodily materiality allowed him to transition easily from his prewar avant-garde poetry to Marxist commitment from the early 1950s. His *Cantos iberos* (*Iberian Songs*, 1954) is a call to collective action. Proclaiming poetry to be "un arma cargado de futuro" (a weapon loaded with the future) in a poem famously set to music in the mid-1960s by Paris-based singer-songwriter Paco Ibáñez, Celaya declares poetry to be the daily bread of the poor. This social vein would be advanced in the 1960s by the younger poets José Agustín Goytisolo (elder brother of novelist Juan) and Jaime Gil de Biedma, both children during the war. Gil de Biedma was brutally frank about the motives of protest poets from wealthy Nationalist backgrounds, like himself and José Agustín: "señoritos de nacimiento/ por mala conciencia escritores/ de poesía social" (sons of privilege/ out of a guilty conscience writers/ of social poetry).

It does not seem coincidence that the major representatives of committed poetry were Basques (Otero, Celaya), Catalans (José Agustín Goytisolo, Gil de Biedma), or women, all of whom bore the brunt of Francoism. Ángela Figuera Aymerich (also Basque) started to publish only in 1948, aged 46, having been purged from her prewar teaching position. A rare woman writer who expresses anger, she rethinks femininity as toughness ("lo recio femenino"). Having read her poems on Radio Madrid in 1935, Gloria Fuertes published in book form from 1950. Her committed poetry shares the playfulness of her prolific output of children's literature, departing from the seriousness of male committed literature. Her use of colloquial language stems from her working-class origins and lack of higher education. (For Fuertes's later feminist writing, see chapter 12.)

Most of the "angry young men" who emerged as opposition novelists in the mid-1950s were radicalized at university, thanks to Communist infiltration of the Falangist student union, SEU (Sindicato Español Universitario / Spanish University Union). They were preceded by two young women novelists, both from Barcelona: Carmen Laforet and Ana María Matute. The existentialist title of Laforet's 1944 *Nada* (*Nothing*) picks up on the sense of impotence of the postwar years. Matute's first novel *Los Abel* (*The Abel Family*, 1948), set before the war, shows her potential for female-focused social critique. Her 1959 *Primera memoria* (translated as *The Island*) explores class hatred during the Civil War, including the persecution of Majorca's Jews (*chuetas*). Her most political novel, *Los hijos muertos* (*The Dead Sons*, 1958), establishes a dialogue between a winner and a loser of the war – perhaps the only Spanish-language novel that has attempted a conversation between enemies.

Discussion of the opposition novels that emerged in the mid-1950s has been obfuscated by unhelpful terminology. The most frequent term used, "social realism," was a way of saying "socialist realism" – a banned Marxist term. The only novels that really fit this category, all by members of the clandestine Communist Party, are Jesús López Pacheco's 1958 *Central eléctrica* (*Power Station*), Antonio Ferres's 1959 *La piqueta* (*The Pickaxe*), Armando López Salinas's 1960 *La mina* (*The Mine*), and Alfonso Grosso's 1960 *La zanja* (*The Trench*), with their workerist subject matter. The other term used was "objectivism," popularized in Juan Goytisolo's 1956 essays in *Destino* (book version *Problemas de la novela* / *Problems of the Novel*, 1959) and the Catalan critic José María Castellet's 1957 *La hora del lector* (*The Hour of the Reader*), both of which relate contemporary Spanish fiction to current French literary debates. What Goytisolo and Castellet understand by "objetivismo" is a muddle of postwar France's interest in the deadpan narration of 1920s–1930s American fiction (Dos Passos, Hammett) and in Italian neorealist cinema, and the phenomenologically oriented French New Novel – all of which reject psychological analysis, seen as an expression of bourgeois individualism, for the external "materialist" depiction of characters' acts and speech as if through a film camera (the Spanish "objetivo," used as a noun, means "camera lens"). The screening of Italian neorealist cinema at the 1951 First Italian Film Week in Madrid changed the course of Spanish cinema (social novelist Jesús Fernández Santos was also a film critic). But no 1950s Spanish novels show influence of the hermetic French New Novel; their authors' concern was to produce an accessible literature of denunciation. "Objectivism" was useful to 1950s social novelists in the different sense that eliminating narratorial comment helped them evade the censor.

Goytisolo identifies as "objectivist" Camilo José Cela's *La colmena* (*The Hive*; written 1945; published Buenos Aires 1951), Fernández Santos's *Los bravos* (*The Untamed*, 1954), and Rafael Sánchez Ferlosio's *El Jarama* (1955). This led to critics' inclusion of *La colmena* in the 1950s social novel, but its objectivism is precisely a refusal to adopt a position – as in Cela's earlier *La familia de Pascual Duarte* (*The Family of Pascual Duarte*, 1942) whose Cervantine unreliable narration undermines any attempt to read it as social critique. *La colmena* was banned until 1955 regardless, as was López Salinas's *Año tras año* (*Year after Year*, 1962), whose objectivist depiction of the difficult survival of a large cast of working-class characters, across two generations, from the war's end to the 1950s appeared with Paris-based exile publisher Ruedo Ibérico. *Los bravos* and *El Jarama* combine lack of narratorial comment with social critique, but at the expense of fatalism since social and political causes are elided. The most successful social novels of the 1950s and early 1960s do engage in psychological analysis, including those by Goytisolo. Critique of pseudo-rebellious bourgeois youth unites the early novels of the bourgeois Goytisolo, the communist Juan García Hortelano, and the working-class Juan Marsé. From *Duelo en el Paraíso* (*Mourning in Paradise*, 1955), Goytisolo's novels of the 1950s are primarily concerned with their adolescent male protagonists' inability to connect with the lower classes; read in the light of his later work (see chapter 12), their homoeroticism is clear.

Committed theater of the 1950s and 1960s has also been called realist – misleadingly since, to circumvent drama's heavy censorship because of its direct contact with audiences, playwrights engaged in indirect statement. Realist drama was acceptable only in *costumbrista* form, as in Antonio

Buero Vallejo's *Historia de una escalera* (*History of a Staircase*, 1949), *Hoy es fiesta* (*Today's a Holiday*, 1956), and *Las cartas boca abajo* (*Cards Face Down*, 1957), which won major theater awards despite their author's commuted death sentence and imprisonment till 1946. To convey a political message, Buero Vallejo regularly resorted to allegory, often using historical or non-Spanish settings and sometimes incurring censorship nonetheless – as in *En la ardiente oscuridad* (*In the Burning Darkness*; written 1946, banned until 1950), *Un soñador para un pueblo* (*A Dreamer for the People*, 1958), *Las meninas* (1960), *El concierto de San Ovidio* (*An Orchestra for St. Ovid*, 1962), and *El sueño de la razón* (*The Dream/Sleep of Reason*, 1969, banned until 1970). His most hard-hitting plays are set in a fictional Surelia ("pais derrotado" / a defeated country): in *Aventura en lo gris* (*Adventure in Grey*, written 1954, banned until 1963) assorted characters try to cross the frontier on the country's occupation. *La doble historia del doctor Valmy* (*The Double Story of Dr. Valmy*, written 1964, banned until 1976) probes torture by the political police.

In 1960, the younger dramatist Alfonso Sastre accused Buero Vallejo of "posibilismo": self-censorship in order to get performed. Playwrights who grew up after the Civil War tended to be more confrontational, in line with increasing student and worker protest. Much of the realist theater of Lauro Olmo was banned, an exception being *La camisa* (*The Shirt*, 1960, performed 1962), unique in dealing with working-class emigration to Germany. José Martín Recuerda, too, saw his plays banned or cut, and from 1966 to 1971 lived overseas. His best-known works – *Las salvajes en Puente San Gil* (*Wild Women in Puente San Gil*, 1961, performed 1963) and *Las arrecogías del beaterio de Santa María Egipcíaca* (*The Inmates of the Convent of St. Mary of Egypt*, 1970, banned until 1977) – are choral pieces with musical interludes that have little to do with realism. Sastre himself refused to compromise with the censor, opting for non-Spanish settings that make his plays more allegorical than realist. His plays typically explore moral dilemmas in revolutionary situations; all were banned for several years if not for the dictatorship's duration. His 1965 *Anatomía del realismo* (*Anatomy of Realism*) argues for a tragic theater that rejects both avant-garde nihilism and Brechtian estrangement. His most successful play *La sangre y la ceniza* (*Blood and Ash*, written 1962–5, banned until 1976) makes brilliant use of, precisely, Brechtian techniques. Another option for dramatists was exile: Fernando Arrabal would move to Paris in 1955 where his absurdist plays were performed in his wife's French translations; most remained unstaged in Spain until after Franco's death.

In the course of the 1960s, opposition writers reassessed strategies, realizing that their work was not producing political change. At the 1963

Madrid conference on realism, the foreign writers present found the Spanish participants' defense of realism outdated. The one Spanish speaker who criticized realism was Luis Martín-Santos (Gracia and Ródenas 2011, 142–3, 519), whose 1962 novel *Tiempo de silencio* (*Time of Silence*) had shown that political commitment could be expressed through literary experimentation. From 1962 Barcelona became the major publishing center for the novels of the Latin American boom, which would render realism obsolete. Most Spanish novelists fell silent for several years, reinventing themselves as experimental writers. The younger generation of novelists that emerged in the early 1970s, promoted by publisher Carlos Barral under the label "La Nueva Novela Española" (The New Spanish Novel) – of whom Javier Marías has been the most enduring – equated being modern with cosmopolitanism and intellectual sophistication rather than analysis of Spanish society. They took as their mentor Juan Benet, whose creation of a mythical Región in his novels from *Volverás a Región* (*Return to Region*, 1967) onwards signaled a rejection of engaged literature for modernist experiment with a strong philosophical bent. The young poets featured in Castellet's 1970 anthology *Nueve novísimos poetas españoles* (*Nine New Spanish Poets*) were more interested in pop culture than politics.

Catalan Writers and the Struggle for Cultural Survival

The political commitment of writers in the Catalan-speaking territories from the 1930s to the 1960s was shaped by the significance that the very act of writing and publishing in Catalan had acquired in the previous decades. *Noucentista* encouragement of writers, thinkers, educators, and other cultural workers to collaborate institutionally with the Mancomunitat to create a modern, educated, civil, and cohesive community combined with the violence and repression experienced by Catalan society in the same period to produce a generation whose commitment to writing was often driven equally by social, political, and cultural concerns. Barcelona's late nineteenth- and early twentieth-century reputation as a city of bombs or *Rosa de foc* (Rose of Fire) meant that it had undergone numerous periods of intense censorship and martial law even before the 1923 advent of the Primo de Rivera dictatorship (Kaplan 1992). In some cases, as in the previously mentioned 1906 response to military censorship of the Lliga Regionalista satirical paper *Cu-cut*, or the negotiation over a draft autonomy statute in 1918–19, this led to collaboration between Catalanist political parties and cultural activists. In other cases, as in the aftermath of the 1909

Tragic Week and the series of strikes following that of La Canadenca in 1919, the response was far more divided, due largely to the reluctance of the Lliga Regionalista's more conservative elements to make any concessions to the growing labor movement that might undermine their own economic hegemony. Catalan intellectuals' relationship to the state was throughout this period marked by the need to navigate a complex sociopolitical map in which at times the Spanish central government would ally itself with the radical republican violence advocated by Alejandro Lerroux, in order to undermine Catalanist action and policies, whereas at other times more right-wing, bourgeois Catalanists would turn to the state for help in "winning" the labor wars of 1919–23. Similar divisions and alliances of convenience, where political, religious, or economic interests were out of step with linguistic or cultural identifications, would re-emerge during the Second Republic and Civil War, as attested in divergent postwar testimonies such as the compelling memoirs of communist Teresa Pàmies and anarchist Federica Montseny, or Joan Sales's extraordinary novel *Incerta glòria* (*Uncertain Glory*, 1956, 1969) in which different ideological visions of the war and its aftermath are intertwined.

Nevertheless, the Catalan cultural field's prevailing characteristic between 1906 and 1939 was one of intellectual collaboration to underpin literary production and dissemination in the Catalan language, through creation of the necessary linguistic tools, libraries, and educational programs and networks; broad-based resistance to the 1923–30 Primo de Rivera dictatorship's repressive measures; or continued commitment to educational and status planning, enshrined in the left-wing Republican Generalitat's cultural policy from 1932 (Campillo 1994; Foguet i Boreu 2008). By the start of the Civil War, there were numerous daily and weekly publications in Catalan, from the conservative *La Veu de Catalunya* and *La Humanitat* to the more left-wing *La Publicitat* and *La Nau*; cultural journals like *La Revista de Catalunya*, *D'Ací i d'Allà*, and *Mirador*; a thriving satirical press that included *L'Esquella de la Torratxa*, *La Campana de Gràcia*, *Papitu*, and *El Be Negre*; children's magazines like *En Patufet*; sports papers like *La Rambla* and *Xut!*; and party-political mouthpieces such as *L'Opinió*, *Solidaritat Obrera*, and *L'Hora*. Furthermore, there was a wide, varied literary marketplace that, despite the continuing institutional privileging of high cultural production, included crime novels and children's fiction.

With the outbreak of the Civil War followed by social revolution in Catalonia, political divergences led to cases of radical re-positioning. Writers who had previously aligned with the Lliga Regionalista, or were threatened or repulsed by revolutionary violence, either left Catalonia in

1936 (Sagarra, Josep Pla, Joan Estelrich) or stopped writing until after the war (J. V. Foix, Josep Maria Junoy, Marià Manent, Joaquim Folch i Torres). However, the majority – including Antoni Rovira i Virgili, Nicolau d'Olwer, Josep Carner, and Joan Puig i Ferreter – remained loyal to the Republic, out of social and political conviction but also as the best way of protecting Catalan culture (Campillo 1994). Some (Avel·lí Artís Gener, Ferran de Pol, Pere Calders, Vicenç Riera Llorca) enlisted to fight against the Francoist forces. Others (Pompeu Fabra, Armand Obiols, Carles Riba, Xavier Benguerel, Francesc Trabal, Joan Oliver, Mercè Rodoreda) were coopted to educational and cultural projects like the Consell de l'Escola Nova Unificada (New Unified School Council), Consell de Cultura (Cultural Council), Institució de les Lletres Catalanes (Institution for Catalan Letters), and the Commissariat de Propaganda de la Generalitat (Generalitat Propaganda Commissariat). The same commitment to the need to protect linguistic and cultural diversity that had underpinned the foundation of a Catalan branch of PEN International in 1922 (Subirana 2018, 160) fed into the unionization of writers with the UGT Agrupació d'Escriptors Catalans or the CNT Grup Sindical d'Escriptors Catalans, as well as their collaboration with the Alianza de Intelectuales para la Defensa de la Cultura and involvement in the Barcelona and Valencia legs of the Second International Congress of Antifascist Writers in 1937. Women writers (Aurora Bertrana, Maria Lluïsa Algarra, Anna Murià, Carme Montoriol, Maria Teresa Vernet) were involved in organizing the 1937 Women's Congress in Barcelona and the feminist magazine *Companya* (1937–8), aimed at a female antifascist readership (Real 2006).

The Catalan cultural field's increasing dynamism in the 1930s was lost with the arrival of Francoist forces from early 1939. The awareness of what was to come – attested by severe repressive measures against Catalanist cultural manifestations in Majorca in summer 1936 – led many Catalan intellectuals from across the political spectrum to work to protect different aspects of the cultural archive. Members of the Institució de les Lletres Catalanes remained in Barcelona until January 1939 to continue this task, transporting key archives north before joining the half million evacuees who crossed the border into France fleeing the advancing Nationalist troops (Campillo 1994; Guillamon 2008).

The Franco regime's repressive measures, including a ban on the public use of Catalan as well as a decade of intense cultural purification through book burning, the dismantling or Castilianization of cultural institutions, and the reassignment of civil servants and educators to other parts of Spain, came as a shock even to Catalan regime supporters (Segura 2006; Larios

2014). Whilst some, like Pla, presented no resistance to writing in Castilian, though remaining committed to mapping the disappearing Catalan land-scape in his dialectically rich prose, others opted for silence or continued to write in secret, sometimes publishing their work in clandestine journals such as *Ariel* (1946–51). Still others lobbied for publications in Catalan to be permitted, beginning with pre-standardization editions of work by medieval and *Renaixença* Catalan poets and religious texts, and gradually obtaining permission for the publication of contemporary poetry which regime censors considered a minority genre (Samsó 1994–5).

Although more wide-ranging publication of other genres would not be permitted until the end of the 1950s, publishers found ways around the censors, backdating to the prewar years works like Josep Maria de Sagarra's translations of Shakespeare or smuggling in texts published by Catalan publishing houses in exile. Other forms of resistance included the organization of literary readings in private homes and later the formation of amateur theater groups such as the Agrupació Dramàtica de Barcelona or the Escola d'Art Dramàtic Adrià Gual, where cultural activists like Maria Aurèlia Capmany and Ricard Salvat organized rehearsals and productions of adaptations of Catalan works and translations.

The lack of a daily press or public access to popular literature and education in Catalan meant that a whole generation grew up with primarily oral access to the language. This led to the emergence of radical writers whose mode of literary expression was Castilian, such as Juan Goytisolo and later Juan Marsé. These difficult sociocultural circumstances meant that, until the late 1950s, poetry was the main vehicle of Catalan linguistic resistance to the Franco regime. So, for instance, Riba's *Elegies de Bierville*, written in exile in 1941–3, began to circulate as a cult testimony to the need for individual and collective cultural resistance even before his own decision to return to Catalonia. Salvador Espriu, who had only published prose works before the war, would through his poetic evocation of the ruins of the mythical world of Sinera and his calls for intercultural tolerance and understanding in the more realist *La pell de brau* (*The Bull-hide*, 1960) become the poetic voice of Catalan cultural resistance. He would achieve a wider popular following in the 1960s through the setting of his poetic texts to music by singer-songwriters associated with the Catalan *nova cançó* (New Song), in particular the Valencian Raimon who became a prominent voice of the late 1960s and early 1970s. The ghosts and ruins of Espriu's Sinera (backwards spelling of his coastal hometown, Arenys de Mar) would be brought to life in productions of *La primera història d'Esther* (*The Story of Esther*, 1962) and *Ronda de mort a Sinera* (*Death Round in Sinera*,

1965) directed by Ricard Salvat, mediated by the latter's radical Brechtian aesthetics and evoking interior exile as a reflective space of resistance for all Catalans. Perception of Espriu's role, alongside that of other poets, in the civic duty of "saving the words" (as Espriu himself put it) for future speakers, writers, and readers of Catalan would be enshrined in the symbolic significance of the Festival de la Poesia Catalana al Price, organized at the Gran Price stadium on April 25, 1970 as an act of protest against the Franco dictatorship, which included participants from across the Catalan-speaking territories – Vicent Andrés Estellés (Valencia), Guilem d'Efak (Majorca), Jordi Pere Cerdà (Perpignan) – as well as writers who had been in exile – Joan Oliver, Agustí Bartra, Jordi Sarsanedas, and Josep Palau i Fabre. The role of the poet as a redemptive voice would remain prevalent long after this period, notwithstanding the contributions of more experimental and counter-cultural poets and movements from Joan Brossa onwards.

From *Galeguismo* to Galaxia: The Freezing and Thawing of Galician Literary Culture

The work during the 1920s of the Xeración Nós (Nós Generation), discussed in chapter 8, transformed the ambition and reach of Galician-language literature but, unlike in Catalonia, the publishing industry remained small and Galician made only limited inroads into the wider public and cultural spheres. The most prominent Galician-language periodicals were published by political groupings; the best known – the Irmandades da Fala's fortnightly *A Nosa Terra* (*Our Land*) which survives online today – is estimated to have sold between 1,000 and 2,000 copies at that time. As the 1930s dawned, Galician-language writers continued to look to the high-cultural models established in the 1920s, with an emphasis on stylized poetry such as the neo-troubadouresque verse of Fermín Bouza-Brey and Álvaro Cunqueiro, or the Greek- and Latin-inspired work of Aquilino Iglesia Alvariño (Vilavedra 1999).

The Republic's advent hastened the foundation of the first Galicia-wide nationalist political party, the Partido Galeguista (PG), in December 1931. Like today's Bloque Nacionalista Galego, the PG was an umbrella for organizations across the nationalist spectrum, uniting over 20 groups, including liberals, conservatives, republicans, socialists, and a minority of independence supporters from Galicia and the diaspora. The party leaders included members of the Xeración Nós (Castelao, Ramón Otero Pedrayo, Vicente Risco, Antonio Vilar Ponte) and up-and-coming thinkers who would make their name during the 1940s and 1950s (Plácido Castro, Ricardo Carvalho Calero, Cunqueiro). The older generation's influence ensured continuity with the policies of the proto-nationalist Irmandades da Fala, particularly regarding their call for Galician self-determination within a federal Spain and official status for the Galician language. A key project, begun in 1932, was to draft the first Galician Autonomy Statute.

At the 1933 elections, the PG had its first local success and gained international recognition from the Congress of European Nationalities (part of the League of Nations) but won no national parliamentary seats. The chasm between the party's left and right was exacerbated by the new right-wing Madrid parliament's suppression of the Galicianist movement, and in 1934 the right broke away under Risco's leadership to form Dereita Galeguista (Galeguista Right). The following year, Ramón Otero Pedrayo published *Devalar (Flowing)*, an experimental novel framed as four seasons in the life of contemporary Galicia. Otero acknowledged as his inspiration a landscape sketch "Devalando" by Castelao; recent critics have signaled the novel's debt to Virginia Woolf, signposted by its central character, Miss Agnes Woolf (Palacios 2002). The novel's stylistic experimentation and lyrical evocation of the landscape are infused with optimism about Galicia's future.

The optimism seemed well founded when, in 1936, Castelao, Ramón Suárez Picallo, and Vilar Ponte won seats in the Madrid parliament, charged with securing approval of the Autonomy Statute, backed by referendum on a 75 percent turnout. The Statute was presented to the Spanish Parliament by Castelao on July 15, 1936; two days later, their fellow-Galician, General Franco, announced the military coup that launched the Civil War and ended the PG project. The close-knit group now traveled (physically and intellectually) in different directions. Risco clinched his rightwards drift by distancing himself from *galeguistas* facing Nationalist reprisals and would become a mouthpiece for the rebels (awarded a medal by Franco in 1963). Otero Pedrayo, sacked from his schoolteacher position, retired to Ourense but, after winning a position at Santiago University, would become a key figure in postwar cultural renewal. Castelao, caught by the war in Madrid, fled to Barcelona and later Buenos Aires where, as party president in exile, he became the postwar Galician political movement's figurehead (Carballal 2017).

In the Franco regime's early years, with the ban on public use of all languages other than Castilian, intellectual and cultural production in Galician was restricted to the South American exile communities led by Castelao and Luis Seoane (see chapter 10). Only in the late 1940s did tentative projects become possible, such as the *Colección Benito Soto*, a bilingual poetry series named after an infamous Galician pirate and directed by Emilio Álvarez Negreira, Manuel Cuña Novás, and Sabino Torres Ferrer, which published some 15 volumes between 1948 and 1952, including works by Celso Emilio Ferreiro, Luis Pimentel, Cunqueiro, Tomás Barros, and Ricardo Carvalho Calero. High-profile Galician writers such as Camilo José Cela, Gonzalo Torrente Ballester, and Elena Quiroga, whose work featured Galician themes and settings, chose to write in Castilian. Cunqueiro – like Cela and Torrente, a Nationalist supporter during the war but breaking with the Falange in 1943 – successfully navigated a bilingual literary career; he remains best known for his ironic, fantastic tales in Galician.

The 1950s saw a slow thawing of the Galician cultural scene, led by the intellectuals known as the Xeración Galaxia (Galaxia Generation) because of their connection with the Editorial Galaxia publishing house. This publishing project aimed to continue the prewar cultural and political work of the Xeración Nós and Partido Galeguista, within the limited possibilities of Franco's Spain (Vilavedra 1999). Created at a banquet presided over by Otero Pedrayo on July 25, 1950 (St. James's Day and Galicia's national holiday), its first publication in April 1951, *Antífona da cantiga*, an anthology of popular *cantigas* with a prologue by poet Ramón Cabanillas, connected with the interrupted prewar tradition and, through the octogenarian Cabanillas, with early twentieth-century institutionalization projects.

Galaxia, directed by Ramón Piñeiro and Francisco Fernández del Riego with an advisory board headed by Otero Pedrayo, became the primary focus for cultural and linguistic regeneration in Galicia, always within the limitations prescribed by the dictatorship. Its cultural magazine *Cadernos Grial*, created in 1951, was almost immediately banned (it reappeared in 1963, continuing today). The project developed the Xeración Nós's internationalizing outlook, promoting Galicia as a fully European culture and Galician as a language suitable for use in all areas of knowledge. Just as the translation of James Joyce into Galician had signaled the Xeración Nós's ambition in the 1920s, so in the 1950s Piñeiro and Celestino Fernández de la Vega's translation of Martin Heidegger's *Essence of Truth* as *Da esencia da verdade* demonstrated their successors' equally grand vision.

The Galaxia group's cultural focus was perceived as dangerously apolitical both by the exile community in South America and by the younger generation that emerged in the 1960s. The open hostility of the new young nationalists is reflected in Xosé Luís Méndez Ferrín's allegorical "murder" of the patriarch Ulm Roan – assumed to represent Piñeiro – in his 1971 novel *Retorno a Tagen Ata* (*Return to Tagen Ata*). The Galaxia group's legacy has thus been somewhat problematic, although Piñeiro's naming as dedi-catee of the 2009 Dia das Letras marked a notable shift.

Basque Culture: Resistance and the Fight for Modernity

The generation of nationalist poets known as Olerkariak (The Poets, 1930–6) revitalized Basque poetry through modernist influences. The leading figures Jose Maria Agirre ("Lizardi") and Estepan Urkiaga ("Lauaxeta") were members of the PNV (Partido Nacional Vasco / Basque Nationalist Party) and committed participants in the cultural association Euskaltzaleak (The Bascophiles, founded 1927), whose project included promoting the Basque language in education, journalism (with the bilingual newspaper *El Día*, 1930–6), and literature (with the magazine *Yakintza*, 1933–6). The poems in Lizardi's acclaimed *Biotz-begietan* (*Heart and Eyes*, 1932) are dedicated to Euskara, the homeland, and nature and love. Lauaxeta, a charismatic writer and nationalist activist who participated actively in the Civil War, was taken prisoner after the bombing of Gernika and executed. His first Romantic- and Symbolist-influenced poetry collection, *Bide barrijak* (*New Directions*, 1931), was hailed for its novelty; the second, *Arrats beran* (*At Dusk*, 1935), made an even greater impact, incorporating stylistic elements of Basque popular lyric poetry, especially ballads and traditional folk songs. The influ- ence of Federico García Lorca's *Romancero gitano* (1928) is notable in poems like "Langile eraildu bati" (A Murdered Worker) (Kortazar 1986). The priest José Ariztimuño ("Aitzol") was fundamental to Euskaltzaleak's activities, drawing inspiration from Finnish and Provençal to enhance Basque litera- ture's cultural capital through publications, theater performances, poetry days, and *bertsolaris*. The 1933 poetry collection *Euskaldunak* (*The Basques*) of Nikolas Ormaetxea ("Orixe") – an active Euskaltzaleak member and author of important translations, who would go into exile after the Civil War – might have provided the foundational national poem called for by Aitzol had it not remained unpublished till 1950. As Aitzol admitted, a major handicap for 1930s Basque-language literary production was its limited reading public. This was aggravated by the Olerkariak poets' adoption of Sabino Arana's purist poetic precepts, which drove a wedge between oral and literary competence. Aitzol would move away from the highbrow poetry he had originally defended, championing a more popular literature rooted in traditional songs, ballads, and *bertsolaritza*.

The repression following Franco's victory in the Civil War had drastic con- sequences for Basque culture. The banning of all public use of Basque and the censorship that, despite its official demise in 1977, continued at varying levels of intensity into the 1980s, sought to eliminate any cultured use of the language (Torrealdai 1995). The result was cultural impoverishment, self-censorship, and an aggravation of the rift between everyday linguistic usage and a strategically deployed poetic hermeticism. The censors' tolerance with regard to Basque-language publications was limited to works of religious edification, popular literature, and folklore. As the 1950s progressed, new publishing and cultural initiatives attempted to revitalize the depleted Basque literary system. The Itxaropena publishing house's Kulixka Sorta series (1952) developed an important list of Basque-language works and translations, while the journals *Karmel* (1950), *Anaitasuna* (1953), and *Jakin* (1956), and the Auspoa publishing house (1961) directed by Antonio Zavala published key works of popular Basque literature, including testimonies of Basque Civil War combatants such as Sebastian Salaberria's *Neronek tirako nizkin* (*I Fired the Shots*, 1964). A new generation of writers emerged in the 1950s with Gabriel Aresti, Jon Mirande, and the novelist Jose Luis Alvarez Enparantza ("Txillardegi") who in 1957 published the first modern Basque novel, the existentialist *Leturiaren egunkari ezkutua* (*Leturia's Secret Diary*). He would continue to publish existentialist novels in the 1960s, as well as political novels in the 1980s, both of which reflected his left-wing Basque nationalist activism (he was a founder of the separatist group ETA). Thanks to these writers, Basque literature began to incorporate modern European literary trends, putting aesthetic criteria before subservience to politics, religion, or folklore. Mirande was the first to break with Basque poetry's pre-1950s latent religiosity. An exceptional polyglot, he learnt Basque at the age of 20. His eclectic philosophical and literary reading (the Stoics, Nietzsche, Spengler, Poe, Baudelaire, Kafka, Yeats) permeates his prose and poetry. An iconoclast and nihilist, his *Haur besoetakoa* (*The Goddaughter*, 1970) has been seen as a Basque *Lolita* and his poetry admired for its daring eroticism.

In the 1960s, economic and industrial development, the establishment of Basque schools (*ikastolas*), the creation of a unified Basque language, anti-Franco political activism, and campaigns for Basque language instruction created a favorable environment for literary renewal. Important in this respect was the 1965 creation of the Durango Book Fair. Gabriel Aresti and Jorge Oteiza, in the literary and art fields respectively, contributed to the creation of a modern cultural movement that embraced the latest European trends together with anti-Franco political militancy. Their revolutionary impact on the Basque cultural world was complemented by the linguist Koldo Mitxelena as the driving force behind the unification of the

Basque language, making possible the creation of a modern Basque litera-ture. The 1960s emergence of Basque theater groups like Jarrai broke old nationalist molds, and Basque social poetry was boosted by modern music groups such as Ez dok amairu (literally, There Is No Thirteen, 1965–72), influenced by the Catalan *nova cançó*.

The role played by Gabriel Aresti in this process was especially impor-tant. His career as writer, publisher, translator, and linguist – authoring short stories, poetry, and drama and translating Boccaccio, Eliot, and Hikmet, among others – inspired the next generation, as Bernardo Atxaga and Ramon Saizarbitoria have attested. His cultural activism included col-laborating with the theater group Jarrai, new publishing houses like Kriselu and Lur, and music groups like Oskorri (Red Sky), as well as his role in the debates on Basque linguistic standardization. After a first Symbolist-inspired poetry collection *Maldan behera* (*Downhill*, 1960), his move to social poetry, influenced by Blas de Otero, brought him a wide cross-generational Basque-speaking readership. *Harri eta herri* (*Rock and Core*, 1964), seen as influenced by the Galician poet Celso Emilio Ferreiro's *Longa noite de pedra* (*Long Night of Stone*, 1962), was followed by *Euskal harria* (*Basque Stone*, 1967) and *Harrizko herri hau* (*This City of Stone*, 1970), both heavily censored. The poems in *Harri eta herri* have urban settings and use simple language to convey a clear message. Echoing his friend Celaya, Aresti defined poetry as a hammer. The poem "Nire aitaren etxea" (The Family Home) in *Harri eta Herri* would become a political rallying-cry for a nation struggling against Francoist repression: "Nire aitaren etxea/ defendituko dut./ Otsoen kontra,/ sikatearen kontra. . . ./ Ni hilen naiz,/ nire arima galduko da,/ baina nire aitaren etzeak/ iraunen du/ zutik." (I'll defend/ the family home;/ from wolves,/ from drought. . . ./ I'll die,/ I'll lose my soul,/ my kin will stray,/ but my father's house/ will stand.).

10

Spain beyond Spain:
Exile and Diaspora (1939–1980s)

This chapter focuses on the Republican refugee exodus triggered by defeat in the Spanish Civil War, setting it in the context of earlier and later waves of migration.

The Aporetic Place of Exile

The place of exile in contemporary Spanish literary historiography has been long debated (Balibrea 2002–3; Blanco Aguinaga 2006), in part because the (re)institutionalization of Spanish literature – as literature exclusively in Castilian – during the Franco dictatorship largely left out writers who had gone into exile at the end of the Civil War, including them only insofar as their prewar writings fitted generational badges like that of the 1927 Generation, as was the case with Rafael Alberti, José Bergamín, and Pedro Salinas; and in part because the way in which exile was hypostasized as a mythical figure of a sundered Spain led to an assumption that the return of certain emblematic writers and intellectuals during and after the transition to democracy would suture that fissure. This division of Spain was reflected in one of the prevalent intellectual discourses of exile around the moral superiority of "la España peregrina" (itinerant Spain) – the journal *España Peregrina* was created in Mexico in 1940 – when compared with territorial Spain under Franco (Caudet 1976, 1992). On the one hand, this meant that Spain's problem continued to be seen as a conflict between "dos Españas" (two Spains), as in Antonio Machado's formulation, disregarding the evidence of extensive splintering in both "traditions" before and after the war (Ealham and Richards 2005). On the other hand, as official representations of the Civil War shifted from that of a crusade against the red, separatist, masonic, and semitic infidel to that of a fratricidal war (Richards 2013), it supposed that "itinerant Spain" could be almost seamlessly incorporated after the dictatorship's end. The return in 1977 of representative figureheads like the President of the Generalitat in Exile, Josep Tarradellas, and the emblematic 1927 Generation poet and member of the newly legalized Spanish Communist Party, Rafael Alberti, and in 1984 of the philosopher María Zambrano, was thus presented as plugging a temporal gap between the democratic tradition of the 1930s and the 1970s. Their individual journeys home became ways of performing some sort of continuity with the pre-Francoist past, by symbolically recognizing a tradition that had been all but silenced until the "return" of democracy.

Perhaps the clearest case of such an operation was that surrounding the internationally acclaimed writer Francisco Ayala who, though he had returned annually to Spain from 1960, only made it his permanent residence in 1980. Ayala's stellar intellectual trajectory was recognized in his election to the Real Academia Española in 1983, followed by the Premio Nacional de las Letras Españolas in 1988, the Premio Cervantes in 1991, and the Príncipe de Asturias award in 1998. The speeches at the Cervantes award ceremony, dovetailing with the build-up to the 1992 celebrations which would present the "discovery" of the Americas as the origin of a postnational, pan-Hispanic global network, reflected precisely how Ayala's self-representation as a rootless, cosmopolitan, and independent intellectual throughout his exile depended on forgetting the material conditions of expulsion, migration, and diaspora. His own answer to his 1949 rhetorical question "¿Para quién escribimos nosotros?" (For whom do we write?), which calls for Spanish Republican writers to rise above the material conditions of their exile (Ayala 1971), is one that is not accepted by many of the politically committed writers discussed in the previous chapter. It is important to contrast Ayala's position with that of Zambrano's 1984 declaration "amo mi exilio" (I love my exile) (see also Zambrano 2009, 2014). If Ayala's embrace of the role of rootless, cosmopolitan exile feeds into postnational narratives of inbetweenness and hybridity, it arguably does so because of the position from which this (re)writing of the imbrication between personal and political takes place, as a tenured professor in the US university system. In contrast, Zambrano's commitment to the intellectual emancipation provided by exile is one in which the suffering and tragic losses of embodied material existence produce a change in disposition towards the Other, as dramatized in *La tumba de Antígona* (*The Tomb of Antigone*, 1967), where the heroine's enclosure and privation in the dark cave results in rebirth rather than suicide, through her ability to listen, to empty the self and embrace silence, in order to find new (empathic, erotic) ways of knowing through the emotions – what Zambrano elsewhere calls "poetic reason": "Nosotras no sabíamos y sabíamos, sentíamos" (We did not know and we knew, we felt) (Zambrano 1967).

Not only did this transfiguration of exile (in the singular) involve a general lack of engagement with the often radically critical and resistant nature of work by Spanish Republican exiles (in the plural) vis-à-vis some of the dominant political, economic, and cultural discourses of the long twentieth century, as has been recognized in recent re-reading and intensive re-engagement with the legacy of Max Aub and Zambrano especially, but it was also an ideological operation that many exiles resisted and resented. The classic case was José Bergamín, whose dissatisfaction with what he saw as the empty, self-congratulatory culture of the transition led him to adopt increasingly radical counter-cultural positions, including an alignment with ETA's political rejection of the legitimacy of the Spanish state in the Basque Country (Balibrea 2008). In other cases, exiles who returned were almost completely invisible, particularly if they could not easily be coopted as lost cultural treasures because they had not been recognized internationally as such. Aub is a case in point: his aborted return in 1969 arguably confirmed the doubts, hesitations, and rejection of return rehearsed in many of his writings – in particular, his plays (notably, the trilogy of one-act plays on return: *La vuelta 1947*, *La vuelta 1960*, and *La vuelta 1964*) and diaries – from the late 1940s onwards. The long diary he composed on his return to Mexico, *La gallina ciega* (*Blindman's Buff*, 1971), records the same personal disappointment he felt as Ayala on his 1960s visits to Spain, at the lack of recognition of his work among a community he had hoped would be his readers; yet it also presents a searing critique of the mediocrity, political contradictions, ambivalence, and inwardness of a Spanish society in the process of incorporation into neoliberal modernity.

This work was relaunched to new audiences in the mid-1990s, in the aftermath of the self-congratulatory 1992 celebrations (Barcelona Olympics, Seville Expo, and the "Discovery"), and arguably contributed to later revisions of the significance and place of exile in Spanish culture, which increasingly became marked by notions of tragic loss, absence, failure, and melancholia. For instance, Jerónimo López Mozo's 2002 play *El olvido está lleno de memoria* (*Forgetting is Full of Memory*), based on the return of exiled actor Edmundo Barbero in 1980, imagines his existential anguish at representing nothing for Spanish audiences; he is an absent presence on the Madrid scene, with his previous performances in major roles in Latin American theater and film not even ghosted on stage except for his own spectral spectatorship of his social invisibility. More problematically, Àngels Aymar's *Trueta* (2009) recovers the figure of the famous Catalan orthopedic surgeon Josep Trueta, who had himself published an awareness-raising volume during his exile in England (*The Spirit of Catalonia*, 1946), by focusing almost completely on his experiences in the 1930s and 1940s, with a melancholy epilogue that testifies to a largely "tragic" experience of return, even though in reality he resumed his career in Spain (Buffery 2011).

Haciendo Justicia (Doing Justice): Remembering and Recovering Exile through Spanish Republican Exile Historiography

The historiography of Spanish Republican exile has attempted to set right these injustices, by recovering the texts, histories, and stories of this parallel tradition from the late 1980s onward. While the initial focus was on writers who were already considered classics but whose works in exile were insufficiently known – such as the poetry of Juan Ramón Jiménez, Jorge Guillén, Luis Cernuda, and León Felipe; the theater of Alberti, Bergamín, and Salinas; the narrative of Ayala, Ramón J. Sender, Paulino Masip, Aub, Esteban Salazar Chapela, Arturo Barea, and later Jorge Semprún – increasingly there was a shift in focus to include wider constituencies and to collect oral testimonies, diaries, and memoirs, in part due to the increasingly collaborative interdisciplinary work between literary scholars and social and political historians. If at first it was largely the 1989 and 1999 anniversaries of the major Republican exodus in January–February 1939 that galvanized work on Spanish Republican exile historiography, activity intensified at the beginning of the twenty-first century (coinciding with the historical memory boom, see chapter 13), introducing new focalizations: the diverse political, cultural, and linguistic communities in exile; the experiences of women and children; second-generation exiles. The majority of women writers in exile hardly featured in the Spanish literary landscape before 2000, even though works by women had been key to pro-Republican propaganda in the immediate postwar years: Isabel de Palencia's *Smouldering Freedom* (1946), Constancia de la Mora's *In Place of Splendor* (1939), Federica Montseny's *El éxodo – pasión y muerte de los españoles en el exilio* (*Exodus – Passion and Death of Spaniards in Exile*, 1949–50), though Dolores Ibárruri's *They Shall Not Pass: The Autobiography of La Pasionaria* (1966) came out in an extended Spanish version in 1984. Even what is now recognized as one of the most detailed, complex, and affecting testimonies of the Spanish Republican refugee crisis over the first six months of 1939, Silvia Mistral's *Éxodo. Diario de una refugiada española* (*Exodus: Diary of a Spanish Female Refugee*, 1940) was not republished in its entirety until 2009. Other women writers/intellectuals whose works in exile had been only partially known but have since been republished include Margarita Nelken, María Teresa León, Concha Méndez, Ernestina Champourcin, Rosa Chacel, Luisa Carnés, María Luisa Elio, Cecilia Guilarte, Maria Lluïsa Algarra, and Teresa Gracia.

In parallel with this commitment to expanding the archive by restoring previously excluded individuals, communities, and histories to their "proper" place in Spanish literary historiography, there have been important debates around the politics and ethics of exile historiography. How far can Spanish Republican exile traditions be reinserted into national literary historiography when, as Carlos Blanco Aguinaga insisted (2006), these were writings that developed largely beyond the purview of the nation – "con un pie fuera de tiempo" (with one foot outside of time), as Ramón J. Sender expressed it in his 1968 rewriting of the *Don Juan* myth (Lonsdale 2011). For increasing numbers of cultural critics, the assumptions and tools of national literary historiography simply cannot deal with Spanish Republican exiles, whose very existence draws attention to the nation's limits. Their writings expose the exclusions and vanishing points in the construction of national narratives, are governed by alternative and at times oppositional spatio-temporal coordinates, and often provide radically different paths through the cultural and political landscape of modernity (Balibrea 2017).

The work of Aub after the Civil War, for instance, presents an almost constant and unflinching witnessing of the injustices and exclusions of twentieth-century history. His six-volume cycle of realist testimonial novels *El laberinto mágico* (*The Magic Labyrinth*, 1943–68) – *Campo cerrado* (*Field of Honor*, 1943), *Campo de Sangre* (*Field of Blood*, 1945), *Campo abierto* (*Open Field*, 1951), *Campo del Moro* (*Moorish Field*, 1963), *Campo francés* (*French Field*, 1963), and *Campo de los Almendros* (*Field of Almond Trees*, 1968) – aims to recover the history of the 1930s and 1940s from below, interweaving the experiences of often humble protagonists with political decision-makers (and destiny-makers). His numerous plays of the 1940s, 1950s, and 1960s represent different aspects of the conflicts, exclusions, forced migrations, and repression he witnessed in Europe, always drawing attention to the need not only to bear witness but also to remain committed to the struggle against injustice. So, his *"San Juan"* (1943) depicts the persecution of the Jewish community in Europe in the 1930s through the fictionalized scenario of a cargo ship carrying 600 Central and Eastern European Jews, who are turned away from every port. The only people saved are a small group of politically committed young men, who jump ship to fight in the Battle of the Ebro in June 1938. His *Morir por cerrar los ojos* (*Dying through Blindness*, 1944) evokes the inhumane conditions in southern French detention camps in order to draw attention to the gulf between French revolutionary ideals of liberty, equality, and fraternity, as captured in *La Marseillaise* – sung in protest by the main female protagonist at the play's end – and the actual treatment of Spanish political refugees. Once again it is the moments of solidarity, social justice, and community resistance that are presented as alternatives to the nation-state's political exclusions and economic self-interest. In other works, Aub explores alternative, politically disruptive temporalities, such as his spoof speech on fantasized election to the Spanish Royal Academy (1959) in which he presents an alternative history whose members include Federico García Lorca and Ramón del Valle-Inclán, privileging the creative voices excluded from the nation since the Civil War. Most biting amongst these more satirical works is his 1960 short story "La verdadera historia de la muerte de Francisco Franco" (The True Story of the Death of Francisco Franco), in which an exasperated Mexican barman, Nacho Jurado Martínez, decides to take his first vacation in 20 years in 1959 in order to visit Spain and assassinate the dictator, so that he no longer has to hear the same old boasts, stories, and infighting of the Republican refugee groups who occupy the Café Español day in day out. On his return to Mexico, Nacho is faced with the same scenario, only the faces have changed to a gaggle of conservatives, traditionalists, and Falangists.

A basic example of the way in which the confrontation with exile requires historians to rethink criteria of inclusion/exclusion would be the case of Maruxa Vilalta, who is included with other second-generation exiles educated in Mexico (Manuel Durán, Ramón Xirau, Angelina Muñiz-Huberman, Núria Parés, Tomás Segovia, for example) in a number of studies (e.g., Mateo Gambarte 1996), but always stands out because she self-identifies to interviewers as Mexican rather than Spanish. As a successful journalist and playwright in Mexico in the 1960s and 1970s, her "choice" might simply reflect, as with Ayala, the extent to which identity positions are shaped by material and economic conditions. How far is it possible to achieve success as a Mexican writer without professing one's Mexicanness? Or conversely, how far can a writer be recovered by Spanish Republican exile historiography if they do not self-identify as Spanish? Closer attention to Vilalta's writings reveals not only that some of her early works – the short stories "El meu dia foll" (My Crazy Day) and "Diferència" (Difference, 1958) – are published in Catalan exile journals, but that many of her plays – from *Un país feliz* (*A Happy Country*, 1964) to *1910* (2000) – contain the imprints of the particular Republican memory associated with her family history, her father, uncles, and paternal grandmother all having affiliated to Esquerra Republicana de Catalunya (Buffery 2016). Thus, even though she wrote in Spanish, she cannot be simply reintegrated into national literary historiography (whatever the nation) but draws attention to the presence and interplay of multiple, overlapping affiliations and temporalities. The problem of where to locate writers who self-translate all or part of their work (including in "self-translation" the forced shift to another language) is, of course, not exclusive to second-generation Spanish Republican exiles – in some ways, it is the same debate that emerged at the Guadalajara and Frankfurt book fairs when Catalan culture was the guest of honor in 2004 and 2007 respectively, or that leads to Samuel Beckett being studied as a French-language writer in France and as an English-language Irish writer in the English-speaking world. Nor is it a problem that can be solved by expanding or collapsing the limits of the nation: what is required is multiple perspectives, the shuttling between languages and contexts, the capacity to attend to blind spots and to listen for the silences.

Important recent work challenging the "exile paradigm" has sought to engage ethically and politically with the phenomena of Spanish Republican exile(s), stressing their exposure of the nation's limits – a Spain or Spains beyond Spain (Epps and Cifuentes 2005) – and the mechanisms by which they resist reincorporation (Balibrea 2017). To begin to apprehend the vanishing points of exile, it is necessary to recognize the challenges it presents through its multiple temporalities, geographies, languages, identities, communities, histories, politics, and projects, and also to allow it to trouble the overarching temporality of modernity. In many ways, exile – in this chapter, Spanish Republican exile – is paradigmatic of the problematics we have faced in composing the present volume as a whole: the attempt to reconcile diverse temporalities, the story of an entity that is constituted only in the very process of telling stories, that calls for multiple positionalities, for the effort to see beyond particular vanishing points, but that is nevertheless ephemeral, a performance and an attitude rather than a new monument or canon.

This is, then, a very different project than the many attempts to call into question the beyondness of exile, whether by insisting that the literature of exile was never excluded under the dictatorship and that we have to thank certain intellectuals under the Franco regime (for example, Dionisio Ridruejo or Camilo José Cela) for acting as bridges between interior and exterior, or in the suggestion of more general histories that exile is a constituent feature of Spanish identity (Kamen 2008). This is not to deny that experiences of exile, migration, and diaspora have been important elements of Spanish cultural history, whether the early nineteenth-century liberal exiles mentioned in chapter 1, or the numerous waves of republican exile throughout the nineteenth and early twentieth centuries in response to urban violence and the repression of republicanism and the labor movement. Many Catalan republicans had to go into exile in the 1890s and 1910s, for instance, and then again during the Primo de Rivera dictatorship, with some, for example Antoni Rovira i Virgili and Ramon Vinyes, experiencing multiple exiles. The continued political commitment and activism of these earlier exiles in the Americas is often what helped to finance pro-republican campaigns in the 1920s. Economic migration, ultimately not so far from political exile, also played a key role in the constitution of the modern state, both regarding internal rural to urban mobility, and in the production of major diasporas in the Americas or some cases north Africa, from Galicia, the Basque Country, Andalusia, the Canaries, the Balearic Islands, and Aragon. All of these processes of voluntary or forced mobility contributed to shape ideas of identity, belonging, and community, as we will see below, especially in the cases of Galicia and the Basque Country. These earlier diasporas would have an impact on the experiences and integration of the half million refugees that fled Spain at the end of the Civil War. Although this chapter deals fundamentally with the post-1939 Republican exile, we have included discussion of the earlier Basque and Galician economic diasporas in the Americas.

Basque Diaspora and Exile: The Eighth Province

The Basque diaspora is commonly referred to as "the eighth province," supplementing the seven historic provinces of the French and Spanish Basque Country. Large-scale Basque emigration to the Americas dates back to the 1830s, when the newly independent Latin American republics sought to recruit European labor. From 1850, with the Californian gold rush, this migratory flow moved northwards to the American West, where Basque emigrants established themselves thanks to their herding skills. Sheep herders would be the protagonists of the first novels about Basque emigration, José Manuel Etxeita's *Jayoterri maitia* (*Beloved Homeland*, 1910) and Resurreccion Maria Azkue's *Ardi galdua* (*The Lost Sheep*, 1918). Like the winning poem at the first 1853 Floral Games (see chapter 6), they equate emigration with loss of Catholic faith and nostalgia for the homeland. In the early twentieth century, emigration was viewed with alarm by the Basque nationalist press, reporting on the 400,000 Basque emigrants in the Americas (Álvarez Gila and Tapiz Fernández 1996). In the 1920s the most influential Basque journalist of the day, Aitzol (penname of José Ariztimuño) campaigned against this population drain in the

French Basque Country, as did the short stories of Kirikiño (penname of Ebaristo Bustintza), *Abarrak* (*Branches*, 1918) and *Bigarren Abarrak* (*More Branches*, 1930). Negative views of emigration would persist through to Nemesio Etxaniz's (notably sexist) 1966 novel, *Ameriketan galdua* (*Lost in the Americas*, 1966). Emigrants to the United States wrote about their experiences in Basque-language weeklies such as *Escualdun Gazeta* (1885–6) and *California'ko Eskual-Herria* (1893–7), both published in Los Angeles, which did not circulate in the Basque Country.

The Basque diaspora today comprises around 4.5 million people, 1.5 times more than the current population of the French and Spanish Basque Country combined, with major concentrations in Argentina, Uruguay, and the United States. Robert Laxalt's English-language novel *Sweet Promised Land* (1957) was the first to elaborate a Basque-American identity that was not tied nostalgically to the Basque homeland. Its Basque sheep-herder protagonist faces the same alienation on his return to the French Basque Country as he had experienced in Nevada. The Basque sheep herder has become as a literary archetype in novels set in the American West in recent decades by Basque-American writers Frank Bergon, Monique Laxalt, Gregory Martin, and Martin Etchart (Río Raigadas 2007). A legacy of this successful emigration is the William Douglass Center for Basque Studies founded in 1967 at the University of Nevada in Reno, which has the largest collection of Basque-related materials outside the Basque Country (www.unr.edu/basque-studies). Few novels have been written in the Basque Country itself about this economic migration. Exceptions are Aingeru Epaltza's *Lur Zabaletan* (*In the Fields*, 1984), Jesus Mari Olaizola Txiliku's *Indianoa* (*The Emigrant*, 1983), and Bernardo Atxaga's "Bi letter jaso nituen oso denbora gutxian" (Two Letters All at Once; the first of his *Two Basque Short Stories*, 1984) which depicts its sheep-herder protagonist's hybrid English-Basque linguistic identity.

If a small amount of nineteenth-century Basque emigration was for political reasons (resulting from the Carlist Wars), in the twentieth century political factors – the Spanish Civil War and, later, ETA terrorism – would be overwhelmingly responsible. Over 100,000 Basques went into exile after the Civil War. Basque-language literature, virtually eradicated at home by massive Francoist cultural repression, was revitalized by exile publishing houses like Ekin, founded in Buenos Aires in 1942, and journals such as *Euzko Gogoa* (1950–5; 1956–9), founded in Guatemala by the exile Jokin Zaitegi, moving in its second period to Biarritz. In its first period *Euzko Gogoa* published over 100 volumes; in its second period, when it published entirely in Basque, it hosted the most interesting creative writers of the

1950s and 1960s, including Orixe (penname of Nikolas Ormaetxea), Juan Mari Lekuona, and Santiago Onaindia. It also published Basque translations of classical Greek authors and Shakespeare, demonstrating the Basque language's ability to render key texts in the Western literary canon. Basque-language writing was kept alive by Telesforo Monzon, a member of the Basque government-in-exile, with his poetry collections *Urrundik* (*From Afar,* 1942) and *Gudarien egiñak* (*The Gudaris' Exploits,* 1944). The Ekin publishing house issued the first postwar novels in Basque: Jon Andoni Irazusta's *Joanixio* (1946) and *Bizia garratza da* (*Life Is Bitter,* 1950), set in the Civil War; and José Eizagirre's *Ekaitzpean* (*In the Storm,* 1948), which explored the conflictive pull experienced by many Catholic Basques during the Civil War thanks to the Carlists' alliance with Franco's Nationalists and Basque nationalists' alliance with the defenders of the Republic.

The work of returning exile Martin Ugalde marked a milestone in the treatment of political repression and exile for many Basques, starting with his 1961 short stories *Iltzalleak* (*The Killers,* 1961, published in Venezuela), awarded the first Basque Government-in-Exile Prize. Following his 1969 return to the Basque Country, his production in Basque outstripped that in Spanish. His autobiographical 1990 *Itzulera baten historia* (*Story of a Return*) is the first Basque-language novel to narrate the impossibility of return; focusing on two generations of a Basque exile family in Venezuela, it explores the gap between the first and second generation who identify with different homelands.

While political exile has become a less frequent theme in recent Basque literature, it is repeatedly referenced in Joseba Sarrionandia's poetry collections *Izuen gordelekuetan barrena* (*In the Recesses of Fear,* 1981), *Hnuy illa nyha majah yahoo* (1985–95), and *Prisons and Exiles: Poems* (2019). The three stories entwined in his novel *Lagun izoztua* (*The Frozen Friend,* 2001) illustrate the dislocation experienced by successive waves of political exiles, whether escaping the Francoist repression or the later radicalization of Basque nationalism with ETA (see chapter 13 for Bernardo Atxaga's exploration of exile as a way of extricating oneself from ETA terrorism). Garazi Goia's *Txartel bat (des)herrira* (*A Ticket to Exile,* 2013) brings together political exile and economic migration through her depiction of motley uprooted Basque characters in contemporary London, one of them a child evacuee to Britain during the Spanish Civil War. Kirmen Uribe would return to the topic of Basque Republican exiles in his last two novels: *Mussche* (2012; translated into five languages) and *Elkarrekin esnatzeko ordua* (*The Hour of Waking Together,* 2016; National Critics Prize). *Mussche* is a tribute to the Flemish writer, translator, and activist Robert Mussche, who disappeared during the

Nazi occupation of Belgium, having taken in a female Basque child refugee. The novel adopts a postmemory perspective, with the past pieced together in a creative mosaic of memory fragments by Mussche's adoptive daughter. *Elkarrekin esnatzeko ordua* narrates the extraordinary lives of the Basque nationalist exiles in Venezuela, the nurse Karmele Urresti and her husband Txomin Letamendi, a trumpeter and captain of the Basque nationalist *gudaris* who fought for the Republic in the Spanish Civil War, with Txomin finally dying in a Francoist jail. The investigation and rewriting of the past by the fictional character Uribe, drawing on assorted documents and testimonies, highlights the ethical commitment to record the injustices of the Francoist repression and to recover the Basque nationalist political project, represented by the Basque government-in-exile headed by José Antonio Agirre.

Galicia: Displacement and Deterritorialization

In Galicia's case, too, the Republican exile must be set in the context of the foundational role of Galicia's overseas communities in the development of modern Galician literature, putting displacement at the core of the Galician cultural imaginary (Hooper 2011; Romero 2012). During the half century before the Republican exiles' arrival in Buenos Aires, Montevideo, or Havana, the Galician communities in those cities had been central to the funding, publication, and circulation of countless Galician literary works, notably Rosalía de Castro's *Follas novas* (*New Leaves*, 1880), which not only takes emigration as a central subject but was published in Havana and dedicated to that city's Sociedade de Beneficencia d'os Naturales de Galicia (Galician Beneficent Society).

The postwar exile complicates the traditional narrative of the relationship between the "two Galicias." If we are accustomed to thinking of this relationship as an exchange of economic capital earned in emigration for cultural capital provided by the homeland, the developments of the 1940s and 1950s shifted the balance. Back in Galicia, Galician-language cultural production had been reduced to almost zero by the intense repression of the early Franco years, re-emerging only with the foundation of Editorial Galaxia in 1950. The exiles, on the other hand, remained politically and culturally active throughout the 1940s. A number of political parties formed, although not all were willing to recover the trajectory of the prewar Partido Galeguista or to recognize the authority of Castelao and others who had held political office at home. These differences were exacerbated with the establishment of the Consello de Galiza (1944) and the Galician government-in-exile (1945).

The manifesto of the postwar exile movement, subsequently adopted by nationalists in the homeland and now considered the foundational text of modern Galician nationalism, is Castelao's vast four-part anthology *Sempre en Galiza* (*Forever in Galicia*). First published in Buenos Aires in 1944, later editions would include his political writings from 1936 to 1948. The introductory section, written for *A Nosa Terra* during Castelao's internal exile in Badajoz in 1935, sets out his leftist ideology as distinct from the hitherto dominant conservatism of his colleague and rival Vicente Risco. The text is divided into four "Books," each written at a different stage of Castelao's exile and reflecting on a particular aspect of the embattled nationalist project. The contents of Libro I, written in the first years of the Civil War between 1936 and 1938, place Castelao's project in its social and historical context. Libro II, which updates the ideas expounded in Libro I, was begun in New York in 1940 and completed en route to Argentina later that year. Libro III, written in Argentina 1942–3, captures the optimism of *galeguistas* who believed, erroneously, that an Allied victory in World War II would oust Franco, allowing return to their homeland. Libro IV, included from the 1961 second edition, was written in 1947–8 on Castelao's return to Argentina from Mexico; it outlines his support for a federalist structure (Carballal 2017). The book's unifying theme is Castelao's belief in Galicia's right to self-determination. While it contains plenty of examples of his famously mordant wit, it is an absolutely serious contribution to his country's political future. The book's symbolic importance remains undimmed; its 70th anniversary was formally marked by the Galician Parliament.

In the cultural field, the *galeguista* project swiftly coalesced around a group of writers and intellectuals in Buenos Aires, where Castelao, Rafael Dieste, Luis Seoane, and other postwar exiles worked alongside those, such as Eduardo Blanco Amor, who were already established in the city, or younger *galeguistas* such as Isaac Díaz Pardo who arrived in the 1950s. After Castelao's death in 1950, Seoane became the lynchpin of the Buenos Aires circle (Devoto and Villares 2012). Like Castelao, whose Galician-language upbringing had marked him out among the Xeración Nós, Seoane had an unusual background that gave him added credibility: born of emigrant parents in Buenos Aires, he had come to Galicia as a child before returning to Argentina as an exile in 1936. A member of the Partido Galeguista during the Republic, he remained politically active in exile through the Republican consulate in Buenos Aires. Throughout the 1940s, he spearheaded a series of cultural initiatives designed to give public visibility to Galician cultural and intellectual production, including book series (Hórreo, Dorna), magazines (*Correo Literario, Galicia Emigrante*), and publishing houses (Editorial Nova, Botella al Mar, Citania). A renaissance man – poet, artist, dramatist, and essayist – Seoane worked primarily in Galician but was pragmatic enough to understand the advantages of incorporating Castilian-language production into Galicia's literary history. He worked closely with Díaz Pardo, co-founding the Laboratorio de Formas (1963), which became an important focus for the cultural activity of the Grupo Sargadelos, today one of Galicia's canonical cultural organizations (Volkova 2017).

Despite the efforts of Castelao, and later Seoane and Díaz Pardo, to maintain contact between *galeguistas* in Galicia and overseas, the different conditions under which the two groups worked inevitably led to tensions. By the 1960s, when political activism re-emerged in Galicia, the assumptions of the last two decades were no longer tenable. Things came to a head in 1966, when the poet and activist Celso Emilio Ferreiro, author of the famous anti-Franco poem "Longa noite de pedra" (Long Night of Stone), emigrated from Galicia to Venezuela to take up the post of Culture Secretary to the Caracas Galician Society. Having expected to become part of a thriving, committed *galeguista* community, he was pulled into a series of political maneuverings by Franco sympathizers, which left him angry and disillusioned. His disgust is colorfully articulated in the satirical poetry collection *Viaxe ao país dos ananos* (*Journey to Dwarf Land*, 1968), which questions emigrants' right to pronounce on the future of a Galicia they no longer know.

Ferreiro's attack on the Galician emigrant community was hugely controversial and denounced by contemporaries, including Seoane. Nonetheless, his point about the detachment of longstanding emigrant and exile communities from the realities of life "at home" remains relevant. The traditional, sentimentalized narrative of emigration has real political consequences, as during the 2005 Galician elections, whose outcome depended on an overseas vote cultivated extensively by the Galician right through the celebration of a nostalgic, essentialized view of Galician culture (Hooper 2006). Since the 1970s, a number of Galician writers, such as Carlos Durán (*Galegos de Londres / Galicians in London*, 1978), Ramiro Fonte (*A rocha dos proscritos / Rock of Outlaws*, 2005), Xelís de Toro (*Os saltimbanquis no paraíso / Jugglers in Paradise*, 1998), Manuel Rivas (*A man dos paiños / The Hand with the Sea-Kites*, 2000), and Xesús Fraga (*A-Z*, 2004) have produced works that problematize that narrative, dealing with more complex issues of deterritorialization, diaspora, and the difficulties of return, often prioritizing the experience of the economic migrants of the 1960s and 1970s as a counterpoint to the traditional narrative (Hooper 2011). Since the 1990s, Galicia has also, for the first time, become a destination for migrants, which has revitalized the longstanding practice of *alófono* or non-native writers, the most prominent of whom include Marilar Aleixandre, John Rutherford, and Victor Omgbá.

Catalan Literature in Exile / Exile Literature in Catalan

In the first six weeks of 1939, nearly half a million refugees fled advancing Francoist troops across the Catalan border with France, the majority of them spending subsequent weeks in makeshift detention camps on the southern French coast. Of these, up to half would return to Spain in the course of the same year, but others, including some 70,000 Catalans, would remain in exile. Many of these Catalan exiles were members of the political, cultural, and intellectual elites whose collaboration with the autonomous government of Catalonia meant they were threatened with reprisals under the February 1939 Law of Political Responsibilities. They included figures like the Esquerra Republicana de Catalunya Generalitat president Lluís Companys, who would be captured by the Gestapo, returned to Spain, tortured and executed in 1940; the prominent anarchist Federica Montseny, who spent the ensuing years touring Europe to denounce the Franco regime's illegality; and Communist Party members like Teresa Pàmies, who after spending part of her exile in Mexico, settled in Prague where she produced radio broadcasts in Spanish and Catalan. The double title of this section is intended as a reminder that virtually all the foremost Catalan writers of the 1930s went into exile at the end of the Civil War.

Many of the most important Catalan writers of the twentieth century would write key works in exile, from Josep Maria de Sagarra's *La ruta blava* (*The Blue Route*, first published in Castilian translation in 1942, in Catalan only in 1964), written during a brief exile at the Civil War's start, to Carles Riba's emblematic *Elegies de Bierville* (*Bierville Elegies*, 1943), which represent the journey from personal and spiritual loss and melancholy to recognition of the poet's cultural responsibility to return and speak for the collective. The hope that the international community would extend the fight against fascism to overturn the Franco regime meant that many Catalans joined the French resistance against Nazi Germany, whilst others were deported and sent to concentration camps such as Mauthausen, as catalogued in Joaquim Amat Piniella's testimonial novel *K.L. Reich* (1963, 2001), which he began to write in Andorra in 1946, and in Montserrat Roig's

1977 oral history *Els catalans als camps nazis* (*Catalans in the Nazi Camps*). Representatives of the different political parties came together to re-form political and cultural institutions in exile, including the Generalitat, which after the detention and execution of Companys was headed by Josep Irla and later Josep Tarradellas; the rival Consell de Catalunya; and the Front Nacional de Catalunya, which was created by members of Estat Català (Catalan State) to organize resistance against the Franco regime. Cultural associations, journals, and publishing houses were set up in Europe and Latin America, sometimes building on the existing diasporic infrastructure of Casals (Community Centers) and Orfeons Catalans. Whilst these, like participation in anti-fascist journalism and radio broadcasts during World War II, were initially intended as temporary measures, alongside political lobbying, to secure international aid in reinstating democratic institutions, from 1946 they took on the longer-term role of maintaining cultural production in the Catalan language. Journals like *Pont Blau*, *Xaloc*, *La Nostra Revista*, and *Quaderns de l'exili*; literary prizes and festivals like the *Jocs Florals*; publishing houses like those of Bartomeu Costa-Amic in Mexico City; educational associations like the Anglo-Catalan Society in the UK: all of these contributed to maintain some sort of cultural infrastructure in which writers could continue to publish.

Thus, writers like Mercè Rodoreda, Agustí Bartra, Josep Carner, and Pere Calders were able to find outlets for short publications or benefitted from translation commissions passed to them through publishing networks in exile. Even so, it was difficult for them to make a living from writing in Catalan, and they often combined literary creation with other roles. Translation was a key option (Bacardi 2009), whether working for the United Nations in Geneva, like Rodoreda, or translating contemporary British and North American poetry into Spanish, as in the case of Bartra, which he complemented with parallel versions in Catalan. Self-translation was also attempted by some writers in order to reach an audience beyond the Catalan-speaking exile community, but, if this was accepted in the cases of Josep Trueta and Víctor Alba (penname of Pere Pagès i Elies) who sought to bring the plight of Catalonia and the Second Republic to wider anglophone audiences, it provoked controversy in the case of writers who chose to publish in Spanish. Carner's Mexican play *Misterio de Quanaxhuata* (*The Quanaxhuata Mystery*, 1943) was widely criticized because he composed it in Spanish, notwithstanding his defense of the need to engage with communities in the host country (Roser i Puig 2011). When he later re-wrote the play in Catalan, having settled in Brussels, he transformed it into a fascinating reflection on intercultural encounter, evoking the complex space inhabited by the exiled intellectual. Negotiations by cultural activists inside and outside Catalonia to get Carner nominated for the Nobel Prize for Literature show how Catalan cultural resistance in this period depended on achieving international visibility (Subirana 2018, 87–90). Rather than the response of a minority culture to the pressures of globalization, this was a struggle to counterbalance the effects of Francoist repression on the internal marketplace, consigned to silence and invisibility.

The activities in exile had relatively little impact in Catalonia itself, leading certain writers and publishers, such as Joan Sales and Xavier Benguerel, to return in the 1950s to continue their promotion of Catalan literature in Spain. Through the Club Editor, created in 1955, they would publish some of the period's most emblematic texts, including key novels by Llorenç Villalonga and Rodoreda. Other bridging figures in this period, such as Ricard Salvat, Manuel de Pedrolo, and Joan Fuster, sought to maintain links with Catalan cultural institutions in exile. However, the lack of possibilities for sustained dialogue throughout the Franco dictatorship's early decades ultimately meant that internal and external resistance had taken parallel paths. One key indicator of this is the greater receptivity of the 1960s Barcelona publishing world to the products of expatriate Latin American writers (such as Mario Vargas Llosa and Gabriel García Márquez), followed by Southern Cone exiles in the 1970s and 1980s (such as Cristina Peri Rossi) (Santana 2000). The ironic result is that Latin American "magic realism" found audiences before the work of homegrown writers like Pere Calders and Tísner (penname of Avel·lí Artís Gener), whose absurd vision and original blend of psychological realism and Surrealism, including Calders's *Cròniques de la veritat oculta* (*Chronicles of a Hidden Reality*, 1955) and Tísner's extraordinary reverse conquest narrative *Paraules d'Opoton el vell* (*Words of Opoton the Old*, 1968), were produced in exile in Mexico. Another indicator of this spatio-temporal dislocation is the sense of alienation experienced by many exiles when they returned to Catalonia, often finding their former home – and language – to be an unrecognizable phantom of the past. This led to the obsessive re-writing of works by Catalan prewar writers such as Salvador Espriu, Sales, and Benguerel (Cornellà-Detrell 2011). It also produced one of the most affecting chronotopes of the period: Mercè Rodoreda's *La plaça del Diamant*.

Published in 1962, Rodoreda's best-known work has been the subject of numerous and diverse critical readings. It marks a return to novel-writing after a long period of relative silence. The 1960s Catalan literary establishment tended to read the novel as if its naive, impressionable, helpless, and victimized narrator transmitted the "woman's" language and voice of its author. Rodoreda's own stance during this period contributed to such a reading: her often subtly ironic, self-deprecating interviews, her insistence on rejecting the five successful prewar novels she had published in Catalan, her dedication to re-writing the only one she was prepared to recognize as her "offspring" (*Aloma*, 1938). However, there was not a complete rupture in her literary and aesthetic production. She continued to write throughout her period of exile, although the upheaval of her experience as a refugee in France, plus the need to eke out a living as a seamstress in the 1940s, meant that her primary focus was on painting and poetry, the latter finding its way into festivals and publications in exile (Ibarz 2008). The letters held at the Fundació Mercè Rodoreda in Barcelona show that she was a constant writer, exploring and revisiting formal and thematic ideas. The short stories she wrote in the 1950s are not just a laboratory for the preparation of her masterpiece; they display immense literary and cultural knowledge, with intertexts that range from the modernist literary canon to anthropology, mythology, visual arts, and even natural history, as well as the different refugee testimonies of her peers. The *Vint-i-dos contes* (*Twenty-Two Stories*, 1958) of this period have been rightly identified as her most sustained investigation of the experiences of violence, dislocation, rupture, and transformation that characterize exile writing.

Why *La plaça del Diamant* was read as it was in the 1960s has much to do with the diffuse and resistant characteristics of the Catalan cultural field in that period, which would have long-term effects on subsequent critical production and legitimization processes through the critical, educational, and publishing institutions that were beginning to be forged. For instance, the tendency to read the novel in almost testimonial terms as the unmediated voice of the author's experience as a Catalan woman, born in Barcelona to a lower-middle-class background, was as much a product of literary critical trends of the period, particularly in its perception of the narrator Natàlia's voice as something new in Catalan literature, as it was of the structural misogyny enshrined by the Francoist marginalization of women since 1939. There are other possibilities for reading the novel, more sensitive to aesthetic and sociocultural specificity, that offer more convincing insights into its continuing popularity amongst readers and into the aesthetic and political significance of its content and form. As many critics have recognized, the novel was written in exile in Geneva but after Rodoreda had begun to make tentative return journeys to her homeland in the 1950s. The alienated, hallucinatory, and impressionistic vision of the city presented in the novel, transmitted through the narrative of a traumatized subject who has gone through extreme deprivation and pain (Buffery

2015), also transmits the effects of the experience of return to a city that is no longer recognizable to the exile, either physically or socially, where people do not even speak the same language. In such a light, Rodoreda's decision to return in her novel to Barcelona before the Spanish Civil War, as a Catalan-speaking space that has been lost but is haunted by ghosts of the past, is incredibly significant. The attempt to recover this dwelling-place as one that is Catalan-speaking and gendered (Resina 2008; Bou 2013) mediates the sense of disorientation, loss, and dislocation experienced by interior and exterior exiles. It is important to recognize that this "lost" space – that of the Republic – is not merely evoked with the nostalgia, mourning, and melancholy characteristic of more testimonial and autobiographical Spanish Republican exile writing, although there are compelling passages that hint at the Republic's revolutionary potential and the sense of liberation it engendered, even for relatively alienated women like Natàlia. We see clearly how the experience of sociopolitical space is determined by gender, class, education, political positioning, sexuality, ideology, and language, as well as simple things like the material reality of the dwelling-place and access to basic human needs such as food, light, warmth, or human contact. In the ruins of Barcelona, and the ruins of Natàlia's life, excavated in this novel, we find a space of reflective nostalgia that provides the opportunity to think these spaces differently.

The Places and Temporalities of Exile

In considering Republican exile literature in general, we should note the importance of the spatial and temporal coordinates that shaped particular experiences (Balibrea 2017). The geographical diversity of the countries where Spanish Republicans found refuge was immense. Many political figures were granted asylum in France, Belgium, Switzerland (especially after the outbreak of World War II), the UK, the US, or the USSR, depending on their political affiliations. Mexico and Chile opened their borders to large numbers of Republican refugees and transatlantic liners were arranged to facilitate evacuation from France. Other Latin American countries that received refugees before and during World War II were Cuba, the Dominican Republic, Venezuela, Colombia, Uruguay, and Argentina, although these destinations often depended on evidence of family or employment contacts. After 1946, refugees were taken in by the Eastern bloc. For writers in Castilian, asylum in Latin America opened up greater possibilities for continued literary production; Mexico City and Buenos

Aires became key cultural centers of the Hispanic world in the 1940s and 1950s, especially with regard to the publishing market and theater. As we have seen, the situation was more complex for writers in Catalan, Basque, and Galician, although in the last case the presence of a significant diaspora in Cuba and Argentina provided a ready-made (though not always receptive) audience, and in the case of the first two there was the option of returning to settle in the Basque- and Catalan-speaking regions of southern France once the Vichy regime had been removed.

Many key places of memory recur again and again in the literature of exile. The most prevalent are those relating to La Retirada, the crossing of the Pyrenees in winter (which led to the death and burial of Antonio Machado shortly after arriving in France), and the concentration camps on the beaches of southern France, where hundreds of thousands of political refugees were held without adequate shelter, water, or food, in many cases into the early 1940s, with some forcibly repatriated or later deported to Nazi concentration camps (Cate-Arries 2004). Among the works dedicated to these major places of memory are Aub's previously mentioned *Morir por cerrar los ojos*, Luis Suárez's *España comienza en los Pirineos* (*Spain Begins at the Pyrenees*, 1944), Manuel Andújar's *St Cyprien, plage . . . campo de concentración* (*St Cyprien, beach . . . concentration camp*, 1942), and Agustí Bartra's *Cristo de 200.000 brazos* (*Christ of 200,000 Arms*, 1943; published in Spanish and Catalan). Other key sites of memory are Spanish Republican exiles' involvement in the French Resistance, and the networks of intra-community support and solidarity they established in French, North African, and Nazi camps, on the transatlantic crossings to the Americas, and in the countries of reception. The commitment to transmitting the Republic's political and cultural legacy included the construction of particular literary myths, with Federico García Lorca's memory maintained in exile through the stage productions and readings of Margarida Xirgu (M. Delgado 2003) and later Rafael Martínez Nadal's commitment to publishing Lorca's controversial *El público*. Writers like Álvaro Custodio, María Teresa León, Alberti, and Aub continued to rewrite versions of Spanish classics (Montiel 2011; Mainer 2006); to take one example, the screenplay by Alberti and León for the 1947 Argentine film adaptation of Lope de Vega's *La dama duende* sets the action in an aesthetically Goyesque eighteenth-century Spain, facilitating a reading in terms of the clash between Catholic traditionalist landowners and the emancipatory exuberance of the popular classes (Wheeler 2011).

The temporalities of exile are also important, in that the literary production of Spanish Republican exile writers is affected by historical developments in the countries of reception and by alternative milestones to those in Spain. Between 1939 and 1945 the Republican exile community was focused on resistance, on maintaining institutional legitimacy, and on the potential liberation of Spain at the end of World War II. From 1946 onwards this optimism was lost, leading to the commencement of other projects. It is telling, for instance, that Ayala's question "For whom do we write?" is from 1949, whereas the collection of stories he published earlier in 1944 was very much focused on experiences related to the Spanish Civil War. Another telling example of these shifting temporalities is Alberti's 1944 play, *El adefesio* (*The Horror*). Completed in Argentina and premiered by Margarida Xirgu's company in Buenos Aires in the same season as Alejandro Casona's *La dama del alba* (*The Lady of the Dawn*) and the world premiere of Lorca's *La casa de Bernarda Alba* (*The House of Bernarda Alba*), *El adefesio* presents a similar story of a young woman trapped in an oppressive household, where the hypocritical, reactionary Catholic morality of her elders drives her to suicide. In the play's original version, the main oppressive force, Gorgo, who takes on the trappings of masculine authority (literally wearing her dead brother's beard), expresses doubt, anxiety, and remorse at the tragic events she unleashes. When Alberti rewrote the play for performance in Madrid in 1976, with Gorgo played by another great symbol of Spanish Republican exile, the Galician-born and French-domiciled Maria Casares, almost any hint of regret or humanity was removed (Buffery 2011). The first 1944 version perhaps reflects the optimism with which exiles awaited the outcome of World War II; the second in 1976 is rewritten from hindsight, knowing that the oppressor was never overthrown.

It is similarly interesting to compare Silvia Mistral's 1940 account of the Retirada and the camps in *Éxodo*, which focuses on the solidarity and companionship of the women in exile and the hope with which the protagonist eventually faces her journey to Veracruz, with Teresa Gracia's later, more elegiac play *Las Republicanas* (*Women of the Republic*, 1978), based on her memory of being taken by her mother to St Cyprien and Argelès in 1940, in search of her father, in which the overlapping, intermingling voices of the women and children with whom she shares this space are transmitted as if through the gaping mouths of the fish who are their only witness. In Mistral's diary we witness the process by which the individual refugee becomes part of the collective, through interacting and engaging with their stories and becoming part of a network of camaraderie and solidarity. In Gracia's play, the alienated, dislocated individual of her earlier long autofictional poem *Destierro* (*Exile*, published 1982) is left with just the fragments of voices, the remnants, traces, and ruins of a now-forgotten community.

11

Catalan, Galician, and Basque Literatures: Recovery and Institutionalization (1960s–1990s)

Manuel de Pedrolo's *Mecanoscrit del segon origen* (*Typescript of the Second Origin*, 1974) imagines a post-apocalyptic scenario in which most of the global population has been wiped out by alien invasion, and it is left to two adolescents to find a way to survive and construct an alternative future for humanity. Just as part of that (re)construction involves the central protagonist Alba sifting through volumes in a ruined Barcelona library in order to preserve an inclusive range of books for future readers, so Pedrolo's novel became one of the most widely read works of Catalan fiction of the subsequent decade, due to its adoption in Catalan secondary education as a text that promoted ethnic diversity, gender equality, and civic responsibility. As we have seen in previous chapters, one of the effects of the Franco dictatorship on Catalan, Galician, and Basque cultures was the obliteration of their literary fields. For all three, cultural production in the postwar period was dispersed due to the large numbers of writers and artists in political exile, and the road to recovery was shaped by the relationship to this often critical outside interlocutor. The relaxation of restrictions on languages other than Castilian and changes in the Francoist censorship from the late 1950s enabled efforts to re-establish these peripheral literary fields, which drew on a climate of increasing economic liberalization and concerted political resistance. Together these provided the momentum for continued recovery under the regime emerging from the 1975 restoration of the constitutional monarchy, whose political decentralization, within the constraints of the 1978 Spanish Constitution, created the conditions for the implementation of cultural policies in Catalonia, Galicia, and the Basque Country. It is important to recognize that many of the cultural institutions that emerged after 1978 were underpinned by developments in the 1960s and early 1970s; it was political and cultural resistance to the Franco regime that laid the grounds for decentralization. In the three cases explored in this chapter, autonomy was achieved under Article 53 of the Constitution between 1979 and 1980; all three regions introduced Laws of Linguistic Normalization, supplemented by campaigns to extend use of the respective local language.

The relative success of education and status planning was inflected by the different social, political, and demographic contexts in each of the so-called "historical autonomies," each of which presented different challenges, not least of which was violent opposition from sectors that saw any form of devolution as a threat to the organic unity of Spain. It should not be forgotten that there were attacks on Catalan-language publishing houses throughout the Catalan-speaking territories nor that the February 23, 1981 attempted coup responded to military concerns about the direction of the "Estado de las Autonomías" (State of Autonomous Communities, as Spain was defined in the 1978 Constitution). However, in all three regions certain patterns were repeated since, to minimize resistance and dissent, the easiest way forward was often to "recover" historical precedents or to mimic what was happening in other regions. Thus, gradual institutionalization was achieved through the creation of libraries, publishing houses, and education institutions; the writing of literary histories and inclusion of vernacular literary texts in educational syllabi; and support for literary creation through prizes, subventions, media adaptations, promotion, and dissemination. Nonetheless, as we shall see, the trajectory followed by literary production has varied in each case.

Imagining a Future for Catalan Culture:
From Resistance to Normalization and Beyond

The reconstruction of the Catalan literary field gained momentum at the end of the 1950s with the emergence of journals like *Serra d'Or* from 1959, followed by *Tele-Estel* and *Presència* in the 1960s; the creation of key publishers like Club Editor (1955) and Edicions 62 (1962); the completion of projects like the Diccionari Alcover-Moll by Editorial Moll in 1962; the commencement of work on a multi-volume Catalan-language encyclopedia, the *Gran enciclopèdia catalana* (1965); and the proliferation of independent theater companies in the 1960s. Simultaneously, the Catalan cultural field was radicalized as a means of resistance to the dictatorship and through its centrality to an increasingly vocal and progressive university student movement. As glimpsed in chapter 9, this meant that even poetry had the capacity to evoke mass cultural resistance, as mediated by the protest singers of the 1960s. In the same period, there was increasing commitment to a literature of experience that reflected the social concerns of the time. Associated above all with the so-called Barcelona School of mainly Spanish-language poets influenced by Jaime Gil de Biedma, this trend impacted on the development of the Catalan literary scene through the work of writers and critics like Gabriel Ferrater and Josep Maria Castellet who, alongside more materialist critics like Joaquim Molas formed in the Romance Philology program at the University of Barcelona under Martín de Riquer, sought to modernize the study of Catalan language and literature, often influenced by periods of residence or connections abroad. The Escuela de Barcelona poet, Carlos Barral, took over his family publishing house in the 1950s to form Seix Barral, becoming one of the most influential publishers of the 1960s, with lists that included Latin American boom writers and prizes to stimulate new writing. Barcelona's increasingly prominent position in the publishing world created a network of support for publication in Catalan, too. However, such writing continued to be subject to censorship; permissions were often granted to novels in Catalan only if a Spanish translation was released simultaneously (Cornellà-Detrell 2011).

Though some scholars (e.g., Vilarós 2018) have emphasized the gulf between Catalan culturalist resistance to the dictatorship and more socially progressive, Marxist-inspired movements associated with the re-emergence of an independent labor movement (Commissions Obreres / Workers' Commissions) and the PSUC (Partit Socialista Unificat de Catalunya / Unified Catalan Socialist Party), a key structural change in the 1960s was the shift to more unified platforms. So, for instance, Òmnium Cultural was founded in 1961 to promote educational, cultural, and political activities that brought together neighborhood associations, political pressure groups, and educational movements to mitigate the effects of Francoist repression on the status of the Catalan language and culture. Its headquarters at the Palau Dalmases hosted the first clandestine Estudis Universitaris Catalans (Catalan-language University Studies) in the late 1960s, giving a new generation of radicalized students the opportunity to re-engage with Catalan cultural texts from varied perspectives. Many would become key players in the Catalan cultural revival of the 1980s and 1990s, such as Jordi Castellanos who structured the study of Catalan literary history at the Universitat Autònoma de Barcelona, and Josep Maria Benet i Jornet who would go on to become the most influential Catalan dramatist of the late twentieth century as a mentor for later generations of Catalan playwrights and writer for Catalan Television in the 1980s (with serials like *Nissaga de poder* / *Line of Power*) (Feldman 2009). From the 1960s the PSUC, with the return of Gregori López Raimundo, husband of Teresa Pàmies, and influenced by Manuel Sacristán's dissemination of Gramscian ideas at the University of Barcelona, embraced a Catalanist agenda that attracted sectors of Catalan society, especially more radicalized student groups. This marriage between Marxism and Catalanism is central to understanding the path taken by Catalan culture in the transition to parliamentary democracy.

Many cultural actions were underpinned by recognition of the manifold role of culture in society, leading to identification of the need for popular forms and of methods and discourses to resist and overcome repression. Writers like Francisco Candel drew attention to the living conditions of generations of immigrants to Catalonia in works like *Los otros catalanes* (*The Other Catalans*, 1963; later translated into Catalan); Montserrat Roig logged the histories of women's experiences through the twentieth century in the trilogy *Ramona, adéu* (*Goodbye, Ramona*, 1972), *Els temps de les cireres* (*The Time of Cherries*, 1977), and *L'hora violeta* (*The Violet Hour*, 1980); and Terenci Moix began to collapse the boundaries between high and popular culture in novels like *El dia que va morir Marilyn* (*The Day Marilyn Died*, 1969). There was considerable focus on the creation of a popular cultural market, with new journals and genre novel collections such as Pedrolo's "La Cua de Palla" for Edicions 62, and increasing attention to Catalan cultural and political content in previously pro-regime press outlets such as *Destino* and the *Correo Catalán*. Publishers like Edicions 62, Aymà, and Ariel gave wider visibility to Catalan culture with projects like the previously mentioned *Gran enciclopèdia catalana* and key histories of Catalan culture such as the 11-volume *Història de la literatura catalana*, initiated with medieval volumes edited by Martín de Riquer and completed with the contemporary volumes of Antoni Comas and Joaquim Molas. Molas played a notable role as general editor of Edicions 62's series of cheap popular editions of classic texts from 1978: the "Millors Obres de la Literatura Catalana" (Best Works of Catalan Literature) and "Millors Obres de la Literatura Universal" (Best Works of World Literature, in Catalan translation). The former included a wide range of prewar texts and postwar works by Pedrolo, Joan Fuster, Josep Maria de Sagarra, Llorenç Villalonga, Blai Bonet, Pere Gimferrer, Mercè Rodoreda, Roig, Baltasar Porcel, Joan Brossa, Vicenç Riera Llorca, and Tísner, as well as anthologies of contemporary poets and prose writers (including Jaume Cabré, Jordi Coca, Carme Riera, Joan Margarit, Narcís Comadira, and Francesc Parcerisas, all of whom remain influential figures in the Catalan canon today).

A salient feature of the Catalan cultural resistance of the late 1960s and 1970s was its internationalization, whether through the Gauche Divine which engaged with modern artistic and media developments beyond Catalan borders, or the focus of writers and scholars like Ferrater on the latest trends in modern literary and linguistic scholarship. Above all the period saw the creation and consolidation of international and Pan-Catalan platforms, drawing both on networks created in exile and on confluences with the internationalizing discourse of late 1960s liberation movements. These included the Universitat Catalana d'Estiu (Catalan Summer University) in Prades de Conflent, the Associació Internacional de Llengua i Literatura Catalanes (International Association of Catalan Language and Literature, 1968), and the PSAN (Partit Socialista d'Alliberament Nacional / Socialist National Liberation Party, 1968) inspired by crucial figures like the Valencian Joan Fuster in *Nosaltres els Valencians* (*We Valencians*, 1962) and *Qüestió de noms* (*A Question of Names*, 1962), in which he defended the Pan-Catalanist idea of the Països Catalans (Catalan Countries, embracing Valencia, the Balearic Islands, Languedoc-Rousillon, Alghero, and the Franja de Ponent in Aragon, as well as Catalonia).

Fuster's writings reflect on the relationship between language, culture, territory, and identity, exploring how processes of linguistic and cultural shift and subordination are produced by the operation of power and struggles for hegemony. Unlike the regionalism of long-standing Valencian-Catalan associations like Lo Rat Penat and even the vision of culture later presented by Catalonia's Generalitat under Convergència i Unió (Convergence and Union, CiU; center-right Catalan Nationalist Coalition), the work of Fuster is forward-looking, pointing to the need for progress in imagining the shape of Valencian identity but breaking from the dependency produced by insufficient awareness of history. Yet his direct criticism of the provincial myths of local and official culture in Valencia led to violent opposition to his work and even threats to his person. His ideas, together with the radical ideas emerging from liberation movements elsewhere in the world that focused on the emancipation of groups previously subordinated due to gender, sexuality, social class, culture, or ethnicity, underpinned the development of double, triple, or multiple militancy, often reflecting different underlying levels of identification and affiliation. So, writers like Maria-Mercè Marçal (see chapter 12) referred to her triple oppression due to gender, nation, and class, and was militant on all three fronts, affiliating with the PSAN and becoming active in the difference feminist movement in Catalonia.

Roig, in her above-mentioned trilogy exploring the turbulent events of Catalonia's twentieth century through different generations of the same family, shows, in each novel, the underlying tensions and struggles produced by different processes of identification and affiliation, the pull between social expectations, community actions, and individual beliefs and desires. For instance, in *Els temps de les cireres*, Natàlia's subordination as a Catalan woman is complicated by her family's reaction to her abortion, forcing her to flee abroad. *L'hora violeta* explores the transition to democracy as a period of inbetweenness, mutation, and transformation, drawing attention to the pressures and tensions produced above all by the triple militancy between gender, nation, and class. Both novels show how the emancipation of women is generally subordinated to the Marxist politics of main parties like the PSUC. This sense of loss or betrayal in the translation of the various 1970s demands for liberation to parliamentary democracy is reflected in criticisms of the new political, social, and cultural structures throughout the 1980s. Roig's work shows an immensely ethical responsibility to negotiate these different pressures, from her journalism, interviews, and commitment to recover invisible voices in her study of the Catalan victims of the Nazi concentration camps, *Els Catalans als camps nazi* (*Catalans in the Nazi Camps*, 1977), to her many essays on feminism and contemporary women's experience, including *Tiempo de mujer* (*Woman's Time*, 1980) and *Mujeres hacia un nuevo humanismo* (*Women toward a New Humanism*, 1982).

It is important to recognize that the institutionalization process that took place from the 1980s onwards, after Catalonia regained its autonomy statute in 1979, was underpinned by broad consensus on the need for Catalan national and social emancipation – around the slogan "Llibertat, amnistia, estatut d'autonomia" (Liberty, Amnesty, Statute of Autonomy) – and by the effectiveness of the different forums, fronts, and organizations set up during the 1970s in planning for regime change. From a cultural and literary perspective, the most important of these was undoubtedly the Congrés de Cultura Catalana (Catalan Cultural Congress) set up by the Col·legi d'Advocats de Barcelona (Barcelona Bar Association) in 1975 (Fuster 1978). The main issues for debate were the defense of national heritage, the demarcation of Catalan territory, official use of Catalan, revitalization of popular culture and folklore, and the recovery and creation of Catalan institutions. Involving over 1,500 different associations and institutions and some 15,000 individual contributors, the Congress ran for two years and contributed to campaigns for the recovery and promotion of Catalan language and culture. Broad consensus around its proposals underpinned the election of Catalanist formations in the 1980 regional government elections and the creation of institutions by which to deliver the necessary social and cultural changes, ranging from the linguistic normalization program, reinstitution of the Institut de les Lletres Catalanes, creation of a Catalan television station, and other aspects of educational and cultural policy taken forward by CiU after its victory in the first autonomous elections in 1980 (Crameri 2008). The relative success of these measures in Catalonia as compared to the Balearic Islands, and the even more extreme case of

Valencia where the culture wars spilled on to the streets in the 1970s and early 1980s, underpin the importance of the broad operation of multiple militancy. In Valencia, the leftist position of Catalanist action was perceived as a threat to existing economic and cultural interests and resulted in violent attacks on Catalan-language bookstores, language centers, and even individuals such as Eliseu Climent and Fuster (Martí 1997).

The shape of Catalan culture since then has, of course, continued to be contested, although in the 1980s there was a high level of consensus around cultural policies to rectify the structural disadvantage of Catalan language and culture after the long years of Francoist repression (Crameri 2008). However, some aspects of cultural policy weakened the Catalan cultural market, precisely because it was perceived to be dependent on government support for its survival. The excessive concern with high culture in order to gain visibility also contributed to a crisis of legitimization expressed in the growing unease of critics and writers about Catalan culture's direction (J.-A. Fernàndez 2008, 46–83).

Part of the problem, as with the other post-1980 autonomous communities, is that the process of canon formation is always contested, if anything more so with smaller cultures where opportunities and resources are more limited, so that differences of opinion are inevitably politicized. The negotiation of enforced bilingualism proved particularly problematic; even in a case like that of Catalonia where diglossic practice had not been as widespread as in other regions, the greater prestige of the Spanish-language market is often presented as one of the main reasons for not supporting Catalan. Furthermore, the economic strength of the transnational Spanish-language market meant that Catalan literature continued to be excluded from the mainstream media and education system, contributing to a continuing lack of visibility at and beyond state level. The various methods introduced locally to counter this – the subvention of translations to and from Catalan; the funding of popular culture; the creation of a highly visible cultural canon of "Catalans universals"; the incorporation of Catalan texts and history into the education system – were the main strategies to compensate for structural weaknesses. However, if a great deal was achieved, the rapid globalization of culture and the strength of the publishing industry in Spanish have limited Catalans' ability to overcome their subordinate position with respect to the Spanish cultural market (Crameri 2008; J.-A. Fernàndez 2008, 120–43).

A complex issue here is the relation of cultural policy to identity politics, particularly with the postmodern turn to a concept of identity as performance in which even essentialist notions of identity come to be seen as strategically adopted. Catalan theater – whether text-based drama by authors such as Pedrolo, Brossa, Benet i Jornet, the Sirera brothers, and Sergi Belbel, or performance-based companies such as Dagoll Dagom, Comediants, Els Joglars, or La Fura dels Baus – has been particularly important for developing performative notions of identity, which may draw on Catalan sources and motifs but are concerned to explode all notions of fixed identity (Feldman 2009). The drive towards experimentation in 1970s Catalan fiction yielded similar effects, which evolved into forms of postmodern narrative in the 1980s by writers such as Quim Monzó, whose formal games from *Uf, va dir el* (*Oof, Said He*, 1978) to *El perquè de tot plegat* (*The Meaning of Everything*, 1993) left very little room for essentialist models.

One of the most visibly resistant figures to the normalizing and essentializing pressures of the institutionalization of Catalan culture in the 1980s and 1990s is undoubtedly Albert Boadella, in his work with Els Joglars and more controversially in his various memoirs, including *Adiós Cataluña* (*Goodbye Catalonia*, 2007). The theater collective Els Joglars was co-founded by Boadella in the 1960s; like other independent theater groups of the period, it turned to non-textual forms to resist and protest against subordination. Its continued political radicalism after the dictatorship's end is often attributed to the 1977 persecution of the company after its production of *La torna*, which satirized the military. However, unlike other 1970s and 1980s performance groups, Els Joglars have maintained their critique of official culture, becoming increasingly uncomfortable for Catalan institutions from the 1990s onward because of their attacks on Catalan politics and politicians and resistance to what they saw as excessively monolithic and essentialist views of Catalan identity (Buffery 2013). Their notion of the nation as a performative space is exemplified most clearly in *El Nacional*. First performed in Girona in 1993, the play was devised explicitly to contest current national and regional cultural policy. The focus on a marginal space, occupied by social outsiders and faced with demolition to make way for new use, provides commentary on the side-effects of the public redeployment of existing cultural infrastructure as well as exploring the very ontology of cultural practice, stripping theater back to consider the relationship between art and life – whether in the Andalusian cleaning lady's transitions into her other role as opera singer in a poor version of *Rigoletto*, or in mirroring the "real" death of the architect on stage in the mimicry of the actors.

The play emerged from a context of widespread debate around the politics of cultural funding and the tendency in contemporary Spanish theater to focus on highly visible, big-budget spectacles based in capital cities rather than spreading the funding across different geographical locations and social strata. Ironically, *El Nacional* was awarded the Premio Nacional de Teatro, one of the institutions against which it was reacting; Boadella refused the prize. At a local level, the play almost certainly responded to the immediate context of the Generalitat's project to create a Catalan National Theater – the Teatre Nacional de Catalunya, eventually completed and inaugurated in 1997 to highly vocal criticism (M. Delgado 2003; Buffery 2006). While the Teatre Nacional de Catalunya emerged from government concern with visual display, reflected in the building's "transparent" glass structure designed by Ricard Bofill, Els Joglars' "national" theater provides an inverted mirror to the national, with a dark, degraded, ruined space occupied by tramps, streetworkers, minimum-wage earners, and pickpockets, directed by the former usher of an opera house, whose mistrust of official "actors" underpins the play's critique. Revived in 2011 to celebrate the 50th anniversary of Els Joglars' founding (Buffery 2013), *El Nacional* presents an intriguing case study of the imbrication between processes of subordination, resistance, and institutionalization in shaping the relationship between the different languages and cultures of the Spanish state.

Literature in Galician: Politics, Peripheries, and Postmodernism

By the 1960s, the institutionalized model of Galician literary history was firmly monolingual, conforming to the "criterio filolóxico" (linguistic criterion) developed by the historian Ricardo Carballo (later Carvalho) Calero, according to which only literature written in Galician can be considered part of Galician literature. The vexed question of bilingualism is illustrated by the case of novelist and politician Alfredo Conde: an independent socialist deputy in the Galician parliament 1981–93 and *conselleiro de cultura* (cultural counsellor) 1987–90, Conde established himself as a Galician-language novelist in the 1970s and 1980s with works such as *Xa vai o griffón no vento* (*The Griffon*, 1984), which won Spain's Premio Nacional de Narrativa in 1986. His switch to Castilian with his 1991 novel *Los otros días*, awarded the Premio Nadal, provoked his repudiation as the archetypal traitor by the Galician left and his works are largely elided from Galicia's institutional literary history.

We have seen in the last two chapters how young writers such as Xosé Luis Méndez Ferrín and Celso Emilio Ferreiro strained against the expectations of older generations, at home and in exile. During the 1960s and 1970s, they became part of Galicia's new, politicized generation of writer-activists, including the poet Manuel María and novelists María Xosé Queizán and Carlos Casares. One of their achievements was to reinvigorate Galician fiction, which had long been considered poetry's poor relation. From the late 1950s, the movement known as the *nova narrativa galega* (New Galician Fiction) sought to challenge this assumption, drawing on the French *nouveau roman* as well as modernist and experimental models from world literature. Its key characteristics, designed in part to disrupt the stereotypical view of Galician-language narrative as *costumbrista* or unimaginatively realist, include rejection of linear narrative, inclusion of multiple intertwined perspectives, and frequent use of interior monologue. This innovative tendency began with Gonzalo Rodríguez Mourullo's *Nasce unha arbore* (*A Tree Is Born*, 1954) and includes Queizán's *A orella no buraco* (*The Ear in the Hole*, 1965; only the second full-length novel in Galician by a woman); Casares's *Xoguetes pra un tempo prohibido* (*Toys for a Forbidden Time*, 1975); Camilo Gonsar's *Cara a Times Square* (*Facing Times Square*, 1980) and, more controversially, Xohana Torres's female-centered *Adiós, María* (1971).

Méndez Ferrín is perhaps the most prominent figure of this generation. He caught the public's eye in 1957 with his first poetry collection, *Voce na néboa* (*Voice in the Fog*), and has since been a constant presence in both the Galician nationalist movement and the Galician cultural sphere, as a political and cultural organizer. In 1958, he became a member of the nationalist literary collective known as the Grupo Brais Pinto and in 1964 co-founded the Marxist political party Unión do Povo Galego, thus becoming a political target; he spent part of the 1970s in hiding and underwent several spells in prison, on the last occasion in 1980 on charges of illegal possession of weapons, of which he was later absolved. Initially a poet, Méndez Ferrín is best known for his fiction, especially his short stories. These – including *Percival e outras historias* (*Percival and Other Stories*, 1958), *Elipsis e outras sombras* (*Ellipsis and Other Shadows*, 1974), and *Amor de Artur* (*Love of Arthur*, 1982) – combine experimental narrative techniques with fantastical imagined geographies and idiosyncratic Celtic-influenced mythologies that allow him to explore pressing issues at a remove from the realism often considered to taint early Galician narrative. This approach, which makes him something like an overtly politicized Cunqueiro, is crystallized in two of his best-known works, *Retorno de Tagen Ata* (*Return from Tagen Ata*, 1971) and *Bretaña, Esmeraldiña* (*Brittany, Little Emerald*, 1987), which are biting allegories of the contemporary Galician political situation, set in the mythical land of Tagen Ata. Since the 1990s, Méndez Ferrín has focused more on the cultural field, although he remains involved with political formations such as the *Frente Popular Galega*. In 1990 he founded, and continues to edit, *A Trabe de Ouro* (*The Golden Beam*), a critical review that continues the project of the Nós and Galaxia groups to make Galician a medium for cultural discourse at the highest levels. In 1999, he was nominated by the Galician Writers' Association for the Nobel Prize for Literature, and in January 2010 was elected President of the Real Academia Galega (RAG), cementing his position at the heart of the Galician cultural establishment.

Méndez Ferrín's journey from enemy of the state to President of the RAG shows the extent of the cultural field's transformation during Galicia's three-and-a-half decades of democracy (Vilavedra 2010). On an institutional level, this transformation has been underpinned by the creation in 1980 of the Comunidade Autónoma de Galicia, under its parliament, the Xunta de Galicia, which has direct control over Galicia's education system and linguistic policy. The establishment in 1982 of a standard form of the Galician language, under the auspices of the RAG and the Instituto da Lingua Galega (ILG), and its introduction for the first time as a co-official language within the autonomous community, paved the way for a concerted drive to embed the language in the Galician public sphere. The drawback is that, while the Xunta is able to legislate for use of Galician in the civil service and in public life, its powers – not to mention its willingness – to intervene in the cultural field are rather more limited.

Despite the enduring fragility of the institutional frameworks for supporting Galician cultural production during the 1980s and 1990s, these decades saw a rapid and unprecedented diversification. During the 1980s, a radically experimental cultural movement sprang up around figures such as the novelist Suso de Toro and the multifaceted musician, writer, and filmmaker Antón Reixa, leader of the poetry collective *Rompente* (1975–83) and the rock group *Os resentidos* (1983–94). Known as the Galician *Movida* for its resonance with the Madrid movement of the same name, its participants joined actively in debates on Galician culture by developing highly theorized oppositional notions of Galician identity through the pastiche of traditional stereotypes based on a combination of ruralism, social realism, and nostalgia. Works such as *Silabario da turbina* (*ABC of the Turbine*, 1978), *Galicia sitio distinto* (*Galicia a Different Place*, 1990–1), and *Ringo Rango* (1992) are characterized by the juxtaposition of multimedia techniques, performance, and guerrilla tactics in addition to conventional textual or audio production (Baltrusch 2011). This self-consciously experimental approach also characterizes the early career of novelist Suso de Toro, who burst onto the literary scene in 1983 with *Caixón desastre* (*Disasterbag*). This novel, like its successors *Polaroid* (1986) and *Land Rover* (1988), incorporates a dense web of multimedia and self-reflexive microtexts that undermine facile projections of "Galician" identity. This trajectory peaks in *Tic Tac* (1993), in which reinvigorated Joycean narrative strategies centered around Toro's narratorial self-projection "Nano" are woven together with biting critiques of institutionalized histories and identities, whether local, national, state, or global. The experimental work of Reixa and Toro confirms Galicia's insertion into a cosmopolitan postmodernity, as well as the diversification of artistic forms in the Galician cultural field.

The Consolidation of the Basque Literary System

Chapter 9 has traced the importance of Basque language and culture for the resistance to the Franco regime in the 1950s and 1960s. In the 1970s, the Basque publishing world experienced significant growth with the creation of new publishing houses such as Gordailu (1969), Lur (1969), Etor (1970), Iker (1972), Gero (1973), and Elkar (1973). Thanks to the influence of Gabriel Aresti, committed poetry remained a key cultural force with the work of Bittoriano Gandiaga and Juan Mari Lekuona, and the younger Xabier Lete and Joxean Artze. (See chapter 12 for the early 1970s emergence of Basque-language women poets.)

The major shift of the 1970s was the take-off of Basque fiction. Keen to enhance their visibility, Basque novelists looked to international trends. Latin American magic realism proved an attractive model with its mix of political critique and fantasy, as in Anjel Lertxundi's stories *Hunik arrats artean* (*Until Nightfall*, 1970) and novel *Ajea du Urturik* (*Something Is Lacking in Urturi*, 1971), or Joan Mari Irigoien's *Oilarraren promesa* (*The Rooster's Promise*, 1976). Basque fiction would achieve international recognition in 1988 with Bernardo Atxaga's *Obabakoak*. Translated into 33 languages, it put Basque literature on the world literature map, in the process becoming the first Basque work to win the Spanish National Fiction Prize. Atxaga's earlier avant-garde writing had moved toward the fantastic with a number of early 1980s stories and a novella set in the fictional town of Obaba. *Obabakoak* (meaning "people or stories of Obaba") is itself a collection of interrelated stories. The affective landscape of Obaba is a virtual realm in which the narrator's memory weaves a suggestive pattern of tales combining metanarrative reflection with strategies taken from fantastic fiction. This is, above all, an intertextual literary journey: a tribute to world masters of the short story genre, with quotes and retellings ranging from Somerset Maugham and Evelyn Waugh to Chekhov, Maupassant, and Villiers de l'Isle Adam (to mention a few). The mix of a magical childhood landscape where logical causality does not obtain with sophisticated literary games created an image of Basque literature as cosmopolitan and postmodern, while seemingly ingenuous. It was a winning formula (Olaziregi 2005, 98–153).

The turn to experimental writing had been anticipated by Ramon Saizarbitoria – who would also become a highly political writer – in his first impressive novel *Egunero hasten delako* (*Because It Begins Every Day*, 1969). His second novel *Ehun metro* (*One Hundred Meters*, 1976), which uses different narrative levels and cinematographic techniques, was also pioneering in being the first of what would become many novels on the topic of ETA terrorism (see chapter 13). His third novel, the metafictional *Ene Jesus* (*Oh Jesus!*, 1976), claims affinity with Beckett's *Malone meurt* (1951). Experimentalism would permeate Basque literary production in the 1970s, exemplified by Patrizio Urkizu's novel *Sekulorum Sekulotan* (*For Ever and Ever*, 1975), which comprises a single interior monologue without commas or periods, or Koldo Izagirre's novel *Zergatik bai* (*Because I Say So*, 1976). Atxaga's 1976 *Ziutateaz* (*About the City*, 1976) is a hybrid text including poems and dramatic fragments. The city is a dystopian paradise, indirectly reflecting the return to harsh repression of the Franco dictatorship's final years, with references to Hölderlin, Artaud, Jarry, and Van Gogh. Experimental theater also emerged in the 1970s, with the creation of theater groups such as Intxitxu and Cómicos de la Legua. This theatrical renaissance was theorized by Atxaga in his essay "Euskal Theatro Berria(ren bila)" ([In search of a] New Basque Theater, 1974); Atxaga's own avant-garde dramatic contribution would be *Borobila eta puntua* (*The Circle and the Point*, 1972).

The 1970s avant-garde spirit manifested itself in counter-cultural magazines such as *Panpina ustela* (*Rotten Doll*, January 1975), created by Atxaga and Koldo Izagirre, whose manifesto "Ez dezagula konposturarik gal, halere" (Let's Not Lose Composure, at Any Rate) proposed a radical renovation of the Basque literary scene. Demands for literary autonomy intensified with the magazine *Pott* (*Kiss/Failure*, 1978–80), founded by Atxaga in Bilbao with writers Joxe Mari Iturralde, Manu Ertzilla, and Joseba Sarrionandia, singer Ruper Ordorika, and scholar Jon Juaristi. The group adopted the provocative stance of the early twentieth-century Dadaists, defending a literary autonomy that did not isolate art from society. The *Pott* group defined themselves as heirs of the modernist masters, with abundant references to Kafka, Pound, Eliot, and Borges. *Pott* published Atxaga's *Etiopia* in 1978, which took the poetic establishment by storm. The book, characterized by savage irony, is a collage of poems and stories in which Atxaga addresses the end of modernity and the impossibility of poetic language.

The arrival of democracy in Spain in 1975 made possible the establishment of a Basque literary field, at least in the Spanish Basque Country. With the 1978 Spanish Constitution, the 1979 Autonomy Statute, and the 1982 Law for the Normalization of the Use of the Basque Language in the Basque Autonomous Community and in 1986 in the Foral Community of Navarre, Basque became co-official with Spanish in those territories. The 1980s thus offered the material conditions needed to realize the push for literary autonomy that had begun in the 1950s, led by Jon Mirande and Gabriel Aresti (see chapter 9): an increase in potential consumers; the professionalization and economic autonomy of artists and producers; and the diversification of agencies of recognition (academies, networks, markets, etc.). For the first time in its history, Basque ceased to be a persecuted language. In the course of the decade, grants for writers and publishers, obligatory bilingual education at pre-university level, and literacy campaigns increased the reading public. These years saw the creation of Basque Public Radio and Television (EITB, 1982) and of the Basque-Language Writers Association (Euskal Idazleen Elkartea, EIE, 1982), Basque-Language Publishers Association (Euskal Editoreen Elkartea, EEE, 1984), and Basque-Language Translators, Editors, and Interpreters Association (Euskal Itzultzaile, Zuzentzaile eta Interpreteen Elkartea, EIZIE, 1987).

Basque Philology Studies, established at the University of Deusto in 1976 and the University of the Basque Country in 1978, produced its first graduates in the 1980s. These graduates, trained in contemporary literary theory and criticism, would contribute to the institutionalization of Basque literature, as well as teaching in the public-school system, which from 1980 offered classes on Basque language and literature, no longer confined to the private network of ikastolas (Basque-medium schools). While previously there had been Chairs of Basque Language and Literature at the universities of Bordeaux-Montaigne (since 1948), Salamanca (since 1952), and Navarre (since 1963), in the 1980s Basque literary studies took a qualitative leap thanks to Professors Koldo Mitxelena (University of the Basque Country), Jesús María Lasagabaster (University of Deusto), and Jean Haritschelhar (Bordeaux-Montaigne University). Lasagabaster (2005) used the term "literatures of the Basques" to refer to the multilingualism of Basque literature, written in Basque, Castilian, and French. In practice, despite occasional postnational definitions, Basque literary history continues to follow the model set by Koldo Mitxelena's *Historia de la Literatura Vasca* (*History of Basque Literature*, 1960), which limited itself to literature written in the Basque language (Mitxelena 1988 [1960]). Regardless of problems of definition, Basque literary criticism has unquestionably been institutionalized, indicated by the Basque government's creation of the Euskadi Prize for Literature in 1989.

The increase in book production has been notable: from 1876 to 1975, an average of 31.5 books in Basque were published annually, while from 1976 to 1994 the figure rose to 659.2 books per year (Torrealdai 1997). A consequence of the consolidation of the publishing market was the dominance of fiction from 1980, compared to the dominance of poetry until the mid-1970s. Of the 1,500 books in Basque published annually, 14 percent are literary works, of which 60 percent is fiction. The increase in the 1980s of literary competitions that favored short fiction, as well as the demands of new readers, boosted sales of short stories, as did the creation of literary journals – *Oh Euzkadi!* (1979–83), *Susa* (1980–94), *Maiatz* (1982–), and *Idatz & Mintz* (1981–) – that offered springboards for new writers. The translation of Basque literary texts into other languages of the Spanish state since the 1980s has been an important measure of recognition.

A major development of the 1980s was the emergence of four women writers who would consolidate their career in later decades: Arantxa Urretabizkaia, Mariasun Landa, Laura Mintegi, and Itxaro Borda (see chapter 12). The 1980s also saw the beginning of modern Basque children's and young adult literature with the publication of Atxaga's *Chuck Aranberri dentista baten etxean* (*Chuck Aranberri at the Dentist*, 1980), Lertxundi's *Tristeak kontsolatzeko makina* (*The Happiness Machine*, 1988), and Mariasun Landa's *Txan fantasma* (*Karmentxu and the Little Ghost*, 1984).

In summary, the embrace of magic realism in the early 1980s deconstructed the rural world that traditional Basque nationalism had promoted as the essence of everything Basque. This permitted a fluid concept of Basque identity that broke with earlier *costumbrista* representations. By the mid-1980s, the experimental, avant-garde phase had come to an end. A sign of "normalization" was the increasing eclecticism of literary trends, with no one tendency dominating. The 1990s would be marked by a wave of novels that turned to the conflictive historical past (see chapter 13).

12

Rewriting Gender and Sexuality (1970s–2020)

This chapter – covering literature written in Spain from the 1970s to 2020, with back-reference to the earlier work of older writers – focuses on three related forms of literary production: first, writing by women that offers a female perspective; second, texts that question traditional gender roles and compulsory heterosexuality; and third, writing that explicitly explores sexuality.

The transition to democracy in the late 1970s saw the recuperation of earlier women and queer-identifying writers who had been marginalized, forgotten, or discussed without considering the importance of gender or sexuality in their writing. An extreme case was that of the homoerotic works of Federico García Lorca: his play *El público* (*The Audience*, written 1930), published in the UK in 1976, was not performed professionally in Spain till 1987; the first complete edition of his *Sonetos del amor oscuro* (*Sonnets of Dark Love*, written 1935) appeared in 1984.

The legal changes during the transition affecting Spaniards' intimate behavior were momentous, formalizing demands voiced since the late 1960s. On victory in the Civil War, Franco rescinded the Second Republic's legalization of divorce and civil marriage. Throughout the dictatorship (1939–75), women could not hold a bank account, own property, or obtain a passport or driving license without their husband's permission (*permiso marital*); abortion and birth control were illegal. The *permiso marital* was abolished in 1975. The 1978 Democratic Constitution granted equal rights to women, decriminalized adultery and birth control, and legalized civil marriage. Divorce was legalized in 1981, and abortion in limited circumstances in 1985. Same-sex acts between men were not formally penalized till the Primo de Rivera dictatorship's 1928 Penal Code, though they could be prosecuted under legislation against indecent behavior, corruption of minors, or public scandal; same-sex acts between women were deemed not to exist. The Republican Constitution decriminalized homosexuality. In 1954 the Franco dictatorship amended the Republic's 1933 Vagrancy and Delinquency Law, which had instituted preventive measures to "save" at-risk individuals from criminality, to authorize arrest of males suspected of sexual deviance; the 1970 Law of Social Danger and Rehabilitation prescribed their internment in rehabilitation centers. Homosexuality was decriminalized in 1979, though the term was eliminated from legislation on public scandal only in 1983 and the Law of Social Danger was fully repealed only in 1995 (Mira 2004).

Belated Recognition

While it is not uncommon for women to have interrupted careers or achieve recognition late, this was exacerbated in Spain by nearly 40 years of Francoism. For women who had begun to write in the 1930s, at a time of new sexual freedoms, Franco's victory in the Civil War meant opting for exile or navigating the imposition of retrograde gender norms at home. The literary careers of Mercè Rodoreda (see chapter 10) and Rosa Chacel were disrupted by exile; both embarked on a new creative phase on return in the early 1970s. Chacel's rejection of the category of femininity is illustrated in her 1976 *Barrio de Maravillas* (*The Maravillas District*; Premio de la Crítica), which follows her exile masterpiece *Memorias de Leticia Valle* (*Memories of Leticia Valle*, 1945) in exploring the subjectivity of young girls who respond to the world as gender-neutral thinking and feeling subjects. It also builds on the depiction of female friendship introduced in her 1972 autobiographical *Desde el amanecer*; the first-person stream-of-consciousness of *Barrio*'s two 13-year-old protagonists articulates an asexual erotic engagement with the world through bodily sensation. The homosexual exile Juan Gil-Albert, cofounder of the Republican wartime journal *Hora de España*, suffered prolonged interior exile on return to his native Valencia in 1947, resuming publication with his 1972 poetic anthology *Fuentes de la constancia* and 1974 autobiographical *Crónica general*, followed by nine further books of poetry. His writing, steeped in references to classical Greek culture and contributing, like Cernuda, to the cultural construction of a homoerotic Mediterranean, dissociates male same-sex desire from effeminacy, insisting that, in excluding women, it is an ethics of virility.

Carmen Conde, already an established poet in the 1930s and a participant in the Republic's Misiones Pedagógicas, stayed in Spain after the war despite an order for her arrest, at the price of concealing her lifelong relationship with Amanda Junqueras and of obtaining recognition as a conventional female love poet (awarded National Poetry Prize 1967; elected first woman member of the Spanish Royal Academy 1978). Retrospective readings of her work reveal a critical exploration of femininity, evident in *Mujer sin Edén* (*Woman without Eden*, 1947) and the privately published *Canto a Amanda* (*Song to Amanda*, 1951). Gloria Fuertes's early poetry is discussed in chapter 9; her defense of women's rights became vocal in her transition-era work, which empathizes with transvestites and queers. Never voicing her publicly known lesbianism explicitly in her poetry, she refused to define herself in terms of the male–female binary: her last book of poetry, playing on the phrase "hombre de pelo en pecho" (man with hair on his chest), is titled *Mujer de verso en pecho* (*Woman with Poetry on Her Chest*, 1995). A prolific author of children's literature, she achieved mainstream recognition during the transition as the host of children's television programs.

Against all the odds, an extraordinary crop of young women novelists began to publish in Spain from the mid-1940s, most of whom would continue to publish after the dictatorship. Carmen Martín Gaite and Josefina Aldecoa married male novelists (Rafael Sánchez Ferlosio, Ignacio Aldecoa) in the early 1950s, and blossomed as writers after separating or becoming widowed. The early novels of Barcelona-based Carmen Laforet and Ana María Matute (see chapter 9) were re-read in the 1990s as feminist classics (Nichols 1992). These readings drew attention to the reversal of gender roles in Laforet's *Nada* (*Nothing*, 1944), with the female narrator-investigator Andrea coolly observing her emotionally unhinged uncles, and to the strength of Andrea's intimate relationship with her friend Ena. Matute's *Primera memoria* (*The Island*, 1959; Premio Nadal) was re-interpreted as the first-person narration of its 14-year-old protagonist Matia's sexual awakening. On election to the Spanish Royal Academy in 1996 (its third woman member) in belated recognition of a career consolidated in the 1950s and 1960s, Matute resumed writing after a 23-year gap, developing an earlier interest in children's literature by exploring the fantastic.

The most successful of this generation of women writers was Carmen Martín Gaite, whose career blossomed under democracy (1978 National Fiction Prize for *El cuarto de atrás* / *The Back Room*; 1988 Prince of Asturias Literature Prize; 1994 National Literature Prize) (Brown 2013). Her 1958 début novel *Entre visillos* (*Behind the Curtains*) anticipates the reflections on her own provincial upbringing under Francoism in the 1978 novel that made her name: *El cuarto de atrás* (*The Back Room*; National Fiction Prize). The female focus of her work intensified after her construction of a female literary genealogy in *Desde la ventana* (*Looking out of the Window*, 1987), written in 1980 during the first of many US Visiting Professorships, which introduced her to feminist criticism. *Nubosidad variable* (*Variable Cloud*, 1992), her first novel for 14 years since *El cuarto de atrás*, explores female–female relations through two schoolfriends who, in later life, address texts to each other. The mother–daughter relationship is central to *Lo raro es vivir* (*Living's the Strange Thing*, 1997), while *La Reina de las Nieves* (*The Snow Queen*, 1994) explores the mother's importance for the son. In the 1990s, Martín Gaite rehabilitated the author of the prewar *Celia* children's stories, Elena Fortún (penname of Encarnación Aragoneses), whose lesbian novel *Oculto sendero* (*Hidden Path*) was published posthumously in 2016. The mother–daughter relationship is fundamental to the first two novels in Josefina Aldecoa's 1990–7 memory trilogy (see chapter 13), which belatedly established her reputation at the age of 64. The gap between her first 1961 short story collection and her return to creative writing in 1984 makes Aldecoa a classic case of an interrupted female career path.

Coming Out

Under the Franco dictatorship, same-sex desire could not be acknowledged publicly. Vicente Aleixandre successfully continued his prewar poetic career, winning the Premio de la Crítica in 1963 and 1969, at the expense of concealing his bisexuality in his writing and public life. The 1977 award of the Nobel Prize for Literature belatedly recognized a career going back to the late 1920s. His love poems to fellow poet Carlos Bousoño were published only in 2015 on the latter's death. The younger Francisco Brines, a child during the Civil War, remained reticent about public expression of his sexual orientation despite drawing on Gil-Albert's and Cernuda's construction of a homoerotic Mediterranean in his poetry from the 1960s to the 1980s.

Other poets of Brines's generation would be less reticent about their sexual orientation. For Jaime Gil de Biedma and Juan Goytisolo – both sons of the Barcelona Castilian-speaking bourgeoisie – the relationship between political and sexual dissidence was complicated. Gil de Biedma was denied membership of the clandestine Catalan Communist Party (PSUC) on the grounds of homosexuality. Goytisolo's discovery in the 1960s of the labor camps for homosexuals in Castro's Cuba led to his break with Marxism; from *Juan sin tierra* (*John the Landless*, 1975), his work denounces both right- and left-wing totalitarianism for enforcing compulsory heterosexuality. Both Gil de Biedma and Goytisolo wrote autobiographical texts that are candid about their sexuality: Gil de Biedma revised his diary *Retrato del artista en 1956* (*Portrait of the Artist in 1956*, 1991) for posthumous publication shortly before his 1990 death from AIDS; Goytisolo's memoirs, *Coto vedado* (*Forbidden Territory*, 1985) and *El reino de taifas* (*Realms of Strife*, 1986), narrate his "coming out." In these memoirs, both writers discuss their attraction to non-Western male bodies: Asian in the case of Gil de Biedma, who was company secretary of his father's Compañía de Tabacos de Filipinas; Arab in the case of Goytisolo, who from 1965 lived between Morocco and Paris, residing exclusively in Morocco after the 1996 death of his life-partner, French novelist Monique Lange.

The erotic verse in Gil de Biedma's collected poems *Las personas del verbo* (*Persons of the Verb*, 1975) is explicitly carnal but discreet. By contrast, the posthumous *Retrato* is fulsome in its descriptions of his sexual encounters with male prostitutes and multiple Asian male lovers during his first stay in the Philippines and Hong Kong in 1956. While he expects them to be available for his pleasure, he describes them as returning his colonial gaze (Vilaseca 2000).

The blatant sexual dissidence of Goytisolo's later experimental fiction is anticipated by the attraction to working-class males of the boy protagonists of his 1950s fiction. In *Reivindicación del conde don Julián* (*Count Julian*, 1970), *Juan sin tierra* (*John the Landless*, 1975), and *Makbara* (1980), the exaltation of sodomy is not so much an expression of homoerotic desire as the infliction of violence on the bourgeois body. Goytisolo's explicit depiction of sexuality pays homage to a scatological tradition of Spanish literature – *El libro de buen amor*; Quevedo; *La lozana andaluza*; the parodic poem *Carajicomedia* in Goytisolo's 2000 novel of that name – excised or sanitized in Spanish literary histories. In *Makbara*, despite the Angel's sexual indeterminacy, the perverse sexual activity is a form of phallus worship that confirms traditional masculinity. Gender boundaries are, however, disturbed in *Las virtudes del pájaro solitario* (*Virtues of the Solitary Bird*, 1988) – a celebration of Spanish and Islamic mysticism – whose narrative voice mutates between male and female in a mystical search for loss of self, problematically related to AIDS (Epps 1996, 379–449). In his autobiography, Goytisolo admits his attraction to virile males; he did not support gay identity politics.

Born in the immediate postwar period, Álvaro Pombo, like many young Spaniards of his generation, escaped Francoist sexual repression for London (the principal setting of his first short story collection) from 1966 to 1977. It has been noted that Pombo's fiction depicts male same-sex relationships that are asymmetrical in terms of age and class (Martínez Expósito 2004, 118). The use of stream-of-consciousness gives an intense depiction of the internalization of guilt; the same-sex affairs in his novels mostly end tragically. Pombo's novels do not fit today's celebration of gay pride. His masterpiece *Contra natura* shows that there are many kinds of same-sex desire.

Writers born in the late 1940s experienced 1960s generational revolt under Francoist political immobilism, generating conflicted attitudes to sexuality. The flaunting of abjection in the psychoanalytically inflected poetry and stories of bisexual writer Leopoldo María Panero, son of the postwar Francoist poet Leopoldo Panero, confirms taboos in the act of breaking them. Much of Panero's prolific work, dating from 1968, was written during his 28 years of psychiatric internment. The sexual exploration of the early 1970s is depicted in the first and last novels of Rafael Chirbes, who started to publish late at the age of 39 (see chapters 13 and 14). *Mimoun* (1988), loosely based on Chirbes's year in Morocco, depicts sexuality (hetero- and homo-) as a disturbing force. His posthumously published *Paris-Austerlitz* (2016), written over 20 years and completed shortly before his death, returns to his pre-Morocco year in Paris at the age of 20. The protagonist fails to assuage his guilt over his abandonment of the terminally ill older French worker who had taken him in as his lover; the intense physical descriptions of their sexual relationship make this perhaps Chirbes's most powerful novel.

Lesbian desire is delicately explored in the first novel *Julia* of Ana María Moix, published in 1970 at a time of increasing student dissent. Its first-person stream-of-consciousness navigates the sexual and gender uncertainties of female adolescence, including the protagonist's attraction to her female university professor. *Julia*'s troubled sexuality makes her queer at a time when the term was not yet current. 1972 saw the arrival in Barcelona as political refugee of Uruguayan poet, novelist, and activist Cristina Peri Rossi, a Spanish citizen since 1975. Her prolific novelistic and poetic output in Spain celebrates lesbian desire and unstable sexual identities. Much of her work was published by Lumen, the Barcelona-based publishing house of Esther Tusquets (to whom Moix's *Julia* is dedicated). Tusquets's début novelistic trilogy *El mismo mar de todos los veranos* (*The Same Sea as Every Summer*, 1978), *El amor es un juego solitario* (*Love Is a Solitary Game*, 1979), and *Varada tras el ultimo naufragio* (*Stranded*, 1980) contains explicit descriptions of lesbian sexuality. Born in 1936 to a right-wing Catalan family that in the postwar period had close links with the Franco regime, Tusquets is another case of a woman taking up creative writing late. The trilogy's stream-of-consciousness expresses the mid-life crisis of female protagonists who, having been brought up to center their lives on marriage, flounder when marriage fails. Despite the trilogy's lack of puritanism – it was written at the time of the *destape* (obsession with female nudity) – the explicit sex scenes resort to metaphor.

Camping up the Transition

If camp became a dominant cultural mode during the transition, it was perhaps because the rapidity of social change generated a sense of acting out new identities. In Spain, where gay rights campaigners were integrated into the broad 1970s pro-democracy movement, the term "gay" never implied an essential gay identity, unlike post-Stonewall gay identity politics in 1970s America. In many ways Spanish culture of the transition anticipated the notion of identity as performance that underlay the development of queer theory in the 1990s Anglo-American academy – not least in the prominence it gave to the figure of the *travesti* (literally "transvestite" but including transgender persons in a broad sense). In this respect, Terenci Moix (older brother of Ana María) was a pioneer. After the realist coming-out novel *El dia que va morir Marilyn* (*The Day Marilyn Died*, 1969), Moix turned to over-the-top camp with *Món mascle* (*Macho World*, 1971), the first of many popular novels – from 1983 moving from Catalan to Castilian – influenced by Hollywood epics and Italian peplum films. His 1990–8 autobiography chronicles the impact of such movies on his sexual imaginary as a boy growing up under early Francoism. His fascination with a Hollywood-mediated ancient Egypt generated a series of best-selling historical fantasies written 1986–2002, which tone down his earlier outrageous camp – a reflection of the "normalization" under democracy of the wilder sexual energies of the 1970s. By contrast, for Luis Antonio de Villena, camp takes the form of a dazzling display of high-cultural intertextual references to queer writers and artists from Catullus to Pasolini. His first three books of poetry – *Sublime Solarium* (1971), *Hymnica* (1975, rev. 1979), *El viaje a Bizancio* (*Journey to Byzantium*, 1976, rev. 1978) – follow Cernuda, Gil-Albert, and Brines in constructing a homoerotic Mediterranean. Villena has been important also for his recovery of earlier queer writers, including Antonio de Hoyos and Álvaro Retana (see chapter 6), as well as Luis Cernuda and Gil-Albert.

It was the popular-cultural version of camp that would connect with political change. The first published novel of gay activist Eduardo Mendicutti, *Una mala noche la tiene cualquiera* (*Anyone Can Have a Bad Night*, 1982), explicitly associates gay lib with the new democracy as its transvestite first-person narrator anxiously awaits the outcome of the February 23, 1981 attempted military coup. Some of Mendicutti's popular novels have a serious subtext beneath their camp pastiche: *Los novios búlgaros* (*Bulgarian Boyfriends*, 1993) depicts eastern European migrants supporting themselves through male prostitution.

We return at the chapter's end to engagements with gender and sexuality by younger Spanish-language writers.

Cartographies of Desire: Rewriting Gender and Sexuality in Catalan

Many of the Spanish-language writers discussed above grew up in postwar Barcelona – an indication of the city's tradition of progressive attitudes to gender and sexuality. Given that public use of Catalan was forbidden during the Franco regime's early years, it is not surprising that the literary sphere should have seen the almost complete disappearance of women writers from Catalan-language publication. Of the many women publishing in Catalan before 1939 – Carme Monturiol, Irene Polo, Mercè Rodoreda, Maria Antònia Salvà, Caterina Albert, Maria Teresa Vernet, Aurora Bertrana, Anna Murià, Maria Lluïsa Algarra, Rosa Maria Arquimbau, Clementina Arderiu, Silvia Mistral – most went into exile where they had difficulty continuing their writing careers. Women writers faithful to Catalan who remained or returned in the 1940s found it especially hard to get published; Caterina Albert (penname "Victor Català") self-translated some of her works into Castilian but her numerous short stories in Catalan, written through the 1960s, were hardly known. Poets like Arderiu and Rosa Leveroni were eclipsed by their male contemporaries, as were the Valencian Maria Beneyto and Carmelina Sánchez-Cutillas, who published in Castilian and Catalan. Although Montserrat Abelló's first collection appeared in the 1960s on her return to Barcelona from exile in Chile, she came to public prominence only in the 1990s.

One of the most visible changes in the Catalan-language literary scene since the 1970s has been the relative influence of women writers, exemplified in the impact of early works by Montserrat Roig and Carme Riera, with the latter's *Te deix, amor, la mar com a penyora* (*I Leave You, My Love, the Sea as a Keepsake*, 1975) running to multiple editions within the first year of publication. Their emergence was partly fueled by a particular context of feminist activism led during the dictatorship by figures such as Maria Aurèlia Capmany, who sought to recover earlier women's voices alongside an international tradition from Virginia Woolf to Simone de Beauvoir to contemporary Anglo-American feminism. Active on a number of fronts,

Capmany translated and penned her own versions of famous women's texts and lives, with numerous other women finding recognition through the combination of gynocentric criticism and feminist activism. Even Rodoreda, who on definitive return to Catalonia in the 1970s moved to the remote village of Romanyà de la Selva, was brought into contact with an emerging network of women writers, performers, and artists through Araceli Bruch's women's theater collective Bruixes de dol (Witches in Mourning), which commissioned the play *El maniquí* (*The Mannequin*, 1979). The play's second act focuses on the bodies and memories of three old ladies living on society's margins, who are explicit about their sexual fantasies and irrepressible hunger for life (Buffery 2018). Later Bruch would join with celebrated lesbian poet Maria-Mercè Marçal, Abelló, and other members of the Catalan PEN Club's Women Writers' Committee to reclaim a feminine literary tradition, bringing together Catalan and non-Catalan women writers in a series of performative workshops, the "Cartografies del Desig" (Cartographies of Desire, 1997–8).

Catalan women's writing of this time was underpinned by a network of activists who were often doubly or triply militant in national, social, and gender emancipation movements, drawing in women from across the Catalan-speaking territories, most notably Isabel-Clara Simó (Valencia), Maria Antònia Oliver (Manacor in Majorca) and Mercè Ibarz (from the Catalan-speaking Baix Cinca area of Aragon). For Roig and Marçal, as for many others, the vindication of a silenced Catalan cultural tradition required a re-writing of (his)story that incorporated the embodied experience of women. This was Roig's project in her novelistic trilogy: the fictional representation of past and more recent Catalan history from a female perspective (see chapter 11). Riera left Majorca to study at the University of Barcelona in 1965, becoming an important Spanish literary scholar and pioneering feminist critic; her fictional works draw on a wide range of intertexts from Catalan, Spanish, and world literature. Yet she has continued to write in the Majorcan dialect of Catalan, at times focusing closely on her homeland's culture and identity, as in *Dins el darrer blau* (*Into the Last Blue*, 1994) which investigates the impact of Inquisitorial persecution on Majorca's *xueta* (Jewish) community, or *Cap al cel obert* (*To the Sky and Beyond*, 2000), whose exploration of migration focuses on Majorca and Cuba as "repeating islands" (Benítez-Rojo 1997) for a woman, again of *xueta* heritage, uprooted from home and family and faced with mirrored histories of colonial oppression and marginalization. Centering on the largely failed attempts of her female protagonists to shape their own destiny, Riera probes the capacity of writing for expressing layered affiliations in which gender intersects with location, cultural identity, class, age, education, and ethnicity (Buffery and Lonsdale 2011).

Recognition of the role of female social networks (Real 1998, 2006) – the journalism of early twentieth-century figures like Dolors Monserdà and Carme Karr; associations like the Lyceum Club from the mid-1920s; women teachers, librarians and translators – in the emergence of canonical writers such as Albert and Rodoreda underpinned the development of contemporary institutional supports such as the Institut Català de la Dona (now Institut Català de les Dones; Catalan Institute for Women), the Fundació Maria Aurèlia Capmany, and numerous academic programs, libraries, bookstores, and journals. These have been key to the recovery of many older women's voices, from poets such as Arderiu, Leveroni, Abelló, and Beneyto, to translators and travel writers like Bertrana, or educators and librarians like Rosa Sensat and Aurora Diaz-Plaja. Most important of all were the endeavors of writers and critics like Roig, Riera, and Marçal to cross disciplinary, social, and generic boundaries in order to explore the space of women's writings and social worlds.

The poetry of Marçal has been particularly influential in relating women's bodies to their spatio-temporal landscape, from reflective, poetic prose on the spaces of her childhood and education in writings on the geopolitical configuration of Barcelona – as in "Viratges i reminiscències" (Turns and Returns) from the volume *Barceldones* (contraction of *Barcelona Women*, 1990) – to the tracing in her poetry of the changing landscape of poet and lover's body through the passage from childhood to maturity, including some of the most explicit explorations of lesbian sexuality in contemporary Spanish writing. Marçal's novel, *La passió segons Renée Vivien* (*The Passion of Renée Vivien*, 1994), published four years before her death from cancer, brings together all of the above concerns: the writer's relationship to a female writing tradition; the relationship between body, desire, sexuality, and writing; the recovery of women's history and its connection to gynocriticism; the sense of identity as layered and multiple, shifting according to language, social space, geographical landscape, and relation with the world. The novel can be seen as part of a tradition of queer writing in Spain indebted to writers like the previously mentioned Terenci Moix and others in the 1960s and 1970s, whose work locates the emergence of modern LGBTQ subjectivities in Catalonia within the context of the large-scale social and cultural changes of the 1960s. The 1977 foundation of the Catalan Gay Liberation Movement (Front d'Alliberament Gai de Catalunya, FAGC) gave rise to writing of a more experimental, transgressive nature (Biel Mesquida, Lluís Fernàndez) and to poetic and theatrical explorations of homoerotic sexual desire (Jaume Creus, Blai Bonet, Narcís Comadira, Josep Maria Miró, Marc Rosich).

In recent decades, women's writing in Catalan has continued to develop and expand, from Marçal's contemporaries Maria Barbal and Imma Monsó to more recent radical feminists like Bel Olid, and includes writers of non-Catalan origin like Patricia Gabancho, Monika Zgustová and, most famously, Najat El Hachmi. *L'últim patriarca* (*The Last Patriarch*, 2008) was the first novel by a North African migrant to be awarded a major literary prize in Spain, and explicitly interweaves different literary and cultural traditions, from the oral histories of El Hachmi's Amazigh heritage to contemporary Catalan literature, with Rodoreda, especially, presented as stimulating the narrator's formation as a writer, and reference to parallel migration writing experiences like that of Zadie Smith in the UK (Buffery 2015). Women are prominent in other genres, too; for example, Teresa Solana in detective fiction and Paula Bonet in graphic novels, while in theater Lluïsa Cunillé is one of the most respected of the burgeoning group of contemporary Catalan women playwrights that runs from Bruch, Àngels Aymar, Mercè Sarrias, and Beth Escudé to Marta Buchaca, Helena Tornero, and Victoria Szpunberg.

Girl (and Boy) Interrupted: The Fragmented Story of Galician Writing on Gender and Sexuality

Rosalía de Castro's importance in the emergence of modern Galician literature has led to a perception that women occupy a less marginal place in the Galician literary system than elsewhere in Spain. This is not true. Few women writers before the 1950s had access to Galician-language cultural circles, and fewer still, for various personal and institutional reasons, chose to write in Galician. The majority of those who did were poets such as Avelina Valladares and Filomena Dato Muruais in the nineteenth century, and Carmen Prieto Rouco in the early twentieth, none of whom occupies a secure place in the Galician canon. Women's narrative in Galicia has had an intensely fractured history (Hooper 2003; Barbour 2020). Castro's prologues to *Cantares gallegos* and *Follas novas* and the unpublished story known as "Conto gallego" aside, the only woman prose writer before 1920 to publish regularly in Galician was Valentina Lago Valladares (penname of Hipólita Muíño), who contributed to the regionalist journal *Revista Gallega* in the early twentieth century. After Francisca Herrera Garrido's 1920 first female-authored novel in Galician, *Néveda*, the second, María

Xosé Queizán's *A orella no buraco* (*The Ear in the Hole*), appeared only in 1965 (March 2018).

Queizán is unquestionably Galicia's most influential female writer after Castro, for her creative work and sustained campaign to create an institutional space for women's voices in Galicia. In fiction, Queizán has made it her mission to chronicle women's experience across time. Two decades after *A orella no buraco*, she returned with *Amantia* (1984), which reconstructs the life of the fourth-century Christian Exeria, popularly regarded as Galician, whose *Itinerarium Egeriae*, a letter describing her pilgrimage to the Holy Land, is one of the earliest known written texts by a European woman. Her subsequent *Amor de Tango* (*Tango Love*, 1992) provides a uniquely female-centered perspective on the Civil War; *O solpor da cupletista* (*Twilight of the Cabaret Singer*, 1995) is a novelized biography of the Galician-born Paris dancer and courtesan Carolina "La Belle" Otero; while *Ten o seu punto a fresca rosa* (*Every Rose Has Its Thorn*, 2000) follows the intertwined lives of three women of different social classes in 1970s Vigo. In 1983, Queizán created the monthly journal *Festa da Palabra Silenciada* (*Festival of the Silenced Word*), with a first monographic issue on Rosalía de Castro; under her editorship, it continues to record Galician women's experience and to introduce into Galicia continental feminist theory and women's writing from across the globe.

The press and academy see the establishment of a strong women's literature in Galician as a prerequisite for "normalization," but Queizán's creative work has been largely ignored institutionally. In 2011, a polemic developed around the failure to nominate her (or any woman) for one of the Galician Royal Academy's three vacant seats. Nonetheless, important gains have been made in recent decades, particularly in narrative. Since Marilar Aleixandre became the first woman to be awarded the prestigious Premio Xerais in 2001, a further nine women have won the prize, the most distinguished being the academic, essayist, and novelist Teresa Moure in 2005 (Barbour 2020). Although the media have celebrated the popularity of Moure's creative work as ushering in the long-awaited "normalization," her supposedly radical feminism makes virtually no advance on the position Queizán has defended since the late 1970s. In narrative, the radical feminist mantle has been taken up by the writer-activist and translator María Reimóndez, with her powerful female-centered fictions *O caderno de bitácora* (*Ship's Log*, 2004), *O club da calceta* (*The Knitting Club*, 2006), and *Pirata* (*Pirate*, 2009). In poetry, we might look to poet-activist Chus Pato whose experimental, transgeneric works *m-Talá* (2000) and *Charenton* (2004) are translated into English by the Canadian poet of Galician extraction, Erin

Moure; to poet and media personality Yolanda Castaño, who exploits her own mediatized image in *O libro da egoísta* (*Book of the Egotist*, 2003); or to poet and theorist María do Cebreiro Rábade Villar, whose thoughtful *Non son de aquí* (*I'm Not from Here*, 2008) prises open the crevices of female subjectivity.

If gender is slowly becoming a topic of informed critical discussion, sexuality has largely been elided in Galician literary criticism, though there are signs of change (Barreto 2017). For example, the works of Eduardo Blanco Amor are increasingly being re-read from a perspective attuned to sexuality, largely because of his involvement in Lorca's *Seis poemas galegos* (*Six Galician Poems*, 1935). Nevertheless, critics of Antón Lopo's novel *Ganga* (2001), featuring probably Galician fiction's first explicitly gay protagonist, rarely mention the issues of sexuality that are crucial to the plot (McGovern 2011). Male same-sex desire has been most clearly portrayed in women's writing, for example in Queizán's 1988 novel *A semellanza* (*The Likeness*), whose protagonist must work his way through different versions of sexuality to find the sexual and emotional "likeness" he seeks, resisting dominant heterosexual social structures. The potential for a "minor" literature to draw a connection between queer sexual identities and non-traditional textual forms is made explicit in the most ambitious queer poetic project to date: Antón Lopo and Ana Romaní's collaborative tripartite work *Pronomes* (Lopo), *Arden* (Romaní) and the co-authored *Lob*s* (*Pronouns / They Burn / [S]He-Wolves*, 1998). Teresa Moure has brought these debates into the institutional sphere with her prizewinning 2011 essay collection *Queer-emos un mundo novo. Sobre cápsulas, xéneros e falsas clasificacións* (*Let's Queer a New World: On Capsules, Genders/Genres, and False Classifications*).

Feminist and Gay Writing in Basque

A striking feature of the 1970s and 1980s was the greater number and visibility of Basque women writers. The process began in the 1960s with Marijan Minaberri's short stories *Itxulingo anderea* (*The Woman of Itxulin*, 1961) and her pioneering *Xoria Kantari* (*Songbird*, 1963); and the plays of Lurdes Iriondo, a well-known singer in the group *Ez dok amairu*, whose *Martin arotza eta Jaun deabrua* (*Martín the Carpenter and Mister Devil*, 1973) and *Sendagile maltzurra* (*The Wicked Doctor*, 1973) incorporated popular songs and national folklore, renovating children's and young adult literature in Basque. These were years of political and cultural activism, with the Basque feminist movement holding its first meeting in Leioa, Bizkaia in 1977. In 1981, the Seminar on Women's Studies was established at the University of the Basque Country, publishing key scholarship questioning the myth of Basque matriarchy nurtured by Basque nationalism (Del Valle 1985). In 1971, the poet Amaia Lasa's co-authored *Poema bilduma* (*Poems*, 1971) had demanded a new language to rescue women's voices from silence. The 1970s also witnessed the emergence of key feminist author Arantxa Urretabizkaia. Following her poetry collections *San Pedro bezperaren ondokoak* (*After St. Peter's Eve*, 1972) and *Maitasunaren magalean* (*Under Love's Wing*, 1982), which speak of female desire via allusions to historical figures like Joan of Arc and Simone de Beauvoir, her lyrical novel *Zergatik Panpox* (*Why, Darling?*, 1979) narrates a day in the life of a mother abandoned by her husband. Drawing on French difference feminism, the novel explores the female body through a psychoanalytic critique of Freudian phallocentrism. Her later exploration of political militancy and motherhood in *Koaderno gorria* (*The Red Notebook*, 1998) points to a political commitment that avoids the masculinizing ethos of ETA, in which men are the warriors and women the supportive wives and mothers (Olaziregi 2021). The novel can be seen as inspired by the life of Yoyes (María Dolores González Katarain), one of ETA's few female leaders, who was assassinated after leaving the organization.

The 1980s saw a greater socialization of feminist debates, with the Second Feminist Meeting in Leioa and the emergence of a new generation of women writers thanks to the growing number of feminist journals, studies, and anthologies. The French Basque poet and novelist Itxaro Borda's first novel *Basilika* (*Basilica*, 1984) evidences the transgressive critical spirit that would pervade her work. If her *100% Basque* (2001; Euskadi Literary Prize) critiqued French-Basque society's traditionalism, her 1992–2012 pentalogy of thrillers featuring the Leninist lesbian detective Amaia Ezpeldoi rewrote the genre. Laura Mintegi's *Nerea eta biok* (*Nerea and I*, 1995) stressed the strictures that Basque society places on lesbian relations. Among the new Basque children's and young adult literature that emerged in the 1980s, Mariasun Landa's *Txan fantasma* (*Karmentxu and the Little Ghost*, 1984), *Iholdi* (1992), and *Krokodilo bat ohe azpian* (*A Crocodile under the Bed*, 2003; Spanish National Prize for Children's and Young Adult Literature) have critiqued sexist stereotypes.

Basque feminist criticism has become institutionalized since the 1990s thanks to the Center for Basque Studies at the University of Nevada and the University of the Basque Country, giving female-authored works greater visibility. The Igartza Saria award of the Elkar publishing house has boosted the careers of already established women writers – for example,

Karmele Jaio whose novel *Amaren eskuak* (*Her Mother's Hands*, 2006) treats the mother–daughter relationship. Works by contemporary female writers explore motherhood, confinement to the private sphere, communication problems between the sexes, female desire and the body, or reclaim agency for female characters. Lourdes Oñederra's novel *Eta emakumeari sugeak esan zion* (*And the Serpent Said to the Woman*, 1999; Spanish Critics' Prize for Fiction in Basque, Euskadi Literary Prize, Euskadi Silver Prize) reflects on the difficulty of using a language that does not belong to women. Miren Agur Meabe's poetry collection *Azalaren kodea* (*The Code of the Skin*, 2000; Spanish Critics' Prize for Poetry in Basque) has explored the female body as a geography of pleasure; the titular prosthesis of her extraordinary *Kristalezko begi bat* (*A Glass Eye*, 2013) stands for multiple losses suffered by the autofictional female narrator.

The Basque gay, lesbian, bisexual, and transgender liberation movement EGHAM (Euskal Herriko Gay-Lesbianen Askapen Mugimenda) was founded in 1977 and recognized by the Basque Government in 1983. Its meetings and the literary biography *Gay nauzu* (*Diary of a Gay Teenager*, 1999) by Iñigo Lamarka, Basque ombudsman in 2004–15, have helped to create social acceptance of sexual and gender diversity. Rikardo Arregi Diaz de Heredia's poetry collections *Kartografia* (*Cartography*, 1998) and *Bitan esan beharra* (*Say It Twice*, 2012), both awarded the Critics' Prize for Poetry in Basque, wrestle with language to express a cartography of gay desire. Literary works with queer characters include Iñaki Mendiguren's *Haltzak badu bihotzik* (*The Alder Has a Heart*, 1990), Bernardo Atxaga's story "Un traductor en Paris" (A Translator in Paris, 1996), and Daniel Landart's *Batita Haundia* (*Big Batita*, 1994) which analyzes prejudice against same-sex relations in the rural French Basque Country. Hasier Etxeberria's thriller *Mutuaren hitzak* (*The Words of the Mute*, 2005) depicts a gay crime of passion, while Juanjo Olasagarre's *Ezinezko maletak* (*Impossible Suitcases*, 2004) reflects on national and gay identity by contrasting the 1980s Basque Country with London. Very few literary works in Basque have depicted transgender characters (Retolaza and Egaña 2016, 38–40).

Female Bodies in Transition: The Personal and the Political

To conclude the chapter, we return to writing in Spanish, focusing on writers born after 1950 who started to publish under democracy. In the late 1970s and 1980s, Spanish critics began to speak of a "women's fiction boom" – a label that included women writers explicitly committed to feminism as well as others who rejected that category yet explored themes such as women's role in society and the workplace, the demands of motherhood, and female subjectivity. The 1975 censorship statutes permitting nudity in films and the 1984 legalization of pornographic movie theaters resulted in a conspicuous sexualization of the public sphere, evident in the constant exhibition of women's bodies (a phenomenon known as *destape*).

In 1977, with the transition in full swing, the erotic literature book series and prize *La Sonrisa Vertical* was created by the Barcelona-based Tusquets publishing house. The aim was to bring explicitly erotic literature out of the closet. The series published works by classic international authors (Henry Miller, the Marquis de Sade, Georges Bataille, Marguerite Duras) and established Spanish-language writers, mostly male (Mario Vargas Llosa, Camilo José Cela, Francisco Umbral), to new voices, including several women. After two decades of commercial success, the series ceased publication in 2004, by when eroticism was fully integrated into the literary mainstream and easily accessible online.

La Sonrisa Vertical's greatest hit was *Las edades de Lulú* (*The Ages of Lulu*, 1989) – the début novel of Almudena Grandes, who would become a major writer in the Spanish literary landscape. Grandes was preceded as a post-dictatorship woman writer of erotic literature by Mercedes Abad and María Jaén, with the latter's Catalan-language *Amorrada al piló* (*Pinned to the Pylon*, 1986) enjoying considerable success. Yet, it was *Las edades de Lulú* that became emblematic of the imaginary of the transition. The protagonist is a 15-year-old schoolgirl when she begins a relationship with her older brother's friend, twice her age, its eroticism sustained by her emotional and aesthetic infantilization (shaved pubis, use of bibs). They marry but, in her thirties, she leaves him for a phase of extreme sexual experimentation that leads her to the verge of self-destruction, prompting her willing return to the role of little girl protected by her husband/father. Lulú's sexual fantasies and practices can be interpreted as a break with normative morality, or as a reproduction of heteronormative behavior patterns linked to traditional pornography. The novel reworks the plot structure of fairy tales, whose gender dichotomies Grandes would deploy in later, more politically engaged works such as *Malena es un nombre de tango* (*Malena is a Name from a Tango*, 1994).

Set in the Madrid of the dictatorship's last years and early transition, *Las edades de Lulú* is imbued with the hedonism and desire to break taboos that typified the *Movida*, the post-1975 (initially) counter-cultural movement that released a cathartic wave of unbridled artistic creativity. By the 1980s, however, the movement had become institutionalized and commercialized, its disruptive political edge giving way to a depoliticized emphasis on individualist consumerist pleasures – an evolution consistent with the broader context of neoliberalism (Nichols and Song 2013; Vilarós 2018). Grandes's later work celebrates a pleasure-filled heterosexuality and a type of "choice feminism" that today seems lacking in complexity.

Another key generational novel is *Crónica del desamor* (*Absent Love: A Chronicle*, 1979; re-issued 2009), by journalist Rosa Montero. Her women in transition deal with gender violence, work precarity, harassment, illegal abortion, machismo, drugs, and the impossibility of juggling employment with the demands of single motherhood. Despite the novel's somewhat schematic realist aesthetic, it gives a glimpse into the hopes and disenchantments of the transition years. In her later career, Montero would explore different genres, from the historical novel to science fiction; in all of them female characters, subjectivities, and bodies are central. Her writing makes an explicit connection between private desires and fantasies (principally female), material realities, and social issues.

Lucía Etxebarría became a media phenomenon with her first novels *Amor, curiosidad, prozac y dudas* (*Love, Curiosity, Prozac, and Doubts*, 1997) and *Beatriz y los cuerpos celestes* (*Beatriz and the Heavenly Bodies*, 1998; Nadal Prize), both of which mixed fiction and autobiographical elements in an exploration of womanhood, eroticism, and consumerism. Etxebarría has continued to write novels, poetry, and essays, which range from explorations of bisexuality and queer sexuality to the social construction of motherhood and gender. Her narratives and public persona, more ideologically ambivalent than her explicitly feminist declarations might suggest, reflect the complex position of Spanish women writers of her generation in the literary market.

An erotic equivalent in poetry to *Las edades de Lulú* is the early work of Ana Rosetti. Like Grandes, Rosetti won the *Sonrisa Vertical* award, for her short story collection *Alevosías* (*Duplicities*, 1991). Despite having worked across different genres (fiction, children's literature, stage works) and artistic registers, it is her poetry that has earned her wide acclaim. Her early poetry collections *Los devaneos de Erato* (*Erato's Pursuits*, 1980), *Devocionario* (*Prayer Book*, 1985), and *Indicios vehementes* (*Vehement Signs*, 1985) were groundbreaking in their brazen, playful sexuality, elaborating a camp aesthetic derived from a mix of American mass culture, fashion, and Andalusian popular Catholicism. In several of her best-known texts, the sexual orientation of the poetic voice is unmarked or there is a double-voiced discourse that dismantles sexual and textual dichotomies, including that of desiring subject/object. In her later poetry – for example, *Punto*

Umbrío (*Shadow Place*, 1995) – her early almost narcissistic focus on bodily pleasures gives way to an engaged social consciousness, without forgoing sensuality (Robbins 2004).

Feminism Comes into View

The reluctance of many women writers in the transition's early years to align themselves publicly with feminism waned as a new wave of women authors began to explore their gendered location and sexed selves unapologetically. As the twenty-first century progressed, feminism as a movement gained extraordinary traction in Spanish society; by the end of its first decade, discussion of gender ideology had become mainstream and on the agenda of all political parties. Visible outcomes were legislation against gender violence (2004); legalization of gay marriage and adoption rights for same-sex couples (2005); automatic parental leave for both spouses after birth (2006); the "Gender Equality Law" ensuring electoral parity (2007); and the expansion of legal access to abortion (2010). Symptomatically, the bestselling autobiography of gay novelist Luisgé Martín, *El amor al revés* (*Love in Reverse*, 2016), ends its painful coming-out story with the happy end of gay marriage. Spain now has a robust network of LGBTQ bookstores and publishers, including children's literature dealing with same-sex parents and gay, lesbian, and transgender issues, though gay male writers generally find it easier to break into the literary mainstream than lesbian authors.

Spanish feminism has finally come into full view, aligned not just with traditional demands (equal pay, protection from gender violence, abortion rights) but also with broad intersectional social and political struggles, including immigration, racism, LGBTQ rights, animal rights, and environmentalism. While Spain is one of the highest-ranked countries for acceptance of same-sex relationships and transgender rights, discrimination became more visible and violent in the twenty-first century's second decade, supported by far-right homophobic discourse and some feminist sectors' opposition to trans-inclusivity. The so-called "wolf pack" (*la manada*) rape case of 2017–19 – involving a young woman raped by five men, one a policeman and another a Civil Guard, all of whom boasted about it on social media – generated an unprecedented wave of protests that, building on the #Metoo movement (#Cuéntalo), peaked on International Women's Day in 2018 when over five million women took to the streets (the association Afroféminas refused to join on the grounds that the demands of black and racialized women were not adequately represented). The march was galvanizing for feminism but contributed to the previously insignificant far-right party Vox – committed to reversing the progressive gender legislation of recent years – gaining 52 seats in Congress at the November 2019 general elections.

Jordi Casanovas, known for his documentary dramas, wrote *Jauría* (*The Pack*) about the "wolf pack" case in 2019. Feminism, gender (including disagreements over trans-inclusive or trans-exclusive policies), LGBTQ rights, and masculinities continue to be at the center of public debate and policies (Amorós and de Miguel 2005; Amorós and Posada Kubissa 2007, 71–84; Bermúdez and Johnson 2018).

Unseemly Bodies: Illness, Aging, Disability

Many works written in the wake of the 2008 economic crisis question the logic of normalized (individual or collective) identities and explore alternative models of sexuality and community (see chapter 14). This questioning has led to an important focus on the body, understood in relation not only to individual pleasure and desire but also to the cultural construction of subjectivities. Many of today's Spanish women writers investigate the body's cultural significance for the social construction of the "normal" and the "natural."

The commodification of sexuality and reproduction – as well as the political dimension of pharmaceutical industries aimed at transforming the body (estrogen, birth control, Viagra, Prozac, doping) – was explored by Paul B. Preciado in *Testo Junkie: Sex, Drugs and Biopolitics in the Pharmacopornographic Era* (2013). Published originally in Spanish (*Testo Yonqui. Sexo, drogas y biopolítica*, 2008) under the name Beatriz Preciado, the text is a "body-essay" documenting the author's female-to-male transitioning and the bodily and affective impact of his voluntary process of "self-intoxication" with testosterone. It is also a philosophical exploration of sex and gender in relation to "pharmacopower" and new medical technologies. Elizabeth Duval – a successful transgender activist since the age of 14, poet, playwright, essayist, and performer – published the autofictional *Reina* (*Queen*, 2020) which recounts her life in Paris as a philosophy student, taking issue with Preciado's claim to non-binarity for not taking into account the privileges associated with the male body or the fact that the intellectual spokespersons for transgender rights tend to be male. In her poetry (*Excepción* / *Exception*, 2020), essays (*Después de lo trans. Sexo y género entre la izquierda y lo identitario* / *After Trans: Sex and Gender between the Left and Identity Politics*, 2021), and op-ed pieces, Duval has continued to engage, theoretically and creatively, with issues of identity, performance, media exposure, and political activism.

An increasing concern is the capitalist construction of a certain type of able body, and the neoliberal commodification of bodies connected to a notion of citizenship based on radical individuality and economic, physical, and emotional self-reliance, resting on a culturally sanctioned fantasy of "wholeness" (McRuer 2018; Federici 2020). In this context, writing by women in particular has shown a marked interest in illness, disability, queerness, and aging. Literary works – fictional or autobiographical – exploring illness and aging have become a distinct genre in Spain as elsewhere in the Western world. Illness (physical or mental) and the aging process anchor a broader reflection on the complex relationship between capitalism, the body, and work (remunerated or not) – key issues in contemporary Spain given the consequences of economic recession since 2008 for the public health service, work precarity, and the care needs of an aging population with a high life expectancy.

A noteworthy early example of the literary exploration of illness was the poetry of Isla Correyero. Her poems in the key anthologies *Las diosas blancas* (*The White Goddesses*, 1985) and *Ellas tienen la palabra. Dos décadas de poesía española* (*Women's Turn to Speak: Two Decades of Spanish Poetry*, 1997) reflect on the hedonism of the transition when, like so many of her contemporaries, she explored the new social and sexual freedoms. Some of her poems shocked critics with their explicit language – as in "Coño azul" (Blue Pussy) or "Terciopelo" (Velvet) – and the brutal lucidity of her depiction of the burdens of homoerotic and heterosexual love, including abuse and violence, as in *Ámbar* (*Amber*, 1984), *Amor tirano* (*Tyrannical Love*, 2003), and *Divorcio* (*Divorce*, 2015). Perhaps her best work relates to corporeality in a very different way: *Diario de una enfermera* (*A Nurse's Diary*, 1996) was based on her experience as a nurse dealing with her father's illness and death in a public hospital. A philosophical meditation on the complexity of pain and suffering, it reflects on the physical and emotional labor provided by exhausted, overworked caregivers. Framed temporally by the night shifts that Correyero had to cover, the poems lay bare the ravages of illness on bodies and minds through their focus on a public hospital's medical and administrative routines. The result combines almost hallucinatory images with colloquial and medical language, defying traditional distinctions between "social" and "avant-garde" poetry.

Correyero's poetic register is conveyed by the title of her anthology of contemporary poetry, *Feroces. Radicales, marginales y heterodoxos en la última poesía española* (1998): fierce and radical, but also tender and empathetic. Contemporary Spanish poetry by women continues to develop the connection between the deeply personal and the political/collective, while exploring new languages of affectivity and divergence – as in the innovative, nonconformist poems by Pilar Adón, María Eloy-García, Txus García, and Elena Medel in the anthology *Insumisas. Poesia crítica contemporánea de mujeres* (*Insubordinate: Contemporary Critical Poetry by Women*, 2019). Begoña M. Rueda's *Servicio de Lavandería* (*Laundry Service*, 2020) exposed the harsh reality of hospital laundry workers (of which Rueda was one) before and particularly during the COVID-19 pandemic, in language that is at the same time sensitive meditation and angry social denunciation.

The link between compulsory able-bodiedness and compulsory heterosexuality is exposed in Isabel Franc's graphic novel *Alicia en un mundo real* (*Alice in a Real World*, 2010; illustrated by Susanna Martín). Franc's first novel *Entre las mujeres* (*Among All Women*, 1992) had won Tusquets's *Sonrisa Vertical* prize for its female protagonist's visionary erotic encounters with the Virgin Mary. This graphic novel – a genre increasingly popular in today's Spain (see chapter 14) – creates a fictional cancer memoir based on Franc's experience. The novel tells the story of a middle-aged lesbian woman's diagnosis and fight against breast cancer, probing the politics of illness and health in neoliberal societies. The narrative realism and humor contrast ironically with the super-hero imagery used to depict the protagonist's resilience through illness, treatment, and a recovery that includes reclaiming her joy and sexualized queer body (DiFilippo 2019). Cancer also anchors Gabriela Ybarra's autobiographical novel *El comensal* (*The Dinner Guest*, 2018; see chapter 14), which combines the story of her grandfather's kidnapping and murder by ETA with that of her mother's later terminal illness – a connection consistent with the frequent metaphorization of Basque separatism as a cancer.

Elvira Navarro's *La trabajadora* (*A Working Woman*, 2014) foregrounds the connection between material and mental precarity in a context of severe economic recession, aggravated by the alienation resulting from loss of community, social, and economic networks. The work of the remarkable poet, essayist, and novelist Marta Sanz showcases the inscription of social and political reality on the body. Her novel *Susana y los viejos* (*Susana and the Elders*, 2002), revolves around the crisis of care afflicting contemporary capitalist societies, with material and affective labor carried out by (usually immigrant and female) workers who earn minimal wages and have no social protection. In *Clavícula* (*Collarbone*, 2017), Sanz reflects on bodily pain, as well as the difficulties of becoming an older woman in a society that prescribes impossible ableist ideals of successful, productive maturity. In *pequeñas mujeres rojas* (*little red women*, 2020), the last novel in a noir trilogy, she weaves a complex narrative from several perspectives, including that of a middle-aged, disabled female protagonist whose commitment to unearthing historical truths exposes the overlapping of political and domestic gender violence.

13

Memory and Forgetting (1970s–2020)

This chapter discusses the literary recovery of painful pasts in the light of contemporary memory discourses that stress the ethical obligation to do so. If chapter 5 discussed the uses of the past for the nation-formation project that, beginning in the late eighteenth century, traversed Spain's nineteenth century, this chapter looks at works set in the past that have the function of rescuing instances of suffering and injustice from oblivion, recognizing that the nation's history has not always been exemplary. Painful pasts are not easy to acknowledge; we will see how much of this writing is problematic. The issues are complex in the case of Spain's historic nationalities which, as seen in chapter 11, were engaged in institutionalizing a sense of national identity in the 1960s to 1990s. That identity could be reinforced by recovering local painful pasts for which the central state was responsible, but acknowledgment was more difficult when the responsibility was local (as in the case of Basque writing on ETA terrorism). Needless to say, not all works set in the past qualify as "memory texts" in the reparative sense outlined here.

As Maurice Halbwachs explained (1992), memory is not the registration in the mind of a past event but the construction of the past, whether witnessed personally or not. It does not give us the past as it was but its meaning for those recalling it in the present. "Collective memory" is not the product of a supposed "collective mind" but the memory of individuals as members of a particular group; hence Halbwachs's alternative term "social memory." There is no such thing as purely individual memory, since all memories are shaped by the "social frames" (group identifications) that give our existence meaning. These social frames encourage remembrance of some things and not others; memory is by definition a selection process that depends on a complementary process of forgetting. The past keeps changing because each historical period constructs different versions.

The global memory boom that began in the 1990s has been seen as the other side of a neoliberal culture of amnesia, with the loss of the past produced by compulsory obsolescence leading to a compensatory proliferation of museums, memorials, exhibitions, and cultural representations that all too often had a market-driven celebratory function (Huyssen 1996). An example was the 1992 quincentennial commemorations of Castile's patronage of Columbus's "discovery" of America, conquest of Spain's last Muslim kingdom of Granada, and expulsion of the Jews, which largely "forgot" those events' catastrophic consequences for non-Christian populations. But the 1990s also saw increasing demands for investigation of the Francoist wartime and postwar repression. The turn to memory in Spanish-language cultural production since the 1990s (including film adaptations of many literary works) has focused overwhelmingly on this topic.

Recovering Silenced Memories of the Francoist Repression

Contemporary Western memory texts seeking to make reparation for violent pasts have adopted various narrative strategies: testimonial recuperation of the past; postmodern play that questions the boundary between the fictional and the real; or recreation of the fragmented, non-linear temporality of memory or its traumatic dislocation. In Spain, the first two have dominated. The third option, characteristic of 1980s Southern Cone fiction on the effects of military repression, is largely limited to writing from the late 1960s to the 1980s. The abolition of censorship in December 1977 produced an increasing desire to "tell it all"; this testimonial imperative, plus the coincidence of the 1990s memory boom with a growing bestseller culture, encouraged a realist aesthetic. The one form of literary experimentation found in recent novels on the Francoist repression is the blurring of fiction and reality through postmodern play; this exposes the constructed nature of all versions of history but undermines the possibility of talking about the past.

Under the Franco dictatorship, pro-Republican memories of the Civil War and its aftermath were silenced through brutal repression. In their place, Spaniards were fed a topsy-turvy official memory according to which the Republic had started the war and the Nationalist victors were the victims of the defeated; that is, of Republican violence. Thus, the memories that needed to be recovered after the return to democracy were those of the war's losers. The year 2000 saw the creation of the Asociación para la Recuperación de la Memoria Histórica (Association for the Recovery of Historical Memory; ARMH) as a civic organization facilitating the exhumation of victims of the Francoist wartime and postwar repression from the mass graves that litter the national territory. The ensuing media "memory war" between political right and left over how or whether the violent past should be remembered peaked during the parliamentary debate on the Socialist government's modest 2007 Historical Memory Law. Post-dictatorship literary production on the Civil War and its aftermath has, by contrast, been exclusively from a left or center-left perspective. The term *memoria histórica* (historical memory) has become shorthand in today's Spain for the memorialization of the victims of the Francoist wartime and postwar repression.

Two international factors have affected this process. First, the discourse on the Holocaust – central to the 1990s Western memory boom – which stressed the memorialization of victims. Second, the emergence also in the 1990s of transitional (that is, post-dictatorship) justice culture, which grew out of the establishment of Truth and Reconciliation Commissions in (among other countries) Argentina (1983–4) and Chile (1990–1). The 1998 creation of the International Criminal Court spurred Spanish judge Baltasar Garzón to secure the arrest in London of Chile's former dictator Pinochet. This prompted many Spaniards to ask why legal processes had not been initiated to deal with the Francoist repression. The heroic vision of the Republican fight against fascism that dominated in the transition years would, from 1999, give way to an emphasis on Republican victims.

A further historical shift has been the questioning of Spain's transition to democracy, previously regarded as exemplary (see chapter 14). Paloma Aguilar Fernández (1996) was the first to note that political debate during the transition was predicated on a tacit agreement not to talk about the violent past – a silencing misleadingly termed a *pacto del olvido* (pact of oblivion). In practice, nothing was forgotten. However, the proliferation of historical studies on the war and dictatorship from the late 1970s did not focus on victims till the late 1990s (Juliá 1999). From that date, the production of novels on the Civil War and its aftermath would become an industry, with practically every novelist contributing. Several of these texts are as much a critique of the transition's sidelining of the past as they are of Francoism.

The Civil War forms the principal backdrop of Juan Benet's pre-memory-boom novelistic output – from *Volverás a Región* (*Return to Region*, 1967) through his unfinished *Herrumbrosas lanzas* series (*Rusty Lances*, 1983–6). Rather than evoke the suffering caused by the war, these texts philosophize about the drives that make aspects of the past taboo, in dense modernist prose that simulates the workings of memory. Modernist prose is, however, used to recreate the suffering of the war and its aftermath by Juan Eduardo Zúñiga, whose first book of stories *Largo noviembre de Madrid* (*Long Madrid*

November, 1980, written in the 1970s) describes the November 1936 onset of the Nationalist siege of Madrid, which he experienced as a boy. The stories recreate traumatic recall through the dislocation of narrative voice, mirroring the spatial dislocation resulting from the air raids and shelling. Zúñiga returned to the topic with his later story collections. Modernist experiment also characterizes Juan Marsé's *Si te dicen que caí* (*The Fallen*, Mexico, 1973; banned in Spain till 1976). The novel mixes direct and reported narration by a group of working-class boys growing up, like Marsé, in 1940s Barcelona, framed by the memories of one of them in the 1960s, and omniscient narration of the story of a group of urban resistance fighters who we discover are the boys' fathers, two of whom in the last chapter look back from the 1960s at their exploits. The different narrative levels leak into one another, such that it becomes impossible to ascertain who is narrating what; the mix of memory and fantasy mirrors a postwar in which truth was replaced by hearsay. Marsé would return obsessively to this postwar scenario in his later fiction from *Un día volveré* (*I'll Return Some Day*, 1982) to *Caligrafía de los sueños* (*Calligraphy of Dreams*, 2004).

The French-language Holocaust memoirs of exile writer Jorge Semprún – *Le long voyage* (*The Long Voyage*, 1963) and *Quel beau dimanche* (*What a Beautiful Sunday*, 1980) – together with his essay *L'écriture ou la vie* (*Writing or Life*, 1994) are classic memory texts. The easing of censorship allowed him to publish his first work in Spanish, *Autobiografía de Federico Sánchez* (*Autobiography of Federico Sánchez*, 1977), comprising the memoirs of his alias as an undercover communist agent in 1950s Spain. The sophisticated understanding of memory's multiple temporalities that this autobiography shares with Semprún's earlier French-language texts is unparalleled in Spanish literature, with the possible exception of Juan Goytisolo's memoirs (see chapter 12). Semprún's late Spanish-language novel *Veinte años y un día* (*Twenty Years and a Day*, 2003) returns to the Civil War but with political analysis replaced by postmodern play.

The late 1970s and 1980s also saw theater turn to the topic. Fernando Fernán Gómez's *Las bicicletas son para el verano* (*Bicycles Are for Summer*; written 1977, staged 1982) gives a *costumbrista* account of life in wartime Madrid. More radical was the minimalist political theater of José Sanchis Sinisterra's Barcelona-based Teatro Fronterizo (Frontier Theater, founded 1977). His *Terror y miseria en el primer franquismo* (*Fear and Misery in Early Francoism*, 1979–2002) – referencing Brecht's *Fear and Misery of the Third Reich* (1938) – comprises nine dramatic fragments probing the corrosion of defeat. The play that clinched his reputation was *¡Ay, Carmela!* (premièred 1987). Unlike Carlos Saura's 1990 film version, it has a retrospective narrative frame, leaving us unsure whether the show that variety artists Carmela and Paulino are obliged to perform for the Nationalist troops, culminating in Carmela's execution, is a representation of what happened, a memory of Paulino, or a posthumous account by Carmela's ghost.

Novelistic output on the Civil War from the 1980s on has privileged the thriller genre, which can cater to realism (by revealing the truth about the crime) or to the postmodern questioning of the relation between fiction and reality (by showing the impossibility of doing so). In these novels, the investigator-protagonist (often the narrator) is not a detective – the 1977 Amnesty Law prohibits prosecutions in Spain – but an academic, journalist, ghostwriter, and / or relative bent on uncovering a family secret. The schoolteacher narrator of Benjamín Prado's *Mala gente que camina* (*Bad Men Walking*, 2006) investigates the "stolen babies" taken from imprisoned Republican mothers. Veteran thriller writer Alicia Giménez Bartlett's *Donde nadie te encuentre* (*Where No One Shall Find You*, 2011) chronicles a French psychology professor's attempt to track down the intersexual rural resistance-fighter La Pastora, still holding out in 1956. A journalist investigator-narrator is used in Javier Cercas's *Soldados de Salamina* (*Soldiers of Salamis*, 2001), which became a bestseller thanks to its polemical subject matter: the escape from a Republican firing squad of the Spanish fascist intellectual Rafael Sánchez Mazas. Cercas abandons Sánchez Mazas's story for the politically safer option of tracking down the Republican soldier who let him go. Cercas's text questions all historical accounts by exposing their constructed nature, displacing the role of hero onto the investigator-narrator (called Javier Cercas). The use in several novels of a ghostwriter-investigator, reconstructing the past for a paymaster, allows critique of democratic Spain's sell-out to the market. This format is used by longstanding communist thriller writer Manuel Vázquez Montalbán in his 1992 *Autobiografía del general Franco* (*Autobiography of General Franco*) and by Isaac Rosa in his 2007 *¡Otra maldita novela sobre la guerra civil!* (*Another Wretched Novel on the Civil War!*, 2007). By making his novel a critical reworking of his earlier *La malamemoria* (*Badmemory*, 1999), Rosa makes history the pretext for a clever metafictional game, foregrounding the author's literary tricks.

The format of a relative investigating a family secret has wide resonance in Spain, where parents often hid from their children the fact that relatives had been victims of Francoist reprisals. The current memory movement has largely been driven by victims' grandchildren, who grew up free of the fear that crippled earlier generations, but novelistic investigators of their family past mostly belong to the second generation. This is postmemory in the sense of Marianne Hirsch's revision of her original 1997 term to include not only memories transmitted from parents to children (which in Spain mostly did not happen) but also the attempts by later generations to "re-embody" memories with which the connection has been lost (Hirsch 2012). Antonio Muñoz Molina inaugurated this theme with his first novel *Beatus Ille* (*A Manuscript of Ashes*, 1986), whose doctoral student investigator Minaya visits his uncle in Mágina (Muñoz Molina's birthplace Úbeda) to conduct research on the (fictitious) local Republican poet Solana, supposedly shot by civil guards in 1947. Minaya's investigation shifts to the private tragedy of the 1937 shooting of his uncle's bride, falling for the clues planted by Solana who, in a postmodern twist, turns out to be alive and to have engineered Minaya's encounter with his supposedly lost manuscript *Beatus Ille* – possibly the novel we are reading – which he is writing in the present. Muñoz Molina's 1991 *El jinete polaco* (*The Polish Rider*) again sidelines its initial political investigation in order to probe a private drama, but the postmodern literary games are now replaced by an intricate study of postmemory as the interpreter-narrator Manuel and his half-American girlfriend Nadia reconnect with their family pasts in Mágina. Almudena Grandes's *El corazón helado* (*The Frozen Heart*, 2007), written well into the memory boom, tackles the silenced stories of those who profited financially from Francoism and the bitter memories of those who were cheated out of an inheritance.

The redemptive urge to overcome the rift between present and past is shown most clearly in novels that opt for first-person testimony, encouraging reader identification. Julio Llamazares's first novel *Luna de lobos* (*Wolf Moon*, 1985) drew on stories about the *maquis* (resistance-fighters) he heard as a child in rural León. Narrated by the sole survivor of a Republican guerrilla group, the novel poetically evokes the group's experiences from 1937 through 1946. It pays tribute to the power of memory not only though the narrator's act of bearing witness, but also by showing that what keeps the group alive is the local community's collective memory of them. Josefina Aldecoa's trilogy *Historia de una maestra* (*A Schoolteacher's Story*, 1990), *Mujeres de negro* (*Women in Black*, 1994), and *La fuerza del destino* (*The Force of Destiny*, 1997) uses first-person narrative to recreate the dislocated structures of memory. It seems not to be coincidence that an older author, born in 1926, should be one of the few contemporary Spanish writers to be interested in the literary recreation of memory processes. The trilogy depicts transmission across three generations: between the Republican schoolteacher protagonist Gabriela and her daughter Juana; and, in the last novel which charts Gabriela's alienation on her return from exile in Mexico to democratic Spain, between Gabriela and her grandson since Juana is too busy campaigning for the 1982 Socialist election victory to be interested in the past.

First-person testimonies (previously published or compiled by herself) were used by Dulce Chacón in her bestselling *La voz dormida* (*The Sleeping Voice*, 2002), the first novel to deal with women in Francoist prisons – appropriately since oral history has been an effective tool for recovering women's voices absent from historical records. Chacón's fusion of omniscient narration with the female characters' thoughts, feelings, and memories combines a sense of testimonial veracity with empathy. But empathy can be a trap, deluding us into thinking we can share the emotions of past victims and potentially blocking analysis (Izquierdo Martín and Sánchez León 2006, 227–76). Chacón's earlier novel *Cielos de barro* (*Skies of Clay*, 2000) avoids this trap by putting the revelations about the village's history of wartime atrocities in the mouth of an illiterate peasant trickster-figure. Almudena Grandes also resorts to first-person narration by a (female or male) character-narrator in her ambitious cycle of six historical novels, *Episodios de una guerra interminable* (*Episodes of an Interminable War*), which pay tribute to Galdós's *Episodios nacionales*, like them focusing on fictional characters ensnared in historical events. The cycle informs readers about a diverse range of "forgotten" aspects of postwar history: in the five novels written before her death, the Republican refugees who joined the French Resistance; the repression of the *maquis*; Franco's penal universe; Nazi war criminals in Spain and Argentina; and Francoist mental institutions. The novels all end in the late 1970s, allowing critique of the transition. Antonio Muñoz Molina's 2009 *La noche de los tiempos* (*In the Night of Time*) similarly relies on the authority of the eyewitness, albeit via third-person narration, by depicting the Republic through its Republican exile protagonist's memories on his late 1936 arrival in the United States.

In all the twenty-first-century fiction on the Civil War discussed so far, clever plots dominate at the expense of psychological complexity. A notable exception is Alberto Méndez's *Los girasoles ciegos* (*The Blind Sunflowers*, 2004), whose four stories relate a succession of "derrotas" (defeats) set in the years 1939–42. The sophisticated use of multiple perspectives explores a psychology of defeat that pushes people to choose death as a way of maintaining dignity. Above all, Méndez's text shows an awareness that the role of memory is not to recover the past but to trace a history of disappearances.

Not all twenty-first-century fiction set in or after the Civil War has a reparative function. The bestselling historical thrillers of Carlos Ruiz Zafón – *La sombra del viento* (*The Shadow of the Wind*, 2001) through *El laberinto de los espíritus* (*The Labyrinth of Spirits*, 2017) – opt for magic realism, converting Spanish history into a Gothic backdrop. Magic realism is also deployed in Luis Mateo Díaz's *Fantasmas de invierno* (*Winter Ghosts*, 2004), *La gloria de los niños* (*The Glory of Children*, 2007), and *La soledad de los perdidos* (*The Loneliness of the Lost*, 2014), whose surreal settings elide political analysis.

Remembering World War II and the Holocaust

The twenty-first century has seen the increasing production in Spain of novels depicting World War II, among them Javier Marías's trilogy *Tu rostro mañana* (*Your Face Tomorrow*, 2002–8); María Dueñas's *El tiempo entre costuras* (*The Time in between*, 2009); Julia Navarro's *Dime quien soy* (*Tell Me Who I Am*, 2012); and Juan Manuel de Prada's *El séptimo velo* (*The Seventh Veil*, 2007). Beneath the ostensible aim of recovering a painful (European and not just Spanish) past, one senses a desire to overcome Spain's isolation from world events by inserting the Spanish protagonists into exciting cosmopolitan adventures (in Britain, Morocco, Portugal, France, USSR, Germany, Poland, Argentina, Mexico), enhanced by a spy story format. Prada's *Me hallará la muerte* (*Death Will Find Me*, 2012) focuses on the División Azul (Blue Division) of mostly Falangist volunteers who fought alongside Hitler's army on the Russian front in 1941–3, debunking heroism as in his earlier *El séptimo velo*, which treats the French Resistance. Agustín Fernández Mallo's 2018 *Trilogía de la guerra* (*War Trilogy*, 2018), whose starting point is the Francoist concentration camp on the Galician island of San Simón, does have a reparative function, achieved by weaving together the many wars, including World War II and the Vietnam War, that are the twentieth century's defining legacy.

The ethical duty to honor victims is seen most clearly in the increasing amount of Spanish fiction about the Holocaust, compensating for an earlier lack of interest on the supposition that Spain had no Jews, having expelled them in 1492. Memorialization of the 9,000 Spanish Republican refugees in France who were interned in Nazi death camps, notably Mauthausen where 5,000 died, has mostly been in Catalan (see chapter 10). The most ambitious Spanish-language attempt to treat the Holocaust is Muñoz Molina's *Sefarad* (2001), which interweaves the voices of victims of Nazi and Stalinist persecution, as well as Spanish Republican exiles. The intertwining of a large number of real-life and fictional stories of displacement creates an equivalence between suffering on very different scales; Spain's expulsion of the Jews is sidelined.

Like Muñoz Molina, the playwright Juan Mayorga has balanced the denunciation of Nazi crimes with those of Stalinism. *Cartas de amor a Stalin* (published and staged 1999) dramatizes the writer Bulgakov's writing of protest letters to Stalin, binding him to tyranny as the object of his attentions. Mayorga's internationally successful *Himmelweg* (*Way to Heaven*; performed 2003, published 2004) stages the (real-life) "performance" that the inmates of Theresienstadt concentration camp were obliged to put on to dupe an International Red Cross delegation. His later *El cartógrafo* (*The Map Maker*; published 2010, staged 2013 in Warsaw) interweaves a present-day attempt to map the disappeared Warsaw ghetto with its mapping by a Jewish girl shortly before it was destroyed. Mayorga, like Méndez in *Los girasoles ciegos*, appreciates that memory does not recover the past but maps a history of disappearances. The real-life heroine of Antonio G. Iturbe's *La bibliotecaria de Auschwitz* (*The Auschwitz Librarian*, 2012) was also from the Warsaw ghetto. The novel reiterates the problematic if attractive trope of culture as salvation from barbarism, treated also in Maria Àngels Anglada's earlier 1994 Catalan-language novel *El violí d'Auschwitz* (*The Auschwitz Violin*), again based on a true story. The most imaginative treatment of Nazi atrocities is found in Ricardo Menéndez Salmón's *La ofensa* (*The Offence*, 2007) and *Medusa* (2012), which reflect on how ordinary German citizens could become accomplices to evil. The burden of memory of Holocaust survivors is treated by Juana Salabert (a second-generation exile born in France) in *Velódromo de Invierno* (*Vélodrome d'hiver*, 2001), whose dislocated narrative structures mimic traumatic recall – the only one of these texts to explore the workings of memory.

The civic organization Amical de Mauthausen, which commemorates Spanish victims of the Holocaust, has also triggered a literary response, thanks to the 2005 revelation that its president, Enric Marco, was never in a Nazi camp but had volunteered to work in the Nazi arms industry under Franco's 1941 agreement with Hitler. Maria Barbal's subtle analysis of "victim envy" in her 2014 Catalan-language fictionalization of Marco's story, *En la pell de l'altre* (*In the Skin of the Other*), was eclipsed by publication later that year of Javier Cercas's docufiction *El impostor*, based on interviews with Marco. Faithful to his postmodern credentials, Cercas concludes that "we are all impostors" since we all turn our lives into a fiction.

Exposing the Underside of the "Development Years" and
Transition to Democracy

The 1960s, presented by the Franco regime as the "Development Years"
and by the left as a period of strong political opposition, have also undergone fictional critique. In Muñoz Molina's thriller *Beltenebros* (1989), a
Republican exile charged by the Spanish Communist Party with assas-
sinating an alleged traitor in the 1960s questions his mission as memories
return of the assassination he undertook in the 1940s. The aim is to expose
the Spanish Communist Party's unacknowledged Stalinist past. The left
is critiqued also by the younger Isaac Rosa in *El vano ayer* (*The Futile Past*,
2004), whose novelist-narrator's self-reflexive failed reconstruction of 1960s
student activism debunks heroic stereotypes of the anti-Franco opposition.
By contrast, Rafael Chirbes's major novel *La larga marcha* (*The Long March*,
1996) recovers the suffering of a large cast of the defeated in the Civil War
over the three subsequent decades, stressing the generation gap between
them and their children, who have grown up in the cities to which their
parents migrated.

The mass migration from countryside to city that transformed 1960s
Spain, making possible Spain's "economic miracle" at the expense of
immense dislocation, has been memorialized in Luis Landero's autobiographical *El balcón en invierno* (*Balcony in Winter*, 2014), and was due to be
treated in the last of Grandes's planned *Episodios*, interrupted by her death.
The resulting rural dereliction was addressed by Llamazares in novels preceding the memory boom that look back at the past through first-person
narration. *La lluvia amarilla* (*The Yellow Rain*, 1988) recreates the fissured
interior monologue of the dying last inhabitant of an abandoned village.
Escenas de cine mudo (*Scenes of Silent Cinema*, 1994) explores photographs of
Llamazares's childhood in a Leonese mining village, reconstructing what
he was looking at when photographed, that is, what was excluded from
representation. His travelogue *El río del olvido* (*The River of Oblivion*, 1990)
charts his journey upstream – against the flow of history – to a rural interior
(his native León again) that contemporary Spain has forgotten.

Critiques of the transition have multiplied in recent years. The topic was
anticipated by Vázquez Montalbán's *El pianista* (*The Pianist*, 1985), which
looks back from the 1982 Socialist election victory at the postwar repression
and prewar avant-garde. The reverse chronology uncovers the destroyed
potential that has been forgotten. The same author's *Galíndez* (1990) uses
the thriller format to investigate the 1956 disappearance in New York of the
exiled Basque nationalist Jesús Galíndez, inviting comparison between the

CIA, which murders the American doctoral student researching Galíndez's death, and the GAL death squads clandestinely organized in the mid-1980s by Spain's Socialist government to eliminate Basque terrorism. Prado's *Operación Gladio* (2011) also indicts the transition for collusion with terrorism by exploring the undercover NATO network Operation Gladio linked to the 1977 assassination of labor lawyers in Atocha, Madrid. Cercas explores conspiracy theories relating to the transition in his bestselling docufictional account of the February 23, 1981 attempted coup, *Anatomía de un instante* (*Anatomy of a Moment*, 2009; see chapter 14). Chirbes anticipated today's analysis of the continuity between Francoist urban speculation and that of the democratic period in *La buena letra* (*Good Handwriting*, 1992) and *Los disparos del cazador* (*The Hunter's Shots*, 1994), described by him as a denunciation of the 1990s New Left's "trueque de verdad por dinero" (trading of truth for money).

Rewriting the Distant Past

The historical novel, foreign and homegrown, dealing with a remote past is also a bestselling genre in Spain, catering largely to a taste for exoticism – as in Magdalena Lasala's novels set in al-Andalus – or for light entertainment – as in veteran bestseller-writer Arturo Pérez-Reverte's novels written for the bi-centenary commemorations of the Battle of Trafalgar, the Dos de Mayo uprising against Napoleonic occupation, and the 1812 Constitution, or his seven *Alatriste* novels (1996–2011) charting the picaresque exploits of a seventeenth-century Spanish soldier-adventurer in Flanders, Madrid, and the Mediterranean. Some of these recreations of the distant past do, however, have a reparative function. Antonio Gala's *El manuscrito carmesí* (*The Crimson Manuscript*, 1990), narrates through its last ruler's eyes the Islamic Kingdom of Granada's fall to an intolerant, primitive Christian Castile. In 1998 Miguel Delibes's *El hereje* (*The Heretic*) exposed the Inquisition's extermination of Spanish Protestants. The well-researched bestsellers by Ildefonso Falcones – *La catedral del mar* (*The Cathedral of the Sea*, 2006) through *Los herederos de la tierra* (*They Shall Inherit the Earth*, 2016) – foreground the persecution of ethnic minorities in medieval, sixteenth-century, and Enlightenment Spain, showing particular sensitivity to the plight of women.

Empire largely remains a blind spot in Spanish fictional inquiries into the past. One of the few novels to tackle the topic – Prada's 2014 *Morir bajo tu cielo* (*To Die under Your Sky*) – misses the opportunity to explore the

Philippine War of Independence from the perspective of the colonized by repeating the celebration of Spanish military heroism in the 1945 patriotic film *Los últimos de Filipinas* (*Last Stand in the Philippines*). An exception is Sanchis Sinisterra's *Trilogía americana* (written 1977–8, first performed 1985–91). Moving between past and present and including indigenous voices, the plays undo teleology through fragmentation, improvisation, and farce.

Catalan Literature "in the Skin of the Other": Other Histories, Other Voices, Other Bodies

One of the most important features of the 1970s was the return of the past, with the transition to autonomous status in Catalonia marked by the recovery of pre-1939 institutions (Generalitat, Institut d'Estudis Catalans, Institució de les Lletres Catalanes, among others); the publication of major cultural histories; the inclusion of key texts about the Civil War and exile in accessible paperbacks; and the excavation of hidden and silenced histories, such as Montserrat Roig's recovery of the experiences of Catalan political prisoners in the Nazi camps (see chapter 10). Manuel de Pedrolo's magnum opus *Temps obert* (*Open Time*, 11 vols., 1963–9), re-edited in the 1970s, traced the different possible narrative outcomes stemming from the aerial bombardment of a residential block in Barcelona in March 1938. In one version, the protagonist overcomes the tragic loss of his family to become a novelist who goes on to write the cycle's final volumes, centering on the 1960s. In another, he is caught up in postwar black-marketeering, becomes a petty criminal, and then gets involved in property speculation. Other versions see him killed in the bombing, evacuated to the countryside, or taken to New York where he scoffs at the older generation of exiles who remain loyal to the culture of their homeland. Rodoreda's *Mirall trencat* (*Broken Mirror*, 1974) plots the rise and fall of three generations of a bourgeois Barcelona household from the turn of the century to the postwar, recovering a lost world from myriad perspectives, including that of the rats who occupy the building as it awaits its final transformation into a building site. While this novel reconstructs a place of memory definitively erased by the Civil War, her subsequent novels *Quanta, quanta guerra* (*War, So Much War*, 1983) and the posthumous *La mort i la primavera* (*Death in Spring*, 1986) center on dystopian landscapes irrevocably transformed by violence. The society depicted in the latter is sustained by its denial of history and censorship of community memory. The definitive 1981 version of Joan Sales's novel on the Civil War, *Incerta glòria* (*Uncertain Glory*, previously issued in 1956 and 1969), began to reach wider audiences only in the twenty-first century, especially after Peter Bush's 2014 translation into English. The novel presents a graphic, ideologically multi-layered vision of the cruel struggles for survival over the war's course, at the Aragonese front and in the Barcelona of the rearguard, interspersed with philosophical and religious meditations. Though by no means ideologically neutral (the author is a Catalanist who has turned from anarcho-communism to Christianity), Sales's novel is even-handed in portraying the war's corruption of all youthful ideals and the uneasy compromises of the survivors in the postwar decades (at home or in exile).

Although many novels and plays of the 1980s and 1990s were drawn to cosmopolitan settings, in line with an institutional obsession with mimicking international trends, a number of novels attempted to recover a forgotten local past, though they were often marketed otherwise. Thus, the works of Jesús Moncada and Mercè Ibarz, which evoke the Catalan-speaking Franja de Ponent on Catalonia's western border with Aragon, were read as rural novels thanks to the center-periphery dynamic resulting from the contemporaneous institutional focus on Barcelona. Moncada's best-known novel *Camí de sirga* (*The Towpath*, 1988) tells the story of Mequinensa, one of the Ebro communities obliterated during the Franco dictatorship in order to build a dam. The novel's overlapping multiple perspectives and temporalities range from the late eighteenth-century revolutionary wars to the impact of the settlement's forced abandonment in the 1950s, which we slowly realize is a punishment for its history of political resistance and insubordination. Ghosts of past and present intermingle in the different community spaces, becoming indistinguishable from the ruins of the built environment. Based on memories and stories gathered from the inhabitants of this lost place, the novel anticipates the concerns with the unburied dead and unmetabolized remains of the past that would become such a feature of the early twenty-first-century cultural marketplace (Crameri 2011). Carme Riera's *Dins el darrer blau* (*Into the Last Blue*, 1994) and *Cap al cel obert* (*To the Sky and Beyond*, 2002), discussed in chapter 12, recover the hidden histories of the Inquisition's late-fourteenth-century persecution of the Majorcan *xueta* (Jewish) community and the Majorcan diaspora in nineteenth-century Cuba. Both novels are explicitly framed as challenges to simplistic historical representations of Catalan victimhood.

Other Catalan writers have drawn attention to the need to recover the experiences of mid-twentieth-century immigrant and refugee communities. Maria Barbal's *Pedra de tartera* (*Stone in a Landslide*, 1982) and *Carrer*

Bolívia (*Bolivia Street*, 1999) tell stories of rural to urban migration produced by the devastation of communities in the postwar period, as experienced by peasant women – from the Catalan Pyrenees and rural Jaén respectively. The world of "els altres catalans" (the other Catalans) – as Francisco Candel (1974) called the Spanish-speaking migrants often forced to live in informal housing or tower blocks on the city outskirts – is explored from the perspective of different characters, some of whom choose to integrate, with others becoming politically active in the labor movement, uncovering the key role played by these communities in the articulation of broad-based oppositional demands for social justice. Julià de Jòdar likewise focuses on the histories of 1960s immigrant communities in his trilogy *L'atzar i les ombres* (*Fate and the Shadows*, 1998–2001).

In Catalonia, political recognition of an unpaid debt to the past culminated in the 2007 creation of Memorial Democràtic, providing an institutional framework for recovering hidden cultural and political histories of the period 1931–80. Its activities have ranged from creating a network of sites of memory, including the Museu Memorial de l'Exili (MUME), to organizing commemorative events, awarding prizes for memory texts, and facilitating the identification and forensic excavation of mass graves. As far as literary production is concerned, the most famous Catalan novels of the Civil-War-related memory boom are Jaume Cabré's *Les veus del Pamano* (*Voices of Pamano*, 2004), which excavates the layers of conflicting trauma narratives that have marked a remote Pyrenean village; Emili Teixidor's *Pa negre* (*Black Bread*, 2003), which explores the ways in which the lessons of the war shape and twist the subjectivity of the adult/child narrator (Ryan 2014, 117–37); and Jordi Coca's *Sota la pols* (*Under the Dust*, 2001), which maps the bodily imprints of repression and violence in postwar Barcelona. Teixidor and Cabré have a long track record of writing novels about different aspects of Catalan history; the latter's 1,000-page *Jo confesso* (2011) takes up the question of personal responsibility in the face of institutional violence across a panoply of European historical crimes ranging from the Inquisition to colonialism and the Shoah. It is a novel that Cabré himself recognizes would not have been possible without *Les veus del Pamano*, and whose continual return to the question of what we do with memory objects – the material culture we exchange, transmit, preserve, or covet – brings into focus the banality of evil and the moral duty to witness and remember. All three writers focus on the embodied, intergenerational transmission of trauma.

This has been a feature of recent plays about past political violence. Argentine-Catalan playwright Victoria Szpunberg's *La fragilidad de la memoria* (*The Fragility of Memory*, 2008–10) focuses on how the traumatic experiences of Argentine exiles are transmitted through the bodies of subsequent generations, whereas Helena Tornero's *No parlis amb estranys* (*Don't Talk to Strangers*, 2013) explores different scenarios of transgenerational transmission by victims and perpetrators of violence. There have also been a number of Catalan texts that offer an ethical and political critique of the appropriation and reactivation of violence and trauma. A key example is Carles Batlle's 2009 play *Zoom*, played out on a film set in which we witness the multiple perspectives underlying different actors' reconstruction of an already mediated story. Engaging with the memories of the author's grandfather, the play becomes a vehicle for questioning the memory boom's nostalgic focus by projecting a more critical, interstitial space. In fiction, the narrator of Carme Riera's *La meitat de l'ànima* (*Half of a Soul*, 2004) ends up choosing her preferred outcome for her dead mother's double life of cross-border liaison and espionage in the 1940s and 1950s, while recognizing alternative possibilities in which there are no innocent victims. Empar Moliner's novel *La col·laboradora* (*The Collaborator*, 2012) is a dark comedy of a ghostwriter asked to falsify the history of a woman killed during the Civil War, so that she fits the profile of the innocent Republican victim that the Catalan politicians and Memorial Democràtic committee wish to see honored on a commemorative plaque. Like Barbal's previously mentioned *En la pell de l'altre*, these self-reflexive works carefully negotiate the multiple demands activated by the (voluntary or involuntary) excavation of the past, exploring competing calls to make other bodies legible in the present and the effect that speaking with the dead has on their own bodies, their own sense of self.

Memorialization of the more distant past has more recently centered on a particular cultural trauma narrative, that of the 1714 siege and fall of Barcelona during the War of the Spanish Succession. This was partly triggered by the 2014 tricentenary, generating commemorative events, publications, and spectacular theatrical productions with titles such as *1714: Tres-cents anys de setge* (*1714: 300 Years of Siege*); *Fang i setge* (*Mud and Siege*); *Crònica d'un setge* (*Chronicle of a Siege*), and *La roda i el foc 1714–2014* (*The Wheel and the Fire 1714–2014*). The prior excavation of extensive remains of the vanquished city, culminating in the inauguration of a Center for Memory and Culture in the former Born district market, led to parallels being drawn with the erased memories of the victims of the Spanish Civil War and Francoist repression, contributing to the sense of injustice underpinning pro-independence sentiment. Novels such as Alfred Bosch's *1714* trilogy (2002) and Albert Sánchez Piñol's *Victus* (2012) set out to challenge myths around the heroism of figures such as Rafael Casanova (commander-in-chief of Catalonia during the siege) and the role of Catalan institutions, giving greater protagonism to the community's participation in Barcelona's defense (Crameri 2015).

Galician Memories: Local Histories, Global Stories

In Galicia, as elsewhere in Spain, the question of who has the right (not to mention authority) to shape the stories admitted to collective memory remains a topic of discussion. The immense institutional weight carried by Galicia's suppressed national history, absent from the school curriculum until the 1970s, has led some Galician historians to reject literary recreations of the past as a threat to the version of history promoted by "proper" historians (e.g., Villares 2007). This shows how close to the surface is the continued institutional need to control what is admitted to collective memory; it also highlights the immense institutional weight of an authorized history that is not yet four decades old. One consequence of this protectionist approach to Galician history is the exclusion of voices marked as different from a national voice erroneously regarded as universal. As a result, creative writing has become a powerful outlet for exploring alternative, often profoundly painful histories and memories – as, for example, with the female-centered historical novels of activist María Xosé Queizán (see chapter 12).

As early as the 1970s, Galician writers were experimenting with genre and narrative technique as a means of evoking painful, often recent traumas inaccessible to historians. For example, both Isaac Diaz Pardo's illustrated chapbook *O crimen de Londres* (*The London Crime*, 1977) and Carlos Durão's novel *Galegos de Londres* (*London Galicians*, 1978) use the dislocation of 1970s Galician migrants in London to decry the psychological and linguistic traumas of forced rural depopulation and its devastating consequences, graphically expressed through the fragility of the not-yet-institutionalized Galician language in which they are written (Hooper 2011). When Diaz Pardo's Varela family are expelled from their land so a US company can build an oil refinery, daughter Carmen takes a job as a maid in London. Three years later, adrift in a world she cannot decipher and berated by an employer she cannot understand, she breaks and strangles the woman to death. Durão's Fermín is a schoolteacher in London; as he gradually loses his mind and, crucially, his language, the reader must piece together a collage of scraps of official and personal documents to understand that he is about to lose his Galician home to an enormous concrete dam and reservoir. In both cases, the erasure of the Galician landscape stands for the potential erasure of Galicia's history and identity by modernizers with larger agendas – both before and after the return to democracy. A more recent exploration of rural depopulation is Xurxo Borrazás's *Ser ou non (To Be or Not to Be*, 2004), a metafictional narrative tracing the erotically charged relationship between a young writer and an elderly woman in an abandoned village. This crucial thread of Galician memory writing received the institutional seal of approval with the award of the 2019 Premio Xerais to Amador Castro Moura's experimental novel *Shanghai a Barcelona (Shanghai to Barcelona*, 2019), which uses a collage of techniques, including multivocalism and haiku, to convey the trauma and ongoing effects of Orlando's emigration from his dying Galician village to the Catalan capital.

The Civil War has inevitably drawn the attention of novelists in Galicia, most famously Manuel Rivas, whose *O lapis do carpinteiro (The Carpenter's Pencil*, 1998) was a crossover hit in Galician and Castilian, since translated into multiple languages worldwide. Rivas, a journalist, novelist and short-story writer, is widely accepted as Galicia's contemporary bard, and *O lapis* is one of a cluster of mid-1990s literary reflections he made on Galician memory, along with *El salvaxe compaña (In the Wilderness*, 1994) and the short story collection *Qué me queres, amor? (What Do You Want of Me, Love?*, 1995; filmed by José Luis Cuerda as *La lengua de las mariposas (Butterfly's Tongue*, 1999) (Romero 2012). *O lapis do carpinteiro* combines several narrative threads, chiefly a journalist's interview with the returned Republican exile Dr. Daniel da Barca, and the conversation between Da Barca's former prison guard Herbal and a young Luso-African prostitute, Maria de Visitacão, to whom he tries to explain his obsession with the doctor. The eponymous pencil acts as a material anchor for the transmission of memories; Herbal's obsession begins when he takes the pencil from the corpse of a prisoner he has shot, an artist whose voice and drawings reverberate in Herbal's mind, urging him to keep Da Barca close. Conflicted by his growing dissatisfaction with his Falangist orders and his simultaneous hatred and fascination for Da Barca, whose life he saves on several occasions, Herbal's complexities remind us that even the apparently black-and-white arena of war is shaded gray. At the end of the novel, he hands the pencil to Maria de Visitacão, not only drawing a line under his own story and giving her the tool to begin telling hers, but also connecting Galicia's historical trauma to the contemporary conflict that has driven Maria to Galicia.

When Spain's Socialist government declared 2006 the Year of Historical Memory, the Xunta de Galicia coordinated hundreds of events under the banner "Ano da Memoria." This triggered a plethora of novels in Galician dealing with the Civil War, including Rivas's mammoth *Os libros arden mal* (*Books Burn Badly*, 2006). The novel ranges over 90 chapters and 130 years, with a cast of hundreds, including nineteenth-century British traveler George Borrow and Republican Prime Minister Santiago Casares Quiroga. Centered around the Falangists' burning of pyres of books on the beaches of A Coruña in August 1936, it offers an ambitious, multivocal depiction of Rivas's native city and the transmission of memory across generations. Suso de Toro, who had made his name in the 1980s as Galicia's first explicitly postmodernist novelist (see chapter 11), revived his novelistic alter ego Nano in *Home sen nome* (*Man without a Name*, 2006), in which Nano spends two days at the bedside of a dying violent Franco sympathizer as he narrates the story of his crimes. The following year, the prestigious Xerais literary prize for 2007 went to debut novelist Rexina Vega, whose *Cardume* (*Shoals*, 2007) sweeps through the history of the Republic, Francoism, and its aftermath in Vigo, in what she calls "un álbum de recordos novelados" (an album of novelized memories) (R. Vega n.d.). For some, the "ano de memoria" was transformative: Xabier Quiroga, who describes his 2009 novel *O cabo do mundo* (*The End of the Earth*) as a "novel of political terror," has stated that it was inspired by what he learned that year about the Nationalists' dawn firing squads in his hometown (Quiroga 2010).

The "novela da memoria" is now firmly established as a sub-genre of Galician fiction, and it has provided an outlet for diverse explorations of Galicia's local and, importantly, global past. Some of the most interesting publications in recent years have sought to embed the recuperation of Galicia's own traumatic twentieth century within the wider Iberian, European, or transatlantic currents without which Galician literary history cannot be understood. For example, the protagonist of Inma López Silva's 2008 novel *Memoria de cidades sen luz* (*Memoir of Lightless Cities*) witnesses the murder of his family as a child in wartime A Coruña and is haunted by his memories through years of exile in Barcelona, Paris, Buenos Aires, and New York. The inclusion of the "novela da memoria" in the circuits of institutional acclaim was confirmed with the award of the 2009 Premio Xerais to Rosa Aneiros's novel *Sol de inverno* (*Winter Sun*) which weaves together the threads of conflict and exile that comprise Galicia's global twentieth century. The protagonist Inverno (Winter) leaves her dying village Antes (Before) for Barcelona, flees the Civil War for France, absorbs the memory of migration in revolutionary Cuba and experiences the hopeful violence of 1968 Paris. This cosmopolitan mode of writing Galicia's memory into global currents is now firmly institutionalized; subsequent Premios Xerais have included novels that provide an inherently Galician perspective on religious colonialism in the Pacific (Xavier Queipo, *Extramunde* / *Out of this World*, 2011); conflict journalism (María Reimóndez, *Dende o conflito* / *From the Conflict*, 2014); and the violent power struggles of medieval Europe (Santiago Lopo, *A arte de trobar* / *The Troubadour Art*, 2017).

Basque Memories: A Double Violence

Since 1990, the Basque Country has experienced a boom in fiction about the Civil War that, in addition to recovering stories of the losers, raises questions about the transmission of Basque nationalist ideas and the radicalization of Basque politics under the Francoist repression. The terrorist organization ETA (Euskadi Ta Askatasuna / Basque Country and Freedom) has been central to reflection on literature's relation to violence. This contemporary Basque memory literature is formally eclectic, often includes a postmodern questioning of the boundary between reality and fiction, and takes the opportunity to rework the historical novel genre. It has been endorsed by award of the Euskadi Literary Prize and supplemented by critical studies and research groups. Mikel Ayerbe's anthology *Our Wars: Short Fiction on Basque Conflicts* (2012) and short-story writer Iban Zaldua's award-winning essay *This Strange and Powerful Language: Eleven Crucial Decisions a Basque Writer is Obliged to Face* (2016), both published in English, are just two of the many reflections on violence by Basque writers.

The *maquis* are treated in Bernardo Atxaga's *Behi euskaldun baten memoriak* (*Memoirs of a Basque Cow*, 1991), based on the legendary Cantabrian anti-Franco resistance fighter, Juan Fernández de Ayala (Juanín), and in Edorta Jimenez's *Azken fusila* (*The Last Gun*, 1994). Other novels, such as Joxe Mari Iturralde's *Izua hemen* (*Fear Here*, 1990), focus on the Basque children evacuated overseas during the war. Inazio Mujika Iraola's *Gerezi denbora* (*Cherry Times*, 1998) and *Sagarrak Euzkadin* (*Apples in Euzkadi*, 2007) are based on real-life testimonies: the former on the memoirs of Alberto Onaindia, a progressive Basque nationalist priest who witnessed the bombing of Gernika; the latter on oral history accounts. Other novels that have addressed the Spanish Civil War include Aingeru Epaltza's *Tigre ehizan* (*Chasing Tigers*, 1996; Euskadi Literary Prize); Andoni Egaña's *Pausoa noiz luzatu* (*When to Take the Next Step*, 1998); Joseba Sarrionandia's *Kolosala izango da* (*It Will Be Colossal*, 2003), which narrates the war from a child's point of view; Iñigo Aranbarri's *Zulo bat uretan* (*Digging Water*, 2008), whose transnational memory narrative links the mass graves of the Civil War to the Argentine *desaparecidos*; and Luis Garde's *Ehiztariaren isilaldia* (*The Silence of the Hunter*, 2016; Euskadi Literary Prize), which narrates, through a self-reflexive narrator-investigator who draws on multiple documentary sources, the escape by Republican prisoners from a fort in Navarre. The sexualization of the Francoist repression and the evacuation of Basque children to Britain during the war are explored by the young women novelists Uxue Alberdi (*Aulki jokoa* / *Musical Chairs*, 2009), Garbiñe Ubeda (*Hobe isilik* / *Better Keep Quiet*, 2013), and Garazi Goia (*Txartel bat (des)herrira* / *A Ticket to Exile*, 2013), among others.

Other Basque novels have memorialized international conflicts. Xabier Montoia's trilogy *Hilen bizimoldea* (*Lifestyles of the Dead*, 1999–2005) has treated World War I, World War II, and the Algerian War. World War II and the Holocaust are memorialized in Harkaitz Cano's *Belarraren ahoa* (*Blade of Light*, 2005; Euskadi Literary Prize), a uchronic narrative in which Hitler has won World War II and, after conquering Europe, sets his sights on Manhattan followed by the whole American continent; and Anjel Lertxundi's *Ihes betea* (*Full of Escape*, 2006), whose German Nazi protagonist discovers he is Jewish.

Two war-related works of fiction stand out: Ramon Saizarbitoria's *Bihotz bi: Gerrako kronikak* (*Two Hearts: War Reports*, 1996) and *Gorde nazazu lurpean* (*Keep Me Buried*, 2000; Euskadi Literary Prize, Spanish Critics' Prize for Fiction in Basque). Both pay tribute to the *gudaris* (Basque nationalist soldiers) as losers in the Civil War; the latter's five stories reflect on the legacy of Basque nationalism. The vast majority of Basque novels on the Civil War depict the losers' perspective and some, especially Bernardo Atxaga's remarkable *Soinujolearen semea* (*The Accordionist's Son*, 2003) and Jokin Muñoz's *Antzararen bidea* (*The Way of the Goose*, 2007), link the radicalization of Basque politics to the Francoist postwar repression. In *Soinujolearen semea*, David, from his Californian ranch, recounts his memories of his childhood in Obaba and his painful discovery of what happened during the Civil War and its aftermath. The two utopian places that the novel describes – Obaba and Stoneham Ranch in California (named after the refugee camp at Stoneham Fields that housed the 4,000 Basque child evacuees to Britain), where the protagonist goes into self-exile after leaving ETA – help the narrator reflect on a past that feels alien and ask to start again. The novel explores the influence of a traumatic past on successive Basque generations that have seen their lives conditioned by a repressive dictatorship and the rise of ETA terrorism. Muñoz's novel tells the story of Lisa, the mother of an ETA terrorist killed while handling a bomb. Lisa looks after the elderly descendant of a landowning family from the imaginary Navarrese town of

Trilluelos, who suffered Falangist persecution during the Civil War. The memory of her son's death becomes entwined with testimonies of horrific wartime executions in Trilluelos.

Fiction on ETA terrorism has been a key feature of recent Basque literature (Olaziregi 2017). Apart from works like Saizarbitoria's 1976 *Ehun metro* (*One Hundred Meters*), fiction addressing ETA only started to blossom in the 1990s. Today over 70 Basque-language novels have been written on the topic. Their treatment of this difficult subject matter has tended to be more nuanced than that of Basque authors writing in Spanish – a case in point is Fernando Aramburu's phenomenally successful Spanish-language *Patria* (2016), which gives a Manichean depiction of armed conflict as well as perpetuating the Basque matriarchal myth fed by earlier Basque nationalism. Important Basque-language novels of the 1990s were Atxaga's *Gizona bere bakardadean* (*The Lone Man*, 1993) and *Zeru horiek* (*The Lone Woman*, 1995) and Saizarbitoria's *Hamaika pauso* (*Innumerable Steps*, 1995). Atxaga's award-winning and much translated novels, both constructed as psychological thrillers, invite readers to enter into the loss of revolutionary ideals by a former male ETA member and the difficult return home from prison of a former female ETA member. Saizarbitoria's *Hamaika pauso* is a novel of metamemory about the Basque generation that, from 1973 to 1984, went from clandestine resistance to the Franco regime to terrorist radicalization. His most explicit rejection of ETA's legacy is the award-winning *Martutene* (2012; Euskadi Literary Prize). With the formal sophistication and metafictional reflection characteristic of Saizarbitoria's work, the novel narrates the characters' itineraries through streets and bars marked by the memory of ETA victims and those living under threat of violence from the organization. (For Arantxa Urretabizkaia's gender critique of ETA, see chapter 12.)

Representations of ETA in Basque fiction have moved from explorations of the perpetrator's point of view to an increasing focus on victims, as in Lertxundi's *Zorion perfektua* (*Perfect Happiness*, 2002) and *Etxeko hautsa* (*Dirty Linen*, 2011). Others have condemned Basque society's equidistance or silence during the years of conflict, as in Uxue Apoalaza's *Mea Culpa* (2011) or the story "Isiluneak" (Silences) in Muñoz's award-winning *Bizia lo* (*Lethargy*, 2003), which depicts the unspoken suffering of parents who fear the tragic death of their son. Short-story writer Iban Zaldua has repeatedly addressed the conflict, for example in *Gezurrak, gezurrak, gezurrak* (*Lies, Lies, Lies*, 2000) or in *Sekula kontatu behar ez nizkizun gauzak* (*As If It Were All Over*, 2018), with an ironic style favoring Borgesian metaliterary games or Cortázarian fantasy embedded in everyday life. By insisting on the need for self-analysis, ethical reflection, and a collective memory that recognizes the pain suffered and contributes to peaceful coexistence, Basque fiction is helping to prevent the re-mythologization of the terrorist by countering the stereotypes disseminated by the media and politicians over the decades. Notable in this respect is Harkaitz Cano's metafictional *Twist* (2013), which focuses on victims not of ETA but of the dirty war waged by the state-sponsored GAL death squads, with clear allusions to the disappeared in the Southern Cone, its multiple perspectives including what was not recorded. The novel's fantasy poetics condemns unpunished past crimes through the spectral presence of the tortured body.

14

Normalization, Crisis, and the Search for New Paradigms (1975–2021)

The timeline of this final chapter is different for the various literatures. The discussion of literature in Spanish picks up from the examination in chapter 9 of the opposition culture of the late Franco era by considering the "culture of the transition," continuing with the impact of the 2008 economic crisis. The sections on literatures in Catalan, Basque, and Galician pick up from the discussion in chapter 11 of the linguistic and cultural normalization processes that, by the 1990s, had completed the institutionalization of literatures in those languages, tracing their story in the twenty-first century. For the specific issues of gender and sexuality and historical memory in the contemporary period, in all four literatures, readers are referred to chapters 12 and 13 respectively.

The Transition as Interpretative Matrix

Until the late 1990s, Spain's transition to democracy was narrativized as a model for export. It was a story of great men (Adolfo Suárez, Juan Carlos I, Santiago Carrillo, Manuel Fraga, Felipe González, the seven "fathers of the Constitution"): political leaders with opposed ideological positions whose ability to put first the needs of the state enabled them to forge agreements based on a pact of reconciliation and forgetting, thanks to which a new democratic consensus was born (Tusell and Soto Carmona 1996; Molinero and Ysàs 2018). Like all good stories, this narrative had a climax: the failed military coup of 1981, involving the army and Civil Guard. Members of the latter held hostage the country's political representatives, at the time swearing in a new prime minister in the Congress of Deputies. After a night of uncertainty, King Juan Carlos I appeared on television, in his military uniform as Captain General of the Spanish Armed Forces, to uphold the besieged democratic regime. That mise-en-scène consolidated the role of the monarchy as unquestionable guarantor of political stability in an otherwise polarized country. After so many previous cases of the armed forces crushing civil society, Spain's story had – ostensibly – a happy ending.

In 2009, renowned novelist Javier Cercas would recreate the memory of that watershed episode in *Anatomía de un instante* (*Anatomy of a Moment*), with his characteristic mix of archivally documented fact, journalism, autofiction, and fiction, blurring the boundaries between historical and moral truths (Song 2016, 49–87). Cercas's overall focus on, and sympathetic interpretation of, the role of (male) elite political actors is consistent with the period's master narrative. The representational absence of other sectors of society contradicts their documented participation in the grass-roots movements and social mobilizations of the 1970s; in the case of women, it obscures their role in what was, for them, a "double transition": personal and political (Larumbe Gorraitz 2004; De Diego González 2008; Nash, Torres, and Ortega López 2009, 71–88). The female narrator of Belén Gopegui's *Lo real* (*The Real*, 2001) argues for the need to look beneath the democratic façade, and in *El azar de la mujer rubia* (*The Luck of the Blonde*, 2007; withdrawn and re-issued 2013), novelist Manuel Vicent offered a fictional account of the progressive, feminist, environmentalist politician Carmen Díaz de Rivera, influential leader of Adolfo Suárez's cabinet and yet nicknamed "the Transition's muse." Marta Sanz's 2013 *Daniela Astor y la caja negra* (*Daniela Astor and the Black Box*) undercuts the disregard for women's intellectual and social contribution to the transition, manifested blatantly by the period's objectification of the naked female body (known as *destape*).

Cercas's *Anatomía de un instante* won the 2010 National Award for Narrative. Its success coincided with a severe national economic and social crisis, and widespread criticism of the "regime of 1978" – referring to the consensus politics that had produced the 1978 Constitution. The country's economic situation, the corruption scandals involving all political parties, King Juan Carlos I's 2014 abdication, and the strength of new social movements would change the Spanish political climate. The fractures in the transition's discursive scaffolding are exposed by novelists like Rafael Chirbes (*La caída de Madrid* / *The Fall of Madrid*, 2000), Francisco Casavella (*El día del watusi* / *The Day of the Watusi*, 2002–3), Benjamin Prado (*Operación Gladio* / *Operation Gladio*, 2011), and Belén Gopegui (*Acceso no autorizado* / *Access Denied*, 2011). As the hegemonic view of the transition came under critical scrutiny, the period's complexity began to emerge (Song 2016), including considerable political violence (Baby 2018) and the role of civil society and of the radical left and its active counterculture (Threlfall 2008; Radcliff 2011; Wilhelmi 2016; Labrador Méndez 2017; Solis Galván 2019).

The 2021 commemorations of the 1981 foiled coup's 40th anniversary took place in the absence of former King Juan Carlos I, who left Spain in 2020 amid accusations of tax evasion, his role in the transition also questioned.

The State of Culture

The state's role as sponsor of national culture is specified in the 1978 Constitution's Article 149.2. This tutelary cultural role has remained undiminished, despite the 1985 devolution of cultural competencies to the autonomous communities. Culture was seen as the indispensable glue holding together opposing ideologies and sensibilities, and cementing Spain's integration into an ideal modern, European, democratic normalcy (Marzo Pérez 2010; L.E. Delgado 2014, 99–194). The endorsement of deliberate forgetfulness, depoliticization, and individualism would later be conceptualized as "the CT paradigm" (CT standing for "culture of the transition") (Martínez 2012). During the first Socialist governments (1982–96), Spanish culture was substantially identifiable with the culture of the state, which subsidized it generously at national and local levels through state positions, prizes, and fellowships (Quaggio 2014). While state or autonomous government sponsorship aided public visibility and the distribution of resources beyond Madrid, it also limited artistic pluralism. The combination of uncontrolled public spending and aggressive marketing techniques in the promotion of a culture spectacular enough, and de-politicized enough, to be palatable to all was criticized by writer Rafael Sánchez Ferlosio in a famous 1984 article, "La cultura, ese invento del gobierno" (Culture, That Government Invention). And yet, state arts sponsorship undoubtedly had benefits, in Spain as in other European countries. This is particularly evident in theater, which survived successive economic crises and the pressures of new technologies and television-on-demand thanks to public financial support at municipal, regional, and state level, or to officially funded institutions such as the Centro Dramático Nacional, Centre Dramàtic de la Generalitat de Catalunya, Centro Dramático Galego, or Centre Dramàtic de la Generalitat Valenciana. Theater magazines throughout this period debated the distorting effects of subsidies and the prioritization of major dramatic spectacles. Nonetheless, alternative models continued to be pursued, as in the satirical political modes pursued by Els Joglars (see chapter 11) or the minimalist, elliptical forms inspired by José Sanchís Sinisterra's Teatro Fronterizo (Frontier Theater), among others. While dependence on official patronage leads to the over-promotion of certain authors and genres and a lack of engagement with radical proposals and new talent, private sponsorship is no more neutral. In 2012, under conservative governments, a coalition of state and private actors joined forces to promote a strongly centralist and nationalist type of nation branding ("la marca España") firmly anchored in a neoliberal ethos of economic profit (the initiative has continued with a marked global emphasis).

In the late 1980s, neoliberalism's extension from economic and political ideology to sociocultural practices was marked by mergers in the publishing sector and the rise of multinational media conglomerates – an ongoing trend. At the same time, the 2010s saw an increase in specialist independent presses (Lengua de Trapo, Valdemar, Bartleby, Pre-textos, Acantilado, Periférica, La Bella Varsovia, Periscopi, Males Herbes, Txalaparta, Pasazaite, Susa, Edicions Laiovento, Irmás Cartoné) that support promising authors but operate on narrow profit margins.

Intellectuals and the Renewal of the Essay

A pressing need for the new democratic regime was the configuration of a public sphere that emphasized the role of civil society, while also establishing the state's function as cultural mediator with the autonomous regions and as promoter of democratic consensus, modernization, and Europeanization. The democratic normalization of Spain was seen as in need of enlightened elites, whose intellectual expertise and moral authority would guide and legitimize the process (Moreno Caballud 2015, 53–104). From the late 1970s, the essay emerged as a key genre for what, deploying methods suited to the late twentieth century, was a nation-building process; this explains the number of essays – by Julián Marías, Jon Juaristi, Fernando Savater, Juan Pablo Fusi, Victoria Camps, among others – centered on issues of national identity, civics, and ethics. For most of the democratic period, Spanish public debate was dominated by a select number of (male) public intellectuals, with the political essay being a particularly male domain. Not until 2006 was a woman awarded the National Essay Prize: Celia Amorós, for her 2004 essay on feminism, *La gran diferencia y sus pequeñas consecuencias . . . para las luchas de las mujeres* (*The Big Difference and Its Small Consequences . . . for Women's Struggles*). Since then, four more have received the award, none for a political essay: Victoria Camps (2011), Adela Cortina (2014), María Xesús Lama (2018), and Irene Vallejo (2020).

Early landmarks in the essay genre were Carmen Martín Gaite's *Usos amorosos del XVIII en España* (*Love Customs in Eighteenth-Century Spain*, 1972) and *Usos amorosos de la posguerra española* (*Courtship Customs in Postwar Spain*, 1987), whose incisive yet accessible analysis of love practices as gendered experiences offered a new model of cultural analysis; and Manuel Vázquez Montalbán's 1971 *Crónica sentimental de España* (*Sentimental Chronicle of Spain*) and 1985 *Crónica sentimental de la Transición* (*Sentimental Chronicle of the Transition*), which link memory and affect. Rafael Sánchez Ferlosio's essays stand out for their stylistic originality and acerbic critique.

The best-known essays published between 1978 and 2000 started as opinion pieces in the press, particularly the national newspaper *El País* which was very influential from its creation in 1976 to the end of the century, when it became increasingly conservative as well as politically and economically dependent. *El País* launched the first "op-ed" piece in Spain in 1976 (Seguín forthcoming). The connections between opinion writing and literary production are striking in the case of contemporary Spain's "novelist intellectuals" – for example, straddling different ideological positions, Juan José Millás, Rosa Montero, Javier Marías, Antonio Muñoz Molina, Suso de Toro, Manuel Rivas, Fernando Aramburu, Almudena Grandes, Javier Cercas, Belén Gopegui, and Marta Sanz. The emergence from 2011 of new social movements, the impact of feminism on public debate, and the rise of social technologies and online media, which created alternative spaces for views not dependent on media conglomerates or institutions, have reconfigured the Spanish public sphere (Jiménez Torres and Villamediana González 2019; Pereira-Zazo and Torres 2019, 181–5). That reconfiguration coincides with new perspectives on social and political issues visible in the work of essayists such as José Ovejero, Fernando Broncano, Daniel Bernabé, Daniel Innerarity, Edgar Cabanas, Edgar Straehle, Josep Ramoneda, Santiago Alba Rico, Marina Garcés, Remedios Zafra, and Alicia Puleo.

The Literature of Consensus: Private Conflicts and the Occlusion of the Social

If social realism had emphasized Spain's "difference" from other European countries, writers of the early democratic period aspired to create a literature with universal reach (Gracia 2000, 2001). The dominant literary discourses of the democratic period's first two decades centered on a postmodern, post-ideological, and post-political urban world of cosmopolitan individuals. It is not coincidence that key works – Muñoz Molina's *El jinete polaco* (*The Polish Rider*, 1991) and Javier Marías's *Corazón tan blanco* (*A Heart So White*, 1992), for example – often have multilingual protagonists who are translators/interpreters, journalists, or professors who, in reflecting on the past, are concerned with their own distinctive subjectivity (A. Fernández 2015). The literary preference for the domestication (or elision) of uncomfortable historical truths through a focus on metaliterary plots and autofiction, and the recurrence of conflicts centered on middle- or upper-class (mostly urban male) psychological crisis, thus sidelining political or collective concerns, relates both to the specific development of Spanish democracy and to the global consolidation of neoliberal ideology (Becerra Mayor 2013, 2015). Various combinations of these traits are shared by major authors of the democratic period (Cercas, Marías, Muñoz Molina, Andrés Trapiello, Enrique Vila-Matas, Millás, Luis Landero).

Poetry of the same period similarly focused on the expression of private experience. The dominant poetic mode, termed the "poetry of experience," initially linked to a Marxist sense of historicity, soon lost its rebellious political impetus to focus on down-to-earth, accessible verse for regular ("normal") people put off by difficult late modernist poetry (Mayhew 2009). Professor and poet Luis García Montero forged a realist aesthetic with sustained critical and popular appeal in works such as *Habitaciones separadas* (*Separate Rooms*, 1984) and *La intimidad de la serpiente* (*Intimacy of the Serpent*, 2003). Also acclaimed by critics, but less influential than García Montero, were Felipe Martínez Reyes, Vicente Gallego, Carlos Marzal, Juaristi, and Ángeles Mora. The success of the poetry of experience paralleled a broader boom in self-writing in poetry, narrative, and diaries.

In the 1990s a diverse set of poets – including Jorge Riechman, Antonio Orihuela, Isla Correyero (see chapter 12), Antonio Méndez Rubio, and the Valencian collective Alicia Bajo Cero (Alicia Sub Zero) – grouped under the label "poetry of critical consciousness" reclaimed the power of poetic language to contribute to a new political imagination, focusing on history and social engagement, sometimes publishing in collaboration with activist associations. Ethical commitment marks the work of two remarkable, very different poets, who both started to write earlier: Chantal Maillard and Antonio Gamoneda. For the Belgian-born philosopher Maillard, poetry and philosophy are coterminous, as illustrated in *Hainuwele* (1990) or the award-winning *Matar a Platón* (*Killing Plato*, 2004). Gamoneda's 1977 *Descripción de la mentira* (*Description of a Lie*) merged ethics and aesthetics in everyday language. He would continue to write about the intersections of personal and collective concerns (love, family, aging, rural depopulation, immigration, economic need) throughout the democratic period, including *Blues castellano* (*Castilian Blues*, 1983; written in the 1960s but unpublished due to Francoist censorship), *Frío de límites* (*Cold of Limits*, 2000) and *Arden las pérdidas* (*Losses are Burning*, 2003). Gamoneda's public visibility increased in the twenty-first century when his poetry's ethos was better suited to the new context of generalized crisis.

The Shifting Scapes of Contemporary Catalan Writing

Convergència i Unió's loss of control of the Catalan Generalitat after 23 years, following autonomous government elections in September 2003 and the retirement of its leader Jordi Pujol, was perceived as the end of an era, leading to widespread reflection on the impact – and failings – of the cultural nationalist project known as *Pujolisme*. The successive coalitions between the Catalan Socialists (PSC), Left Republicans (ERC), and eco-socialist Iniciativa per Catalunya-Verds (Initiative for Catalonia-Greens) that held power under Socialist presidents Pasqual Maragall (2003–6) and José Montilla (2006–10) inaugurated a period of renewed debate around the present, past, and future of Catalan culture and society that included reimagining Catalonia's political fit within Spain. Initially enabled by the socially reformist PSOE government of prime minister José Luis Rodríguez Zapatero, Catalonia's proposed new autonomy statute, ratified by referendum in 2006, met with widespread consternation on the political right and was eventually curtailed by the Spanish constitutional court. These debates and consequent social mobilizations, reflected in literary production of the period, respond to a crisis in the models of representation that had been prevalent in the 1990s, which in turn finds its roots in the rapid acceleration of demographic, environmental, economic, and technological change.

For example, the 2003–4 theater cycle at the Sala Beckett, "L'acció té lloc a Barcelona" (The Action Takes Place in Barcelona), broke with dominant paradigms in dramatic writing to shine a light on everyday life in the city (Buffery 2007; Feldman 2009), in previous years depicted mainly in audiovisual media products such as the Catalan television (TV3) soap *Poblenou* (1994). Internationally acclaimed playwright Lluïsa Cunillé, known for her preference for dislocated settings, situated her play *Barcelona, mapa d'ombres* (*Barcelona, Map of Shadows*, 2004) in a dated apartment in Barcelona's Eixample, sublet by its aging owners to various occupants whose relationship to the city is marked by alienation and marginality. Published together with actor/playwright Pau Miró's *Plou a Barcelona* (*It's Raining in Barcelona*, 2004), which focused on an immigrant prostitute's life in the central Raval district, both plays capture the daily struggle for survival in a city undergoing radical transformation, to the detriment of spaces of care, solidarity, and community. Likewise, Sergi Belbel's *Forasters* (*Strangers*, 2004) was more firmly located in local urban space than any of his previous work, linking the characters' estrangement to the lack of shared spaces for intersubjective understanding resulting from rapid social, economic, and environmental change. Juxtaposing different generations of the same Catalan family, the play drew attention to the ethical challenges of an increasingly multiethnic society and to the impact of interruptions in intergenerational transmission on any possibility of a shared cultural heritage.

Other theatrical creations that reflected on the ethical responsibility toward alterity include Carles Batlle's *Oasi* (*Oasis*, 2001) and *Temptació* (*Temptation*, 2003), Manuel Molins's *Abu Magrib* (*Abu Maghreb*, 2001), Guillem Clua's *La pell en flames* (*Skin in Flames*, 2004), and Cunillé's *Après moi, le deluge* (2007). The questions raised by Cunillé about the limits of speaking for the racialized, sexualized, and/or gendered Other have become a major concern for subsequent writers. In Najat El Hachmi's novelistic trilogy about the experience of south–north migration to Catalonia – *L'últim patriarca* (*The Last Patriarch*, 2008), *La filla estrangera* (*The Foreign Daughter*, 2015), and *Mare de llet i de mel* (*Mother of Milk and Honey*, 2018) – the narrative of the daughter's emancipation via intercultural literacy through learning the Catalan language is permeated with intersectional awareness of a layered legacy of physical and symbolic violence, in which the mother's generation remains an unvoiced cypher until the final novel. Similar disruptions in transmission are staged in Josep Maria Benet i Jornet's play *Salamandra* (*Salamander*, 2005), where unresolved and intermingled histories of political violence, trauma, exile, and dislocation result in an unfathomable present; the play ends with the evocation of Barcelona as little more than an exotic, cinematic backdrop, where Catalan language and culture are in just as much danger of extinction as the salamander of the play's title.

This sense of a crisis in representation is perhaps most fully captured in Julià Guillamon's influential study *La ciutat interrompuda* (*The Interrupted City*, 2001), in which the critic noted the relative paucity of realist representations of the Catalan capital in Catalan when compared with the Spanish-language writings of Juan Marsé, Manuel Vázquez Montalbán, Félix de Azúa, and Eduardo Mendoza, among others. Guillamon's urban literary historiography both anticipates later shifts toward a more plurilingual definition of Catalan culture and provides an essential guide to continuing critiques of neoliberal capitalism's dispossessive processes from within the Catalan-speaking territories, ranging from the mordacious experimental narratives of Barcelona-based Majorcan poet Miquel Bauçà (*Carrer Marsala*,

1985) to Joan-Francesc Mira's anthropological insights into urban speculation in Valencia (*Els treballs perduts* / *Labors Lost*, 1989; *Purgatori* / *Purgatory*,
2003), and Arcadi Espada's exposé of the impact of extractivist urbanism
on inner city communities (*Raval: De l'amor als nens* / *Raval: On the Love
of Children*, 2000). Nevertheless, it needs to be supplemented by attention
to the multipolarity of a cultural field traversed by competing institutional interests and their relative standing in a global marketplace, and the
diversity of "scapes" – ethnoscapes, technoscapes, mediascapes, finances-
capes, ideoscapes – that frame and constitute contemporary subjectivities
(Appadurai 1996).

Phenomena like the Sala Beckett cycle and *Forasters* should also be seen
as a symptom of, and reaction to, the culture of normalization associated
with the first two decades following Spain's transition to democracy. As
seen in chapter 11, the term normalization was adopted by Spain's "historic
autonomies" from sociolinguistic usage to denote a process of educational,
corpus, and status planning designed to combat the effects of imposed
diglossia. The Catalan version of linguistic and cultural normalization
is interpreted very differently depending on one's ideological positioning. Opponents of institutional supports for Catalan have construed it as
a Convergència i Unió (CiU)-engineered hegemony, characterized by a
focus on cultural nation-building and integration rather than multicultural
diversity and inclusion. Others understand it as a by-product of the asymmetrical legitimization channels enshrined in the State of the Autonomies
(see, especially, Articles 145 and 149 of the 1978 Constitution), which
limited the cultures of the periphery to looking inwards rather than out-
wards. A common critical complaint is that the excessive institutional focus
on quantitative improvements – numbers of books published, translation
subventions, commemorative events, and awards for "universal" Catalans
– has had an inverse relation to literary quality and caused market satura-
tion. Canonization of certain figures – Baltasar Porcel as the great novelist;
Miquel Martí i Pol for poetry; Josep Maria Flotats as a man of the theater
– has tended to produce resentment, and up-and-coming Catalan writers
have complained of the excessive focus on the consecration of selected classics. While these reparative measures are understandable in the context of
a minoritized language and culture, the size of the market and neoliberal
pressures favoring free-market capitalism have exacerbated internal tensions (J.-A. Fernàndez 2008).

The scenario that emerged from the late 1990s might, then, be seen
as a series of culture wars, particularly over the relationship between
Catalan- and Castilian-language expression and production. Just as the 1983

Linguistic Normalization Law was opposed by some 2,300 public figures hostile to any legal requirement to learn Catalan, so the rationale for a new Linguistic Policy Law in 1998 was contested by the Foro Babel, created in 1996 to protest the perceived exclusivity of official Catalan cultural policy. This culminated in the 2005 creation of the political party Ciutadans de Catalunya (later Ciudadanos), with the participation of writers like Espada, Xavier Pericay, Teresa Giménez Barbat, Azúa, and Albert Boadella as founders and literary apologists, precisely at a moment when Catalan culture was becoming more outward-looking. Debates over the limits of Catalan culture climaxed over the question of who should be sent to international book fairs – like those of Guadalajara (2004) and Frankfurt (2007) – at which Catalonia or Catalan culture were guests of honor. Crime writer Teresa Solana provides a humorous take on this scenario in her 2006–16 detective series, one of whose twin-brother investigators invents a Spanish-language patrician genealogy so as to hobnob with Barcelona high society.

Even before this, the crisis of normalization had provoked a plurality of political, cultural, and social responses. This is the period of the emergence and visibility of writers born outside Catalonia who chose to publish in Catalan, such as Najat El Hachmi, Laila Karrouch, Saïd El Kadaoui, Agnès Agboton, Patricia Gabancho, Joan-Daniel Bezsonoff, Matthew Tree, Victòria Szpunberg, and more recently Denise Duncan. The increasing mobilization of civic society around social, environmental, and cultural issues began to translate into politically activist platforms, such as philosopher Marina Garcés's Espai en blanc (Blank Space), and the creation of alternative publishing houses, cultural centers, and online media, from *Vilaweb* (1995) to *Ara* (2010), which offered more sustained spaces of engagement for writers and readers in Catalan. Such developments would provide the networks that helped to sustain Catalan cultural production and social and political activism in the following decades, nurturing a diversity of voices – from established poets, novelists and philosophers like Sebastià Alzamora, Empar Moliner, and Josep Ramoneda to the critical journalism of Vicent Partal, Carles Capdevila, Toni Soler, and David Fernàndez.

While essayists such as Jordi Amat (*El llarg procés* / *The Long Process*, 2015) retrospectively blame the cultural nation-building of Jordi Pujol for the subsequent rise of separatist discourse in Catalonia, this ignores the aggressive recentralization policies of the 1996–2004 Partido Popular legislatures under José María Aznar and the shift away from CiU at the end of the twentieth century. In the literary field this was a time of convergence and concentration in the book market, with Planeta acquiring key Catalan-language publishing houses like Columna and later helping to prop up

Grup 62; the consolidation of Random House Mondadori (later Penguin Random House) as a leading literary imprint for Spain and Latin America; and Barcelona's reinforcement of its leading position in book production and distribution in the Spanish-speaking world. While these developments underpinned invitations to book fairs and Barcelona's successful bid to become a UNESCO City of Literature in 2015 (as "a publishing capital in two languages"), they undoubtedly increased the unequal competition between Catalan and Castilian for readers in the same geographical space. For Guillamon (2019, 348), the relentless pressures to adapt to a changed sociocultural environment were represented in Quim Monzó's short story "Davant del rei de Suècia" (Before the King of Sweden) in *El millor dels mons* (*The Best of All Worlds*, 2001). By 2007 Monzó had ceased publishing fiction in Catalan, and in 2009 Carles Casajuana issued a novel entitled *L'últim home que va escriure en català* (*The Last Man to Write in Catalan*). Yet this was also a period when bestsellers written in Spanish, such as Javier Cercas's *Soldados de Salamina* (*Soldiers of Salamis*, 2001) or Carlos Ruiz Zafón's *La sombra del viento* (2001), were routinely translated into Catalan, and works by writers such as Care Santos or Lolita Bosch were released in both languages simultaneously, without necessarily specifying the original language of composition.

The case of celebrated poet Joan Margarit – the first Catalan-language poet to be awarded the Premio Cervantes (announced in 2019, at the end of a year in which the Premio Nacional de las Letras went to the Basque writer Bernardo Atxaga, the Premio Nacional de Poesía to Galician poet Pilar Pallarés, and the Premio Nacional de Traducción to the Catalan Dolors Udina) – is revealing. The fact that much of his work since the late 1990s was published bilingually made him a convenient counter-symbol to Catalan separatism and perceived cultural exclusivisms. In contrast, Albert Sánchez Piñol's switch to writing his 2012 novel *Victus* in Castilian, after the international successes of *La pell freda* (*Cold Skin*, 2002) and *Pandora al Congo* (*Pandora in the Congo*, 2005), met with widespread consternation in Catalonia, even though the Catalan version was released soon afterwards.

The most sustained engagement with the shifting scapes of contemporary Catalan writing, in a series of eco-anthropological reflections on a society in crisis, is that of Francesc Serés. His trilogy *De fems i de marbres* (*On Manure and Marble*, 2003) was inspired by Jesús Moncada's *Camí de Sirga* (*The Tow Path*, 1988) and Mercè Ibarz's *La terra retirada* (*The Land Withheld*, 1993) in tracing the disappearing spaces, communities, and livelihoods of his childhood in the Catalan-speaking Franja d'Aragó, on the Aragonese–Catalan border, via the voices of different generations of rural inhabitants, contributing to the literature of rural dispossession and abandonment that would become so prevalent in the subsequent decade (Resina and Viestenz 2012; Dasca 2018). In *La força de la gravetat* (*The Force of Gravity*, 2006) and *La matèria prima* (*Raw Material*, 2007) his focus shifts, like that of Jordi Puntí in *Els castellans* (*The Castilians*, 2011) and Adrià Pujol Cruells in *Picadura de Barcelona* (*The Barcelona Itch*, 2014), to urban, suburban, and rururban spaces, and the invisible and precarious lives of those who live and work there. In *La pell de la frontera* (*The Skin of the Frontier*, 2014), Serés returns to interview the new workers and inhabitants of his former rural home: immigrants from North Africa, Asia, and Eastern Europe, living in ever-worsening conditions due to the 2008 economic crisis. His major auto-fictional novel *La casa de foc* (*The House of Fire*, 2020) charts the multi-layered impact of the crisis on rural Girona, mapping the effects of property specu-lation, corruption, and substance abuse from a deep temporal perspective. The novel ends with hope pinned on an eco-feminist future, represented by the rural patriarch's granddaughter.

Younger writers – Marta Rojals in *Primavera, estiu* (*Spring, Summer*, 2011) and *L'altra* (*The Other Woman*, 2014); Eva Baltasar in *Permagel* (*Permafrost*, 2018); Alícia Kopf in *Maneres de (no) entrar en casa* (*Modes of [Not] Entering Home*, 2011) and *Germà de gel* (*Brother of Ice*, 2015); Irene Solà in *Els dics* (*The Dykes*, 2017) – have used autofictional techniques to chronicle the disrup-tion, precarity, and indignity of lives blighted by lack of access to secure work, housing, social care, and a living wage: broken families, homeless-ness, alcoholism, drug abuse, economic migration, attempted suicide, social isolation. While the response of some writers to the devastation of familiar landscapes is to resort to nostalgia for a somehow better (whether more radical or idyllic) past, others have imagined alternative spaces projected into the future. Between 2009 and 2012, coinciding with the civic-society-organized local consultations on independence, a cluster of novels imagined a politically independent Catalonia: some of them using the tech-niques of speculative fiction, such as Toni Soler's *L'última carta de Companys* (*Companys' Last Letter*, 2009); others providing a retrospective journalistic chronicle of the desired events, such as Patricia Gabancho's *Crònica de la independència* (*Chronicle of Independence*, 2009). More recently, the chronicles and testimonies that followed the October 1, 2017 disputed referendum on Catalan independence continue to fuel communities of resistance, united by a sense of injustice and grievance against the Spanish state but also by the experience of sharing the same spaces cooperatively and collabora-tively. One of them, philosopher Marina Garcés's *Ciutat Princesa* (*Princess City*, 2018), provides an alternative history of the experience of urban social protest in the city from 1997 to 2017 – one that links the counter-cultural squats of the 1990s with the anti-war movement, feminist mobilizations, environmental activism, the 15-M protests of 2011, and latterly the pro-independence demonstrations, celebrating them as transversal, strategic, and precarious communities under threat who come together to imagine different ways of sharing the same space.

Change of Skin: The Basque Literature of Afterwards

Basque nationalism in its different dimensions has been the driving force behind Basque institutional life since 1975. Indeed, experts talk of the period 1998–2009 as a pro-self-rule era, under the lehendakari (president) Juan José Ibarretxe who defended the Basque people's right to decide their political future. Yet, the most important political development in the Basque Country during the last decade has undoubtedly been ETA's definitive cessation of armed activity in October 2011. Its decision to disarm came years later, in April 2017, followed by its dissolution in 2018. By that time, the twenty-first century had witnessed politically restless years with the banning of left-wing nationalist parties by the 2003 Ley de Partidos (Political Parties Law). The Basque Country weathered the 2008 economic crisis better than the rest of Spain, thanks to the strength of its industry and exports, and its lesser dependence on the construction sector, which meant that the real estate bubble hit the Basque economy less severely. In 2012, the unemployment rate was 14.5 percent (the lowest in Spain).

The economic crisis did, however, hit the Basque book sector, with a 35 percent contraction in turnover in 2008, partly offset by an 8.8 percent increase since 2014 ("El sector del libro" 2020). These figures cover a network of 118 publishers, 102 of them private and very small, and 70 percent of them located in the Basque Autonomous Community (Gobierno Vasco 2020). Independent bookstores – responsible for 56 percent of Basque-language book sales – subsist with difficulty, many absorbed by chains like FNAC or macro book-and-leisure stores. Nevertheless, digital libraries such as eLiburutegia, financed by the Basque Government, or platforms such as Booktegi have succeeded in attracting Basque readers. Of the 2,138 books published in Basque in 2018 (1,855 in print editions), 34.7 percent were books for children and young adults and 29.3 percent were textbooks, with adult literature comprising 14.7 percent (compared to 18.5 percent in Galician, 21.4 percent in Catalan, and 20.7 percent in Spanish) (Eizagirre Gesalaga 2020). This is not a good outlook for the professionalization of

Basque-language writers, who have to turn to national and international consortia to achieve wide recognition. Some writers' early careers were boosted by literary awards at Spanish state level, as with the National Fiction Prize won by Atxaga in 1989 and by Kirmen Uribe in 2009, producing tensions in the Basque literary field over the state's promotion of their work in Castilian translation, often without mention of the Basque originals. In this respect, the creation in 2010, endorsed by the Basque Parliament, of the Etxepare Basque Institute, whose mission is to promote Basque language and literature overseas, has been crucial, leading to an exponential increase in the presence of Basque writers at major international book fairs and to translations of their work into other languages (in many cases translated directly from Basque).

The internationalization of Basque literature in the twenty-first century is illustrated by the trajectory of Kirmen Uribe (Olaziregi and Elizalde 2021). His first book of poems, *Bitartean heldu eskutik* (*Meanwhile Take My Hand*, 2001; Spanish Critics' Prize), whose micro-stories convey through small gestures what lies beyond language, has been translated into five languages. His multimedia project *Jainko txiki eta jostalari hura* (*That Tiny Playful God*, 2013) was premiered in New York. His prize-winning first novel *Bilbao-New York-Bilbao* (2008), translated into fifteen languages, recounts a plane trip from Bilbao to New York, framing the story of three generations of the author's family and mixing textual formats (emails, dictionaries, diaries, poems, letters) and temporalities in a postmodern poetics. (For Uribe's novels on Basque Republican exiles, see chapter 10.)

A new generation of young Basque fiction writers has focused on the economic precarity that has badly affected young people in particular, with a 2019 Basque unemployment rate of 25.5 percent for those under 25. Harkaitz Zubiri's *Etxekalte* (*The Spendthrift*, 2012) uses a thriller format to chronicle the corruption enveloping a crisis-hit company, some of whose workers have contracted asbestos-related diseases. Ana Jaka's novel *Ez zen diruagatik* (*It Wasn't for the Money*, 2014) explores its protagonists' psychological uncertainty and loss of roots. Fermin Etxegoien's earlier *Autokarabana* (*Mobile Home*, 2009; Spanish Critics' Prize for Fiction and Euskadi Literary Prize) sarcastically narrates the mid-life crisis of its antihero, whose mobile home figures dispossession and instability. Ana Malagon's *Gelditu zaitezte gurekin* (*Stay with Us*, 2017) chronicles its characters' financial problems and emotional limitations. The stories in Eider Rodríguez's brilliant *Bihotz handiegia* (*Heart Too Large*, 2017; Euskadi Literary Prize, Euskadi Silver Prize) explore the traps of domesticity for women and anxieties about the threat of falling out of the middle class (González-Allende 2019). By contrast, Irati Elorrieta's choral tales *Neguko argiak* (*Winter Lights*, 2018; Euskadi Literary Prize) depict the nomadic lifestyle of a group of young people from different nationalities and backgrounds in a cosmopolitan Berlin, stressing friendship and resistance.

Recent poetry collections, too, address subjective as well as economic and social facets of the crisis. Luis Garde's *Eremuen birkalifikazioa* (*Land Rezoning*, 2014) conveys precarity through images of abandoned housing developments or subjects seeking employment. Particularly powerful are Iñigo Astiz's *Baita hondakinak ere* (*The Waste Too*, 2012) and *Analfabetoa* (*Illiterate*, 2019). The poetic voice in the latter expresses its bewilderment at the material and affective incoherence of everyday life, reflecting on "the end of the reign of things" signaled by the closed factories and stationary cranes seen from the window. Contemporary Basque theater has echoed this sense of uncertainty, notably through Xabier Mendiguren Elizegi's 2014 adaptation and translation into Basque of *Hamlet*, directed by Ximun Fuchs with a cast headed by actor and drama scholar Ander Lipus, set in a twenty-first-century Basque Country torn by power struggles, betrayals, and inheritance wrangles.

The contradictions of neoliberalism have been addressed in a relatively small number of dystopian narratives, which denounce consumerism and social and environmental degradation. Itxaro Borda's novel *Kripton 85*, for example, chronicles a lesbian couple's attempt to flee a tyrannical world threatened by nuclear disaster. Surprisingly, given the Basque Country's concern with protection of the environment, biodiversity, and recycling, Basque literary production has not seen the turn to the rural evidenced in the other literatures of Spain and in Basque cinema (Roberto Caston's 2009 *Ander*; Asier Altuna's 2015 *Amama*; Joaquín Calderón's 2018 *Basque Selfie*).

The topic that has dominated cultural creativity in every sphere is the end of ETA, raising the issue of how to narrate the suffering of the different categories of victim and focusing not so much on the past conflict (see chapter 13) as on its consequences for inhabitants of the Basque Country today. Victims and perpetrators haunt the Basque collective memory, often signaling the spectral presence of a past that has not attained closure and is susceptible to traumatic replay. Gabriela Ybarra's Spanish-language novel *El Comensal* (*The Dinner Guest*, 2015), mentioned in chapter 12, points through the unoccupied place-setting at the family table to the spectral presence of the autofictional narrator's grandfather, Javier Ybarra, kidnapped and killed by ETA. As a member of the postmemory generation – the bearer of her parents' memory – Gabriela reconstructs, via photographs, press clippings, and letters, the story of her grandfather's disappearance, her grief rekindled by mourning her mother's death from cancer. Illness also induces reflection on a post-ETA Basque identity in Uxue Alberdi's *Jenisjoplin* (2017). The novel's protagonist, nicknamed Jenisjoplin and living with AIDS, belongs to a generation that grew up in the 1980s in a sociohistorical context framed by terrorist violence, unemployment, workers' struggles, and drugs, with a high incidence of AIDS. The novel uses the sick body to symbolize a collective Basque identity that has moved from the epic depiction of heroic violence, with struggle (armed or otherwise), toughness, and anger seen as the markers of national identity, to the exploration of a weak, vulnerable identity that needs to reinvent itself if it is to have a future.

Other recent novels reflect on how the legacy of armed and political conflict is being tackled. Katixa Agirre's road novel *Atertu arte itxaron* (*The Apathetic Tourists*, 2015) brings together the 2004 Islamist bombings in Madrid, the multiple attacks committed by the protagonist's ETA-member father, and the 1976 massacre of striking workers in Vitoria-Gasteiz, exploring the collective responsibility resulting from decades of terrorism, including the injustice of bearing the blame for acts committed by previous generations. The novel also reflects on the promotion of gastronomic tourism as a strategy for a country that does not want to go on being known internationally for the "Basque conflict." Lander Garro's novel *Gerra txikia* (*The Little War*, 2014) is narrated from the perspective of an ETA member's son living in exile in the French Basque Country in the 1980s, at a time of violence on the part of ETA and the GAL death squads, drugs, and labor disputes, addressing the relation between Wars (with capital "W") and the domestic wars (with lower-case "w") they generate at family level.

The institutionalization of feminist cultural studies and debate with the creation of gender studies programs at the University of the Basque Country (UPV-EHU) and University of Deusto has led to an explosion of academic and literary publications. The book series LISIPE of the Susa publishing house (the first Basque-language series devoted to feminist thought) has questioned the conceptual frameworks of Basque history, customs, and thought, with texts on feminism and political change, and on the connection between writing and the body. The shocking statistics on gender violence in Spain have provoked reflection and protest in cultural production. The play *Invisible* (2009; staged at New York's Micro Theater in March 2020) by Aizpea Goenaga – actress, theater and film director, and former director of the Etxepare Basque Institute – transmits the helplessness and pressure felt by the protagonist, hospitalized after being attacked by her husband, in the ensuing legal process, with the multiple (often female) voices of family, work colleagues, and medical staff perpetuating the oppression of the victim of sexual violence. Violence is structural in the 2017 Spanish-language novel *Mejor la ausencia* (*Better Absent*) of Edurne Portela, author of the essay *El eco de los disparos. Cultura y memoria de la violencia* (*The Echo of Gunshots: Culture and Memory of Violence*, 2016) on political violence in the Basque Country. The novel recounts the female protagonist's tumultuous childhood and youth on the industrial left bank of the Nervión estuary and, after a lapse of 17 years, her return and recollection of what happened, connecting social and domestic violence and exploring the ways in which power relations construct gender. Karmele Jaio's 2019 *Aitaren etxea* (*The House of the Father*; Euskadi Literary Prize), similarly analyzes the construction of masculinity and femininity in the Basque context, alluding to political violence insofar as it relates to the delimitation of established gender roles in a heteronormative society. The novel offers a metafictional reflection on writing about gender violence.

Crisis and Its Counterpoints: Galician Analog and Digital Culture since 2008

As with literature in Basque, the financial crisis of 2008 had a severe impact on the fragile institutional infrastructure of Galicia's literary and publishing sectors. According to the Consello da Cultura Galega, the crisis threw the steady growth enjoyed by Galicia's publishing industry since 2000 into sharp reverse. The number of Galician-language books published annually peaked in 2008 at just over 3,000; within five years, it had plummeted to 1,500. Children's and young adult literature in Galician, however, continued to grow during the crisis, comprising more than 21 percent of titles and 30 percent of sales by 2012, according to that year's annual report of the Asociación Galega de Editores (Galician Publishers' Association). Nonetheless, the long-term consequences have been brutal. Figures from Spain's Instituto Nacional de Estadística show that the crisis led to the closure of more libraries in Galicia than in any other autonomous community: 74 were shuttered between 2008 and 2019, far ahead of Aragón, in second place with 54.

The consequences of diminishing access to literature have, inevitably, made their way into contemporary fiction. Manuel Rivas's 2015 novel *O último día de Terranova* (*Terranova's Final Day*) reflects Rivas's conviction, repeated in interviews at the time of the book's publication, that bookstores are a metaphor for human contact and a doorway to immersion in a society and its history. His Terranova (Newfoundland) bookstore, founded by Galician cultural activists in 1930s A Coruña, survived for 60 years as an underground cultural center, contraband book exchange, and point of contact with the American diaspora. Now run by their son Vicenzo, a disabled punk musician and sometime emigrant, Terranova is threatened with closure as its neighborhood is overrun by property speculators and Vicenzo must look for a solution in the books and the histories they evoke. More generally, Galician writers have striven to depict the effects of the crisis on both individuals and communities. Some have tried to understand the everyday consequences of economic breakdown on the individual. For example, Alberto Manuel Ramos Ríos's 2013 novel *Todos os días* (*Every Single Day*) traces a week in the life of unemployed journalist Iván, for whom the realization that "todos os días" are now the same, triggers a psychological and physical breakdown. Miguel Sande's *A candidata* (*The Candidate*, 2016) follows the economic and moral disintegration of a middle-class Galician family from the perspectives of mother, father, and daughter. Meanwhile, Ramón Vilar Landeira's novel/short story hybrid *Un peixe no parqué* (*A Fish on the Parquet*, 2019) depicts the everyday life of a contemporary working-class community trapped in a normalized precarity, arguing that survival depends on a strategy of individual rather than collective "desmemoria" (forgetting).

The shifts we have seen in cultural paradigms across Spain's literatures since 1978, and more intensely since the crisis, have taken on a distinctive shape in Galicia. The turn to ecoliterature was perhaps inevitable in a country whose self-image, rooted since the *Rexurdimento* in an intimate connection with the natural world, was rocked by the disastrous Prestige oil spill of 2002 (which itself generated an intense cultural and literary response). Among the most interesting ecoliterary voices is María Reimóndez, whose 2012 novel *En vías de extinción* (*Endangered Species*) had reached its fourth edition by 2019. The novel traces the journey to self-realization of the translator and interpreter Gaia, a "well-travelled polyglot mountain-woman" who defines herself as a lesbian feminist nationalist but rejects the marginal status those labels might suppose. In its dense polylingual web of texts drawn from multiple genres, rich with botanical and intertextual references (above all to Rosalía de Castro's *Cantares gallegos*), the novel evokes the inherent ecological and social diversity of Galicia's rural way of life, its delicate balance threatened by urban sprawl, and its related cultural values. Others, treading the borders between science fiction and dystopian literature, focus more intensely on the consequences of Earth's diminishing resources. Iolanda Zúñiga's *Natura* (*Nature*, 2018) follows a mother and daughter fleeing the environmental catastrophe of a planet without water. They aim for the safety of Nature, a man-made world-within-a-world that only the Elixidas (Chosen Ones) can enter, but find a repressed domain with no memories, feelings, or free will. Antía Yáñez's self-described 2019 "greenpunk xuvenil" (Young Adult Greenpunk) novel, *Be Water*, depicts another mother and daughter negotiating a society driven underground by the disappearance of water from the Earth's surface. Dialoguing with familiar literary works – its four parts are called *A colmea* (*The Beehive*), *Utopía*, *Grandes esperanzas* (*Great Expectations*), and *A Odisea* (*The Odyssey*) – it depicts underground society as a vast beehive in which humans, like worker bees, have no option for survival other than to work until they die.

Another novel set in a dystopian underground future, María Alonso's 2012 *Despois do cataclismo* (*After the Cataclysm*), is grounded in a biological violence that is part of a wider move toward an acutely critical exploration of violence and its consequences, often along gendered lines. Alonso's novel shares a starting point with those of Zúñiga and Yáñez but with an explicitly feminist and sociohistorical, rather than ecological, focus. Its post-apocalyptic Galician society is under the iron control of the guardians of Tradition who have reinvented the social structures and limited self-expression of Galicia's pre-Roman *castrexo* (Castro) culture, enforced – in a "biopunk" twist – by the implantation of a "Nanochip do Pensamento" (Thought Nanochip) that controls the individual's thoughts and actions. The nameless heroine's story is attentive to the dangerous consequences for women of the authoritarian revival of traditional social and biological roles. Others have taken a more realist approach. For example, Reimóndez's 2016 novel *A dúbida* (*Doubt*) is a chilling psychological study of doubt from the perspective of a woman whose politician husband is arrested for child sex offences, while Ledicia Costas, in *O corazón de Xúpiter* (*Jupiter's Heart*, 2012), explores the psychology of teenage astronomy enthusiast Isla, groomed online by an older man. In *Infamia* (*Infamy*, 2019), Costas follows a professor of Penal Law who investigates a 25-year-old child murder, opening the door to reflection on the consequences of structural and cyclical violence, and the silence it imposes.

The entwined questions of violence and silence intersect with the growing body of Galician *narcoliteratura*, which explores the multi-million-euro, modern-day drug business facilitated by Galicia's more than 1,000 miles of often acutely isolated coastline (Núñez Sabarís 2020). While far from a new topic in Galician or, indeed, Spanish fiction, the discourse around the effect of this largely invisible activity on Galician identity and society was enriched by the publication in 2010 of Manuel Rivas's novel *Todo é silencio* (*All Is Silence*). Far from the hard-boiled depiction of drug crime in the *novelas negras* (detective fiction) of Carlos Reigosa (e.g., *Narcos*, 2000) or Domingo Villar (e.g., *Ollos de auga* / *Water-blue Eyes*, 2006), Rivas's novel combines his characteristic lyrical evocation of place with a sharply critical eye on those facilitating the drug networks' control over a community. Other nuanced explorations of the subject are Manuel Portas's cinematic *Denso recendo a salgado* (*Dense Aroma of Salt*, 2010) or Diego Ameixeiras's female-centered *Todo OK* (*All OK*, 2012). Awareness of Galicia's drug industry was supercharged following the 2015 publication of journalist Nacho Carretero's reportage *Fariña* (*Flour*; slang for "cocaine"), which traces the centuries-long history of Galicia's drug-smuggling "clans." When the book was banned by a Madrid court in 2017 over a libel action by one of the protagonists, an innovative webpage set up by the Madrid booksellers' guild text-mined *Don Quijote* to reproduce all 80,000 words of Carretero's text. The following year, a lightly fictionalized version of *Fariña* set in the 1980s became a hugely popular Netflix TV series under the title "Cocaine Coast." The risks of uncritically dramatizing real, violent criminals were addressed in José Prieto's social theater adaptation of *Fariña*, which debuted in A Coruña in 2019 before touring Galicia. The play employs a range of dramatic techniques to place Galicia, rather than specific criminals, as the story's protagonist, drawing the audience in to reflect on Galicia's collective responsibility for this dark chapter in its history.

The success of non-traditional cultural forms represented by the various iterations of *Fariña* reflects a wider shift away from traditional poetics and modes of authorship that can be attributed as much to the rise of new media as to the shattering effects of the economic crisis. Short-form writing, such as the *microrrelato* (micro-story), is not new but has taken off in Galicia, partly thanks to the success of works such as Iolanda Zúñiga's structurally experimental 2007 *Vidas Post-it* (*Post-it Lives*), written on literal post-it notes while the author was working in a fast-food restaurant. The multitude of micro-stories depict fragments of contemporary lives, from the banal to the brutal; the fragments cohere into a whole that reflects the harshness of everyday life. Zúñiga's follow-up, the polyphonic novel *Periferia* (*Periphery*, 2010), set in a chaotic, post-crisis São Paulo, won Galicia's prestigious Premio Xerais in 2010. The *microrrelato* genre has made a comfortable home for itself online, with web- or Twitter-hosted competitions receiving dozens of entries, but it achieved unprecedented institutional status with the establishment in 2018 of the PuntoGal/Real Academia Galega *microrrelato* competition. Inviting entries of 200 words or less, the explicit aims of this initiative are to connect with technology, to bring in a greater diversity of writers, and to stimulate the use of Galician among the young. The 2019 competition attracted more than 500 entries.

Galician-language cultural producers have not been slow to grasp the opportunities created by burgeoning access to digital tools and online audiences. There is a healthy Galician-language social media community, with roots going back to Vieiros (1996–2010), the first privately owned, Galician-language internet and social media platform. Among the pioneering achievements facilitated by Vieiros was Camilo Franco's *Por conto alleo* (*On Someone Else's Account*, 1999), the first Galician-language digital book, compiled from 50 daily short stories, each based on a two-word prompt from a Vieiros user. Between 2005 and 2008, María Yáñez and Berto Yáñez managed Galicia's first online, open-access publishing project, Ediciós da Rotonda, which published the first online, open-access Galician-language novel, Carlos Meixide's *O home inédito* (*The Unpublished Man*, 2007). In 2015, Fran Alonso released *Poetic@s* (*Poetics*; poetica.gal), a multimedia, multilingual poetry installation drawing on a range of social media activity, which the author described as "participative poetry." Today, Galician cultural practitioners and institutions are highly visible on social media platforms such as Twitter and YouTube, creating original material and "remixing" literary texts both old and new with audiovisual content to create something distinctive. The new media landscape is not welcomed uncritically, however. Suso de Toro, writing in *Dentro da literatura* (*Inside Literature*, 2019) warned that the dominance of US new media, and Spain's inability (let alone Galicia's) to create and sustain its own brands, meant that in new media terms "Spain is a mere North American colony." María Yáñez, one of Galicia's most interesting commentators on digital cultures, argues further that the lack of a convincing digital strategy for supporting creation, distribution, and archiving means that Galicia's thriving digital cultural heritage is at risk of disappearing (Yáñez 2019). Almost 15 years' worth of cultural and literary content on Vieiros, the pioneering Galician-language web platform, was never archived and is now lost for good.

The changing cultural paradigms in post-crisis Galicia reveal how Galician literary culture today continues to bridge the universal and the local, drawing as much on the deep well of Galician culture and history as on global narratives of ecology, feminism, gender, and violence. Crucially, the sustained and innovative production of high-profile female novelists such as María Reimóndez and Iolanda Zúñiga definitively counters the elision of women's voices and experiences during the first decades of the modern Galician novel.

Questioning Normalcy, Imagining Otherwise

Moving back to literary production in Spanish, we conclude by discussing the emergence in the twenty-first century of new cultural paradigms, prompted by political, economic, and social changes. The so-called "Spanish economic miracle" spanning the late 1990s and early 2000s turned out to be a mirage, due largely to the collapse of the real estate bubble, known as the "crisis del ladrillo" (brick crisis). Even during economic expansion, Spain had higher levels of unemployment and labor precarity that most of its European neighbors (during the crisis, double the Eurozone average). Thus, in the twenty-first century, Spain became, once again, a country of emigrants, with many immigrants who had made Spain their home in the 1980s and 1990s forced to return to their countries of origin. Cultural production of the period 2007–20 has reflected on the social and environmental unsustainability of the neoliberal model based on "desarrollismo" (development at all costs), privatization of social services, and exclusive focus on economic profit. Connected to the economic situation but linked to other factors (high levels of corruption, Catalan territorial crisis) was the loss of trust in the institutional and political system. The term that sums up the emotional habitus of the period 2008–14 is "indignation" – the name shared by the Spanish 15-M movement (shorthand for 15 May) with similar movements elsewhere. On May 15, 2011, disillusionment and anger found a public outlet in a mass protest that occupied Madrid's central square, the Puerta del Sol, spreading to involve 6.5–8.5 million Spaniards in cities nationwide and giving rise to subsequent protest "waves" (*mareas*). One of 15-M's most popular slogans was "No nos representan" (They don't represent us), referring to the disconnect between citizens' needs and political and institutional discourses and policies.

The label "literature / culture of crisis" signals a shift to critical examination of the effects – inequality, precarity, social immobility, hyper-individualism, environmental degradation – of neoliberalism's enabling fictions, as well as the emergence of alternative politics and cultural imaginaries (Álvarez Blanco and Gómez López-Quiñones 2016; Bezhanova 2017; Claesson 2019). This shift is illustrated by two 2014 poetry collections – the project *Marca(da) España. Retrato poético de una sociedad en crisis* (*Spain Brand[ed]: A Poetic Portrait of a Society in Crisis*, playing on the state logo Marca España) and Carlos Loreiro, Fran Garcerá, and Merche Ribas's *Calle de las impertinencias* (*Street of Impertinences*) – but goes back to earlier years with Ben Clark's 2006 *Los hijos de los hijos de la ira* (*Children of the Children of Wrath*; a reference to Dámaso Alonso's 1944 *Los hijos de la ira* / *Children of Wrath*).

Novels that have captured the causes and consequences of nationwide crisis include Chirbes's *Crematorio* (*Crematorium*, 2007) and *En la orilla* (*On the Edge*, 2013); Gopegui's *El padre de Blancanieves* (*Snow White's Father*, 2009) and *El comité de la noche* (*The Night Committee*, 2014); Javier López Menacho's *Yo, precario* (*My Precarious Life*, 2013); Elvira Navarro's *La trabajadora* (*The Woman Worker*, 2014), Javier Mestre's *Made in Spain* (2014), and José Ovejero's *Insurrección* (*Insurrection*, 2019). Chirbes's *Crematorio* depicts the rise and fall of property developer Rubén Bertomeu's financial empire which, over the 1990s–2000s, transformed a fictional Mediterranean agricultural enclave into a mass tourist mecca, exposing the effects of his predatory tactics and corruption on his family and the environment. *En la orilla* focuses more closely on destruction and loss, both material and spiritual, local and transnational. Like Chirbes, Gopegui produced her most openly political novels during the crisis, mitigating his pessimism by reflecting on individual and collective agency, female as well as male. Normalized precarity is exposed in Isaac Rosa's *La mano invisible* (*The Invisible Hand*, 2011) and *Tiza roja* (*Red Chalk*, 2020), and Cristina Morales's *Lectura fácil* (*Easy Reading*, 2018) which uses multiple registers, genres, and perspectives to critique institutions, patriarchy, feminism, disability legislation, and even certain forms of activism.

Playwrights such as Juan Mayorga, Angélica Liddell, Rodrigo García, and Roger Bernat had, since the 1990s, made visible the dispossession and marginalization that underpin the constitution of a normalized state. Mayorga's *Hamelin* (2005), Jordi Casanovas's *Ruz-Bárcenas* (2014) based on courtroom transcripts, and Cunillé's *Islàndia* (2017) explore political, financial, and media corruption and injustice. The participatory, documentary theater of Bernat and Simona Levi draw attention to social exclusion, while Liddell and García develop autofictional techniques, often exposing their own bodily vulnerability, to show how the neoliberal system shapes, coerces, and expels bodies considered redundant. Particularly notable in this turn to the political has been a new generation of women dramatists: Laila Ripoll, Itziar Pascual, Beth Escudé, Marta Buchaca, Clàudia Cedó, and the above-mentioned Szpunberg. Recent theater has embraced the use of new media with the growth of "dramaturgia expandida," "inmersiva," or "transmedia" (expanded, immersive, or transmedia dramaturgy), a trend exacerbated by the need to find new ways to reach a confined public during the COVID-19 pandemic – as illustrated by the productions of CaboSanRoque, Grumelot, Marcelo Expósito, Francesc Cuéllar, David Espinosa, and Bárbara Mestanza.

The turn to the digital, in addition to reconfiguring the public sphere, has introduced new modes of literary transmission (blogs, YouTube, tumblr,

Snaptchat, Twitter) that generate new ways of writing (short formats, simple language, use of digital slang) (Saum-Pascual 2018; Rodríguez-Gaona 2019a, 2019b). Poets like Luna Miguel, Elvira Sastre, Marwan, Defreds, Berta García Faet, and Irene X have developed an active social media presence; this, in addition to broadening audiences, has allowed the recovery of poetry's performative dimension and encouraged formal hybridity. Their writing combines emotional self-exploration with strong social overtones. The turn toward a new type of "social poetry" in which collective, personal, and representational concerns intersect (López Fernández, Martínez Fernández, and Molina Gil 2018) is visible in Batania Neorrabioso's 2014 book *La poesía ha vuelto y yo no tengo la culpa* (*Poetry Is Back and It's Not My Fault*), which combines his graffiti poetry with tweets, articles, short stories, and excepts from his blog; Marcos Cantelli's 2016 *Cons ti tu ci ón*, which uses digital experimentation to deconstruct the 1978 Constitution; or the work of Julieta Valero and Carlos Catena Cózar.

Another formal innovation has been the recent boom in graphic narrative (Amago and Marr 2019), whose popular appeal has been used to raise political and social awareness by authors and illustrators such as Susanna Martín and Paula Bonet, Carlos Portela and Sergi San Julián, Alicia Puleo, Rosana Antolí, Jorge Carrión, and Paco Roca. Ana Penyas's *Estamos todas bien* (*We're Doing Fine*, 2017; first female winner of the National Comics Prize) and *Todo bajo el sol* (*Everything under the Sun*, 2021) explore aging and the rise of mass tourism, while Miguel Brieva uses the comics format to imagine sustainable alternatives to the neoliberal ethos of growth. Migrant crossings and racism are depicted in Carlos Spottorno and Guillermo Abril's *La grieta* (*The Crack*, 2016), Javier de Isusi's Basque-language *Asylum* (2017), and Javier Gallego and Juan Gallego's *Como si nunca hubieran sido* (*As If They Had Never Existed*, 2019). Quan Zhou Wu's graphic narratives – beginning with *Gazpacho agridulce* (*Sweet-and-Sour Gazpacho*, 2015) – explore racial and ethnic stereotypes through critical humor.

The examination of layered identities is at the core of novels by children of immigrants who live across languages and cultures: in addition to the previously mentioned El Hachmi, Munir Hachemi (*Cosas vivas* / *Live Things*, 2018), Mohamed El Morabet (*Un solar abandonado* / *An Abandoned Plot*, 2018), Lucía Mbomío (*Hija del camino* / *Daughter of the Road*, 2019), and Margaryta Yakovenko (*Desencajada* / *Unhinged*, 2020). Esther Bendahan explores Sephardic communities in the Maghreb and the diaspora, via her own experiences as a Sephardi Jewish woman raised in Spain. Desirée Bela-Lobedde and Silvia Albert Sopale depict racism and sexism as experienced by Spanish-born children of African descent. To this must be added the work of African-born writers resident in Spain – such as Francisco Zamora Loboch, Agnès Agboton, or Donato Ndongo. All of these authors offer an insider view of the racial tensions in today's Spain that offsets the tendency in earlier writing by Spanish authors to depict immigrants as victims in need of rescue and assimilation.

From 2013 – triggered by Sergio del Molino's essay *La España vacía* (*Empty Spain*, 2013) – novels, poems, and essays started to feature the depopulated rural spaces of the Iberian peninsula's central plateau. Follow-up essays include Paco Cerdá's *Los últimos. Voces de la Laponia española* (*The Last Inhabitants: Voices from Spain's Lappland*, 2017); Virginia Mendoza's *Quién te cerrará los ojos* (*Who Will Close Your Eyes*, 2017); and Víctor Guiu's *Lo rural ha muerto, viva lo rural* (*The Rural Is Dead, Long Live the Rural*, 2019). The impact of Del Molino's book coincides with increased ecological awareness (Beilin 2015; Beilin and Viestenz 2016; Prádanos 2018) and the phenomenon of "neoruralism," referring to city dwellers who visit or move to the countryside in search of an alternative lifestyle, viewing it from an urban standpoint. Several contemporary Spanish neorural narratives focus on individual trajectories and solutions, unable to imagine functional communities outside of the consumerist paradigms that led their protagonists to flee the city in the first place, as in Sara Mesa's *Un amor* (*Love*, 2020) or veteran novelist Rosa Montero's *La buena suerte* (*Good Luck*, 2020). Composed during the COVID-19 pandemic, Julio Llamazares's beautifully written and illustrated *Primavera extremeña. Apuntes del natural* (*Springtime in Extremadura: Sketches*, 2020) picks up on his remarkable 1988 *La lluvia amarilla* (*Yellow Rain*, 1988), among the first novels to focus on rural depopulation, but ends with the family's return to urban normalcy.

An exception to the turn to the rural by urban writers is the rural veterinarian María Sánchez, whose 2019 essay *Tierra de mujeres. Una mirada íntima y familiar al mundo rural* (*Land of Women: An Intimate Family View of the Rural World*) implicitly counters Del Molino's essay by viewing the rural world from the perspective of those (especially the women) who live and work there. Discussing ecological concerns from an eco-feminist perspective, her depiction of the daily lives of the inhabitants of what she prefers to call an "emptied" (rather than "empty") Spain focuses on their often-unrewarded labor but also on their sense of community, creativity, and resilience – a topic also treated in her 2017 poems *Cuaderno de campo* (*Country Log Book*). Her ethics of care focuses on the genealogies of women who sustain those communities and on the semi-forgotten language of rural labor.

The majority of the novels that have turned to Spain's rural areas stress the challenges of extreme weather conditions and lack of material resources.

Jesús Carrasco's outstanding debut novel *Intemperie* (*Out in the Open*, 2013) is a bleak tale of vulnerability and survival, the latter depending largely on knowledge of the landscape. Dystopian tone and archetypes are present in novels such as Jenn Díaz's *Belfondo* (2011), Manuel Darriba's *El bosque es grande y profundo* (*The Forest Is Vast and Deep*, 2013), Lara Moreno's *Por si se va la luz* (*In Case the Lights Go Out*, 2013), Pilar Adón's *Las efímeras* (*The Mayflies*, 2015), Blanca Riestra's *Greta en su laberinto (Una ópera rock)* (*Greta in Her Labyrinth [A Rock Opera]*, 2016), and Iván Repila's *El niño que robó el caballo de Atila* (*The Boy Who Stole Attila's Horse*, 2017). In Spain as elsewhere in the Western world, the popularity of dystopian, even apocalyptic, scenarios is anchored not in visions of the future but in aspects of the present: natural catastrophes, global pandemics, destruction of social bonds, technological surveillance (Palardy 2018; Castro Picón forthcoming).

Not all the novels that turn to Spain's forgotten territorialities focus on its central heartland. Andrea Abreu's *Panza de burro* (*Donkey Belly*, 2020), set in Tenerife, offers a first-person exploration, in one of the island's dialects, of a child's subjectivity, exposing the ecological and cultural impact of mass tourism. In addition to the aforementioned Catalan-language novels that focus on rural life in Catalan-speaking territories, special mention must be made of Irene Solà's award-winning *Canto jo i la muntanya balla* (*I Sing and the Mountain Dances*, 2019) whose original depiction of life in a frontier area of the Pyrenees is narrated not only by its living and undead inhabitants, but also by the natural and animal environment: clouds, mountains, mushrooms, dogs, deer.

The turn to the rural is not always progressive. It may critique neo-liberalism's political and sociocultural normativity while proposing a nostalgic return to an idealized past – as in Ana Iris Simón's successful *Feria* (*Fairground*, 2020). It can come in realist or dystopian forms. It can call for collective action, including the practice of alternative lifestyles, or for individual resilience and self-management. Often it merely offers a temporary reprieve. In other cases, it opens up alternative ways of being in relation to others, emphasizing the interdependence of all forms of life and possibilities of imagining otherwise.

References

Adorno, Theodor W., and Max Horkheimer. [1947] 2002. "The Culture Industry: Enlightenment as Mass Deception." In *Dialectic of Enlightenment: Philosophical Fragments*, edited by Gunzelin Schmid Noerr, translated by Edmund Jephcott, 94–136. Stanford, CA: Stanford University Press.

Agirreazkuenaga, Joseba. 1992. "La tradición historiográfica vasca: su desarrollo en el marco de las ciencias sociales." *Historia Contemporánea* 7: 257–82.

Aguilar Fernández, Paloma. 1996. *Memoria y olvido de la guerra civil española.* Madrid: Alianza. (Updated as *Políticas de la memoria y memorias de la política: el caso español en perspectiva comparada.* Madrid: Alianza Editorial, 2008.)

Alas, Leopoldo. 1991. *Galdós, novelista,* edited by Adolfo Sotelo Vázquez. Barcelona: PPU.

Albareda i Salvadó, Joaquim. 2002. *Felipe V y el triunfo del absolutismo: Cataluña en un conflicto europeo (1700–1714).* Barcelona: Generalitat de Catalunya, Entitat Autònoma del Diari Oficial i de Publicacions.

Alberca, Manuel. 2015. *La espada y la palabra. Vida de Valle-Inclán.* Barcelona: Tusquets.

Albert, Mechthild, ed. 2005. *Vanguardia española e intermedialidad. Artes escénicas, cine y radio.* Madrid: Iberoamericana / Frankfurt: Vervuert.

Albiac Blanco, Maria-Dolores, ed. 2011. *Razon y sentimiento 1692–1800.* Vol. 4 of *Historia de la literatura española,* edited by José-Carlos Mainer. Barcelona: Critica.

Aldekoa, Iñaki. 2004. *Historia de la literatura vasca.* Donostia: Erein.

Álvarez Barrientos, Joaquín. 2003. "La república literaria en Europa: Centro y periferia." In *España entre dos siglos. Sociedad y Cultura,* edited by Antonio Morales Moya, 233–44. Madrid: Sociedad Estatal de Conmemoraciones Culturales.

Álvarez Barrientos, Joaquín. 2005. *Ilustración y Neoclasicismo en las letras españolas.* Madrid: Síntesis.

Álvarez Barrientos, Joaquín. 2006. *Los hombres de letras en la España del siglo XVIII. Apóstoles y arribistas.* Madrid: Castalia.

Álvarez Blanco, Palmar, and Antonio Gómez López-Quiñones, eds. 2016. *La imaginación hipotecada. Aportaciones al debate sobre la precariedad del presente.* Madrid: Libros en Acción.

294 Modern Literatures in Spain

Álvarez de Miranda, Pedro. 1985. "'Proyectos' y 'proyectistas' en el siglo XVIII español." *Boletín de la Real Academia Española* 65, no. 236: 409–30.

Álvarez de Miranda, Pedro. 1992. *Palabras e ideas. El léxico de la Ilustración temprana en España (1680–1760)*. Madrid: Anejos del Boletín de la Real Academia Española.

Álvarez Gila, Óscar, and José María Tapiz Fernández. 1996. "Prensa nacionalista vasca y emigración a América (1900–1936)." *Anuario de Estudios Americanos* 53 (1): 233–60.

Álvarez Junco, José. 2001. *Mater Dolorosa. La idea de España en el siglo XIX*. Madrid: Taurus.

Amago, Samuel, and Matthew J. Marr, eds. 2019. *Consequential Art: Comics Culture in Contemporary Spain*. Toronto: University of Toronto Press.

Amorós, Celia, and Ana de Miguel, eds. 2005. *Teoría feminista. De la Ilustración a la globalización*, 3 vols. Madrid: Ediciones Minerva.

Amorós, Celia, and Luisa Posada Kubissa, eds. 2007. *Feminismo y multiculturalismo*. Madrid: Instituto de la Mujer.

Anderson, Benedict. 1983. *Imagined Communities: Reflections on the Origin and Spread of Nationalism*. London: Verso.

Andioc, René. 1988. *Teatro y sociedad en el Madrid del siglo XVIII*. Madrid: Castalia.

Andioc, René. 2012. "Theatre of the Elites, Neoclassicism and the Enlightenment, 1750–1808." In M. Delgado and Gies, 157–72.

Anguera, Pere. 2003. "Denied Impositions: Harassment and Resistance of the Catalan Language." *Journal of Spanish Cultural Studies* 4 (1): 77–94.

Appadurai, Arjun. 1996. *Modernity at Large: Cultural Dimensions of Globalization*. Minneapolis, MN: University of Minnesota Press.

Aresti, Nerea. 2014. "De heroínas viriles a madres de la Patria. Las mujeres y el nacionalismo vasco (1893–1937)." *Historia y Política* 31: 281–308.

Arkinstall, Christine. 2014. *Spanish Women Writers and the Freethinking Press, 1879–1926*. Toronto: University of Toronto Press.

Ayala, Francisco. 1971. "Para quién escribimos nosotros." In *Los ensayos. Teoría y crítica literaria*, 138–64. Madrid: Aguilar

Baasner, Frank, and Francisco Acero Yus. 2007. *Doscientos críticos literarios en la España del siglo XIX*. Madrid: Instituto de la Lengua.

Baby, Sophie. 2018. *El mito de la transición pacífica. Violencia y política en España (1975–1982)*. Madrid: Akal.

Bacardí, Montserrat. 2009. "La traducció catalana a l'exili. Una primera aproximació." *Quaderns: Revista de Traducció* 16: 9–21.

Baena, Diego. 2020. "La literatura y sus pueblos. Demopoéticas de la España liberal (1834–1854)." PhD thesis, Princeton University.

Balcells, Albert. 2011. *Cataluña ante España. Los diálogos entre intelectuales catalanes y castellanos, 1888–1984*. Lleida: Editorial Milenio.

Balibrea, Mari Paz. 2002–3. "El paradigma exilio." *Nuevo Texto Crítico* 15–16 (29–32): 17–39.

Balibrea, Marí Paz. 2008. "Usos de la memoria de la República durante la transición." In *Plan Rosebud. Sobre imágenes, lugares y políticas de la memoria*, edited by María Ruido, 149–59. Santiago de Compostela: Xunta de Galicia.

Balibrea, Marí Paz, ed. 2017. *Líneas de fuga. Hacia otra historiografía cultural del exilio republicano español*. Madrid: Siglo XXI.

Baltrusch, Burghard. 2011. "The Postmodern Avant-Gardes in Post-1975 Galician Literature: Rompente, Antón Reixa, and Suso de Toro." In Hooper and Puga Moruxa, 237–57.

Barbour, Catherine. 2020. *Contemporary Galician Women Writers*. Oxford: Legenda.

Barreto, Danny M. 2017. "Putting Queerness on the Map: Notes for a Queer Galician Studies." In Sampedro Vizcaya and Losada Montero, 25–38.

Bartrina, Francesca. 2001. *Caterina Albert / Víctor Català. La voluptuositat de l'escriptura*. Vic: Eumo.

Bastons [i Vivanco], Carles. 2006. *Joan Maragall y Miguel de Unamuno. Una amistad paradigmática*. Lleida: Editorial Milenio.

Bastons i Vivanco, Carles, and Lluís Busquets i Grabulosa. 2002. *Castilla en la literatura catalana*. Barcelona: Generalitat de Catalunya.

Becerra Mayor, David. 2013. *La novela de la no-ideología. Introducción a la producción literaria del capitalismo avanzado en España*. Cienpozuelos: Tierradenadie.

Becerra Mayor, David. 2015. *Convocando el fantasma. Novela crítica en la España actual*. Cienpozuelos: Tierradenadie.

Becerra Mayor, David, and Antonio J. Antón Fernández. 2010. *Miguel Hernández. La voz de la herida*. Córdoba: El Páramo.

Beilin, Katarzyna Olga, 2015. *In Search of Alternative Biopolitics in Contemporary Spain: Anti-Bullfighting, Animality, and the Environment*. Columbus, OH: Ohio State University Press.

Beilin, Katarzyna Olga, and William Viestenz, eds. 2016. *Ethics of Life: Contemporary Iberian Debates*. Nashville, TN: Vanderbilt University Press.

Benet, Josep. 1992. *Maragall i la Setmana Tràgica*. Barcelona: Edicions 62.

Benítez-Rojo, Antonio. 1997. *The Repeating Island: The Caribbean and the Postmodern Perspective*, translated by James E. Maraniss. Durham, NC: Duke University Press.

Beramendi, Xusto. 2007. *De provincia a nación. Historia do galeguismo político*. Vigo: Edicións Xerais de Galicia.

Bermúdez, Silvia, and Roberta Johnson, eds. 2018. *A New History of Iberian Feminisms*. Toronto: Toronto University Press.

Bezhanova, Olga. 2017. *Literature of Crisis: Spain's Engagement with Liquid Capital*. Lewisburg, PA: Bucknell University Press.

Bijuesca, Josu. 2010. "Felipe Arrese Beitiaren poesia eta euskaldunen nazio identitatea." *Oihenart* 25: 177–88.

Blanco, Alda. 2001. *Escritoras virtuosas. Narradoras de la domesticidad en la España isabelina*. Granada: Universidad de Granada.

Blanco, Alda. 2003. "Introducción". In *A las mujeres. Ensayos feministas de María Martínez Sierra*, edited by Alda Blanco, 11–35. Logroño: Instituto de Estudios Riojanos.

Blanco Aguinaga, Carlos. 2006. "Problemas que plantea para la historia literaria el exilio español de 1939." In *Ensayos sobre la literatura del exilio español*, 27–72. Mexico: Colegio de Mexico.

Bolufer Peruga, Mónica. 1998. *Mujeres e Ilustración. La construcción de la feminidad en la España del siglo XVIII.* Valencia: Institució Alfons el Magnànim.

Bolufer [Peruga], Mónica. 2016. "Reasonable Sentiments: Sensibility and Balance in Eighteenth-Century Spain." In L.E. Delgado, P. Fernández, and Labanyi, 21–38.

Bolufer Peruga, Mónica. 2018. "New Inflections of a Long Polemic: The Debate over the Sexes in Enlightenment Spain." In *A New History of Iberian Feminisms*, edited by Silvia Bermúdez and Roberta Johnson, 38–49. Toronto: University of Toronto Press.

Bosch, Lolita. 2009. "Prólogo." In Víctor Català, *Soledad*, translated by Basilio Losada. Madrid: Lengua de Trapo.

Botrel, Jean-François. 1974. "La novela por entregas. Unidad de creacieon y consumo." In *Creación y público en la literatura española*, edited by Jean-François Botrel and Serge Salaün, 111–15. Madrid: Castalia.

Botrel, Jean-François. 1981. *Clarín y sus editores, 1884–1893.* Rennes: Université de Haute Bretagne.

Botrel, Jean-François. 1984. "Le succès d'édition des oeuvres de Benito Pérez Galdós. Essai de bibliométrie." *Anales de Literatura Española* 3: 119–57.

Botrel, Jean-François. 1993. *Libros, prensa y lectura en la España del siglo XIX.* Madrid: Fundación Germán Sánchez Rupérez.

Botrel, Jean-François. 2011. "De imaginatura. La adaptación escriptovisual de la narrativa en los pliegos de aleluyas." In *Simposio sobre literatura popular. Imágenes e ideas: la imaginatura*, edited by Joaquín Díaz, 213–46. Urueña: Fundación Joaquín Díaz.

Bou, Enric. 2013. *La invenció de l'espai. Ciutat i viatge.* Valencia: Universitat de València.

Bourdieu, Pierre. [1979] 1996a. *Distinction: A Social Critique of the Judgement of Taste*, translated by Richard Nice. London: Routledge.

Bourdieu, Pierre. [1992] 1996b. *The Rules of Art: Genesis and Structure of the Literary Field*, translated by Susan Emanuel. Stanford, CA: Stanford University Press.

Boyd, Carolyn. 1997. *Historia Patria: Politics, History, and National Identity in Spain, 1875–1975.* Princeton, NJ: Princeton University Press.

Branchadell, Albert. 2006. *L'aventura del català. De les Homilies d'Organyà al nou Estatut.* Barcelona: L'Esfera dels Llibres.

Brown, Joan Lipman. 2013. *Approaches to Teaching the Works of Carmen Martín Gaite.* New York: MLA.

Buffery, Helena. 2006. "Theater Space and Cultural Identity in Catalonia." *Romance Quarterly* 5 (3): 195–209.

Buffery, Helena. 2007. "The 'Placing of Memory' in Contemporary Catalan Theatre." *Contemporary Theatre Review* 117 (3): 385–97.

Buffery, Helena, ed. 2011. *Stages of Exile: Spanish Republican Exile Theatre and Performance.* Bern: Peter Lang.

Buffery, Helena. 2013. "Archaeologies of the National: Boadella and *El Nacional* Revisited." *Digithum* 15: 80–6.

Buffery, Helena. 2015. "Traumatic Translations of *La Plaça del Diamant*: On the Transmission and Translatability of Cultural Trauma." In *Funcions del passat en la cultura catalana contemporània*, edited by Josep-Anton Fernàndez and Jaume Subirana, 197–217. Lleida: Punctum.

Buffery, Helena. 2016. "¿Una voz en el desierto? Espacio, identidad y posmemoria en la obra finisecular de Maruxa Vilalta." In *Escritoras españolas en el exilio mexicano. Estrategias para la construcción de una identidad femenina*, edited by Eugenia Helena Houvenaghel and Florien Serlet, 79–95. Ghent: Universiteit Ghent.

Buffery, Helena. 2018. "A 'Natural History' of Return: Landscape, Myth and Memory in the Late Work of Mercè Rodoreda." In *Catalan Culture: Experimentation, Creative Imagination and the Relationship with Spain*, edited by Lloyd Davies, Gareth Walters, and John Hall, 14–34. Cardiff: University of Wales Press.

Buffery Helena, and Carlota Caulfield, eds. 2012. *Barcelona: Visual Culture, Space and Power.* Cardiff: University of Wales Press.

Buffery, Helena, and Laura Lonsdale. 2011. "Invisible Catalan(e)s: Catalan Women Writers and the Contested Space of Home." In *A Companion to Spanish Women's Studies*, edited by Xon de Ros and Geraldine Hazbun, 287–300. Woodbridge, UK: Tamesis.

Burguera, Mónica. 2012. *Las damas del liberalismo respetable. Los imaginarios sociales del feminismo liberal en España (1834–1850).* Madrid: Cátedra.

Burke, Peter. 1978. *Popular Culture in Early Modern Europe.* New York: Harper & Row.

Cacho Viu, Vicente. 1998. *El nacionalismo catalán como factor de modernización.* Barcelona: Quaderns Crema/Publicaciones de la Residencia de Estudiantes.

Campillo, Maria. 1994. *Escriptors catalans i compromís antifeixista (1936–1939).* Barcelona: Curial.

Candel, Francisco. 1974. *Els altres catalans.* Barcelona: Edicions 62.

Cañizares-Esguerra, Jorge. 2001. *How to Write the History of the New World: Histories, Epistemologies, and Identities in the Eighteenth-Century Atlantic World.* Stanford, CA: Stanford University Press.

Carballal, Ana. 2017. "Castelao: Nationalism, Federalism, and the Postcolonial." In Sampedro Vizcaya and Losada Montero 2017, 179–89.

Carner, Josep. 1996. "La contribució dels escriptors a la llengua de cultura." In *La prosa literària de Josep Carner*, edited by Marcel Ortín, 54–67. Barcelona: Quaderns Crema.

Caro Baroja, Julio. 1980. *Romances de ciego*, 2nd edn. Madrid: Taurus.

Carrera, Magalí M. 2003. *Imagining Identity in New Spain: Race, Lineage, and the Colonial Body in Portraiture and Casta Paintings*. Austin: University of Texas Press.

Casacuberta, Margarida, and Marina Gustá, eds. 2010. *Urban Narratives: The Literary Construction of Barcelona*. Barcelona: Fundació Antoni Tàpies.

Cassany, Enric, ed. 2009. *Panorama crític de la literatura catalana*. Vol. 4: Segle XIX. Barcelona: Vicens Vives.

Cassassas, Jordi, ed. 2016. *En defensa de la cultura. Damunt les espatlles dels gegants*. Barcelona: Arpa.

Castellanos, Jordi. 1983. *Raimon Casellas i el Modernisme*. Barcelona: Curial-Abadia de Montserrat.

Castellanos, Jordi. 2013. *Estudis, edicions, escrits*. Barcelona: L'Avenç.

Castro Picón, Natalia. Forthcoming. "Apocalyptic Visions of the Crisis: The Imaginary of the Flood in Contemporary Spanish Culture." In *The Routledge Companion to Contemporary Spanish Culture*, edited by L. Elena Delgado and Eduardo Ledesma. New York: Routledge.

Cate-Arries, Francie. 2004. *Spanish Culture behind Barbed Wire: Memory and Representation of the French Concentration Camps, 1939–1945*. Lewisburg, PA: Bucknell University Press.

Caudet, Francisco. 1976. *Cultura y exilio. La revista "España peregrina" (1940)*. Valencia: Fernando Torres.

Caudet, Francisco. 1992. *El exilio español en México. Las revistas literarias (1939–1971)*. Madrid: Fundación Banco Exterior.

Charnon-Deutsch, Lou. 1994. *Narratives of Desire: Nineteenth-Century Spanish Fiction by Women*. University Park, PA: Pennsylvania State University Press.

Charnon-Deutsch, Lou. 1995. "Bearing Motherhood: Representations of the Maternal in Emilia Pardo Bazán's *Los pazos de Ulloa*." In *New Hispanisms: Literature, Culture, Theory*, edited by Mark I. Millington and Paul Julian Smith, 69–95. Ottowa: Dovehouse Editions.

Charnon-Deutsch, Lou. 2008. *Hold That Pose: Visual Culture in the Late Nineteenth-Century Spanish Periodical*. University Park, PA: Penn State University Press.

Ciurans, Enric. 2012. "Topografia del teatre barceloní 1860–1900." In *Pensar i interpretar l'oci. Passatemps entreteniments, aficions i addiccions a la Barcelona del 1900*, edited by Teresa-M. Sala, 125–42. Barcelona: Universitat de Barcelona.

Claesson, Christian. 2019. *Narrativas precarias. Crisis y subjetividad en la cultura española actual*. Xixón: Hoja de Lata Editorial.

Conrad, Sebastian. 2012. "Enlightenment in Global History: A Historiographical Critique." *American Historical Review* 117: 999–1027.

Cornellà-Detrell, Jordi. 2011. *Literature as a Response to Cultural and Political Repression in Franco's Catalonia*. Woodbridge, UK: Tamesis.

Costa Carreras, Joan, ed. 2009. *The Architecture of Modern Catalan: Pompeu Fabra (1868–1948), Selected Writings*, translated by Alan Yates. Amsterdam: John Benjamins.

Coulon, Mireille. n.d. "Biografía de Ramón de la Cruz." www.cervantesvirtual .com/portales/roman_de_la_cruz/autor_biografia/

Crameri, Kathryn. 2008. *Catalonia: National Identity and Cultural Policy, 1980–2003.* Cardiff: University of Wales Press.

Crameri, Kathryn, ed. 2011. *Where the Rivers Meet: Jesús Moncada*. Nottingham: Five Leaves Publications.

Crameri, Kathryn. 2015. *Goodbye Spain? The Question of Independence for Catalonia.* Eastbourne: Sussex Academic Press.

Cruz, Jesús. 2011. *The Rise of Middle-Class Culture in Nineteenth-Century Spain.* Baton Rouge: Louisiana State University Press.

Curet, Francesc. 1967. *Història del teatre català*. Barcelona: Aedos.

Dainotto, Roberto M. 2007. *Europe (in Theory)*. Durham, NC: Duke University Press.

Dasca, Maria. 2018. "Representing the Land in Current Iberian Literature." In *Rural Writing: Geographical Imaginary and Expression of a New Regionality*, edited by Mauricette Fournier, 29–44. Newcastle: Cambridge Scholars Publishing.

Davidoff, Leonore, and Catherine Hall. 1987. *Family Fortunes: Men and Women of the English Middle Class, 1780–1850*. London: Hutchinson.

Davidson, Robert A. 2009. *Jazz Age Barcelona*. Toronto: University of Toronto Press.

Davies, Rhian. 2000. *"La España Moderna" and Regeneración: A Cultural Review in Restoration Spain, 1889–1914*. Manchester: University of Manchester.

Davies, Rhian. 2018. "How to Be a Writer for the Press – and How to Write about It." In Ginger and Lawless, 174–86.

Davis, Ryan A. 2017. "Literary Medicine, Medical Literature: César Juarros and *La Novela de Hoy*." In Zamostny and Larson, 99–125.

De Diego González, Álvaro. 2008. *Las mujeres de la Transición*. Madrid: Cortes Generales.

Del Molino, Sergio. 2013. *La España vacía. Viaje por un país que nunca fue*. Madrid: Turner.

Del Valle, Teresa, ed. 1985. *Mujer vasca, imagen y realidad*. Barcelona: Anthropos.

Delgado, Luisa Elena. 2003. "El artista frente al abismo. Modernidad y decadencia de Antonio de Hoyos." In Garín Llombart and Tomás Ferré, 101–23.

Delgado, Luisa Elena. 2008. "Gertrudis Gómez de Avellaneda. Escritura, feminidad y reconocimiento." In *La mujer de letras o la letraherida. Discursos y representaciones sobre la mujer escritora en el siglo XIX*, edited by Pura Fernández and Marie-Linda Ortega, 201–20. Madrid: CSIC.

Delgado, Luisa Elena. 2014. *La nación singular. La cultura del consenso y la fantasía de normalidad democrática española (1999–2011).* Madrid: Siglo XXI Editores.

Delgado, Luisa Elena, Pura Fernández, and Jo Labanyi, eds. 2016. *Engaging the Emotions in Spanish Culture and History.* Nashville, TN: Vanderbilt University Press.

Delgado, Luisa Elena, Jordana Mendelson, and Óscar Vázquez. 2007. "Recalcitrant Modernities: Spain, Cultural Difference, and the Location of Modernism." *Journal of Iberian and Latin American Studies* 13 (2–3): 105–19.

Delgado, Maria M. 2003. *Other Spanish Theatres: Erasure and Inscription on the Twentieth-Century Spanish Stage.* Manchester: Manchester University Press.

Delgado, Maria M., and David T. Gies, eds. 2012. *A History of Theatre in Spain.* Cambridge: Cambridge University Press.

Devoto, Fernando, and Ramón Villares. 2012. *Luis Seoane, entre Galicia y la Argentina.* A Coruña: Biblos.

DiFilippo, Emily. 2019. "Post-Op in the Real World: Cancer and Queer Resistance in Isabel Franc and Susanna Martín's *Alicia en un mundo real.*" In Amago and Marr, 195–219.

Dijkstra, Bram. 1986. *Idols of Perversity: Fantasies of Feminine Evil in Fin-de-Siècle Culture.* New York: Oxford University Press.

Doménech Rico, Fernando. 2012. "Theatrical Infrastructures, Dramatic Production and Performance, 1700–1759." In M. Delgado and Gies, 120–33.

Domingo, Josep M. 2013a. "Els Jocs Florals en la literatura contemporània." *Catalan Historical Review* 6: 179–87.

Domingo, Josep M. 2013b. "Sobre la Renaixença." *L'Avenç* 390: 26–35.

Donato, Clorinda, and Ricardo López. 2015. *Enlightenment Spain and the "Encyclopédie Méthodique".* Oxford: Voltaire Foundation.

Dubet, Anne, and Elena García Guerra. 2009. "Historiadores y arbitristas." In *La Monarquía de Felipe II. La Corte* (vol. 3), edited by José Martínez Millán and María Antonieta Visceglia, 870–6. Madrid: Fundación MAPFRE.

Dufour, Gérard. 2003. "El libro y la Inquisición." In *Historia de la edición y de la lectura en España, 1472–1914,* edited by Víctor Infante, François López, and Jean-François Botrel, 285–91. Madrid: Fundación Sánchez Rupérez.

Dussel, Enrique D. 1995. *The Invention of the Americas: Eclipse of "the Other" and the Myth of Modernity,* translated by Michael D. Barber. New York: Continuum.

Ealham, Chris, and Michael Richards, eds. 2005. *The Splintering of Spain: Cultural History and the Spanish Civil War, 1936–1939.* Cambridge: Cambridge University Press.

Egea, Juan F. 2003. "Imágenes becquerianas o la lírica entre el dinero y la fotografía." *Arizona Journal of Hispanic Cultural Studies* 7 (1): 7–22.

Egea, Juan F. 2004. "Bécquer's Bank: Women, Currency and the Prose of Existence." *Revista Canadiense de Estudios Hispánicos* 28 (3): 501–17.

Eizagirre, Ana. 2008. *Euskaldun zintzoaren etxerako eskuliburua*. Donostia: Utriusque Vasconiae.

Eizagirre Gesalaga, Xabier. 2020. "Euskal liburugintza 2018." *Jakin* 241: 97–120.

Elorza, Antonio. 1984. *La razón y la sombra. Una lectura política de Ortega y Gasset*. Barcelona: Anagrama.

"El sector del libro pide ayudas para sobrevivir a la crisis." 2020. *EITB* (8 April). https://www.eitb.eus/es/cultura/detalle/7153837/coronavirus-covid19-el-sector-libro-vasco-pide-ayudas-sobrevivir/.

Enjuto-Rangel, Cecilia, Sebastiaan Faber, Pedro García-Caro, and Robert Patrick Newcomb, eds. 2019. *Transatlantic Studies: Latin America, Iberia, and Africa*. Liverpool: Liverpool University Press.

Epps, Brad. 1996. *Significant Violence: Oppression and Resistance in the Narratives of Juan Goytisolo, 1970–1990*. Oxford: Oxford University Press.

Epps, Brad, and Luis Fernández Cifuentes, eds. 2005. *Spain beyond Spain: Modernity, Literary History, and National Identity*. Lewisburg, PA: Bucknell University Press.

Escolar, Hipólito. 1987. *La cultura durante la guerra civil*. Madrid: Alhambra.

Espigado, Gloria. 2010. "Las primeras republicanas en España. Prácticas y discursos identitarios (1868–1874)." *Historia Social* 67: 75–91.

Federici, Silvia. 2020. *Beyond the Periphery of the Skin: Rethinking, Remaking, and Reclaiming the Body in Contemporary Capitalism*. Oakland, CA: PM Press.

Feldman, Sharon. 2009. *In the Eye of the Storm: Contemporary Theater in Barcelona*. Lewisburg, PA: Bucknell University Press.

Fernández, Álvaro. 2015. "La domesticación del pasado. *Corazón tan blanco*/*El jinete polaco*: La gran novela de la Transición." In *Estudios de literatura, cultura e historia contemporánea. En homenaje a Francisco Caudet*, edited by Fernando Larraz, 505–30. Madrid: Universidad Autónoma de Madrid.

Fernàndez, Josep-Anton. 2008. *El malestar en la cultura catalana. La cultura de la normalització (1979–1999)*. Barcelona: Editorial Empúries.

Fernández, Luis Miguel. 2006. *Tecnología, espectáculo, literatura: Dispositivos ópticos en las letras españolas de los siglos XVIII y XIX*. Santiago de Compostela: Universidade de Santiago de Compostela.

Fernández, Pura. 2003. "La condición social del artista. La paradoja de Alejandro Sawa." In Garín Llombart and Tomás Ferré, 125–58.

Fernández, Pura. 2016. "Emotional Readings for New Interpretative Communities in the Nineteenth Century." In L.E. Delgado, P. Fernández, and J. Labanyi, 56–76.

Fernández Cifuentes, Luis. 1988. "Signs for Sale in the City of Galdós." *Modern Language Notes* 103: 289–311.

Flitter, Derek. 1992. *Spanish Romantic Literary Theory and Criticism*. Cambridge: Cambridge University Press.

Foguet i Boreu, Francesc, ed. 2008. *Teatre en temps de guerra i revolució*. Lleida: Punctum.

Fontanella, Lee. 1982. *La imprenta y las letras en la España romántica.* Bern: Peter Lang.

Foucault, Michel. [1976] 1987. *The History of Sexuality: An Introduction,* translated by Robert Hurley. Harmondsworth, UK: Penguin Books.

Fradera, Josep M. 2003. *Cultura nacional en una sociedad dividida, 1838–1868.* Madrid: Marcial Pons.

Fradera, Josep M. 2007. "L'intel·lectual abans de l'intel·lectual. Consideracions vacil·lants sobre el cas català entre la revolució liberal i el canvi de segle." In *La projecció social de l'escriptor en la literatura contemporània,* edited by Ramon Panyella, 67–107. Lleida: Punctum.

Fradera, Josep M. 2009. *La pàtria dels catalans. Història, política, cultura.* Barcelona: La Magrana.

Franco, Dolores. 2005. *España como preocupación.* Madrid: Alianza.

Freire López, Ana María. 2003. "La obra periodística de Emilia Pardo Bazán." In *Estudios sobre la obra de Emilia Pardo Bazán,* edited by Ana María Freire López, 115–32. La Coruña: Fundación Pedro Barrié de la Maza.

Fuentes, Yvonne, and Mark R. Malin, eds. 2021. *Protest in the Long Eighteenth Century.* Abingdon, UK: Routledge.

Fusi, Juan Pablo. 1994. "Centralismo y localismo. La formación del Estado español." In *Nación y Estado en la España liberal,* edited by Guillermo Gortázar, 77–90. Madrid: Noesis.

Fuster, Jaume. 1978. *El Congrés de Cultura Catalana: Qué és i qué ha estat.* Barcelona: Laia.

Fuster i Sobrepere, Joan. 2006. *Barcelona i l'estat centralista: indústria i política a la dècada moderada (1843–1854).* Vic: Eumo.

Gallén, Enric. 2012. "Guimerà a Europa i Amèrica." *Catalan Historical Review* 5: 85–100.

García Díaz, Noelia. 2019. "Benito Jerónimo Feijoo in the Initial Stages of the Spanish Public Sphere: Some Considerations." In Jiménez Torres and Villamediana González, 44–69.

García Montero, Luis. 2001. *Gigante y extraño: Las "Rimas" de Gustavo Adolfo Bécquer.* Barcelona: Tusquets.

Garín Llombart, Felipe Vicente, and Facundo Tomás Ferré, eds. 2003. *En el país del arte. La novela del artista.* Valencia: Biblioteca Valenciana.

Garzia, Joxerra. 2012. "The History of *Bertsolaritza.*" In Olaziregi, 43–65.

Gemie, Sharif. 2006. *Galicia: A Concise History.* Cardiff: University of Wales Press.

George, David. 2002. *Theatre in Madrid and Barcelona.* Cardiff: University of Wales Press.

Gies, David T. 1988. *Theatre and Politics in Nineteenth-Century Spain: Juan de Grimaldi as Impresario and Government Agent.* Cambridge: Cambridge University Press.

Gies, David T. 1994. *The Theatre in Nineteenth-Century Spain.* Cambridge: Cambridge University Press.

Gies, David T. 1999. "El XVIII porno." In *Signoria di Parole. Studi offerti a Mario dei Pinto*, edited by Giovanna Calabrò, 298–310. Naples: Liguore Editore.

Gies, David T. 2008. "Very Private Matters: Imagining the Erotic in Eighteenth-Century Spanish Poetry." In *Imagining Selves: Essays in Honor of Patricia Meyer Spacks*, edited by Rivka Swenson and Elise Lauterbach, 70–92. Newark, DE: University of Delaware Press.

Ginger, Andrew. 2019. "The Shape of the Public Sphere in Spain (1860–99): A Dream of Generalities." In Jiménez Torres and Villamediana González, 129–51.

Glendinning, Nigel. 1972. *The Eighteenth Century*. London: Ernest Benn.

Gobierno Vasco. 2020. *Informe de la edición en euskera 2019*. https://www.euskadi.eus/web01-a3kebarg/es/contenidos/informacion/keb_argit_lib_euskara_2019/es_def/index.shtml

González-Allende, Iker. 2019. "Mujeres que trabajan. La economía feminista en la narrativa de Eider Rodríguez." *Symposium* 73: 203–18.

González-Millán, Xoán. 2003. "La reivindicación de un 'diccionario gallego' en el siglo XIX." *RDTP* 50 (8): 5–32.

González Montañés, Julio. 2018. "O 'Entremés gallego' de Salvador Francisco Roel." *A Trabe de Ouro* 108: 135–47.

Gracia, Jordi. 2000. *Los nuevos nombres: 1971–2000*. Supplement 1 of *Historia y crítica de la literatura española*, vol. 9, edited by Francisco Rico and Jordi Gracia. Barcelona: Crítica.

Gracia, Jordi. 2001. *Hijos de la razón. Contraluces de la libertad en las letras españolas de la democracia*. Barcelona: Edhasa.

Gracia, Jordi. 2004. *La resistencia silenciosa. Fascismo y cultura en España*. Barcelona: Anagrama.

Gracia, Jordi, and Domingo Ródenas. 2011. *Derrota y restitución de la modernidad*. Vol. 7 of *Historia de la literatura española*, edited by José-Carlos Mainer and Gonzalo Pontón. Barcelona: Crítica.

Gray, Rockwell. 1989. *The Imperative of Modernity: An Intellectual Biography of José Ortega y Gasset*. Berkeley: University of California Press.

Gubern, Román. 1999. *Proyector de luna. La generación del 27 y el cine*. Barcelona: Anagrama.

Guillamon, Julià. 2008. *El dia revolt. Literatura catalana de l'exili*. Barcelona: Empúries.

Guillamon, Julià. 2019. *La ciutat interrompuda, seguit de El gran novel·loide sobre Barcelona*. Barcelona: Editorial Anagrama.

Guillory, John. 1993. *Cultural Capital: The Problem of Literary Canon Formation*. Chicago: University of Chicago Press.

Guimerá Ravina, Agustín. 2007. *El reformismo borbónico. Una visión interdisciplinar*. Madrid: Alianza.

Gutiérrez García, Santiago. 2014. "Clerics, Troubadours and Damsels: Galician

Literature and Written Culture during the Middle Ages." In Miguélez-Carballeira, 2014, 13–34.

Habermas, Jürgen. [1962] 1992. *The Structural Transformation of the Public Sphere: An Inquiry into a Category of Bourgeois Society*, translated by Thomas Burger with Frederick Lawrence. Cambridge: Polity Press.

Haidt, Rebecca. 1998. *Embodying Enlightenment: Knowing the Body in Eighteenth-Century Spanish Literature and Culture*. New York: St. Martin's Press.

Haidt, Rebecca. 1999. "Luxury, Consumption, and Desire: Theorizing the *Petimetra*." *Arizona Journal of Hispanic Cultural Studies* 3: 33–50.

Haidt, Rebecca. 2003a. "A Well-Dressed Woman Who Will Not Work: Petimetras, Economics, and Eighteenth-Century Fashion Plates." *Revista Canadiense de Estudios Hispánicos* 28 (1): 133–57.

Haidt, Rebecca. 2003b. "The Enlightenment and Fictional Form." In *The Cambridge Companion to the Modern Spanish Novel*, edited by Harriet S. Turnet and Adelaida López de Martínez, 31–46. Cambridge: Cambridge University Press.

Haidt, Rebecca. 2011. "Los Majos, el "españolísimo gremio" del teatro popular dieciochesco. Sobre casticismo, inestabilidad y abyección." *Cuadernos de Historia Moderna* 10: 155–73.

Halbwachs, Maurice. 1992. *On Collective Memory*, translated by Lewis A. Coser. Chicago: University of Chicago Press.

Haritschelhar, Jean. 2012. "The Eighteenth and Nineteenth Centuries: Brides across Borders." In Olaziregi, 109–33.

Harvey, Karen. 2004. *Reading Sex in the Eighteenth Century: Bodies and Gender in English Erotic Culture*. Cambridge: Cambridge University Press.

Highfill, Juli. 2014. *Modernism and Its Merchandise: The Spanish Avant-Garde and Material Culture, 1920–1930*. University Park, PA: Penn State University Press.

Hill, Ruth, ed. 2018. *Other Enlightenments: Spain, from the Atlantic to the Pacific*. Special issue of *The Eighteenth Century: Theory and Interpretation* 51 (2).

Hirsch, Marianne. 2012. *The Generation of Postmemory: Writing and Visual Culture after the Holocaust*. New York: Columbia University Press.

Hobsbawm, Eric, and Terence Ranger, eds. 1984. *The Invention of Tradition*. Cambridge: Cambridge University Press.

Hoggart, Richard. [1957] 2017. *The Uses of Literacy*. London: Taylor & Francis.

Hooper, Kirsty. 2003. "Girl, Interrupted: The Distinctive History of Galician Women's Narrative." *Romance Studies* 21 (2): 101–14.

Hooper, Kirsty. 2006. "Galicia desde Londres desde Galicia: New Voices in the Twenty-First-Century Diaspora." *Journal of Spanish Cultural Studies* 7 (1): 171–88.

Hooper, Kirsty. 2011. *Writing Galicia into the World: New Cartographies, New Poetics*. Liverpool: Liverpool University Press.

Hooper, Kirsty. 2020. *The Edwardians and the Making of a Modern Spanish Obsession*. Liverpool: Liverpool University Press.

Hooper, Kirsty, and Manuel Puga Moruxa, eds. 2011. *Contemporary Galician Cultural Studies: Between the Local and the Global*. New York: MLA.

Hughes, Robert. 1991. *The Shock of the New: Art and the Century of Change*. London: Thames and Hudson.

Huyssen, Andreas. 1996. *Twilight Memories: Marking Time in a Culture of Amnesia*. New York: Routledge.

Iarocci, Michael. 2006. *Properties of Modernity: Romantic Spain, Modern Europe, and the Legacies of Empire*. Nashville, TN: Vanderbilt University Press

Ibarz, Mercè. 2008. *Rodoreda: Exili i desig*. Barcelona: Empúries.

Igartua, Ivan, and Xabier Zabaltza. 2012. *Euskararen Historia. Historia de la lengua vasca. History of the Basque Language*. Donostia: Etxepare Euskal Institutua.

Ilie, Paul. 1984. "Autophagous Spain and the European Other." *Hispania* 67 (1): 28–35.

Izquierdo Martín, Jesús, and Pablo Sánchez León. 2006. *La guerra que nos han contado. 1936 y nosotros*. Madrid: Alianza.

Jameson, Fredric. 2013. *The Antinomies of Realism*. London: Verso.

Jiménez Torres, David, and Leticia Villamediana González, eds. 2019. *The Configuration of the Spanish Public Sphere: From the Enlightenment to the Indignados*. New York: Berghahn Books.

Jorba, Manuel. 1986. "La Renaixença"; "Llengua i literatura 1800–1833"; "El Romanticisme"; "Els Jocs Florals"; "La poesia entre 1859 i 1880." In *Història de la literatura catalana*, vol. 8, edited by Martí de Riquer, Antoni Comas, and Joaquim Molas, 9–222. Barcelona: Ariel.

Juliá, Santos, ed. 1999. *Víctimas de la guerra civil*. Madrid: Temas de Hoy.

Juliá, Santos. 2004. *Historias de las dos Españas*. Madrid: Taurus.

Kamen, Henry. 2008. *Imagining Spain: Historical Myth and National Identity*. New Haven, CT: Yale University Press.

Kaplan, Temma. 1992. *Red City, Blue Period: Social Movements in Picasso's Barcelona*. Berkeley: University of California Press.

Keown, Dominic. 2008. "Joan Salvat-Papasseït: A Revolutionary Domesticated?" *Catalan Review* 22: 253–64.

Kirkpatrick, Susan. 1989. *Las Románticas. Escritoras y subjetividad en España, 1835–1850*. Madrid: Cátedra.

Kirkpatrick, Susan. 1995. "Fantasy, Seduction, and the Woman Reader: Rosalía de Castro's Novels." In *Culture and Gender in Nineteenth-Century Spain*, edited by Lou Charnon-Deutsch and Jo Labanyi, 74–97. Oxford: Oxford University Press.

Kitts, Sally-Ann. 2019. "Spain and Habermas' Public Sphere: A Revisionist View." In Jiménez Torres and Villamediana González, 25–43.

Kortazar, Jon. 1986. *Teoría y práctica poética de Esteban Urkiaga "Lauaxeta"*. Bilbao: Desclee de Brower.

Kristeva, Julia. 1986. "Women's Time," translated by Alice Jardine and Harry

Blake. In *The Kristeva Reader*, edited by Toril Moi, 187–213. New York: Columbia University Press.

Labanyi, Jo. 1993. "Representing the Unrepresentable: Monsters, Mystics and Feminine Men in Galdós's *Nazarín.*" *Journal of Hispanic Research* 1: 227–37.

Labanyi, Jo. 2000. *Gender and Modernization in the Spanish Realist Novel.* Oxford: Oxford University Press.

Labanyi, Jo. 2019. *Spanish Culture from Romanticism to the Present: Structures of Feeling.* Oxford: Legenda.

Labrador Méndez, Germán. 2017. *Culpables por la literatura. Imaginación política y contracultura en la transición española (1968–1986).* Madrid: Akal.

Lamas, Rafael. 2008. *Música e identidad. El teatro musical español y los intelectuales en la edad moderna.* Madrid: Alianza.

Laqueur, Walter. 1990. *Making Sex: Body and Gender from the Greeks to Freud.* Cambridge, MA: Harvard University Press.

Larios, Jordi, ed. 2014. *La cara fosca de la cultura catalana. La col·laboració amb el feixisme.* Palma: Editorial Lleonard Muntaner.

Larumbe Gorraitz, María Ángeles. 2004. *Las que dijeron no. Palabra y acción del feminismo en la Transición.* Zaragoza: Prensas Universitarias de Zaragoza.

Lasagabaster, Jesús María. 2005. *Las literaturas de los vascos.* Bilbao: Universidad de Deusto.

Lewis, Elizabeth Franklin, Mónica Bolufer Peruga, and Catherine Marie Jaffe, eds. 2020. *The Routledge Companion to the Hispanic Enlightenment.* Abingdon, UK: Routledge.

Llorens, Vicente. 1979. *Liberales y románticos*, 3rd edn. Madrid: Castalia.

Lonsdale, Laura. 2011. "Don Juan in Exile." In Buffery, 95–106.

López Casimiro, Francisco. 2011. "La masonería en el siglo XIX. Orto y ocaso." In *Masonería e Ilustración. Del Siglo de las Luces a la actualidad*, edited by José Ignacio Cruz, 107–30. Valencia: Universitat de València.

López Fernández, Álvaro, Ángela Martínez Fernández, and Raúl Molina Gil, eds. 2018. *Lecturas del desierto. Antología y entrevistas sobre poesía actual en España.* Dossier in *Kamchatka: Revista de Análisis Cultural* 11: 7–378.

Louis, Anja. 2005. *Women and the Law: Carmen de Burgos, an Early Feminist.* Woodbridge, UK: Tamesis.

Macpherson, C.B. [1962] 1990. *The Political Theory of Possessive Individualism: Hobbes to Locke*, 13th edn. Oxford: Oxford University Press.

Madariaga Orbea, Juan. 2006. *Anthology of Apologists and Detractors of the Basque Language.* Reno, NV: Center for Basque Studies.

Mainer, José Carlos. 2004. *La doma de la quimera. Ensayos sobre nacionalismo y cultura en España.* 2nd rev. edn. Madrid: Iberoamericana / Frankfurt: Vervuert.

Mainer, José Carlos. 2006. *Moradores de Sansueña.* Valladolid: Universidad de Valladolid.

Mandrell, James. 1995. "'Poesía . . . eres tú', or the Construction of Bécquer and the Sign of Woman." In *Culture and Gender in Nineteenth-Century Spain*, edited by Lou Charnon-Deutsch and Jo Labanyi, 53–73. Oxford: Oxford University Press.

Manzano, Eduardo. 2000. "La construcción histórica del pasado nacional." In *La gestión de la memoria. La historia de España al servicio del poder*, edited by Sisinio Pérez Garzon et al., 33–62. Barcelona: Crítica.

March, Kathleen. 2018. "The Galician Novel." *A Companion to the Twentieth-Century Spanish Novel*, edited by Martha Eulalia Altisent, 235–46. Woodbridge, UK: Tamesis.

Marco, Joaquín. 1977. *Literatura popular en España en los siglos XVIII y XIX*. Madrid: Taurus.

Marfany, Joan-Lluís. 1975. *Aspectes del modernisme*. Barcelona: Curial.

Marfany, Joan-Lluís. 2004. "Minority Languages and Literary Revivals." *Past and Present* 184 (1): 137–67.

Marfany, Joan-Lluís. 2008. *Llengua, nació i diglòssia*. Barcelona: L'Avenç.

Marfany, Joan-Lluís, 2017. *Nacionalisme espanyol i catalanitat (1789–1859). Cap a una revisió de la Renaixença*. Barcelona: Edicions 62.

Martí, Manel. 1997. *La transició al País Valencià*. Special issue of *L'Avenç* 214.

Martí-López, Elisa. 2000. "Autochtonous Conflicts, Foreign Fictions: The Capital as Metaphor for the Nation." *Catalan Review* 14 (1–2): 117–28.

Martí-López, Elisa. 2002. *Borrowed Words: Translation, Imitation and the Making of the Nineteenth-Century Novel in Spain*. Lewisburg, PA: Bucknell University Press.

Martí-López, Elisa, ed. 2020. *The Routledge Hispanic Studies Companion to Nineteenth-Century Spain*. Abingdon: Routledge.

Martí-Monterde, Antoni. 2016. "Rubén Darío i Santiago Rusiñol. Política i periodisme literari en la Barcelona modernista." *Catalan Review* 30: 275–304.

Martínez, Guillem, ed. 2012. *CT o la Cultura de la Transición. Crítica a 35 años de cultura española*. Barcelona: Debolsillo.

Martínez del Campo, Luis. 2018. "How to Be an Intellectual." In *Spain in the Nineteenth Century: New Essays on Experiences of Culture and Society*, edited by Andrew Ginger and Geraldine Lawless, 233–45. Manchester: Manchester University Press.

Martínez Expósito, Alfredo. 2004. *Escrituras torcidas. Ensayos de crítica "queer."* Barcelona: Laertes.

Martínez Martín, Jesús A. 2009. *Vivir de la pluma. La profesionalización del escritor, 1836–1936*. Madrid: Marcial Pons Historia.

Marzo Pérez, Jorge Luis. 2010. *¿Puedo hablar con libertad, excelencia? Arte y poder en España desde 1950*. Murcia: E.P.R. Murcia Cultural.

Mateo Gambarte, Eduardo. 1996. *Los "niños de la Guerra." Literatura del exilio español en México*. Lleida: Pagès Editors.

Mayhew, Jonathan. 2009. *The Twilight of the Spanish Avant-Garde: Spanish Poetry 1980–2000*. Liverpool: Liverpool University Press.

McDonagh, Gary. 1987. "The Geography of Evil: Barcelona's Barrio Chino." *Anthropological Quarterly* 50 (4): 173–84.

McGlade, Rhiannon. 2016. *Catalan Cartoons: A Cultural and Political History.* Cardiff: University of Wales Press.

McGovern, Tim. 2011. "Camping up the Nation: Antón Lopo's *Ganga* and the Queering of Iberia." In Hooper and Puga Moruxa, 166–81.

McRuer, Robert. 2018. *Crip Times: Disability, Globalization, and Resistance.* New York: New York University Press.

Medina, Alberto. 2009. *Espejo de sombras. Sujeto y multitud en la España del siglo XVIII.* Madrid: Marcial Pons.

Medina, Alberto. 2013. "The Institutionalization of Language in Eighteenth-Century Spain." In *A Political History of Spanish: The Making of a Language,* edited by José del Valle, 77–92. Cambridge: Cambridge University Press.

Memorial de Greuges. 1760. https://www.uv.es/correa/troncal/resources/greuges1760.pdf.

Mendelson, Jordana. 2005. *Documenting Spain: Artists, Exhibition Culture, and the Modern Nation, 1929–1939.* University Park, PA: Penn State University Press.

Michonneau, Stéphane. 2002. *Barcelona: Memòria i identitat. Monuments, commemoracions i mites.* Vic: Eumo.

Mignolo, Walter. 2012. *Local Histories/Global Designs: Coloniality, Subaltern Knowledges, and Border Thinking.* Princeton, NJ: Princeton University Press.

Miguélez-Carballeira, Helena. 2013. *Galicia, a Sentimental Nation: Gender, Culture and Politics.* Cardiff: University of Wales Press.

Miguélez-Carballeira, Helena, ed. 2014. *A Companion to Galician Literature.* Woodbridge, UK: Tamesis.

Mira, Alberto. 2004. *De Sodoma a Chueca. Una historia cultural de la homosexualidad en España en el siglo XX.* Madrid: Egales.

Miracle, Josep. 1990. *Àngel Guimerà, creador i apòstol.* Barcelona: Abadia de Montserrat.

Mitchell, Timothy. 1994. *Flamenco Deep Song.* New Haven, CT: Yale University Press.

Mitxelena, Koldo. [1960] 1988. *Historia de la lengua vasca.* Donostia: Erein.

Molas, Joaquim. 1989. "Pròleg." In Jordi Rubió i Balaguer, *Il·lustració i Renaixença,* 5–22. Barcelona: Publicacions de l'Abadia de Montserrat.

Molas, Joaquim. 2009. "Jocs Florals, 1925." In *Homenatge als Jocs Florals de Barcelona. Any LXVII de Llur Restauració,* edited by Grup d'Estudi de la Literatura del Vuit-cents, vii–xiii. Lleida: Punctum.

Molas, Joaquim et al., eds. 2005. *Les avantguardes literàries a Catalunya. Bibliografia i antologia crítica.* Madrid: Iberoamericana/Frankfurt: Vervuert.

Molinero, Carme, and Pere Ysàs. 2018. *Transición. Historia y relatos.* Madrid: Akal.

Monroe, James T. 1970. *Islam and the Arabs in Spanish Scholarship (Sixteenth Century to the Present).* Leiden: E.J. Brill.

Montiel, Francisca. 2011. "An Intertextual Return: Álvaro Arauz's *Entre Medina y Olmedo.*" In Buffery, 57–70.

Morel Borotra, Natalie. 2003. *L'opéra basque (1884–1937).* Baigorri: Izpegi.

Moreno Caballud, Luis. 2015. *Cultures of Anyone: Studies on Cultural Democratization in the Spanish Neoliberal Crisis*. Liverpool: Liverpool University Press.

Mundi, Francisco. 1987. *El teatro de la guerra civil*. Barcelona: PPU.

Muñoz Sempere, Daniel, and Gregorio Alonso García, eds. 2011. *Londres y el liberalismo hispánico*. Madrid: Iberoamericana / Frankfurt: Vervuert.

Murado, Miguel Anxo. 2008. *Otra idea de Galicia*. Barcelona: Random House Mondadori.

Murgades, Josep. 1987. "El Noucentisme." In *Història de la literatura catalana*, vol. 9, edited by Joaquim Molas, 9–72. Barcelona: Ariel.

Murgades, Josep. 2020. "Catalan Noucentisme and Narrative." In *Catalan Narrative 1875–2015*, edited by Jordi Larios and Montserrat Lunati, 216–33. Cambridge: Legenda.

Murray, N. Michelle, and Akiko Tsuchiya, eds. 2019. *Unsettling Colonialism: Gender and Race in the Nineteenth-Century Global Hispanic World*. Albany, NY: SUNY Press.

Nash, Mary, Gemma Torres, and Teresa María Ortega López. 2009. *Feminismos en la transición*. Barcelona: Grup de Recerca Consolidat Multiculturalisme i Gènere, Universitat de Barcelona.

Nichols, Geraldine Cleary, 1992. *Des/cifrar la diferencia. Narrativa femenina de la España contemporánea*. Madrid: Siglo XXI.

Nichols, William J., and H. Rosi Song, eds. 2013. *Toward a Cultural Archive of the Movida: Back to the Future*. Madison, NJ: Fairleigh Dickinson University Press.

Núñez Sabarís, Xaquín. 2020. *Cartografías de narrativa galega contemporánea*. Vigo: Galaxia.

Olaziregi, Mari Jose. 2005. *Waking the Hedgehog: The Literary Universe of Bernardo Atxaga*. Reno, NV: Center for Basque Studies.

Olaziregi, Mari Jose, ed. 2012. *Basque Literary History*. Reno, NV: Center for Basque Studies.

Olaziregi, Mari Jose. 2017. "Literature and Political Conflicts: The Basque Case." In *The International Legacy of Lehendakari Jose Antonio Aguirre's Government*, edited by Xabier Irujo and Mari Jose Olaziregi, 251–78. Reno, NV: Center for Basque Studies, University of Nevada.

Olaziregi, Mari Jose. 2021. "Beyond the Motherland: Memory and Emotion in Contemporary Basque Women's Fiction." In *Memory and Emotion: Basque Women's Stories. Constructing Meaning from Memory*, edited by Larraitz Ariznabarreta and Nere Lete, 263–93. Reno, NV: Center for Basque Studies.

Olaziregi, Mari Jose, and Amaia Elizalde, eds. 2021. *Kirmen Uribe. Escritura y vida*. Berlin: Peter Lang.

Onaindia, Mario. 2002. *La construcción de la nación en España. Republicanismo y nacionalismo en la Ilustración*. Barcelona: Ediciones B.

Otero Urtaza, Eugenio, ed. 2006. *Las Misiones Pedagógicas, 1931–1936*.

Madrid: Sociedad Estatal de Conmemoraciones Culturales/Residencia de Estudiantes.

Outram, Dorinda. 2019. *The Enlightenment*, 4th edn. Cambridge: Cambridge University Press.

Outram, Dorinda. 2022. *The Body and the French Revolution: Sex, Class and Political Culture*. Milton Keynes, UK: Taylor & Francis.

Pagés-Rangel, Roxana. 1997. *Del dominio público. Itinerarios de la carta privada*. Amsterdam: Rodopi.

Palacios, Manuela. 2002. "'A Fastness of Their Own.' The Galician Reception of Virginia Woolf." In *The Reception of Virginia Woolf in Europe*, edited by Mary Ann Caws and Nicola Luckhurst, 281–95. London: Continuum.

Palardy, Diana Q. 2018. *The Dystopian Imagination in Contemporary Spanish Literature and Film*. London: Palgrave Macmillan.

Palomo, María del Pilar, and Jesús Rubio Jiménez, eds. 2015. *Rimas. leyendas y relatos orientales*. Seville: Fundación José Manuel Lara.

Paquette, Gabriel B. 2008. *Enlightenment, Governance and Reform in Spain and Its Empire, 1759–1808*. Basingstoke, UK: Palgrave Macmillan.

Passerini, Luisa. 1999. *Europe in Love, Love in Europe: Imagination and Politics in Britain between the Wars*. London: I.B. Tauris.

Pateman, Carole. 1988. *The Sexual Contract*. Cambridge: Polity Press.

Penrose, Mehl Allan. 2014. *Masculinity and Queer Desire in Spanish Enlightenment Literature*. Farnham, UK: Ashgate.

Pereira-Zazo, Óscar, and Steven L. Torres, eds. 2019. *Spain after the Indignados/ 15M movement: The 99% Speaks Out*. Cham, Switzerland: Palgrave Macmillan.

Pérez Galdós, Benito. 1972. *Ensayos de crítica literaria*, editado por Laureano Bonet. Barcelona: Península.

Pérez Garzón, Juan Sisinio et al. 2000. *La gestión de la memoria. La historia de España al servicio del poder*. Barcelona: Crítica.

Pérez Magallón, Jesús. 2002. *Construyendo la modernidad. La cultura española en el tiempo de los novatores (1675–1725)*. Madrid: CSIC.

Poblet, Josep Maria. 1967. *Frederic Soler, Pitarra*. Barcelona: Aedos.

Prádanos, Luis I. 2018. *Postgrowth Imaginaries: New Ecologies and Counterhegemonic Culture in Post-2008 Spain*. Liverpool: Liverpool University Press.

Prado, Antonio. 2011. *Escritoras anarco-feministas en "La Revista Blanca" (1898–1936). Matrimonio, familia y estado*. Madrid: Fundación de Estudios Libertarios Anselmo Lorenzo.

Prat de la Riba, Enric. 1908. "Importancia de la llengua dins del concepte de la nacionalitat." *Primer Congrés Internacional de la Llengua Catalana*, 665–9. Barcelona: Joaquim Horta.

Pym, Richard. 2007. *The Gypsies of Early Modern Spain, 1425–1783*. Basingstoke, UK: Palgrave Macmillan.

Quaggio, Giulia. 2014. *La cultura en transición. Reconciliación y política cultural en España, 1976–1986*. Madrid: Alianza Editorial.

Quiroga, Xabier. 2010. Interview with Xan Carballa. *El País* (22 January).

Rábade Villar, María do Cebreiro. 2011. "Cultural History and Resistance: The Articulation of Modern Galician Literature." In Hooper and Puga Moruxa, 54–73.

Rabaté, Colette, and Jean-Claude Rabaté. 2009. *Miguel de Unamuno. Biografía.* Madrid: Taurus.

Radcliff, Pamela Beth. 2011. *Making Democratic Citizens in Spain: Civil Society and the Popular Origins of the Transition, 1960–78.* Basingstoke, UK: Palgrave Macmillan.

Real, Neus. 1998. *El club femení i d'esports de Catalunya. Plataforma d'acció cultural.* Barcelona: Abadia de Montserrat.

Real, Neus. 2006. *Dona i literatura a la Catalunya de pre-guerra.* Barcelona: Abadia de Montserrat.

Resina, Joan Ramon. 2000. "The Time of the King: Gift and Exchange in Zorrilla's *Don Juan Tenorio.*" *Diacritics* 30: 49–77.

Resina, Joan Ramon. 2008. *Barcelona's Vocation of Modernity: Rise and Decline of an Urban Image.* Stanford, CA: Stanford University Press.

Resina, Joan Ramon, and William R. Viestenz, eds. 2012. *The New Ruralism: An Epistemology of Transformed Space.* Madrid: Iberoamericana / Frankfurt: Vervuert.

Retolaza, Iratxe, and Ibon Egaña. 2016. "The Gay, Lesbian and Transsexual Basque Novel." In *Contemporary Basque Literature,* edited by Jon Kortazar, 38–41. Reno, NV: Center for Basque Studies.

Richards, Michael. 2013. *After the Civil War: Making Memory and Re-Making Spain since 1936.* Cambridge: Cambridge University Press.

Rigobon, Patrizio. 2013. "Francisco María Tubino: Between Federalism and Iberianism." In *Iberian Modalities: A Relational Approach to the Study of Culture in the Iberian Peninsula,* edited by Joan Ramon Resina, 99–108. Liverpool: Liverpool University Press.

Río Raigadas, David. 2007. *Robert Laxalt: The Voice of Basques in North American Literature.* Reno, NV: Center for Basque Studies.

Ríos-Font, Wadda. 2004. "Literary History and Canon Formation." In *The Cambridge History of Spanish Literature,* edited by David T. Gies, 15–35. Cambridge: Cambridge University Press.

Rivière Gómez, Aurora. 2000. *Orientalismo y nacionalismo español. Estudios árabes y hebreos en la Universidad de Madrid (1843–1868).* Madrid: Universidad Carlos III de Madrid.

Robbins, Jill, ed. 2004. *P/Herversions: Critical Studies of Ana Rossetti.* Lewisburg, PA: Bucknell University Press.

Rodríguez, Francisco. 1990. *Literatura galega contemporánea. Problemas de método e interpretación.* Vigo: Cumio.

Rodríguez de Rivera, Itziar. 2017. "Backward Modernity? The Masculine Lesbian in Spanish Sicaliptic Literature." In Zamostny and Larson, 77–98.

Rodríguez-Gaona, Martín. 2019a. *Decir mi nombre. Muestra de poetas contemporáneas desde el entorno digital*. Lleida: Editorial Milenio.

Rodríguez-Gaona, Martín. 2019b. *La lira de las masas: Internet y la crisis de la ciudad letrada. Una aproximación a la poesía de los nativos digitales*. Madrid: Editorial Páginas de Espuma.

Rodríguez Sánchez, María José. 2004. "Prensa periódica y crítica literaria." In *Se hicieron literatos para ser políticos. Cultura y política en la España de Carlos IV y Fernando VII*, edited by Joaquín Álvarez Barrientos, 25–62. Madrid: Biblioteca Nueva.

Rodríguez Solás, David. 2014. *Teatros nacionales republicanos. La Segunda República y el teatro clásico español*. Madrid: Iberoamericana / Frankfurt: Vervuert.

Rogers, Gayle. 2012. *Modernism and the New Spain: Britain, Cosmopolitan Europe, and Literary History*. Oxford: Oxford University Press.

Romero, Eugenia R. 2012. *Contemporary Galician Culture in a Global Context: Movable Identities*. Lanham, MD: Lexington Books.

Romero Tobar, Leonardo. 1987. "Prensa periódica y discurso literario en la España del siglo XIX." In *La prensa española durante el siglo XIX*, edited by José Simón Díaz, 93–104. Almería: Instituto de Estudios Almerienses.

Roser i Puig, Montserrat. 2011. "Nostalgia and Exoticism in *El ben cofat i l'altre*, by Josep Carner." In Buffery, 145–60.

Ruano de la Haza, José María. 2012. "The World as a Stage: Politics, Imperialism and Spain's Seventeenth-Century Theatre." In M. Delgado and Gies, 57–78.

Rubí, Gemma, and Francesc Espinet, eds. 2008. *Solidaritat catalana i Espanya (1905–1909)*. Barcelona: Editorial Base.

Ruiz Salvador, Antonio. 1971. *El Ateneo Científico, Literario y Artístico de Madrid (1835–1885)*. London: Tamesis.

Ryan, Lorraine. 2014. *Memory and Spatiality in Post-Millennial Spanish Narrative*. Farnham, UK: Ashgate.

Salaün, Serge. 1985. *La poesía de la guerra de España*. Madrid: Castalia.

Salaün, Serge. 2011. *Les spectacles en Espagne (1875–1936)*. Paris: Presses Sorbonne Nouvelle.

Sampedro Vizcaya, Benita, and José A. Losada Montero, eds. 2017. *Rerouting Galician Studies: Multidisciplinary Interventions*. New York: Palgrave Macmillan.

Samsó, Joan. 1994–5. *La cultura catalana. Entre la clandestinitat i la represa pública (1939–1951)*, 2 vols. Barcelona: Abadia de Montserrat.

Sánchez Ferlosio, Rafael. 1984. "La cultura, ese invento del *gobierno*." *El País* (21 November), 11–12.

Sánchez Llama, Íñigo. 2000. *Galería de escritoras isabelinas. La prensa periódica entre 1833 y 1895*. Madrid: Cátedra.

Sánchez Ron, José Manuel. 2016. "La Ilustración española." *Mercurio* 185 (November). http://mercurio.fundacionjmlara.es/ediciones/2016/mercurio -185/la-ilustracion-espanola/.

Sanchis Guarner, Manuel. 1981. *Renaixença al Pais Valencià*. Valencia: Tres i Quatre.

Sansano, Gabriel. 2005. "Some Types of Short Theatre in Eighteenth-Century Valencia." *Catalan Review* 19: 265–84.

Sansano, Gabriel. 2009. *Un cabàs de rialles. Entremesos i col·loquis dramàtics valencians del segle XVIII*. Valls: Cossetània Edicions.

Santamarina, Antón. 2011. "Limiar do Dicionario de Dicionarios." Documentos. *Dicionario de Dicionarios*. Universidade de Vigo. Web.

Santana, Mario. 2000. *Foreigners in the Homeland: The Spanish American New Novel in Spain, 1962–1974*. Lewisburg, PA: Bucknell University Press.

Santonja, Gonzalo. 1993. *La novela revolucionaria de quiosco, 1905–1939*. Madrid: El Museo Universal.

Saum-Pascual, Alex. 2018. *#Postweb! Crear con la máquina y en la red*. Madrid: Iberoamericana/Frankfurt: Vervuert.

Sebold, Russell P. 2000. "Introducción." In José de Cadalso, *Cartas marruecas/ Noches lúgubres*, 15–125. Madrid: Cátedra.

Seguín, Bécquer. Forthcoming. *The Op-Ed Novel: Spain and the Politics of Literary Persuasion*. Cambridge, MA: Harvard University Press.

Segura, Antoni. 2006. *Catalunya any zero*. The Anglo-Catalan Society. www.anglo-catalan.org.

Seoane, Maria Cruz. 1997. "La literatura en el periódico y el periódico en la literatura." In *Periodismo y literatura*, edited by Annelies van Noortwijk and Anke van Haastrecht. Special issue of *Foro Hispánico* 12: 17–26.

Serrano, Carlos. 2000. "El 'nacimiento de los intelectuales'. Algunos replanteamientos." *Ayer* 40: 11–23.

Shaw, Donald L. 1963. "Towards the Understanding of Spanish Romanticism." *Modern Language Review* 58: 190–5.

Shoemaker, William H. 1973. *Las cartas desconocidas de Galdós en "La Prensa" de Buenos Aires*. Madrid: Cultura Hispánica.

Shubert, Adrian. 1990. *A Social History of Modern Spain*. London: Routledge.

Sinclair, Alison. 1977. *Valle-Inclán's "Ruedo Ibérico": A Popular View of Revolution*. London: Tamesis.

Sinclair, Alison. 1998. *Dislocations of Desire: Gender, Identity, and Strategy in "La Regenta"*. Chapel Hill, NC: University of North Carolina Press.

Sinclair, Alison. 2009. *Trafficking Knowledge in Early Twentieth-Century Spain: Centres of Exchange and Cultural Imaginaries*. Woodbridge, UK: Tamesis.

Škrabec, Simona. 2017. *Una pàtria prestada. Lectures de fragilitat en la literatura catalana*. Valencia: Publicacions de la Universitat de València.

Smith, Theresa Ann. 2003. "Writing Out the Margins: Women, Translation and the Spanish Enlightenment." *Journal of Women's History* 15 (1): 118–43.

Smith, Theresa Ann. 2006. *The Emerging Female Citizen: Gender and Enlightenment in Spain*. Berkeley: University of California Press.

Soguero García, Francisco Miguel. 2000. "Los narradores de vanguardia como renovadores del género biográfico. Aproximación a la biografía vanguard-ista." In *Hacia la novela nueva: Essays on the Spanish Avant-Garde Novel*, edited by Francis Lough, 199–217. Oxford: Peter Lang.

Solís Galván, Raúl. 2019. *La doble transición*. España: Libros.com

Song, H. Rosi. 2016. *Lost in Transition: Constructing Memory in Contemporary Spain*. Oxford: Oxford University Press.

Soria, Mar. 2019. "Colonial Imaginings on the Stage: Blackface, Gender, and the Economics of Empire in Spanish and Catalan Popular Theater." In *Unsettling Colonialism: Gender and Race in the Nineteenth-Century Global Hispanic World*, edited by N. Michelle Murray and Akiko Tsuchiya, 135–69. Albany, NY: SUNY Press.

Sosa-Velasco, Alfredo Jesús. 2010. *Médicos escritores en España, 1885–1955: Santiago Ramón y Cajal, Pío Baroja, Gregorio Marañón y Antonio Vallejo Nágera*. Woodbridge, UK: Tamesis.

Stolley, Karen. 2020. "Other Empires: Eighteenth-Century Hispanic Worlds and Global Enlightenment." In Lewis, Bolufer Peruga, and Jaffe, 17–29.

Subirana, Jaume. 2018. *Construir con palabras. Escritores, literatura e identidad en Cataluña (1859–2019)*. Madrid: Cátedra.

Subirats, Eduardo. 1981. *La Ilustración insuficiente*. Madrid: Taurus.

Surwillo, Lisa. 2007. *The Stages of Property: Copyrighting Theatre in Spain*. Toronto: University of Toronto Press.

Terry, Arthur. 2003. *A Companion to Catalan Literature*. Woodbridge, UK: Tamesis.

Threlfall, Monica. 2008. "Reassessing the Role of Civil Society Organizations in the Transition to Democracy in Spain." *Democratization* 15 (5): 930–51.

Torrealdai, Joan Mari. 1995. *La censura gubernativa y el libro vasco (1936–1983)*. Bilbao: Universidad de Deusto.

Torrealdai, Joan Mari. 1997. *Euskal Kultura Gaur*. Donostia: Jakin.

Torrecilla, Jesús. 1996. *El tiempo y los márgenes. Europa como utopía y como amenaza en la literatura española*. Chapel Hill, NC: University of North Carolina Press.

Torrents, Ricard. 2002. *Verdaguer. Un poeta per a un poble*. Vic: Eumo Editorial.

Torrents, Ricard. 2004. *A la claror de Verdaguer. Nous estudis i aproximacions*. Vic: Eumo.

Triadú, Joan, ed. 1950. *Antologia de contistes (1850–1950)*. Barcelona: Selecta.

Tsuchiya, Akiko. 2011. *Marginal Subjects: Gender and Deviance in Fin-de-Siècle Spain*. Toronto: Toronto University Press.

Tsuchiya, Akiko. 2015. "Género, asociacionismo y discurso antiesclavista en la obra de Faustina Sáez de Melgar (1834–1895)." In *"No hay nación para este sexo". La Re(d)pública transatlántica de las Letras: escritoras españolas y latinoamericanas (1824–1936)*, edited by Pura Fernández, 111–30. Madrid: Iberoamericana/Frankfurt: Vervuert.

Tsuchiya, Akiko, and William G. Acree, eds. 2016. *Empire's End: Transnational Connections in the Hispanic World*. Nashville, TN: Vanderbilt University Press.

Tuñón de Lara, Manuel. 1972. *El movimiento obrero en la historia de España*. Madrid: Taurus.

Tusell, Javier, and Álvaro Soto Carmona, eds. 1996. *Historia de la transición (1975–1986)*. Madrid: Alianza.

Ucelay da Cal, Enric. 2003. *El imperialismo catalán. Prat de la Riba, Cambó, D'Ors y la conquista moral de España*. Barcelona: Edhasa.

Ugalde, Mercedes. 1993. *Mujeres y nacionalismo vasco. Génesis y desarrollo de Emakume Abertzale Batza (1906–1936)*. Bilbao: UPV.

Urgell, Blanca. 2018. "Primer vasco moderno." In *Historia de la lengua vasca*, edited by Joaquín Gorrochategui Churruca, Iván Igartua Ugarte, and Joseba Andoni Lakarra Andrinua, 593–716. Vitoria-Gasteiz: Gobierno Vasco.

Uría, Jorge. 2003. "La taberna. Un espacio multifuncional de sociabilidad popular en la Restauración española." *Hispania* 63: 571–604.

Valero, José Antonio. 2002. "Razón y nación en la política cultural del primer dieciocho." *Espéculo: Revista de Estudios Literarios* 22. https://webs.ucm.es/info/especulo/numero22/razon18.html.

Valis, Noël Maureen. 2003. *The Culture of Cursilería: Bad Taste, Kitsch, and Class in Modern Spain*. Durham, NC: Duke University Press.

Vallverdú, Francesc. 1980. *Pompeu Fabra. La llengua catalana i la seva normalització*. Barcelona: Edicions 62.

Van Horne Melton, James. 2001. *The Rise of the Public in Enlightenment Europe*. Cambridge: Cambridge University Press.

Vega, Jesusa. 2010. *Ciencia, arte e ilusión en la España ilustrada*. Madrid: CSIC.

Vega, Rexina. n.d. "Converterse en escritora." Centro de documentación da *Asociación de Escritores en Lingua Galega*. https://www.aelg.gal/centro-documentacion/autores-as/rexina-vega/paratextos/2987/converterse-en-escritora

Venuti, Lawrence. 2019. "Introduction." In J.V. Foix, *Daybook 1918. Early Fragments*, edited and translated by Lawrence Venuti, xiii–xxxii. Evanston, IL: Northwestern University Press.

Vilarós, Teresa M. 2018. *El mono del desencanto: Una crítica cultural de la transición española (1973–1993)*, 2nd edn. Madrid: Siglo XXI.

Vilaseca, David. 2000. "The Ambassadors Goes to Manila: The Postcolonial Gaze in Gil de Biedma's *Retrato del artista en 1956*." *Journal of Spanish Cultural Studies* 1 (1): 75–87.

Vilavedra, Dolores. 1999. *Historia da literatura galega*. Vigo: Galaxia.

Vilavedra, Dolores. 2010. "Political Autonomy and Literary Institutionalization in Galicia." In *New Spain, New Literatures*, edited by Luis Martín-Estudillo and Nicholas Spadaccini, 117–34. Nashville, TN: Vanderbilt University Press.

Villacañas Berlanga, José Luis. 2000. *Ramiro de Maeztu y el ideal de la burguesía en España*. Madrid: Espasa.

Villares, Ramón. 2007. Interview with Camilo Franco. *Culturas. La Voz de Galicia* (11 August), 13.

Villares, Ramón, and Javier Moreno Luzón. 2009. *Restauración y dictadura*. Vol. 7 of *Historia de España*, edited by Josep Fontana and Ramón Villares. Barcelona: Crítica.

Viñao Fraga, Antonio. 1990. "The History of Literacy in Spain: Evolution, Traits, and Questions." *History of Education Quarterly* 30: 573–99.

Volkova, Ekaterina. 2017. "Sargadelos and the Aesthetic Formation of Galician Identity." In Sampedro Vizcaya and Losada Montero, 315–30.

Wheeler, Duncan. 2011. "¿La película duende?: María Teresa León, Rafael Alberti and Alternative Traditions of Resurrecting Golden Age Drama." In Buffery, 71–93.

Wilhelmi, Gonzalo. 2016. *Romper el consenso. La izquierda radical en la transición española (1975–1982)*. Madrid: Siglo XXI.

Williams, Raymond. [1975] 1980. "Base and Superstructure in Marxist Cultural Theory." In *Problems in Materialism and Culture*, 31–49. London: Verso.

Williams, Raymond. [1977] 2009. *Marxism and Literature*. Oxford: Oxford University Press.

Yañez, Maria. 2019. "Cultura dixital. Voluntaria, anónima e poucas veces sustentable." *Praza* (9 February). https://praza.gal/cultura/cultura-dixital-voluntaria-anonima-e-poucas-veces-sustentable.

Yates, Alan. 1975. *Una generació sense novel·la?* Barcelona: Edicions 62.

Yates, Alan. 1998. *Narcís Oller. Tradició i talent individual*. Barcelona: Curial-Abadia de Montserrat.

Zambrano, María. 1967. *La tumba de Antígona*. Mexico City: Siglo XXI.

Zambrano, María. 2009. *Las palabras del regreso*, edited by Mercedes Gómez Blesa. Madrid: Cátedra.

Zambrano, María. 2014. *El exilio como patria*, edited by Juan Fernando Ortega Muñoz. Barcelona: Anthropos.

Zamostny, Jeffrey, and Susan Larson, eds. 2017. *Kiosk Literature of Silver Age Spain: Modernity and Mass Culture*. Bristol: Intellect.

Zanardi, Tara. 2016. *Framing Majismo: Art and Royal Identity in Eighteenth-Century Spain*. University Park, PA: Penn State University Press.

Zubiaurre, Maite. 2012. *Cultures of the Erotic in Spain, 1898–1939*. Nashville, TN: Vanderbilt University Press.

Index

15-M 279, 288
1812 Constitution 16, 21–2, 24–5, 255
1868 Revolution 28, 38, 52, 54, 55, 58, 60–1, 92, 98, 99, 110, 131, 160
1898 Generation 77, 141–4, 161
1978 Constitution 208–9, 221, 223, 269, 275, 290

Abad, Mercedes 238
Abelló, Montserrat 230–1, 232
Abreu, Andrea 292
Abril, Guillermo 290
absolutism 13, 17, 22–4, 28–9, 48–9, 54, 60, 85, 86–7, 89, 90, 151
academies 9, 13, 42, 44–5, 47, 59–60, 71, 91, 97, 159, 221
    Galician Royal Academy 67, 80, 155, 218, 234, 286
    Spanish Royal Academy 28, 34, 44, 50, 59, 63, 86, 136, 189, 193, 224–5
Acuña, Rosario de 60–1, 143
Adema, Gratien (Zaldubi) 83
Adón, Pilar 243, 292
Agboton, Agnès 276, 291
aging 241–2, 272, 290
Agirre, Domingo 82, 97, 159
Agirre, Katixa 282
Aguiló, Marià 72–3, 92
Agustí, Ignacio 172
Aitzol (José Ariztimuño) 116, 185, 195
Alarcón, Pedro Antonio de 51–2
Alas, Leopoldo (Clarín) 37–40, 52–4, 56, 59, 60–1, 126–8, 135
Alba, Duchess of 42, 45
Alba, Duke of 42
Alba, Víctor (Pere Pagés i Elies) 202
Alba Rico, Santiago 271
Alberdi, Uxue 264, 282
Albert, Caterina (Victor Català) 72, 135, 140, 230, 232
Albert Sopale, Silvia 290

Alberti, Rafael 123–4, 131, 167, 170–1, 188–9, 191, 206–7
Alcalá Galiano, Antonio 25
Alcover, Antoni 115
Aldecoa, Ignacio 225
Aldecoa, Josefina 225–6, 250–1
Aleixandre, Marilar 201, 234
Aleixandre, Vicente 226
Alfaro, José María 172–3
Algarra, Maria Lluïsa 180, 192, 230
Alicia Bajo Cero 272
Almirall, Valentí 72, 74, 93–4, 115
Alomar, Gabriel 135
Alonso, Dámaso 174, 288
Alonso, Fran 287
Alonso, María 285
Altadill, Antonio 112
Altamira, Rafael 8
Altolaguirre, Manuel 171
Altzaga, Toribio 117–18
Alvarez Enparantza, Jose Luis (Txillardegi) 186
Álvarez Negreira, Emilio 184
Álvarez Quintero, Joaquín 111
Álvarez Quintero, Serafín 111
Alzamora, Sebastià 276
Amador, Margarita 121
Amador de los Ríos, José 104
Amar y Borbón, Josefa 19, 45
Amat, Jordi 276
Amat Piniella, Joaquim 201
Ameixeiras, Diego 286
Amorós, Celia 270
anarchism 60–1, 94, 115, 120–1, 128, 131, 134, 142, 149, 150–2, 162, 165–8, 179, 201
Andrés y Morell, Juan 14, 88, 104
Andújar, Manuel 206
Aneiros, Rosa 262
Angelon, Manuel 112
Anglada, Maria Àngels 253
Añón, Francisco 76
anticlericalism 60–1, 80, 91, 110, 115, 121, 126

Antolí, Rosana 290
Antonio, Manuel 156
Apoalaza, Uxue 265
Aramburu, Fernando 265, 271
Arana, Sabino 98, 117, 147, 157–8, 160, 185
Arana, Vicente de 84, 97
Aranbarri, Iñigo 263
Aranda, Count of 46–7
Aranguren, José Luis 173
Araquistáin, Juan Venancio 97
Arconada, César M. 124, 129, 167, 171
Arderiu, Clementina 230, 232
Arenal, Concepción 59, 77
Aresti, Gabriel 186–7, 218, 221
Argentina 28, 56, 154, 176, 247, 251–2
    emigration to 138, 155, 198
    exile in 153, 183, 196, 199, 205–7
Aribau, Bonaventura Carles 65, 71, 91–2, 104
Arniches, Carlos 110–11
Arquimbau, Rosa Maria 230
Arrabal, Fernando 177
Arregi Diaz de Heredia, Rikardo 237
Arrese-Beitia, Felipe 83
Artze, Joxean 219
Arús, Rossend 114
Astiz, Iñigo 281
Atxaga, Bernardo 187, 196–7, 219–20, 222, 237,
    263–5, 277, 280
Aub, Max 170–1, 190–3, 206
autofiction 207, 237, 241, 268, 272, 278, 281,
    289
    autobiography 23, 33, 34–5, 149, 191, 197,
        205, 224, 226–7, 229, 239–40, 242–3,
        248, 249, 254
autonomy statutes 208
    Basque 221
    Catalan 147, 178, 213, 273
    Galician 183
avant-garde 79, 100, 101, 123, 128–31, 135,
    154, 167–70, 173–4, 177, 219–20, 222,
    242, 254
Ayala, Francisco 130–1, 167, 189–91, 193, 207
Ayerbe, Mikel 263
Ayguals de Izco, Wenceslao 109–10, 126
Aymar, Àngels 190, 233
Azkue, Resurreccion Maria 68, 84, 117–18,
    158–9, 195
Azorín (José Martínez Ruiz) 53, 142–3, 149
Azpeitia, Julene 159
Azúa, Félix de 274, 276

Balaguer, Víctor 72–73, 93, 112, 132
ballad tradition 25, 90, 103–5, 107–8, 123, 149,
    167, 170–1, 185

Ballot, Josep Pau 92
Baltasar, Eva 278
Barbal, Maria 233, 253, 257, 259
Barbero, Edmundo 190
Barbier, Jean 160
Barea, Arturo 191
Baroja, Carmen 143
Baroja, Pío 99, 121, 128, 142–4, 148–9, 161–2
Baroja, Ricardo 128
Baroja, Serafín 118
Barral, Carlos 178, 210
Barreras, Federico 155
Barros, Tomás 184
Bartra, Agustí 182, 202, 206
Basque literature 62, 67–8, 81–4, 96–8, 116–18,
    157–60, 185–7, 195–8, 219–22, 235–7,
    263–6, 279–83
Batania Neorrabioso 290
Batlle, Carles 259, 274
Bauçà, Miquel 274–5
Bécquer, Gustavo Adolfo 35–6, 50, 52–3, 55, 90,
    108, 136–7
Bécquer, Valeriano 36
Bela-Lobbede, Desirée 290
Belbel, Sergi 215, 274
Belda, Joaquín 122
Bell-Lloch, Maria 93
Bendahan, Esther 290
Benet, Juan 178, 247
Benet i Jornet, Josep Maria 210, 215, 274
Beneyto, Maria 230, 232
Benguerel, Xavier 180, 203
Bergamín, José 169, 173, 188, 190–1
Bergnes de las Casas, Antoni 65, 92
Bergon, Frank 196
Bernabé, Daniel 271
Bernaldo de Quirós, Constancio 144
Bernat, Roger 289
Bernat i Baldoví, Josep 113
Bertrana, Aurora 180, 230, 232
Bertrana, Prudenci 139
bertsolaritza see orality
Bezsonoff, Joan-Daniel 276
Bilintx (Indalecio Bizkarrondo) 118
Blanco Amor, Eduardo 199, 235
Blanco White, Joseph 23–4, 49, 53
Blasco Ibáñez, Vicente 52, 109, 121, 128, 138
Boadella, Albert 215–16, 276
Bofarull, Antoni de 72–3, 92–3, 112
Bofill, Ricard 216
Böhl de Faber, Juan Nicolás 25–6, 107
Bonaparte, Louis Lucien 68
Bonet, Blai 211, 233
Bonet, Paula 233, 290

Borda, Itxaro 222, 236, 281
Borges, Jorge Luis 154, 220
Borrozás, Xurxo 261
Bosch, Alfred 259
Bosch, Lolita 277
Botín Polanco, Antonio 131
Bousoño, Carlos 226
Bouterwek, Friedrich 103
Bouza-Brey, Fermín 182
Brañas, Alfredo 154–5
Brieva, Miguel 290
Brines, Francisco 226, 229
broadsheets 107–8, 116, 123
Broncano, Fernando 271
Brossa, Jaume 134, 162–3
Brossa, Joan 182, 211, 215
Bruch, Araceli 231, 233
Buchaca, Marta 233, 289
Buero Vallejo, Antonio 176–7
Buñuel, Luis 124, 129, 137
Burgas, Josep 114
Burgos, Carmen de (Columbine) 53, 121, 128, 143, 165–6
Bustintza, Errose 159

Caballero, Fernán (Cecilia Böhl de Faber) 37, 54, 108
Caballero Audaz, El (José María Carretero) 122
Cabanas, Edgar 271
Cabanillas, Ramón 184
Cabarrús, Francisco 15, 42, 45
CaboSanRoque 289
Cabré, Jaume 211, 258
Cabrerizo, Mariano 65
Cabriada, Juan de 9, 16
Cadalso, José 8, 18, 20–1, 30, 42–3, 48
café cantante 111, 122–3
Calderón de la Barca, Pedro 25, 46, 106
Calders, Pere 116, 180, 202–3
Calé, Emilia 77
Cámara, Miguel de 52
Cambó, Francesc 144
camp 229–30
Campión, Arturo 84, 117, 159
Campomanes, Pedro Rodríguez de 44, 45
Camps, Victoria 270
Candel, Francisco 211, 258
Canitrot, Prudencio 119
Cano, Harkaitz 264, 266
Cánovas del Castillo, Antonio 86
Cantelli, Marcos 290
Capdevila, Carles 276
Capmany, Antoni de 69, 92
Capmany, Maria Aurèlia 181, 230–1

Caramuel, Juan 16
Cardoso, Isaac 15
Carlism 81, 85, 90, 92–3, 96, 98–9, 116, 148, 150–1, 162, 196–7
Carlos II 18
Carlos III 17, 31, 45–6, 48–9, 103, 106
Carlos IV 107
Carlos V, Holy Roman Emperor (Carlos I of Spain) 8
Carner, Josep 134, 180, 202–3
Carnés, Luisa 130–1, 168–9, 171, 192
Carrasco, Jesús 292
Carré Aldao, Eugenio 155
Carretero, Nacho 286
Carrión, Jorge 290
Carvalho Calero, Ricardo 183–4, 216
Casajuana, Carles 277
Casanova, Sofía 119
Casanovas, Jordi 241, 289
Casares, Carlos 217
Casares, Maria 207
Casavella, Francisco 268
Casellas, Raimon 139, 162–3
Casona, Alejandro 169, 207
Castaño, Yolanda 235
Castelao, Alfonso Daniel Rodríguez 157, 182–3, 198–9, 200
Castellanos, Jordi 210
Castellet, José María 175–6, 210
casticismo 11, 15, 58, 80, 99, 106–7, 110, 135, 143, 147
Castilian, imposition of 1, 10, 12–13, 21, 46, 63–4, 66–9, 103, 113, 155, 159, 180–1, 183, 188, 230, 280
Castro, Plácido 183
Castro, Rosalía de 36–7, 66, 77–81, 96, 120, 136, 155, 198, 233–4, 284
Castro Moura, Amador 261
Catalan independence movement 259, 276–7, 278–9
Catalan literature 63–5, 69–75, 91–4, 111–16, 131–5, 139–40, 160–4, 178–82, 193–5, 201–5, 208–16, 230–3, 256–60, 273–9
Catena Cózar, Carlos 290
Catholicism 25, 28, 35, 54–5, 57, 82, 94, 120, 145–9, 151, 157, 158, 160, 163, 169, 173–4, 195, 197, 206–7, 239
    Catholic Church 6, 14–15, 17, 19, 42, 44, 80, 94, 137, 163, 173
    see also Inquisition
Cebreiro, Álvaro 156
Cedó, Clàudia 289
Cela, Camilo José 52, 176, 184, 194, 238
Celaya, Gabriel 174–5, 187

censorship 16, 23, 36, 46–9, 52, 54, 80, 86, 99,
    115, 164, 165, 176–7, 178, 181, 184,
    186–7, 208, 210, 246, 256, 272
    see also Inquisition
centralization 8, 11–14, 41, 63, 64, 99, 103, 105,
    276
Cercas, Javier 249, 253, 255, 268, 271–2, 277
Cerdà, Jordi Pere 182
Cerdà, Paco 291
Cernuda, Luis 170, 191, 224, 226, 229
Cerquand, François 117
Chacel, Rosa 100, 154, 192, 224
Chacón, Dulce 261
Chaho, Agustin 65, 83, 96–7
Champourcin, Ernestina 192
children's literature 82, 175, 179, 222, 225–6,
    235–6, 239–40, 283
Chirbes, Rafael 228, 254–5, 268, 289
Christianity 26, 89, 91, 97, 174, 257
    see also Catholicism
cinema 121, 122, 130–1, 168, 169, 176, 190, 218,
    238, 256, 259, 281, 282
    adaptations 52, 74, 206, 246, 248, 261
    influence of 124, 129, 135, 229
Claramunt, Teresa 61
Clark, Ben 288
class 3, 27, 39, 43, 102, 106, 113, 130, 143, 152,
    205, 212–13, 227, 232, 284
    middle classes 24, 98, 204, 272, 280
    working classes 58, 60–1, 94, 109–11, 121,
    127–8, 133, 153, 157, 169, 175–7, 248
Clavé, Josep Anselm 114
Clavijo y Fajardo, José 45, 48
Climent, Eliseu 214
Clua, Guillem 274
Coca, Jordi 211, 258
colonialism *see* empire
coloniality 10, 14, 79, 136, 139, 146, 149, 227,
    231, 263
Comadira, Narcís 211, 233
Comas, Antoni 211
Comediants 215
Cómicos de la Legua 220
communism 121, 153, 165, 167–71, 174–6, 179,
    189, 201, 226, 248–9, 254, 257
Companys, Lluís 115, 201–2, 278
Conde, Alfredo 216
Conde, Carmen 59, 224
Conde, José Antonio 88
consensus, culture of 267–70, 271–2
Coromines, Pere 162
Coronado, Carolina 32–3, 136
Correyero, Isla 242–3, 272
Cortada, Joan 86, 91–2, 112

Cortiella, Felip 114, 134, 163
Cortina, Adela 270
cosmopolitanism 26, 32, 99, 117, 132–3, 135,
    147, 154, 160–4, 189, 219–20, 252, 257,
    262, 271, 281
Costa, Joaquín 144
Costas, Ledicia 285
costumbrismo 37, 53, 82–3, 101, 107, 113, 118,
    120, 126, 132, 159–60, 176, 217, 232,
    248
Creus, Jaume 233
Cruz, Juan de la 106–7
Cruz, Ramón de la 10, 21, 42, 106–7, 112–13
Cuba 23, 33, 35, 52, 59, 98, 141, 143, 152, 226
    exile in 205–6
    migration to 79–81, 138, 145, 174, 231, 257,
    262
Cuéllar, Francesc 289
Cuña Novás, Manuel 184
Cunillé, Lluïsa 233, 273–4, 289
Cunqueiro, Álvaro 182–4, 217
Curros Enríquez, Manuel 79–81
Custodio, Álvaro 206

d'Abbadie, Antoine 68, 82
Dagoll Dagom 215
Dalí, Salvador 135
d'Argullol, Josep 93
Darío, Rubén 36, 141–2
Darriba, Manuel 292
Daskonagerre, Jean-Baptiste 97
Dato Muruais, Filomena 233
de los Ríos, Blanca 143
decadence 7, 17–18, 21, 64, 68, 143–4, 146, 149,
    151, 162
d'Efak, Guilem 182
Defreds 290
degeneracy theory 39, 127–8, 143–4, 148
del Molino, Sergio 291
Delgado, Manuel 51
Delibes, Miguel 255
Desclot, Bernat 63
diaspora 182, 195–6, 200–1, 206, 257, 284, 290
    see also migration, emigration; exile
Díaz, Jenn 292
Díaz de Rivera, Carmen 268
Díaz Fernández, José 130, 168
Díaz Pardo, Isaac 199, 200, 260
Díaz-Plaja, Aurora 232
Dicenta, Joaquín 61
Dieste, Rafael 170–1, 199
digital literature 286–7, 289–90
diglossia 64–6, 68, 118–20, 275
Dimas i Graells, Joaquim 113

disability 241–2, 244, 284, 289
do Cebreiro Rábade Villar, María 235
d'Olwer, Nicolau 180
d'Ors, Eugeni (Xènius) 134–5, 163–4
Dueñas, María 252
Duncan, Denise 276
Durán, Agustín 25, 104
Durán, Carlos 200
Durán, Manuel 193
Durão, Carlos 193
Duval, Elizabeth 241–2
dystopia 256, 281, 284–5, 292

Echegaray, José 74
ecology 138–9, 240, 268, 276–9, 281, 284, 287, 291–2
economic crisis 241, 268, 273, 278, 279, 281, 283–4, 286, 288–9
  see also precarity
education 15, 19, 26, 44, 54, 63, 138, 144, 149–50, 153, 169–70
  auto-didact 57, 140, 168, 175
  Basque 68, 84, 117, 158, 185, 209, 221
  Catalan 65, 70, 132, 161–2, 179–80, 202, 205, 208–10, 213–14, 275
  female 47, 55, 166
  Galician 66, 209, 260
  and nation formation 85–6, 103, 105
  see also Castilian, imposition of; literacy
Egaña, Andoni 263
Eizagirre, José 197
El Hachmi, Najat 233, 276, 290
El Kadaoui, Saïd 276
El Morabet, Mohamed 290
Eleizegi, Katalina 158–9
Elio, María Luisa 192
Elizanburu, Jean Baptiste 82–3
Elorrieta, Irati 281
Eloy-García, María 243
empire 1, 11, 22–3, 78, 87, 91, 137, 141, 143, 146, 152, 162–3, 168
  see also coloniality; Cuba; Morocco; Philippines
Enlightenment 12–22, 28–31, 34, 42–6, 48, 58–9, 66, 105–6, 255
environment *see* ecology
Epaltza, Aingeru 196, 263
eroticism 18–19, 30, 36, 120–2, 143, 189, 224, 227, 238–9, 243
Ertzilla, Manu 220
Escalante, Eduard 113
Escudé, Beth 233, 289
Espada, Arcadi 275–6
Espina, Antonio 100, 129

Espina, Concha 121, 138–9, 140, 143
Espinosa, David 289
Espriu, Salvador 181–2, 203
Espronceda, José de 24–6, 30, 32, 51, 90, 100, 108
Estébanez Calderón, Serafín 53, 90, 126
Estellés, Vicent Andrés 182
Estelrich, Joan 180
ETA (Euskadi Ta Askatasuna) 186, 196–7, 220, 236, 243, 245, 263–6, 281–2
Etchart, Martin 196
Etxahun (Pierre Topet) 116
Etxaniz, Nemesio 196
Etxebarría, Lucía 239
Etxeberri, Joanes 68
Etxeberria, Hasier 237
Etxegoien, Fermin 280
Etxeita, José Manuel 159, 195
Etxepare, Bernard 81
Etxepare, Jean 160
exile 22–6, 49, 85, 87, 148, 162, 177, 196–7
  Republican 116, 150, 153, 167, 173, 176, 181–5, 188–207
Expósito, Marcelo 289

Fabra, Pompeu 65, 73, 140, 161, 180
Falange Española 131, 138, 152, 165, 172–5, 184, 193, 249
Falcones, Ildefonso 255
Falla, Manuel de 123
Fandiño, Antonio Benito 76
Faraldo, Antolín 75–6, 95
Farinelli 106
fascism 13, 150–1, 153, 165, 168, 172, 201, 247, 253, 264
  see also Falange Española
Feijoo, Father Benito 8, 14–19, 30, 42, 57
Felipe V 7–8, 11–12, 14
Felipe, León 191
Feliu i Codina, Josep 93
feminism 28, 39, 57, 61, 71, 121, 165–7, 180, 212–13, 225, 230–1, 233–7, 240–1, 268, 270, 279, 282, 284–5, 287, 289, 291
  see also gender
Fernàndez, David 276
Fernández, Lluís 232
Fernández Anciles, Francisco 77
Fernández de la Vega, Celestino 184
Fernández del Riego, Francisco 184
Fernández de Neira, José 76
Fernández Mallo, Agustín 252
Fernández Santos, Jesús 176
Fernández y González, Francisco 91
Fernández y González, Manuel 52, 91, 109

Fernando VI 106
Fernando VII 22–4, 85, 87, 89, 98
Fernán Gómez, Fernando 248
Ferrater, Gabriel 210–11
Ferreiro, Celso Emilio 184, 187, 200, 216
Ferres, Antonio 175
Figuera Aymerich, Ángela 175
Floral Games
    Jocs Florals 64, 71–3, 82, 91, 93–4, 103, 112,
        114–15, 117, 160, 163, 202
    Lore Jokoak 81–3, 158, 195
    Xogos Florais 76
Flotats, Josep Maria 275
Foix, J. V. 139, 180
Folch i Torres, Joaquim 180
folk culture 80, 82, 90, 101, 107–8, 111, 114,
    117, 120, 122–3, 149–50, 159, 169–70,
    185–6, 213, 235
    see also ballad tradition
folletín see serialized novel
Fonte, Ramiro 200
Forner, Juan Pablo 8
Fortún Elena (Encarnación Aragoneses) 226
Fraga, Xesús 200
Franc, Isabel 243
France 44, 47–8, 54, 70, 142, 227, 237
    cultural influence of 63, 110, 112, 145,
        175–6, 217, 236
    hostility to 10, 15–16, 21, 46, 156
    exile in 24–5, 88–9, 148, 177, 180, 192–3, 201,
        205–7, 252–3
    French Basque Country 67–8, 81–3, 99, 116,
        157, 160, 196, 217
    hegemony of 6, 8–10, 14
    see also Peninsular War; War of the Spanish
        Succession
Franco, Camilo 287
Franco, Francisco 148, 172–3
    Franco dictatorship 88, 101, 122, 165, 171,
        172–8, 180, 183, 185, 194, 201, 223,
        246–54, 257
    Francoism 8, 174–5, 196–7, 200, 204, 224–5,
        227–9, 255, 262
    see also censorship; Spanish Civil War
freemasonry 60–1
Freud, Sigmund 38–40, 153
Fuchs, Ximun 281
Fuertes, Gloria 175, 225
Fura dels Baus, La 215
Fusi, Juan Pablo 270
Fuster, Joan 203, 211–12, 214

Gabancho, Patricia 233, 276
Gala, Antonio 255

Galdós *see* Pérez Galdós
Galician literature 65–7, 75–81, 95–6, 154–7,
    182–5, 198–201, 218–19, 233–5, 260–3,
    283–7
Gallego, Javier 290
Gallego, Juan 290
Gallego, Vicente 272
Gálvez, María Rosa 47, 87
Gamoneda, Antonio 272–3
Gandiaga, Bittoriano 219
Ganivet, Ángel 142–3, 146
Garay de Monglave, Francisque-Eugène 97
Garcerá, Fran 288
Garcés, Marina 271, 276, 278–9
García, Rodrigo 289
García, Txus 243
García Balmaseda, Joaquina 55
García de la Huerta, Vicente 87
García Faet, Berta 290
García Gutiérrez, Antonio 26, 50, 89
García Hortelano, Juan 176
García Lorca, Federico 123, 161, 167, 169–70,
    173, 185, 193, 206, 223
García Márquez, Gabriel 203
García Montero, Luis 36, 272
Garde, Luis 264, 281
Garfias, Pedro 171
Garro, Lander 282
Gasch, Sebastià 135
Gayangos, Pascual 88
gay rights 227–30, 232–3, 235, 237, 240
gender 10, 17–22, 27–40, 43, 55, 59–60, 79,
    82–3, 87, 127, 138–40, 205, 223–44, 274,
    282–3, 285, 287
    femininity 21, 33–8, 174, 224–5, 283
    homoeroticism 223–4, 226–7, 229, 233, 242,
        284
    homosexuality 121, 122, 223–4, 226–30
    homosociality 18, 42, 45, 59–60
    lesbianism 167, 226, 228, 231–2, 236, 237,
        240, 281
    masculinity 18–20, 38–40, 143, 148, 227, 283
    queerness 18, 122, 223, 225–9, 232, 235, 237,
        239, 242–3
    see also camp; feminism; gay rights;
        sexuality; transgender rights
género chico see sainete; zarzuela
Germany 9, 48, 145, 152, 177, 201, 252
Gil-Albert, Juan 224, 226, 229
Gil de Biedma, Jaime 174–5, 209, 226–7
Gil y Carrasco, Enrique 26, 90
Gil y Zárate, Antonio 103–4
Giménez Barbat, Teresa 276
Giménez Bartlett, Alicia 249

Giménez Caballero, Ernesto 124, 131, 167–8, 172
Gimeno de Flaquer, Concepción 55
Gimferrer, Pere 211
Goenaga, Aizpea 282–3
Goethe, Johann Wolfgang 32, 38, 163
Goia, Gorazi 197, 264
Goizueta, José María de 97
Golden Age drama 104, 105–6, 147, 170–1
    see also Calderón de la Barca; Lope de Vega
Gómez de Avellaneda, Gertrudis 32–6, 52, 59
Gómez de la Serna, Ramón 53, 121, 124, 129, 131
Gonsar, Camilo 217
Gopegui, Belén 268, 271, 289
Goya, Francisco José de 10, 42, 45, 58, 107
Goytisolo, José Agustín 174
Goytisolo, Juan 165, 175–6, 181, 226–7, 248
Gracia, Teresa 192
Gramsci, Antonio 101, 150, 169, 210
Grandes, Almudena 238–9, 250–1, 254, 271
graphic narrative 233, 243, 290
Grassi, Ángela 37, 55
Graupera, Ángela 121
Grimaldi, Juan de 105
Grosso, Alfonso 175
Grumelot 289
Gual, Adrià 163, 181
Guilarte, Cecilia 192
Guillamon, Julià 274, 277
Guillén, Jorge 191
Guimerà, Àngel 71, 73–5, 114, 139–40
Guiu, Víctor 291
Gustavo, Soledad 121
Guzmán y de la Cerda, María Isidra Quintina 45
gypsies 12–13, 21, 89, 111, 123, 134

Hachemi, Munir 290
Haritschelhar, Jean 221
Hartzenbusch, Juan Eugenio 88, 108
Hernández, Miguel 170–1
Herran, Fermín 84
Herrera Garrido, Francisca 120, 157, 233
Herrera Petere, José 171
Hickey, Margarita 19
Hiribarren, Jean Martin 83, 116
hispanidad 145
historiography
    Basque 96–7
    Catalan 70, 91–3
    Galician 80, 95–7, 260
    national 15–16, 86, 88
    women's 232

workers' 101
    see also literary history
Holocaust 247–8, 252–3
homoeroticism *see* gender
homosexuality *see* gay rights; gender
homosociality *see* gender
Hoyos, Antonio de 122, 229
Huidobro, Vicente 170
Humboldt, Wilhelm von 68, 82, 117

Ibáñez, Paco 174
Ibárruri, Dolores 191
Ibarz, Mercè 231, 257, 277
Ibsen, Henrik 132, 163
Iglesia Alvariño, Aquilino 182
Iglésias, Ignasi 114
illness 40, 242–3, 282
Innerarity, Daniel 271
Inquisition 15, 19, 27–8, 32, 44, 47–8, 54, 90, 255, 257, 258
Insúa, Alberto 119, 122
intellectual property rights 49–52, 109, 166
Intxitxu 220
Iparragirre, José María 116
Irazusta, Jon Andoni 197
Irene X 290
Iriarte, Tomás de 52
Irigoien, Joan Mari 219
Iriondo, Lurdes 235
Isusi, Javier de 290
Iturbe, Antonio G. 253
Iturralde, Joxe Mari 220, 263
Iturralde y Suit, Juan 84
Izagirre, Koldo 220
Iztueta, Juan Ignazio 82, 117

Jaén, María 238
Jaio, Karmele 237, 283
Jaka, Ana 280
Jarnés Benjamín 100
Jarrai 187
Jaume I 63, 113
Jews 11, 87, 89, 90, 110, 161, 175, 192, 231, 246, 252–3, 257, 264, 290
Jimenez, Edorta 263
Jiménez, Juan Ramón 38, 191
Jòdar, Julià de 258
Joglars, Els 215–16, 269
journalism 24, 26, 53–8, 115, 119, 125, 167–8, 185, 213, 232, 263, 268, 276
    see also magazines; press
Jovellanos, Gaspar Melchor de 15–17, 20, 31, 42–3, 45, 48, 52
Joyes y Blake, Inés 19

Juaristi, Jon 220, 270, 272
Junoy, Josep Maria 180

Karr, Carme 232
Karrouch, Laila 276
kiosk literature (novella series) 120–2, 151,
    166–7
Kirikiño (Ebaristo Bustintza) 196
Kopf, Alicia 278
Krausism 144, 169

Laforet, Carmen 175, 235
Lafuente, Modesto 86
Lago Valladares, Valentina (Hipólita Muíno)
    233
Laín Entralgo, Pedro 172–3
Lama, María Xesús 270
Lamarka, Iñigo 237
Landa, Mariasun 222, 236
Landart, Daniel 237
Landero, Luis 254, 272
landscape 83, 94, 96, 129, 132, 136–40, 149, 160,
    181, 183, 232, 261, 292
Lange, Monique 227
Larra, Mariano José de 8, 24, 26, 32, 50–1, 53,
    55, 90, 105, 125
Larralde, Jean Baptiste 83
Larramendi, Manuel 68
Lasa, Amaia 236
Lasagabaster, Jesús María 221
Lasala, Magdalena 255
Latin America *see* Spanish America
Lauaxeta (Estepan Urkiaga) 116, 185
Laxalt, Monique 196
Laxalt, Robert 196
Lázaro Galdiano, José 57
learned societies *see* academies
Lekuona, Juan Mari 197, 219
Lemos, Countess of 42
León, María Teresa 167, 171, 192, 206
Lerroux, Alejandro 151, 179
Lertxundi, Anjel 219, 222, 264–5
lesbianism *see* gender
Lestache, Elisa 77
Lete, Xabier 219
Leveroni, Rosa 230, 232
Levi, Simona 289
Lhande, Pierre 160
liberalism 22, 26, 27–8, 29, 31–2, 38, 49, 54,
    85–6, 90, 92, 99, 114, 152, 165, 169
    liberals 23–4, 43, 60, 72, 87, 163, 172–3, 182,
        194
    questioning of 144, 151, 165, 170
    see also 1812 Constitution; neoliberalism

Liddell, Angélica 289
Liost, Guerau de (Jaume Bofill) 73, 134
Lipus, Ander 281
Lista, Alberto 24, 30
literacy 82, 90, 109, 158, 162, 170, 221
literary canon 2–3, 13, 50, 77, 79, 102–5, 107,
    194, 197, 204, 211, 214, 233
literary history 14, 37, 61, 62, 141, 209
    Basque 160
    Catalan 64–5, 69–70, 111, 163, 210–11
    Galician 66, 77–8, 119, 155, 216
    Spanish 166, 188, 191–5
Lizardi (Jose Maria Agirre) 116, 185
Llamazares, Julio 250, 254, 291
Llanas Aguilaniedo, José María 144
Llanos Gutiérrez, Valentín 90
Llull, Ramon 63
Lope de Vega, Félix 167, 206
López Bago, Eduardo 54
López de Ayala, Ángeles 61
López de la Vega, Joaquina 77
López Ferreiro, Antonio 96
López Menacho, Javier 289
Lopez Mendizabal, Ixaka 158
López Mozo, Jerónimo 190
López Pacheco, Jesús 175
López Raimundo, Gregori 210
López Salinas, Armando 175–6
López Silva, Inma 262
López Soler, Ramón 65, 90–2
Lopo, Antón 235
Lopo, Santiago 263
Lorca *see* García Lorca
Loreiro, Carlos 288
Luna, Elvira 77
Luzán, Ignacio de 12, 29

Machado, Antonio 36, 53, 123, 142–3, 149–50,
    169–70, 173, 188, 206
Machado, Manuel 122–3
Machado y Álvarez, Antonio (Demófilo) 120,
    122, 129
Macías Picavea, Ricardo 144
Madrid, Francisco/Francesc 134
Maeterlinck, Maurice 132, 161
Maeztu, María de 143, 166
Maeztu, Ramiro de 142–6
magazines 53–8, 92, 125, 147, 153–4, 167–70,
    172–3, 188
    Basque 82–3, 118, 159, 185, 196–7, 220, 222
    Catalan 65, 73, 132, 160–3, 178–9, 202, 209
    Galician 155–6, 182, 184, 234
Maillard, Chantal 272
majismo 10, 20–1, 106

Malagon, Ana 280
Mallada, Lucas 144
Manent, Marià 180
Manterola, José 83, 117
Maragall, Joan 133, 163–4
Marañón, Gregorio 122
Marçal, Maria-Mercè 212, 231–3
March, Ausiàs 63
Margarit, Joan 13, 211, 277
María, Manuel 217
Marías, Javier 178, 252, 271–2
Marías, Julián 270
Marichalar, Antonio 173
Marsé, Juan 176, 181, 248, 274
Martí i Folguera, Josep 93
Martí i Pol, Miquel 275
Martin, Gregory 196
Martín, Luisgé 240
Martin, Susanna 243, 290
Martín Gaite, Carmen 225–6, 270–1
Martín Recuerda, José 177
Martín-Santos, Luis 178
Martínez de la Rosa, Francisco 24–6, 52, 88–9
Martínez Nadal, Rafael 206
Martínez Padín, Leopoldo 95
Martínez Reyes, Felipe 272
Martínez Sierra, Gregorio 166
Martínez Sierra, María (María de la O
    Lejárraga) 166
Martorell, Joannot 63
Marwan 290
Marxism 147, 161, 170, 174–5, 210–11, 213,
    217, 226, 272
Marzal, Carlos 272
masculinity *see* gender
Masip, Paulino 191
Massanés, Josepa 71
Massó i Torrent, Jaume 160
Mata, Pere 112
Mateo Díaz, Luis 252
Matute, Ana María 175, 225
Maurras, Charles 146
Mayans, Gregorio 15, 44
Maymón, Antonia 121
Mayorga, Juan 253, 289
Mbomío, Lucía 290
Medel, Elena 243
Meixide, Carlos 287
Meléndez Valdés, Juan 18–19, 30, 42–3, 48
memory 89, 147, 190–91, 193, 198, 206–7, 219,
    226, 245–66, 268, 271, 281, 283
Méndez, Alberto 251, 253
Méndez, Concha 124, 131, 192
Méndez Ferrín, Xosé Luís 184, 216–18

Méndez Rubio, Antonio 272
Mendicutti, Eduardo 229–30
Mendiguren, Iñaki 237
Mendiguren Elizegi, Xabier 281
Mendoza, Eduardo 274
Mendoza, Virginia 291
Menéndez Pelayo, Marcelino 8, 15–16, 64, 70,
    72
Menéndez Salmón, Ricardo 253
Mesa, Sara 291
Mesonero Romanos, Ramón 53, 107, 125–6
Mesquida, Biel 232
Mestanza, Bárbara 289
Mestre, Javier 289
Metge, Bernat 63
Mexico 23, 55, 91, 151, 252
    exile in 116, 188, 190, 199, 201–3, 205–6, 250
Michel, Francisque 117
migration 188–9, 192, 194–5, 278
    emigration 78–9, 83, 138, 155, 158, 177,
        195–7, 198, 210, 231, 262, 288
    immigration 233, 240, 254, 258, 272, 274,
        278, 288, 290–1
    within Spain 84, 125–6, 138, 261
    see also diaspora; exile
Miguel, Luna 290
Milà de la Roca, Nicasio 112
Milà i Fontanals, Manuel 64–5, 72–3, 92
Millás, Juan José 271–2
Minaberri, Marijan 235
Mintegi, Laura 222, 236
Mira, Joan-Francesc 275
Mirande, Jon 186, 221
Miró, Josep Maria 233
Miró, Pau 273
Misiones Pedagógicas 150, 169–70, 224
Mistral, Silvia 191, 207, 230
Mitxelena, Koldo 160, 186, 221
Modernisme 69, 73, 115, 132–3, 140, 141, 161–3
Modernismo 141–2, 145, 151
    see also Symbolism
Mogel, Bizenta 81–2
Mogel, Juan Antonio 82, 117
Moix, Ana María 228
Moix, Terenci 211, 229, 232
Molas, Joaquim 210–11
Moliner, Empar 259, 276
Moliner, María 170
Molins, Manuel 274
Moncada, Jesús 257, 277
Monserdà, Dolors 133, 232
Monsó, Imma 233
Montanyà, Lluís 135
Montengón, Pedro 87

Montero, Rosa 239, 271, 291
Montesquieu, Baron de 8, 20
Montijo, Countess of 42
Montoia, Xabier 264
Montoriol, Carme 134, 180
Montseny, Federica 121, 166–7, 179, 191, 201
Monzó, Quim 215, 277
Monzon, Telesforo 197
Mor de Fuentes, José 32
Mora, Ángeles 272
Mora, Constancia de la 191
Mora, José Joaquín de 25–6, 108
Morales, Cristina 289
Moratín, Leandro Fernández de 19–20, 31–2,
    42–3, 45, 47, 52, 105
Moratín, Nicolás Fernández de 18–19, 21, 43,
    45, 47, 87, 105
Morel, Bénédict 144
Moreno, Lara 292
Morocco 20, 87, 141, 168, 227, 228, 252
    African War 51, 87, 91, 92, 113, 136
Moure, Erin 234–5
Moure, Teresa 234–5
Movida 238
    Galician 218
Mujika, Gregorio 160
Mujika, Tene 159
Mujika Iraola, Inazio 263
Muñiz-Huberman, Angelina 193
Muñoz, Jokin 264–5
Muñoz Molina, Antonio 250–4, 271–2
Muntaner, Ramon 63
Murguía, Manuel 67, 76–8, 80, 95–6, 101–2,
    119, 155–6
Murià, Anna 180, 230
Muslim Spain 9, 11, 62, 87, 88–9, 91, 97, 246
    Arabic studies 87–8, 90–1

Napoleonic occupation *see* Peninsular War
nationalism 24, 26, 63, 99, 141–2, 157
    Basque 81, 83–4, 98–9, 117, 147–8, 157–9,
        185–7, 195, 197–8, 222, 236, 254, 263–5,
        279
        see also ETA
    Catalan 91–4, 141, 147, 160–4, 212, 273
    Galician 95, 119–20, 150, 156, 182–3, 184
    Spanish 11, 18, 21–2, 104, 107–8, 141, 145,
        270
    sub-state 102, 141, 145, 150
    see also hispanidad; Spanishness
nation-formation 13–15, 23, 38, 70–1, 85–99,
    100, 107, 126
    see also literary canon
Navarro, Elvira 243, 289

Navarro, Julia 252
Navarro Villoslada, Francisco 97
Nazarí, Carlos Emilio 124
Ndongo, Donato 291
Nelken, Margarita 166, 192
neoclassicism 12, 21, 24–5, 29–30, 32–3, 46–7,
    86–7, 89, 105–6, 163, 173
neoliberalism 190, 239, 242–3, 245, 270, 272,
    274–5, 281, 288–9, 290, 292
Neruda, Pablo 154, 170
new media 271, 276, 279, 286–7, 289–90
Nietzsche, Friedrich 145, 163, 186
Nifo, Francisco Mariano 48
Nordau, Max 144
normalization
    cultural 222, 229, 234, 267, 269–70, 272, 275,
        288–9
    linguistic 67–8, 156, 208, 213, 221, 267, 275
Noucentisme 69, 73–4, 115, 134–5, 140, 161,
    163–4, 178
nova cançó 182, 187
    see also Raimon
novatores 9, 16–17, 44
Novia Salcedo, Pedro 97

Obiols, Armand 180
Ocampo, Victoria 154
Olaizola Txiliku, Jesus Mari 196
Olasagarre, Juanjo 237
Olavide, Pablo 17, 31, 42
Olerkariak 158, 185
Olid, Bel 233
Oliver, Joan 180
Oliver, Maria Antònia 231
Oller, Narcís 52, 132–3
Olmet, Luis Antón del 119
Olmo, Lauro 177
Omgbá, Victor 201
Onaindia, Alberto 263
Onaindia, Santiago 197
Oñederra, Lourdes 237
opera 41, 46, 106, 110, 118
Opisso, Regina 121
oral history 191, 202, 233, 251, 263
orality 66, 76, 78, 83, 103, 107, 109, 116–17,
    137, 158, 181, 185
    bertsolaritza 82–3, 116–17, 183, 185
    see also ballad tradition; folk culture
Ordorika, Ruper 220
Orihuela, Antonio 272
Orixe (Nikolas Ormaetxea) 160, 185, 197
Oropesa, Countess of 45
Ortega y Gasset, José 53, 100, 122–3, 129, 135,
    142, 152–4, 156, 168–9, 173

Osuna, Duchess of 42
Oteiza, Jorge 186
Otero, Blas de 173–5, 187
Otero Pedrayo, Ramón 157, 182–4
Ovejero, José 271, 289

Palacio Valdés, Armando 136, 138
Palau i Fabre, Josep 182
Palencia, Isabel de 191
Pallarés, Pilar 277
Pàmies, Teresa 179, 201, 210
Panero, Leopoldo 172, 228
Panero, Leopoldo María 228
Parcerisas, Francesc 211
Pardo Bazán, Emilia 28, 34, 37–9, 52–3, 56–7,
    59–60, 109, 120–1, 135–6, 143
Parés, Núria 193
Partal, Vicent 276
Pascual, Itziar 289
Pato, Chus 234
Patxot, Ferran 112
Paz, Octavio 170
Pedrolo, Manuel de 203, 208, 211, 215, 256
Peinador, Enrique 155
Pelai Briz, Francesc 93
Pemán, José María 172
Peninsular War 17, 21–4, 31–2, 42, 48, 64,
    69–70, 78, 85, 92–3, 98, 119, 255
Penyas, Ana 290
Pere IV 63
Pereda, José María de 53, 59, 70, 136, 138
Pérez Galdós, Benito 38–40, 41, 43, 51, 56, 59,
    61, 98–9, 109, 121, 126–8, 136, 143,
    251
Pérez Reoyo, Narcisa 77
Pérez-Reverte, Arturo 255
Pérez y Zaragoza, Augstín 108
Peri Rossi, Cristina 203, 228
Pericay, Xavier 276
Philippines 23, 141, 143, 152
Piferrer, Pau 92
Pimentel, Luis 184
Piñeiro, Ramón 184–5
Pintos, Xoán Manuel 66, 76
Piquet, Jaume 114
Pizkundea (Basque Renaissance) 81–4
Planes, Josep Maria 134
Pol, Ferran de 180
political commitment 73, 115, 130, 150,
    165–87, 195, 206, 213, 236, 273
Polo, Irene 230
Pombo, Álvaro 227–8
Pondal (Eduardo González-Pondal Abente)
    79, 80–1

popular culture 101–24, 150–1, 160, 168, 186,
    211, 213–14, 239
    fiction 60, 64–5, 134, 157, 167, 229
    poetry 35, 92, 167, 184–5
    theater 21, 30, 42–3, 46–7, 59, 69, 143, 167,
        169, 171
    see also ballad tradition; folk culture; kiosk
        literature; orality; serialized novel;
        workers' culture
Porcel, Baltasar 211, 275
Portas, Manuel 286
Portela, Carlos 290
Portela, Edurne 283
Pous i Pagès, Josep 139
Prada, Juan Manuel de 252, 255–6
Prado, Benjamín 249, 255, 268
Prat de la Riba, Enric 144, 164
precarity 239, 242–3, 278, 280–1, 284, 288
Preciado, Paul B. 241
Precioso, Artemio 120
press 60, 142, 149
    Basque 157, 185
    Catalan 64, 70–1, 115–16, 163–4, 179, 181
    Galician 96
    Spanish 41, 48–9, 85, 152–3, 271
    see also magazines
Prieto, José 286
Prieto Rouco, Carmen 233
Primo de Rivera, José Antonio 152, 165
    see also Falange Española
Primo de Rivera dictatorship 73, 75, 146, 148,
    151–3, 156, 162, 178–9, 195, 228
public sphere 14–15, 19, 27, 31–2, 34, 41–61, 62,
    166, 182, 218, 238, 270–1, 289
publishing industry 48, 50–2, 54, 70, 153–4,
    206, 214, 238, 240, 270
    Basque 186, 187, 196–7, 219, 221–2, 279, 282
    Catalan 178, 181, 202, 203, 209–11, 276–7
    Galician 155, 182, 184, 198, 200, 283
Puig i Ferrater, Joan 180
Puigblanch, Antoni 92
Pujol, Jordi 273, 276
Pujol Cruells, Adrià 278
Puleo, Alicia 271, 290
Puntí, Jordi 278

Quadrado, Josep Maria 92
queerness *see* gender
Queipo, Xavier 263
Queipo de Llano, Gonzalo 171
Queizán, María Xosé 217, 233–5, 260
Quintana, Manuel José 24
Quiroga, Elena 184
Quiroga, Xabier 262

race 9, 11, 33–4, 87–92, 95, 97, 123, 130–1, 143,
    146, 148, 152, 158, 240, 274, 290–1
    see also coloniality; gypsies; Jews; migration,
    immigration; Muslim Spain; slavery
Raimon 181
Rambal, Enrique 124
Ramis i Ramis, Joan 87
Ramón y Cajal, Santiago 122
Ramoneda, Josep 271, 276
Ramos Ríos, Alberto Manuel 284
reading public 28, 41, 47, 50, 53–8, 71, 92, 105,
    109, 117, 119, 155, 166, 185, 221
    see also literacy
realism 74, 114, 140, 163, 176–8, 192, 229, 239,
    243, 246, 249, 272, 274, 285, 292
    magic 203, 219, 222, 252
    rejection of 115, 169, 217–18
    social(ist) 167–8, 175, 271
realist novel 29, 37–9, 54, 56, 59, 102, 109, 125,
    132, 135, 137, 143
regionalism 85, 94, 136, 138, 144, 147, 163,
    212, 233
    Lliga Regionalista 134, 161, 163, 178–9
    rexionalismo 67, 150, 154–5
Reigosa, Carlos 286
Reimóndez, María 234, 263, 284–5, 287
Reixa, Antón 218–19
Renaixença 64–5, 69–75, 94, 103, 111, 113, 132,
    134, 160, 164, 181
Renart, Francesc 113
Repila, Iván 292
republicanism 23, 56, 59–61, 82, 93, 94, 109–10,
    113–14, 128, 135, 138, 142, 145, 151,
    157, 160–2, 165, 182, 194–5, 273
    see also Spanish Republic, First; Spanish
    Republic, Second
Restoration 28, 41, 54, 85–6, 96, 100, 144, 150
Retana, Álvaro 122, 229
Rexurdimento 66, 75–81, 95, 119, 155, 264
Ribas, Carles 180–1, 201
Ribas, Merche 288
Ridruejo, Dionisio 172–3, 194
Riechman, Jorge 272
Riera, Carme 13, 211, 230–2, 257, 259
Riera i Bertran, Joaquim 93
Riera Llorca, Vicenç 180, 211
Riestra, Blanca 292
Ripoll, Laila 289
Riquer, Martín de 210–11
Risco, Vicente 156–7, 182–3, 199
Rivadeneyra, Manuel de 104
Rivas, Duke of (Ángel Saavedra) 25–6, 52, 87,
    89–90, 105, 108
Rivas, Manuel 200, 261–2, 271, 283–6

Robert, Robert 114, 132
Robrenyo, Josep 113–14
Roca, Paco 290
Rodó, Enrique 145
Rodoreda, Mercè 180, 202–5, 211, 224, 230–3
Rodriguez, Eider 280
Rodríguez, Francisco Javier 66
Rodríguez Mohedano, Pedro 103–4
Rodríguez Mohedano, Rafael 103–4
Rodríguez Mourullo, Gonzalo 217
Roel, Salvador Francisco 118–19
Roig, Montserrat 201–2, 211–13, 230–1, 256
Rojals, Marta 278
Romaní, Ana 235
Romanticism 23–6, 49, 51–2, 54, 63, 82–3, 92,
    94–5, 107, 117, 168, 185
    drama 37, 50, 58, 105
    interest in the past 65, 69, 71, 87–91, 96–7,
    108, 112, 158
    and subjectivity 28–30, 32–5, 37, 39, 40
Ros, Samuel 131
Rosa, Isaac 249, 254
Rosales, Luis 172–3
Rosetti, Ana 239
Rosich, Marc 233
Rousseau, Jean-Jacques 27–8, 32–3, 87
Rovira i Virgili, Antoni 180, 185
Rubió i Balaguer, Jordi 64
Rubió i Lluch, Antoni 64
Rubió i Ors, Joaquim 64, 71–2, 91–2
Rueda, Begoña M. 243
Ruiz Zafón, Carlos 251–2, 277
rural Spain 37, 74, 78, 82, 84, 101–2, 125–7, 134,
    135–40, 143, 149, 160, 163, 167, 169,
    218, 222, 258
    idealization of 53, 81, 114, 132, 151, 159
    turn to 254, 257, 260, 272, 277–8, 284,
    291–2
    see also ecology; folk culture; landscape
Rusiñol, Santiago 163
Rutherford, John 201
Ruyra, Joaquim 139

Sacristán, Manuel 210
Sáez de Melgar, Faustina 37, 55, 59
Sagarra, Josep Maria de 73, 134, 180–1, 201,
    211
Sagasta, Práxedes Mateo 54
sainete 10, 21, 42, 80, 106–7, 110–11, 143
    sainet 112–13
Saizarbitoria, Ramon 187, 220, 264–5
Salaberria, Sebastian 186
Salabert, Juana 253
Salazar Chapela, Esteban 191

Sales, Joan 179, 203, 256–7
Salinas, Pedro 170, 188, 191
Sallaberry, Jean Dominique Julien 117
salons *see tertulias*
Salvà, Maria Antònia 230
Salvat, Ricard 181–2, 203
Salvat-Papasseït, Joan 123, 135
Samaniego, Félix María 18, 45
San Julián, Sergi 290
Sánchez, María 291
Sánchez-Cutillas, Carmelinas 230
Sánchez Ferlosio, Rafael 269, 271
Sanchez Piñol, Albert 259–60, 277
Sánchez Saornil, Lucía 166–7
Sanchis Sinisterra, Juan 248–9, 256, 269
Sande, Miguel 284
Santos, Care 277
Sanz, Marta 243–4, 271
Sardà, Joan 73–4, 132
Sarmiento, Fray Martín 66
Sárraga, Belén 61
Sarria, Marquise of 42
Sarrias, Mercè 233
Sarrionandia, Joseba 197, 220, 263
Sarsanedas, Jordi 182
Sastre, Alfonso 177
Sastre, Elvira 290
Savater, Fernando 270
Sawa, Alejandro 50
Schlegel, August Wilhelm 25, 92, 104
Schlegel, Friedrich 25, 92, 104, 107
Scott, Walter 71, 90, 92, 97
secularism 8–9, 15–16, 28–9, 39, 55, 87, 152, 157, 173
Segovia, Tomás 193
Seguí, Salvador 121
Semprún, Jorge 191, 248
Sender, Ramón J. 168, 171, 191–2
Sensat, Rosa 232
Seoane, Luis 183, 199–200
Serés, Francesc 277–8
serialized novel 37–8, 50, 52–3, 55–7, 60, 91, 96, 108–10, 112, 121, 159
sexuality 18, 35, 37–40, 121–2, 148, 205, 212, 223–44, 264, 274, 283, 285
    see also eroticism
Simó, Isabel-Clara 231
Simón, Ana Iris 292
Simonde de Sismondi, Jean-Charles-Léonard 103
Sinués de Marco, María del Pilar 37, 55
Sirera, Josep Lluís 215
Sirera, Rodolf 215
slavery 33–6, 47, 59, 78, 89

socialism 28, 60–1, 99, 116, 121, 127–8, 145–6, 165, 168, 182, 216, 273
    Socialist government 247, 255, 261, 269
    Spanish Socialist Party (PSOE) 148, 152, 157, 166, 251, 254
Societies of Friends of the Nation 14, 19, 44
Solà, Irene 278, 292
Solá, Jaime 155
Solá, María 121
Solana, Teresa 233, 276
Soler, Frederic (Serafí Pitarra) 72, 93, 113–14
Soler, Toni 276, 278
Soroa, Marcelino 118
Spanish America 11–12, 22–3, 54–5, 58, 145, 166
    Spanish American literature 56, 61, 110, 137, 141–2, 145, 170, 178, 190, 195, 202–3, 205, 210, 219, 277
Spanish-American War 141–2, 144–5
Spanish Civil War 116, 146, 185, 188, 234, 268
    depictions of 175, 179, 186, 197, 207, 234, 246–52, 256–9, 261–2, 263–4
    Nationalist supporters 148, 172, 174, 183–4, 197
    Republican supporters 180, 188–94, 196–200, 201–7
    see also political commitment
Spanish Republic, First 93, 98, 127, 160, 168
Spanish Republic, Second 115–16, 122, 150, 153, 165–71, 179, 182, 223–4
Spanishness 8–9, 10–11, 13, 16–17, 21–2, 24, 32, 102–3, 122, 146–7, 173
Spottorno, Carlos 290
standardization, linguistic 65, 67, 71, 73, 78, 147, 159, 161, 181, 187
Straehle, Edgar 271
Strindberg, August 132
Suárez, Luis 206
Suárez Picallo, Ramón 183
Sue, Eugène 110, 112
Surrealism 129–30, 135, 167–8, 203
Symbolism 139–40, 141, 163, 185, 187
Szpunberg, Victoria 233, 258–9, 276, 289

Tarradellas, Josep 188, 202
Teixidor, Emili 258
Terradas, Abdó 114
tertulias 9, 19, 42–4, 65, 151
theater audiences 45–7, 58–9
Ticknor, George 103
Tísner (Avel·lí Artís Gener) 116, 203, 211
Tornero, Helena 233, 259
Toro, Suso de 218–19, 262, 271, 287
Toro, Xelís de 200

Torras i Bages, Josep 93–4, 160, 163
Torre, Guillermo de la 131
Torrente Ballester, Gonzalo 172, 184
Torres, Xohana 217
Torres Ferrer, Sabino 184
Torres-García, Joaquím 135
Torres Villarroel, Diego de 16, 18
Trabal, Francesc 180
transgender rights 229, 237, 240–1
transition (to democracy) 229, 237–40, 242,
        247, 251, 254–5, 267–9, 271, 275
Trapiello, Andrés 272
Tree, Matthew 276
Trigo, Felipe 121–2, 137, 143
Trueba, Antonio 78
Trueba y Cosío, Joaquín Telesforo de 90
Trueta, Josep 190–1, 202
Turbino, Francisco Maria 70
Tusquets, Esther 228–9

Ubeda, Garbiñe 264
Udina, Dolors 277
Ugalde, Martin 197
Umbral, Francisco 238
Unamuno, Miguel de 8, 36, 53, 58, 60, 70, 99,
        122, 137, 142–3, 146–9, 151, 158, 161–3
United States 98, 141–5, 196, 251
Unzueta, Sorne 159
Uribe, Kirmen 197–8, 280
Urkizu, Patrizio 220
Urquijo, Julio de 117, 159
Urretabizkaia, Arantxa 222, 236, 265
Urruzuno, Pedro Miguel 160

Valera, Juan 52, 55, 136, 138
Valero, Julieta 290
Valladares, Avelina 233
Valle Inclán, Ramón del 99, 123, 129, 142–3,
        150–2, 156, 193
Vallejo, César 170, 173
Vallejo, Irene 270
Vallmitjana, Juli 114, 134, 163
Valverde, José María 173
Vargas Llosa, Mario 203, 238
Vayreda, Marian 93, 139
Vázquez Montalbán, Manuel 249, 254, 271, 274
Vega, Garcilaso de la 173
Vega, Rexina 262
Verdaguer, Jacint 73–4, 91, 93–4
Verea y Aguiar, José 95
Vernet, Maria Teresa 180, 230

Vicent, Manuel 268
Vicetto, Benito 95–6, 101
Vilalta, Maruxa 193
Vila-Matas, Enrique 272
Vilanova, Emili 114, 132
Vilar Landeira, Ramón 284
Vilar Ponte, Antonio 182–3
Villalonga, Lorenç 203, 211
Villar, Domingo 286
Villena, Luis Antonio de 229
Vinson, Julien 117
Vinyes, Ramon 195
Vivanco, Luis Felipe 172–3

War of Independence *see* Peninsular War
War of the Spanish Succession 7, 11–13, 64,
        69, 93, 259
Webster, Wentworth 117
workers' culture 61, 101, 114, 128, 148
        see also anarchism; socialism

Xeración Galaxia 184
Xeración Nós 95, 119–20, 155–7, 182, 184, 199
Xirau, Ramón 193
Xirgu, Margarida 206–7

Yakovenko, Margaryta 290
Yáñez, Antía 285
Yáñez, Berto 287
Yáñez, María 287
Ybarra, Gabriela 243, 281
Yoyes (Maria Dolores González Katarain) 236
Yxart, Josep 73–4, 132

Zafra, Remedios 271
Zaldua, Iban 263, 265
Zamacois, Eduardo 120
Zamacola, J. A. 96
Zambrano, María 154, 169, 189, 190
Zamora Loboch, Francisco 291
zarzuela 42, 50, 105, 110, 118, 143
        sarsuela 113
Zavala, Antonio 186
Zgustová, Monika 233
Zhou Wu, Quan 290
Zola, Émile 57, 132
Zorrilla, José 26, 33, 40, 50–1, 90, 108
Zubiri, Harkaitz 280
Zúñiga, Iolanda 285, 287
Zúñiga, Juan Eduardo 247–8
Zunzunegui, Juan Antonio 172